NEWGATE NARRATIVES

CONTENTS OF THE EDITION

NEWGATE NARRATIVES

Edited by Gary Kelly

Volume 2
*Richmond; or, Scenes in the Life of a Bow Street Officer, Drawn Up
from His Private Memoranda*

Routledge
Taylor & Francis Group

LONDON AND NEW YORK

First published 2008 by Pickering & Chatto (Publishers) Limited

2 Park Square, Milton Park, Abingdon, Oxon OX14 4RN
711 Third Avenue, New York, NY 10017, USA

Routledge is an imprint of the Taylor & Francis Group, an informa business

First issued in paperback 2017

BRITISH LIBRARY CATALOGUING IN PUBLICATION DATA
1. Newgate (Prison : London, England) – Fiction 2. Newgate (Prison : London, England) – History – Sources 3. Prisons – England – Fiction 4. Prisons
– England – History – 19th century – Sources 5. Crime – England – London
– Fiction 6. English fiction – 19th century
I. Kelly, Gary
823.8'0803556[F]

ISBN-13: 978-1-1387-5561-1 (hbk)
ISBN-13: 978-1-138-11165-3 (pbk)
ISBN-13: 978-1-85196-812-1 (set)

Typeset by Pickering & Chatto (Publishers) Limited

CONTENTS

INTRODUCTION

Richmond; or, Scenes in the Life of a Bow Street Officer, Drawn Up from His Private Memoranda was published in three volumes in early March 1827 by the firm of Henry Colburn, the most prominent publisher of fashionable novels at this time.[1] *Richmond* has been seen as innovative for introducing the figure of the professional police detective as the central character in the novel, since two of its three volumes comprise a series of cases solved by the narrator-protagonist, a 'Bow Street officer', or 'runner'. This was a special kind of policeman operating partly independently and partly under the direction of the magistrate at the Bow Street police office, near Newgate prison, in London. *Richmond* may have been a response to the publication or imminent publication of the supposed memoirs of the notorious Paris police chief, François Vidocq (1775–1857), but *Richmond*'s handling of the subject of crime detection is distinctive and unique. Further, this aspect of *Richmond* is less innovative than the way it novelizes the news, or fictionalizes themes currently or recently in the news at the time the novel was published. The author of *Richmond* was and is unknown, but this attribute is characteristic of novels by the professional journalist Thomas Gaspey (1788–1871). Gaspey, his other novels, and *George Godfrey* are dealt with in separate introduction to Volume 3 of this set. The purpose of this introduction to *Richmond* is not to establish its authorship but to show how it, too, novelizes the news, not only in its themes or content, but also in its development of the novel form, and thereby participates in 'Newgate discourse', or the set of texts, practices and institutions around crime and punishment, symbolized by London's infamous Newgate prison.

Nevertheless, a brief consideration of *Richmond*'s authorship will help highlight its formal and thematic contexts. *Richmond* has been attributed to Thomas Skinner Surr (1770–1847) as well as to Gaspey, though E. F. Bleiler, in his introduction to a modern edition, rejects both Surr and Gaspey as its authors.[2] Against attribution to Gaspey is the fact that *Richmond* is unlike his previous novels in important respects: it is a first-person narrative, it deals with contemporary life, it is more fluently written, it lacks a well prepared and strong closure, it does not contain blocks of information obtained from antiquarian or travel literature and it abandons chapter epigraphs for head-of-chapter summaries. Further, when Gaspey's widow applied for relief to the Royal Literary Fund in 1875, she did not list *Richmond* among her late husband's works.[3] At the same time, *Richmond* does not particularly resemble Surr's previous novels. In favour of attribution to Gaspey is the fact that *Richmond* does resemble his novelistic practice in important respects: it continues the kind of exploration of popular novel forms seen in his previous fiction, it involves a lot of travelling or wandering by the protagonist, it exhibits Gaspey's predilection for puns, it contains songs and poems similar to those in his other novels and to the kind Gaspey published in magazines, it takes up themes that recur in his earlier novels, it resembles *The History of George Godfrey*, published the following year by the same publisher, and which *is* attributed to Gaspey. Differences between Gaspey's previous novels, all published by the firm of Longman, Hurst, Rees, Orme and Brown, and *Richmond* and *George Godfrey*, both published by Henry Colburn, may also be attributable to change in publisher and to changes in Gaspey's professional life. Certainly *Richmond* is, in major ways, more journalistic than novelistic in form and more characteristic of a writer who was by this time an experienced, fully engaged newspaper journalist and editor. Most important, then, like the novels known to be Gaspey's, *Richmond* incorporates a number of related topics of current or recent interest at the time of the novel's publication: it novelizes the news. Indeed, it goes further and attempts to fuse the novel form with journalistic discourse and conventions.

As a novel, *Richmond* is a fictional autobiography in two large movements: the first volume recounts Tom Richmond's life from his childhood to his joining the police force known as the Bow Street 'runners', or 'officers'; the next two volumes recount five of the cases he investigates – the abducted boy, the persecuted clergyman, the smugglers and grave-robbers, the man who tried to reenact Shakespeare's *Taming of the Shrew* in his own marriage, and the genteel gamblers and forgers.

Richmond opens his account with his early years in rural Derbyshire, his childhood pranks, rebellious schooldays and local sweetheart, Anne, and his early employment in a Liverpool counting house, or accounts office. While in Liverpool, he is fascinated by a performance of George Colman the Younger's popular musical play *Inkle and Yarico* (1787), staged by a company of 'strolling' or itinerant actors, and he runs off with his friend Jem Bucks to take up the theatre life. Together Richmond and Bucks ramble about Westmorland and Lancashire, encountering a highway robber named Blore and some country folk, getting arrested and managing to escape, eventually finding work with an itinerant theatre company at Lancaster. Richmond urges Anne to join him. She manages to escape her uncle's vigilance and does so, and they plan to marry. When they are about to perform on stage at Lancaster as Romeo and Juliet, however, she is seized by an agent of her uncle. A troop of gypsies, including an eccentric young gentleman named Wilton and his gypsy lover, Mary, help find her. Anne and Richmond join the wandering gypsy band, but she falls ill and dies. The group then wanders across England to Cambridge, where they befriend a poacher and then help him escape from the game-keepers. While camped outside Cambridge they encounter some gentleman-student gamblers, Lord Blank, Sir Byam Finch and others. Richmond, Wilton and the gypsies continue their roaming and camp on Hampstead Heath, north of London. Here, offended by the parish vestry's notice banning gypsies, vagabonds and similar types, they plan to erect a counter-notice banning the vestrymen. They also discover that the local people are disgruntled by corruption among the vestry council, and Wilton, Richmond and their companions plot to expose them. Wilton then engages in a wrestling match with some prizefighters on Wimbledon Common, which he wins thanks to the strength and endurance he has gained from his vagrant life. After several more years of such wandering, quickly passed over in the narrative, Richmond decides to find a settled profession and, meeting Jem Bucks, who has been taken on by the Bow Street police office in London, he too becomes a police detective, closing Volume 1.

Volume 2 launches Richmond on his career in crime detection with investigating the abduction and possible murder of a boy at Roehampton, south-west of London. The investigation turns up Richmond's former friends, the gypsies, and the robber, Blore, but eventually leads to Jones, a dealer in bodies stolen from graves and sold to commercial anatomy schools – regulations at the time required medical students to study anatomy by dissecting human cadavers, creating a constant demand for them, which was supplied commercially. The boy was not murdered for this trade, but is discovered concealed on a river barge guarded by Jones's accomplice, a dangerously violent Welshwoman. The terrified boy is released but the woman escapes after nearly killing Richmond and his helper. Though Jones is arrested he too manages to get away. Richmond's next case is comical: he is called in by the clergyman of the village of Duckenhurst to solve mysterious hauntings. On investigation, these turn out to be pranks by parishioners disgruntled by their new minister's rapacious policy of exacting tithes – he was formerly a grasping attorney. Though Richmond sympathizes with the parishioners, he exposes their tricks and, in the process, uncovers a gang of body snatchers working with Jones, stealing recently interred bodies and selling them to commercial anatomy schools. The gang are also engaged with Jones in smuggling taxable goods into England from abroad, a widespread practice at the time, sometimes employing entire villages. Assisted by an impetuous but good-hearted Irish labourer, Thady, Richmond breaks up and arrests the gang and sets off to Hampshire, where Jones is operating from a place of concealment in the New Forest. At the smuggling village of Cadenham, Richmond again encounters the gentlemen swindlers, Lord Blank and Sir Byam Finch and, with Thady, secretly defeats their plan to fleece a wealthy Creole named Blizzard. Richmond also meets Maria, who was seduced at Cambridge by Finch and whom Finch is now trying to cast on Blizzard. But Richmond falls for the despondent and repentant woman, deciding to help her and, despite her 'fallen' condition, marry her himself. Thady uncovers Jones's plan for a grand smuggling operation and Richmond prepares to catch the gang red-handed, with the assistance of the gruff but professional lieutenant Frampton, commander of a revenue sloop and an uncorrupted Hampshire magistrate, 'W—m M—d', who can be identified as the actual William Mitford (1744–1827), famous historian of ancient Greece and a Hampshire magistrate.

Volume 3 opens with Richmond's plan in progress and, after a series of nocturnal adventures and fights between the smugglers and the government forces, Jones and his gang are taken and Richmond and Thady are appropriately rewarded. In London, Thady is soon cheated of his money – London was famously a dangerous place for naïve countryfolk and foreigners. Richmond deals with a call into the country to try to deal with an eccentric young husband who is re-enacting Shakespeare's *Taming of the Shrew* in his own domestic sphere. When Richmond returns to London he is drawn in to the case of young Percy, a rich heir plundered of his wealth by sharpers. One of these is a farmer, Grinstead, who has inveigled Percy into appearing to court his daughter and who is extorting money from Percy by a threat of a lawsuit for breach of promise. Another and very different sharper is the glamorous Mrs —. From her house in Mayfair she operates both a fashionable but dishonest private gambling casino and a secret printing press for forged banknotes. Richmond is drawn to the case when he notices her attempting to pass forged notes while shopping. He then intervenes to save Percy from suicide after following him from Mrs —'s house one night. Richmond is now married and settled with Maria and they take Percy in and care for him. While with them, he unfolds his tale of being systematically cheated, first by Grinstead and then by Mrs — and her husband. Again, Richmond lays his plans and, acting with his friend and fellow officer Jem Bucks, surprises and seizes the forgers, while a party of police enter the front of the house to apprehend Mrs — and her husband. They find Mrs — in a concealed room, but she takes laudanum and expires rather than face public exposure and prison. Her husband is later killed in a duel by Percy, who then escapes to the Continent, and the novel closes precipitately with Richmond's assertion that, 'My purpose will be answered if what I have recorded in these volumes shall serve to beguile an idle hour, or show to those, who are inexperienced, the innumerable snares which beset the path of life, particularly in this overgrown and bustling metropolis.'

As this summary indicates, *Richmond* seems to have started out as a pica-resque novel of adventures on the road and then shifted suddenly to being a detective novel. This turn may owe something to the the exploits of François Vidocq, Paris police chief. Vidocq was a controversial character who crossed back and forth over the line between criminal and police and was also able to survive radical changes of political regime in France. This adaptability would have reminded British observers of the best known English criminal-turned-policeman, Jonathan Wild (1683–1725), whose relationship to *Richmond* is discussed later. An edition of what purported to be Vidocq's memoirs was being prepared in Paris in the mid-1820s. Vidocq was not the author of these memoirs, which were probably assembled or rewritten from his notes by Émile Morice and Louis-François L'Héritier. Their contribution seems to have been to enliven or sensationalize François Vidocq's material. A four-volume English translation appeared as *Memoirs of Vidocq* in the series *Autobiography: A Collection of the Most Instructive and Amusing Lives ever Published, Written by the Parties Themselves*, published between 1826 and 1833.[4] The publisher was a conger of the firm of Hunt and Clarke, publishers of plays, travels and books and periodicals associated with reformism, and the firm of Whittaker, Treacher and Arnot, a more miscellaneous publisher but specialists in biographies and autobiographies. Though *Richmond* was published in 1827, information about Vidocq and 'his' memoirs may well have been circulating earlier, given their sensational nature and their supposed author's prominence and career. As a journalist, Gaspey was well situated to hear of such matter and so *Richmond* may owe the idea of a collection of police cases and its first-person narrative form to the *Memoirs of Vidocq*. Otherwise *Richmond*'s material is not as sensational as Vidocq's and is handled in a more matter-of-fact and journalistic way – perhaps more like François Vidocq's own accounts of his cases, before they were popularized by Morice and L'Héritier. Further, British interest in French policing practices in the 1820s was treated less as a subject in its own right than as a matter of comparison related to the larger issues of reform of policing, criminal law and the penal system being intensely debated in Britain itself. 'Vidocq' became very popular in France, with many editions, adaptations and later films and television series through the nineteenth and twentieth centuries. In Britain, however, other detectives, whether policeman or private investigators, would be more prominent. Though perhaps instigated by the appearance of the *Memoirs of Vidocq*, *Richmond* drew thematically and formally not so much on that work as on two large discourses ready to hand, the picaresque novel tradition and the developing practices of journalism.

Formally, *Richmond* can be read in part as a contribution to the long tradition of a kind of crime literature that many 'Newgate novels' drew on – the picaresque romance. This tradition goes back to sixteenth- and seventeenth-century Spanish picaresque or 'rogue-on-the-road' fiction, including the anonymous *Lazarillo de Tormes* (1554), Mateo Alamén's *Guzman de Alfarache* (1599–1604) and Francisco de Quevedo's *El Buscón* (1662), known in English as *The Sharper* or *The Swindler*. This form developed in various ways down to Gaspey's day, including the criminal autobiographies of Daniel Defoe such as *Colonel Jack* (1722) and *Moll Flanders* (1722), Henry Fielding's satirical *Jonathan Wild* (1743), and Tobias Smollett's grim *Ferdinand Count Fathom* (1753). In the last decade of the eighteenth century the form was adapted again, this time by writers with a reformist agenda inspired partly by the English 'constitutionalist' tradition and partly by the early developments of the French Revolution, in such novels as William Godwin's *Things as They Are; or, The Adventures of Caleb Williams* (1794) and Thomas Holcroft's *Hugh Trevor* (1794–7) and *Memoirs of Bryan Perdue* (1805). At this time, anti-Revolutionary writers also adapted the form, depicting the rogue-on-the-road as a conspirator or spy, a traitor or foreign agent out to corrupt virtuous English maids, delude well-meaning young English gentlemen, and overthrow the British constitution, in such novels as George Walker's *The Vagabond* (1799) and Elizabeth Hamilton's *Memoirs of Modern Philosophers* (1800). More recently, there were Gothic novels and Romantic narrative poems that adapted the picaresque rogue novel in new ways, such as C. R. Maturin's *Melmoth the Wanderer* (1820), and Byron's hero-villain poems such as *The Corsair* (1814) or *Don Juan* (1819–24). *Richmond* resembles yet differs from these predecessors.

In particular, *Richmond* participates in a tradition of picaresque fiction in which the protagonist operates on or moves back and forth between both sides of the law. Here the best known example at the time *Richmond* was published would still be Fielding's *Jonathan Wild*, the fictionalized biography of a real-life thief turned thief-taker (1683–1725). There were early nineteenth-century editions of Fielding's book and a chapbook edition of Wild's story in 1825, and Wild continued to appear in successive editions of the *Newgate Calendar*, a compendium of brief biographies of convicted criminals. More broadly, Fielding's novel, with such continuingly popular classics as John Gay's musical drama *The Beggar's Opera* (1728), suggested that the state and its officials and institutions were as vicious and corrupt as, and often in cahoots with, the criminal underworld they pretended to prosecute and punish. *Jonathan Wild* had continued relevance in the early nineteenth century because members of the law enforcement and justice systems were still widely believed to collude with the criminal underworld, and such collusion was exposed from time to time. Tom Richmond's career is not as dark and devilish as Jonathan Wild's, and *Richmond* does not satirize so strongly the world of the establishment and the state as mirrored in and colluding with the underworld of crime and corruption. Richmond's adventures, whether on the road with the gypsies and strolling actors or on the hunt as a police investigator, are more genially comic than in the long tradition of picaresque fiction from the early Spanish novellas to the more recent social novels of the late eighteenth and early nineteenth centuries. Nor does *Richmond* resemble the optimistic picaresque novels of certain late eighteenth-century reformist writers, such as Thomas Holcroft, a point that would align *Richmond* with Thomas Gaspey's cautious sympathy for certain reform causes of the 1820s while supporting the established system. Finally, Tom Richmond remains a largely social character, with relatively little subjective self-examination or inner conflict, unlike the political inquirers, glamorous swashbucklers and satanic protagonists of British political novels of the 1790s and Byronic narrative poems and Gothic romances of the 1810s and 1820s.

Admittedly, the fictitious autobiographical form of *Richmond* is a departure from the third-person form of Gaspeys's novels from *The Mystery* to *The Witch-finder* and his later novel, *The Self-condemned*. Nevertheless, *Richmond* is, like them, designed to address current or recent public events, issues, and controversies, and particularly those in the news during the mid-1820s. Among the topics cast into fictional form in *Richmond* are: police and policing; strolling players, gypsies and vagrants generally; the game laws; corruption in local government; 'body snatching' or the theft of cadavers of the recently deceased, or even murdered persons, to supply anatomy subjects to commercial medical schools; tithes and collection of tithes that supported the established church and clergy; marriage and divorce; various kinds of fraud and deception; forgery in particular; gambling, or gaming; and several others.

As its subtitle indicates, *Richmond; or, Scenes in the Life of a Bow Street Officer* is largely a collection of cases investigated by a member of the police body attached to Bow Street magistrate's office and known under various names and nicknames but particularly as Bow Street 'runners' or 'officers', and as 'robin redbreasts', after the red waistcoats that, with a blue coat, formed part of their dress, but only when assembled as a body and not when on active duty, when they were in effect plain clothes officers. The Bow Street officers as a body were created from foundations laid down in the 1750s by the magistrate Henry Fielding, also author of the criminal biography *Jonathan Wild*, numerous satirical plays, and the widely read novels *Joseph Andrews*, *Tom Jones* and *Amelia*, and then by his brother John Fielding. The Bow Street officers were paid from government funds in an attempt to detach them from the traditional kind of thief-takers, the most notorious of which was Jonathan Wild, who solved crimes for a fee and who were often, like Wild, themselves criminals or in cahoots with criminals.[5] Unlike the largely ineffective policing force known as 'watchmen', who were based in each parish and walked the streets at night to keep order, but who were largely passive in their procedures, the Bow Street officers were meant to be active. They were the magistrate's agents, serving writs and investigating matters assigned to them. They also, however, retained traits of the old-style entrepreneurial thief-takers, who took up cases likely to produce financial rewards for themselves and who, notoriously, often colluded with or created crimes in order to 'solve' them and receive the rewards. In 1816, for example, a Bow Street officer was among a group of six policemen of various kinds who were charged with participating in crimes for this purpose.[6]

In 1816 John Townsend, perhaps the Bow Street officer best known to the wider public, gave testimony as to his and the other officers' duties and way of working to the parliamentary committee 'on the State of the Police of the Metropolis'. He testified that the officers worked out of the Bow Street magistrates' office and that they did not attend at the office every day. His opinion was that an officer could not live on his salary as an officer alone and that officers should be paid one-hundred guineas a year to make them independent. He stated that the officers were often sought at the police office for immediate action by official institutions such as the Excise Office and the Bank of England, and that they would be paid an extra guinea a day for attending at these places. He testified that officers often collected rewards posted for solving crimes, that only the crimes of highway robbery and burglary provided rewards, and that wealthy criminals would attempt to bribe officers. He confirmed that officers occasionally had to leave the country on police business. He was certain that officers had to frequent places of criminal resort or 'flash houses' in order to procure the information necessary to solve crimes. It was his opinion that, despite there being fewer executions than in the past, 'the morals and manners of the lower people' were worse in the past than in the present, that many committed crimes because they could not obtain honest work, that policing diminished the number of crimes, that displaying the bodies of the hanged in public deterred others from crime, and that some years of prison confinement were worse punishment than hanging.[7]

In 1822 John Stafford, clerk of the Bow Street office, gave the parliamentary committee on the policing of London detailed information about his officers. They were John Townsend, John Sayers, John Vickery, Daniel Bishop, Samuel Taunton, William Salmon, George Ruthven and James John Smith. According to Stafford, they were deployed as follows:

> Townsend and Sayers generally attend His majesty [George IV] when he is out of town, they are now at Brighton [where the king had a palace]; Salmon and Ruthven have been upon the Continent in pursuit of persons who have absconded with property belonging to their employers in the city, they are both returned; Bishop has been at a variety of places in the country, I think three or four different places, on business; Taunton has been recently to the Exeter assizes [or periodic criminal trials], and he is now at the Maidstone assizes, a little while before that he followed some offenders to Scotland and brought them from thence; Vickery has been employed a good deal in

making inquiries for the post office relative to some offences that have been committed there, he has been also in Hampshire, and on account of his being very unwell he
applied for permission to stay a little while at Odiham, which, I believe, is his native
place; in fact he has never been well since he was very ill-used some time ago, and
nearly murdered; Smith has been employed in a variety of matters in Kent and at
Norwich, and latterly at Baldock in Hertfordshire.[8]

Of these officers, the one whose activities most closely resemble those of the
protagonist of *Richmond* is perhaps Daniel Bishop. Ironically, a year after *Richmond* was published Bishop was revealed to have colluded with a receiver of
stolen goods and was dismissed from the service, though later reinstated on the
grounds that such practices were commonplace.[9] Stafford went on to tell the
parliamentary committee that much of the Bow Street officers' work was in the
country and that otherwise they were assigned to cases in London; that they
were the police officers most often requested for such service because of their
reputation for perseverance, bravery, initiative and reliability; that they could be
hired to carry out private investigations, as Tom Richmond is; that if additional
officers were needed they were selected from among the best assigned to other
police offices in the metropolis; that what they were paid in salary was regarded
as a retaining fee and not full remuneration; and that 'the constables at the different police offices are left a good deal at their own guidance and discretion, as
to how they dispose of their time'.

By the time *Richmond* was published a number of the Bow Street officers
had become public figures and were in the news as individuals. One of these was
George Ruthven (*c.*1793–1844), who came to prominence through helping to
expose the so-called 'Cato Street Conspiracy' in late February 1820. A group
led by Arthur Thistlewood (1774–1820) planned to assassinate members of the
government as a way to provoke a popular revolution and make way for a government based on the proto-socialist ideas of the radical reformist and publisher,
Thomas Spence (1750–1814). Ruthven, instructed by Bow Street magistrate
Richard Birnie (*c.*1760–1832), disguised himself as a labourer, spied on the conspirators, and then laid a trap for them as they gathered to carry out their plot.
More of a celebrity was John Townsend (1760–1832), who operated within and
beyond London, on official duty and for private hire and who rose to be made
responsible for the security of the royal family. He was often in the entourage of
the Prince of Wales, affected to speak in underworld 'cant' or slang, appeared
often in graphic satires of the time and was a major witness before the parliamentary committee of inquiry into policing in 1816, where he expressed opposition
to the system of payments to police for contributing to successful capital convictions – a practice that connected the police to the corrupt old system of
professional 'thief-takers'. It may well be that the author of *Richmond* obtained
suggestions for the protagonist's cases, or even the cases themselves, from inter-

viewing subjects such as Ruthven, Townsend, or others at the Bow Street office – something Gaspey as a journalist was well situated to do. It is notable, however, that the author of *Richmond* chose not to offer fictional 'political' cases such as Ruthven's Cato Street conspiracy or fictional adventures in high life such as Townsend's association with the King.

The policing of greater London, and the country as a whole, continued to be in the news through the 1820s, especially under the Home Secretary, or government minister for law and order, Robert Peel (1788–1850), who held the office from 1822 to 1827 and again from 1828. Earlier, Peel had been chief secretary of the administration of Ireland, and had established a countrywide police force to suppress the widespread economic and political violence carried out by the disaffected Irish peasantry. This force became a model for similar ones established elsewhere in the empire and eventually, after *Richmond* was published, in London. During the 1820s parliament examined the issue of policing several times, in connection with legal and penal reform, and in the context of widespread public concern about a supposed increase in crime, the inconsistency and harshness of the criminal law, the inadequacy of the prisons and the penal system, and the ineffectiveness of existing kinds of punishment as either deterrent or regime of reformation (see the documents selected in Volume 1 of this series). *Richmond* novelizes issues of policing and certain crimes, in particular; *George Godfrey* would go on to novelize other issues in this broad public, parliamentary, judicial, and administrative reconsideration of crime and punishment in the 1820s. In 1822 parliament issued its *Report from the Select Committee on the Police of the Metropolis*, recording evidence and making recommendations, among which was extension, regulation, and professionalization of the system of Bow Street officers. Robert Peel continued to guide parliamentary consideration of policing and eventually succeeded in passing the Metropolitan Police Act in 1829, two years after publication of *Richmond*. The act established a metropolis-wide police force with many of the positive features of the Bow Street system, in essence the same policing system still in place. Many of the Bow Street officers were absorbed into the new London police force. By its positive and sympathetic portrayal of a Bow Street officer, the novel may have contributed to that development. Certainly Tom Richmond exemplifies the kind of policeman that the act and its consequences created.[10] Yet the positive representation of the Bow Street officer in *Richmond* may also have been intended to oppose the creation of a new police force, which many resisted as a dangerous strengthening of state power, by showing that the Bow Street police were adequate to the job.

In the news alongside policing was the supposed crime wave that a reformed police service was meant to address. Through the 1820s there was a succession of parliamentary reports on numbers of commitments and convictions for criminal offences, in response to the general perception that crime had increased after the end of the Napoleonic wars. The increase in crime was usually attributed to unemployment, exacerbated by other factors such as the practice of supplementing low wages from the poor rate (or parish-based welfare system), and leading to such 'crimes' as poaching, vagrancy, highway robbery and similar crimes of necessity or opportunity committed by the marginalized and distressed. It is these 'crimes' that are represented in the first volume of *Richmond*, as the protagonist roams over half of England with strolling actors and gypsies, encountering poachers and robbers, before he crosses over from outlaw to lawman in the rest of the novel. The problem again provoked public debate and parliamentary action, with a bill 'to amend laws relating to vagrants' in 1821; a bill 'for consolidating and amending laws relating to rogues, vagabonds, vagrants, and disorderly persons' in 1822; returns for the number of 'persons committed under vagrant laws to prisons in England and Wales' in 1824, culminating in a bill 'for more effectual suppression of vagrancy and punishment of idle and disorderly persons' in 1824. In his *Observations* on the act (1824), the lawyer and historian John Adolphus (1768–1845), who had defended the Cato Street conspirators in 1820, criticized its harshness and its definition of vagrant, which included unlicensed 'common stage actors', 'pretended gypsies', 'fortune tellers' – all of which appear in *Richmond* – as well as many others. A writer using the pen-name 'Barrister' also criticized the act in *The Vagrant Act in Relation to the Liberty of the Subject* (1824) and *A Letter to a member of Parliament on the Impropriety of Classing Players with Rogues and Vagabonds in the Vagrant Act* (1824).

In *Richmond* it is in fact Wilton, the gentleman turned 'pretended gypsy', who celebrates the 'liberty' of the vagrant life. Strolling actors had long been treated sympathetically and even glamorized in fiction; in the 1810s and 1820s gypsy life was presented positively, and even as a utopian community, in new editions of the well-known chapbook *Adventures of Bamfylde Moore Carew*, supposedly king of the gypsies; and there were historical and cultural accounts of the gypsies and their customs and language in magazine essays and such books as William Chambers's *Exploits and Anecdotes of the most Remarkable Gypsies in the Southern Counties of Scotland; Together with Traits of their Origin, Character and Manners* (1821, reprinted 1823). Poaching was also widely seen as an 'excusable' crime; as the 1827 parliamentary *Report from the Select Committee of Criminal Commitments and Convictions* observed, 'there is a general feeling both amongst the farmers and amongst the labourers that poaching is not a moral crime'.[11] Poaching for personal consumption was less an issue than poaching for sale, as represented in *Richmond*. Such sale was illegal, but as the 1823 parliamentary *Report from the Select Committee on the Laws Relating to Game* had concluded, existing laws had utterly failed to stop the practice and should be abolished and replaced with legislation establishing licensed sale of legally obtained game. Social commentators also represented the game laws as a form of oppression of the poor, as in Isaac Williams's *Avarice Exposed; or, A Treatise on the Corn and Game Laws* (1826); many law reformers pointed at the notorious 'Black Act', which had made illegally hunting with a blackened face at night a capital offence, a provision later extended to cover protesters outside royal game reserves. In 1825 George Bankes published a pamphlet entitled *Reconsiderations on Certain Proposed Alterations of the Game Laws*, in which he upheld the laws but protested that his aim was not to preserve game but to prevent crime; and in *A Treatise on the Game Laws* (1826), Joseph Chitty rehearsed the many statutes that had criminalized the unauthorized hunting of game over the years. These various categories of vagrant depicted in *Richmond* – the strolling actors, gypsies and poachers – are treated sympathetically, though not uncritically, and even the highway robber Blore is portrayed as acting more out of desperation than depravity.

Perhaps more contentious than suppression of vagrancy and poaching was the imposition of tithes, or the exaction of a proportion of produce or money for the support of the established state church and clergy. Tithes had long been socially divisive, setting clergy and the established church against not only religious dissenters, or those who refused to accept the authority of the established church, but also against property owners, however small, who adhered to the state church but who resented its tax on the produce of their land, investment and labour. In Ireland, where such tithes were exacted from the Catholic majority for the benefit of a Protestant minority, the imposition was widely and often violently resisted by the 1820s, and was a major cause of Irish Catholic political protest and mobilization. But even in England, where the majority belonged to the established church, tithes were unpopular, and becoming more so in the face of increasingly determined attempts by proprietors of tithes to levy them regularly and in full, and to reclaim those that had fallen out of use or that had, perhaps centuries earlier, been settled for a 'composition', usually a fixed monetary sum, which had of course decreased in real value over the generations. In Volume 2, *Richmond* gives full satirical treatment to such proprietors intent on re-establishing the original value of the tithe with the case of the rector of Duckenhurst, formerly a petty attorney who entered the clergy solely to have an easy life on the income of his tithes, and whose despotic insistence on his 'rights' evokes the hostility and harassment of his parishioners. Though Richmond is sympathetic to the parishioners, he does his duty and pursues the troublemakers. Through the 1820s there was a lively and often bitter 'paper war' over tithes, political economists weighed in with arguments on whether or not tithes were a drain on the economy, and reformists held up tithes as an example of a powerful and privileged minority exploiting and oppressing the majority. Not surprisingly, William Cobbett, the tireless critic of economic parasites and the privileged classes, lambasted tithes and those who exacted them, in his March

1822 *Monthly Sermon*. Given the inflammatory nature of the issue, parliament addressed it several times from the 1810s onward – several times a year in the case of Ireland. An 1817 parliamentary Bill for the Amendment of the Law in Respect of Tithes gave relief at law to those benefiting from a long-established composition of the tithe. Parliament continued through the 1820s to monitor the issue and the conflicts arising from it, and in 1827 attempted to make com- mutation of tithes by mutual agreement easier, observing in the preamble to the bill that 'in many places much inconvenience has been found to result from the levying of Tithes, and many disputes have arisen in consequence between the Rectors, Vicars and other Incumbents of Ecclesiastical Benefices and Livings and their Parishioners or other persons liable to pay Tithes to them'.[12]

Another topic that was related to the theme of 'crime', broadly understood, that was often in the news, especially from 1820, and that is novelized in *Rich- mond*, is love and with it marriage and divorce. This topic is represented from a variety of angles in the novel: in the early and almost illicit relationship of Richmond and Anne, the manifestly illicit relationship of Wilton and the gypsy Mary, the bad marriage of the parents of the abducted boy, the illicit relationship of Sir Byam Finch and the naïve Maria, Richmond's marriage to Maria despite her 'fallen' condition, and other relationships. Marriage and divorce were in the news most spectacularly and alarmingly, from a national point of view, in 1820 with the attempt by the then Prince Regent to divorce his estranged wife, Prin- cess Caroline. The cause of Caroline was taken up by the political opposition, reformists, and a disaffected public as a way to force regime change, with large popular demonstrations that, many thought, portended an imminent political revolution. The potential political consequences of this marital dispute were exacerbated when the Prince Regent succeeded to the throne in 1821, making Caroline the Queen and, in the event of her husband's incapacity – not unlikely since his father had been incapacitated by mental illness for many years – possi- bly regent herself, with considerable political power. The issue faded from public attention with Caroline's death in 1822, but the 'Queen Caroline Affair' inten- sified public interest in, and concern over, issues of marriage, divorce, property, and legitimacy through the 1820s, and the early 1820s saw a spate of pamphlets on these subjects, inspired by the public spectacle of royal marriage breakdown.

These issues were not, of course, new. For decades literature had portrayed the conflicts and injustices caused by unequal laws of marriage, divorce, property and child custody. The relationship between love and marriage had long been a subject of conflict in middle-class culture and literature, especially novels. On the one hand there was growing resistance to marriage arranged for family or property reasons and support for a meritocratic ideology of love and marriage based on individual suitability and preference. On the other hand there was fear that personal preference might lead to 'imprudent', exploitative, or unhappy marriages, to seduction and loss of moral reputation, or to sexual promiscuity and bastardy, all affecting the stability, preservation and transmission of property. Lawmakers struggled to regulate marriage and to maintain conjugal power in men's hands. Since the 1790s, led by feminists such as Mary Wollstonecraft, a middle-class political and cultural avant-garde had criticized the patriarchal marriage-property system in their writings and experimented with alternative amorous and conjugal arrangements in private life. Religious and moral commentators denounced the moral degeneracy of the age and middle-class social managers tried to 'reform' and regulate what they saw as lower-class and upper-class 'libertinism', while reform-oriented intellectuals and writers, led by figures such as the poet Byron and the 'Holland House' circle, cultivated and promoted purposely transgressive sexual and marital relations. The upper class were widely perceived as routinely unfaithful maritally and promiscuous sexually, while the lower classes were widely supposed to emulate their 'betters' in these respects. A popular form of cheap literature comprised accounts of lawsuits arising from extra-marital affairs in high society. The publisher John Fairburn specialized in this line of chapbooks in the 1810s and 1820s, reporting lawsuits for what was known as 'criminal conversation' or 'crim. con.' – extra-marital sexual intercourse – and newspapers and magazines regularly carried accounts of such suits. Because divorce was difficult or impossible to obtain in the law courts, parliament received a steady stream of petitions to dissolve marriages, and accounts of these were also published for public amusement, instruction, titillation, or outrage. The interest extended to cultural anthropology and Romantic Orientalism, with their depictions of other cultures' practices of sexuality and marriage; for example, increased interest in the subject led in 1824 to a new edition of James Lawrence's 1811 novel ostensibly about the unconventional marriage practices of a south Indian people, entitled, *The Empire of the Nairs; or, The Panorama of Love*, with the engaging subtitle, 'enlivened with the intrigues of several crowned heads; and with anecdotes of courts, brothels, convents, and seraglios; the whole forming a picture of gallantry, seduction, prostitution, marriage, and divorce, in all parts of the world'.

Attitudes to love and marriage had wide political implications, especially after the 1790s. The Society for the Suppression of Vice, established in 1802 after a royal proclamation against vice in 1787, was instigated by the religious Evangelical and anti-slavery campaigner William Wilberforce and his associates. As commentators of the time pointed out, however, the Society concentrated their attention on the lower and lower-middle classes and on what they saw as the intertwined dangers of sexual immorality, religious free-thinking and 'blasphemy' and political reformism. A particular object of the Vice Society's system of harassment and intimidation was the radical reformer, writer and publisher, Richard Carlile (1790–1843). Carlile was jailed from 1819 to 1825 for republishing the works of Tom Paine and other writings, but his wife and then his sister carried on selling his publications, one of which was *Every Woman's Book; or, What is Love?* (1826), a pamphlet advocating sexual equality, acceptance of sexual pleasure as human and social, and practice of birth control. At the same time, legal and theological discourses were brought to bear in such works as the lawyer Thomas Poynter's *Concise View of the Doctrine and Practice of Ecclesiastical Courts in Doctors' Commons on Various Points Relative to Marriage and Divorce* (1824) and the Rev. Hector Morgan Davies's *Doctrine and Law of Marriage, Adultery, and Divorce* (1826). *Richmond* does not deal directly with issues of marriage, adultery and divorce that were constantly in the news in the 1820s, but it repeatedly represents unconventional or illicit conjugal relationships and unsatisfactory marriages. In doing so, the novel emphasizes the forbearance and sacrifice of women in making and maintaining conjugal relationships, legalized or not, in all the depicted relationships, but most obviously in the case of the man enacting Shakespeare's *Taming of the Shrew* in his own marriage, an episode which otherwise fits oddly into Tom Richmond's dossier of cases. Further, in the one happy marriage that the novel features, between Tom Richmond and the 'fallen' Maria, Richmond expressly raises and dismisses the issue of female sexual chastity as a *sine qua non* of marriage, and while he concedes that Maria's loss of 'respectability' may be a consideration – 'virtuous' women were not supposed to befriend or even visit a 'fallen' woman – he also sets that aside as irrelevant to people in their humble station in life – policemen, like hangmen, were conventionally regarded as social outsiders by profession. In short, *Richmond* treats love and marriage in relation to and as part of a broad and complex topic in the news, touching private and public life, morality and property, and regulation and reform.

Richmond's representation of organized and systemic forms of crime also incorporated certain current news topics as indications of public and institutional interest and concern. There are four main topics absorbed into the novel in this respect. One of these is 'body-snatching', or the theft of the recently deceased from graveyards for sale to commercial anatomy schools. Newspapers carried reports of often violent confrontations between the public and grave-robbers, and between gangs of grave-robbers, and newspapers and cheap pamphlets reported murders carried out as a way to obtain specific kinds of saleable cadavers. The demand for fresh cadavers arose from the requirement to study anatomy in order to qualify to practise medicine, and dissection classes open to the public were also a form of commercial entertainment. Since the eighteenth century, many anatomical subjects had been supplied from the gallows, and legislation provided that the bodies of hanged felons be turned over to anatomy schools, though the practice was widely unpopular and from time to time a mob sympathetic to a particular criminal would try to prevent this. By the mid-1820s, however, increasing demand from anatomy schools, the inability to preserve bodies for very long and diminution in the number of hangings created a crisis of supply, leading to organized theft of the recently interred from graveyards – one of the trades Jones practises in Tom Richmond's first case. Grave-robbing led to gang rivalries and fights, and extraordinary measures were taken by relatives of the deceased to prevent such theft, such as guarding the gravesite or erecting a 'mortsafe' around it.[13] Murders were also committed as part of this traffic, as in the famous case of William Burke and William Hare, who carried out a series of murders in Edinburgh for this purpose in 1827 and 1828, just after *Richmond* was published. In 1828 parliament also investigated the matter, producing the *Report of the Select Committee on Anatomy*, which eventually led to the 1832 Bill for Regulating Schools of Anatomy.

Connected to grave-robbing in *Richmond* is smuggling, a longstanding and, with poaching, perhaps the most pervasive crime of the time. Grave-robbing, poaching and smuggling were similar in being nocturnal crimes usually executed by gangs, which the property owning public seem to have found especially alarming. Poaching and smuggling had particular resemblances of their own. They were among the commonest offences listed in the returns to parliament for criminal convictions and the authorities found both very difficult to suppress. Law manuals for justices of the peace and magistrates all contained instructions on dealing with those apprehended for smuggling, which was a serious crime, yet, like poaching, also widely accepted and even connived at by people in all social classes. The seriousness of smuggling was stated emphatically in the eleventh edition (1825) of a widely used law manual of the time, *Gifford's English Lawyer; or, Every Man His Own Lawyer: Containing a Summary of the Constitution of England, Its Laws and Statutes*:

> This offence is restrained by a great variety of statutes, which inflict pecuniary penalties, and seizure of goods for smuggling, and affix the guilt of felony, with transportation for seven years, upon more open practices. By the [act] 10 Geo. II. c. 34. if three or more persons shall assemble with fire-arms or other offensive weapons to assist in the illegal exportation or importation of goods, or in rescuing the same after seizure, or in rescuing offenders in custody for such offences, or shall pass with such goods in disguise, or shall wound, shoot at, or assault any officers of the revenue when in the execution of their duty, such persons shall be felons without benfit of clergy.[14]

The statement indicates that the offences were frequent enough to require such penalties as deterrents, and these offences are precisely those depicted in *Richmond*. To assist law enforcement and the justice system further, there were regular updates of *An Alphabetical Abridgement of the Laws for the Prevention of Smuggling*, listing statutes from the time of Charles II up to the year of publication. In 1825, parliament passed *An Act for the Prevention of Smuggling*, and the government ordered the publication of James Hume's *The Laws of the Customs*,

Compiled by Direction of the Lords Commissioners of His Majesty's Treasury, and Published by the Appointment and under the Sanction of the Commissioners of His Majesty's Customs, with Notes and Index. Meanwhile, moral and social commentators attempted to persuade the public that purchasing smuggled goods was wrong for a variety of reasons. These pamphlets included *The Sin and Misery of Smuggling Considered in a Sermon* (1819); a reprint of the Methodist John Wesley's *A Word to a Smuggler* (1823); *The Bold Smiggler* (1824), a melodramatic and ostensibly true tale of the exposure of a villainous smuggler; and the prolific Evangelical writer Caroline Fry's *Peggy Lum; or, A Hint to the Purchasers of Smuggled Goods: A Tale* (1825). In a more elaborated and belletristic way, *Richmond* takes its place in this campaign to portray the evils of smugglers and smuggling.

Finally, *Richmond* represents a variety of organized frauds and deceptions that were in the news and before parliament in the 1820s. Two of these, counterfeiting banknotes and crooked gambling, are connected through the same perpetrators, Mrs — and her husband and their accomplices. Richmond first notices the lady attempting to pass forged banknotes in shops, using her genteel appearance and manners to pay for small items with large notes, aiming to receive change in genuine money. While observing her house in a fashionable part of London, Richmond then becomes involved with the wretched Percy, who is stripped of his large inheritance by the crooked gambling carried on at Mrs —'s house and various other frauds she and her accomplices practise on him. This lengthy episode in the novel responds, very broadly, to public concern in the 1820s over what was perceived to be an increase in crimes of fraud and deception, linked to concern over the reliability and stability of the system of public credit and finance.

More particularly, the novel responds to public concern over the counterfeiting of Bank of England notes in the early 1820s. There were two related issues here – the ease or difficulty of forging banknotes, and the reliability and stable value of paper currency. Until 1821, banknotes could not be exchanged for gold and silver currency, exacerbating concern over the genuineness of the paper notes. In 1818 Charles Williams published his *Considerations on the Alarming Increase of Forgery on the Bank of England, and the Neglect of Remedial Measures; with an Essay on the Remedy for the Detection of Forgeries*; this book came out with the firm of Longman, Hurst, Rees, Orme and Brown, soon to be publisher of Thomas Gaspey's first five novels. Williams attributed the supposed increase in counterfeiting banknotes to the same cause of economic distress blamed by commentators on the increase of other crimes, such as poaching and smuggling, referred to earlier. Williams also blamed the Bank of England and the government for insufficient care in making notes counterfeit-proof, declaring, 'The unguarded character of the Bank note seems almost to invite the bold and the unwary to the trial, instead of being fenced about by difficulties, if not sufficient to keep the enterprizing or the desperate from the attempt, at least to give them obstacles to surmount before they venture to immolate themselves' (p. 41). The American inventor Jacob Perkins (1766–1849) came up with a more sophisticated printing method and in 1819 moved to Britain and obtained the contract for producing Bank of England notes. His invention was discussed by Sir William Congreve in his *Analysis of the True Principles of Security against Forgery Exemplified by an Enquiry into the Sufficiency of the American Plan for a New Bank Note* (1820). At the same time, there was public discussion of appropriate punishments for forgery as a crime that threatened the basis of the national economy. Anxiety about banknotes' genuineness persisted, however, and was exacerbated by a perceived increase in frauds and forgeries carried out by those entrusted with a wide variety of documents of value, such as stocks and instruments for establishing or transferring property. In 1819 George Cruikshank and the reformist William Hone issued a burlesque banknote satirizing paper money and the government's attempts to ensure its credibility through legislating harsh punishments for forgery and for passing bad notes. In 1821 an anonymous writer addressed the Lord Chancellor *On the Subject of Forgeries and Bank Prosecutions, and on the Proposed Amelioration of the Criminal Law*. Though technological improvements made forging banknotes more difficult after the early 1820s, confidence in paper money continued to weaken, and by 1825–6 there was a crisis in banking and paper currency, with consequent failure of country banks and bankruptcy of many businesses. The government responded with a banking act in 1826, initiating a process of liberalization in banking and joint-stock companies. One of the commentators on this crisis was the same Thomas Skinner Surr who is sometimes credited with authorship of *Richmond*, in a pamphlet entitled *The Present Critical State of the Country Developed; or, An Exhibition of the True Causes of the Calamitous Derangement of the Banking and and Commercial System* (1826).

The reliability of paper currency and the banking system was related to the reliability of other kinds of paper instruments used to represent or transfer property. This issue is strikingly presented in *Richmond* in the case of Percy, who is bilked of large sums by fraud and the fraudulent passing of his cheques and other instruments of property by Farmer Grinstead and Mrs — and her gang. The most celebrated such case in real life was probably that of Henry Fauntleroy (1784–1824), a banker who financed a lavish lifestyle by forgery and fraud with his clients' property, and who was caught, convicted and hanged outside Newgate prison on 30 November 1824 before a crowd estimated at 100,000. Fauntleroy was fictionalized in Edward Lytton Bulwer's 1828 novel, *The Disowned*, and it may be that Percy in *Richmond* is meant to represent a victim of the fraudster such as Fauntleroy. Legislation did not seem able to keep up with the problem.

In 1823, parliament passed a Forgery Bill consolidating and updating legislation on various kinds of forgery, including wills, legal documents, certain kinds of banknotes and so on. Together, paper money and paper financial instruments, including stocks, deeds, wills and so on, constituted a complex financial system that could both enable and disable economic activity. Political economists weighed in with analyses of the situation and proposals for change, such as Thomas Tooke's *Considerations on the State of the Currency* (1826). The poet Thomas Moore published several satirical poems on currency and finance in 1826 in *The Times* newspaper. Reformers such as William Cobbett had been claiming for years that the currency and finance system was a fraud that benefited and was managed by just such upper-class crooks as Mrs — and her husband. When *Richmond* was published in 1827, all this would be fresh in the minds of readers, and a continuing topic of news, giving additional resonance to the novel's portrayal of forgers and fraudsters.

Banking, banknotes and investment were related in public discussion to the widespread vice of gaming, or gambling, through the identification of both as forms of speculation based on chance rather than knowledge and highly susceptible to, or indeed inseparable from, cheating and fraud. Gaming had long been considered an upper- and lower-class vice, and in the 1820s there were semi-private gambling dens and gambling clubs located in the St James's quarter and elsewhere in London's fashionable west end. Scandal papers frequently reported the enormous losses incurred by the famous and the fashionable, led by George IV when Prince of Wales and subsequently Prince Regent, when his father and parliament paid his debts, in one instance in return for his agreement to marry so as to produce a legitimate heir and thereby ensure the stability of the crown and government. In such ways were gambling and the established order seen as intertwined. As *Richmond* shows in the instances of Percy and the Cambridge student-gentlemen, it could certainly be considered genteel to risk and lose large sums. Middle-class moralists, social commentators, and reformists of course inveighed against the evils of gambling, especially among the lower and upper classes. William Cobbett in his political *Sermon* of 1 October 1821 condemned gaming for hardening the feelings and corrupting society. In the October 1825 issue of the *Newgate Monthly Magazine*, which both sensationalized and condemned lower- and upper-class vice and crime for a middle-class readership, an essayist blamed the upper classes for the recent spread of gambling to the other classes:

> The passion for gaming belongs more particularly to what are called the higher orders of society,—to the titled and the aristocratical portion of the community. Yet so prone is mankind to be dazzled by appearances,—so apt is he to copy the manners and practices of those whom he has been taught to look upon as his superiors,— when we reflect that a great part of what were once exclusively the vices of the rich,

are now become extensively the practices and propensities of the poor, owing solely to their pernicious example,—and when we see the influence which riches every where procure for their possessors,—and that the desire of getting riches acts powerfully on all mankind,—we shall no longer be surprised at the progress which gaming has made, and is still making, upon the useful classes of society.[15]

Even more seductive would be the 'gamestress', such as Mrs —.

The example of the 'fashionable gamester' was considered especially danger-ous for 'mercantile' or middle-class youth; as *The Economist* magazine put it in 1824:

> When the glittering of London pleasures first meets the eye of a young man placed upon the road of a mercantile life, or when he enters any of the multifarious depart-ments in the machine of society which always lead the industrious and prudent to honourable emolument, he too frequently misconceives the fashionable gamester's character, and confounds his crimes with elegant accomplishments.[16]

The dangers of gambling were also associated with perhaps the most famous murder case of the mid-1820s. This was the murder of William Weare by John Thurtell and his accomplices, known as the Radlett or Elstree murder, in October 1823, over a gambling debt owed by Weare to Thurtell. One of the dozen-and-a-half books on the murder was entitled *The Fatal Effects of Gambling, Exemplified in the Murder of Wm. Weare, and the Trial and Fate of John Thurtell . . .; To Which Is Added, The Gambler's Scourge: A Complete Exposé of the Whole System of Gambling in the Metropolis* (1824). In the 'Gambler's Scourge', various suppos-edly 'true-life' incidents are recounted that would together compose the story of Percy in *Richmond*. The picture of 'fashionable' gaming presented by these com-mentators and their judgment of it are similar to those presented by *Richmond*'s narrator-protagonist, though his sympathy for the victim is perhaps greater. More generally, the mid-1820s saw the steady mobilization of middle-class pub-lic opinion, parliamentary legislators and the government to restrict and control gambling, among other 'vices', as a threat to good work habits, prudent domes-tic economy, and thus to the national economy as a whole.[17] In this movement, *Richmond* represents a 'liberal conservative' approach similar to that taken by the government and such leading government figures as George Canning, whose politics Thomas Gaspey seems to have agreed with in other respects. Finally, in *The History of George Godfrey*, published a year after *Richmond*, Gaspey would vividly represent another form of gambling widely deplored for its negative effect on the national economy – speculating in stocks and shares.

Richmond's representation of fashionable gaming as inherently fraudulent and corrupting is set within the broader context of what were known at the time as the 'frauds of London'. These encompassed the widespread practices of fraud and deception, both occasional and organized, that were supposed to characterize everyday life in the metropolis, to victimize foreigners and country visitors in particular, to contribute to the supposed crime wave of the time, and to participate in a network of fraud and corruption pervading all levels of society, reaching into politics and government, and supposedly requiring any number of reforms. Other parts of this network of fraud, from bogus auctions to the stock market, would be depicted in Thomas Gaspey's *History of George Godfrey*. In *Richmond*, the most prominent victim of the frauds of London is the amiable Irishman (and Richmond's assistant) Thady, who is quickly relieved of his reward for helping to catch the gang of smugglers. Warnings about the 'frauds of London' in fact comprised a form of popular literature that was generations old. In the mid-eighteenth century there were works such as *The Cheats of London Exposed* (1769) and *The New Cheats of London Exposed* (1750), and in the 1770s Alexander Hogg, publisher of a popular version of the *Newgate Calendar*, published *The Frauds of London Detected*. The genre seems to have been reinvigorated in the aftermath of the decades of the Revolutionary and Napoleonic wars. In 1815, an 'Old Bow Street Officer' published a twenty-eight-page pamphlet entitled, *The Frauds of London, Displaying the Numerous and Daring Cheats and Robberies Practised upon the Stranger and the Unwary*. A similar work was *The Stranger's Guide; or, The Frauds of London Exposed* (1821). The frauds particular to 'trade', or small business, were of concern to Londoners themselves, and *The London Tradesman* (1819), a manual for shopkeepers, included a section on 'Swindler's Arts'. The frauds of London were also put into narrative form, as in *A Fortnight's Ramble through London; or, A Complete Display of all the Cheats and Frauds Practised in that Great Metropolis . . . Being a Narrative of the Adventures of a Farmer's Son* (1817). *Richmond* absorbs this topic, too, into its narrative, and in fact the novel's closing sentence declares that its purpose is precisely to bring such information to the reading public.

Finally, it is one victim of the 'cheats of London' in the novel, Thady, who also foregrounds one of Gaspey's favourite themes, and a continuing major issue in the news – Ireland and the 'Irish problem'. *Richmond* portrays Thady and the other Irish as representative the entire Irish people; the portrayal is both sympathetic and condescending. On the one hand, Thady is passionate, impulsive, naïve and uncultured; on the other hand, he is loyal, honest, reliable and strong. In the period just preceding publication of *Richmond* the 'Irish problem' had become increasingly pressing. Led by Daniel O'Connell, the Catholic Association had been holding huge demonstrations in various parts of Ireland, demanding emancipation of Catholics from their long-standing civil disabilities, such as exclusion from certain public offices and professions, restrictions on worship and religious education and so on. To achieve this end, the Association demanded an end to the union of Ireland with Great Britain, that is, with England and Scotland. Perhaps most importantly, the organization, size and composition of the Association demonstrated the feasibility of something that alarmed the ruling establishment of the United Kingdom – a coalition of lower and middle classes to demand reforms, in an organization funded by very small individual contributions, mobilized to express their demands with convincingly large numbers – a movement with the manifest potential to carry its demands by force should it choose to do so. Two years after *Richmond* was published, the Catholic Relief Act conceded many of the Association's demands as the only way of avoiding such a violent revolution, though against the continuing opposition of the king, the establishment and most non-Catholics across the United Kingdom. The Catholic Relief Act enfranchised many Catholics, but not most of those who had mobilized in the Catholic Association; in fact, the Act extended citizenship only to more well-to-do, property-owning Catholics, as an attempt to break up the coalition of lower and middle classes that had made the Catholic Association such a powerful force, alarming to the establishment and an example to a similar, emergent coalition in England and Scotland. The same tactic would be used by the establishment in devising and enacting the Reform Bill of 1832.

Gaspey would later give full, if oblique, treatment to the 'Irish problem' of his day, using the form of the historical novel, in *The Self-Condemned* (1836), a quite substantial work of fiction. There he acknowledged the assistance of the Irish-born Protestant civil servant, antiquarian and writer, Thomas Crofton Croker (1798–1854). It is possible that Gaspey already knew Croker in the mid 1820s, when Croker was working at the Admiralty office in London and published his *Researches in the South of Ireland, Illustrative of the Scenery, Architectural Remains, and the Manners and Superstitions of the Peasantry* (1824), and his widely read and admired *Fairy Legends and Traditions of the South of Ireland* (1825–8). Certainly *Richmond* portrays Thady and the other Irish characters in the novel as inhabiting a world of 'superstitions of the peasantry' and 'fairy legends and traditions'. Further, Thady shares a name and a similar character with the narrator of *Castle Rackrent* (1800), Maria Edgeworth's widely read comic novel promoting the Union of Great Britain and Ireland. Both Croker's work and the two Thadys are designed to show the desirability of maintaining a paternalistic and conciliatory relationship between Great Britain and Ireland, in the interests of both. This implication goes beyond Ireland to the empire at large. Through Thady and his compatriots, *Richmond* represents the Irish as an unmodernized 'folk', like the peoples of Britain's other colonies as the British liked to see them: essentially virtuous, well meaning and docile but easily mis-led by appeals to their passions and requiring the direction and management of a supposedly more cultivated, rational and self-disciplined people and government, in order to bring out the best rather than the worst in them. Susceptible to the 'cheats of London' in the broadest sense of exploitation by the unscrupulous and self-serving, Thady, as representative of the Irish, clearly needs a 'union' with the well-meaning and virtuous of Britain in order to be useful to others and do well for himself. Though the issue here is not attribution of *Richmond* to Thomas Gaspey, nevertheless, its view of the Irish and the 'Irish problem' is broadly similar to that set out in the novels known to be Gaspey's.

So too, with the novelistic form of *Richmond*, despite the fact that it seems formally different from Gaspey's earlier novels in major respects. Though *Richmond* is in first-person narrative form, unlike Thomas Gaspey's early novels, this is consistent with the participation of *Richmond* in the picaresque tradition, discussed earlier, major representatives of which were also first-person narratives. Gaspey's early novels were all to some degree historical romances and the usual narrative mode for this subgenre was third-person; both *Richmond* and Gaspey's *George Godfrey* are set in contemporary life, in addition to being picaresque novels and so a change in narrative mode to first-person was appropriate for the conventions of this subgenre. Further, *Richmond* does not use the first-person narrative form to develop a complex and conflicted protagonist, as many other novels of the time in this form did. Tom Richmond remains a relatively straightforward character, not much given to self-reflection, like the protagonists of Thomas Gaspey's early novels. Gaspey's early novels were structured as a braided or criss-crossing narrative, in which the story shifts back and forth from one character or group of characters to another or back and forth from the narrative present to a restrospective explanation of events just recounted; at the novel's closure, the several strands come together. The narrative structure of *Richmond* appears to differ from this, as the story, narrated by its eponymous protagonist, follows his adventures. Nevertheless, this story also shifts focus from time to time as Richmond recounts the background and experiences of one character or another that he encounters in the course of his own adventures. Though in a moderated way, then, the narrative structure of *Richmond* is also based on the braided pattern.

Other aspects of *Richmond* that seem to differ from Thomas Gaspey's novelistic practice in his early novels may be placed more or less directly in relation to Gaspey's employment as a journalist. From *The Lollards* to *The Witch-finder* and the later *Self-condemned*, these novels are larded with antiquarian and historical information, an interest that was Gaspey's sideline or hobby, whereas *Richmond*, especially Volumes 2 and 3 recounting the hero's cases as a Bow Street officer, is filled with anecdotes that could have come from the 'Court News' or 'Bow Street News' sections of the *Morning Post* or *Courier* newspapers, for which Gaspey worked. Antiquarian and historical anecdotes could be regarded as the documented news of past times, and news of the present as the documentation for antiquarian and historical researches of the future. The artistic objectives of including such material, in both the historical romance and the novel of contemporary life, were to create an impression of the authenticity of the represented fictional world, to establish the author's knowledge and reliability in this representation, and to create for the reader an effect of 'real life'. All of these objectives could be reduced to the single one of rhetorical effectiveness—persuading the reader of the 'truth' of the fiction, or its ideological validity, its applicability to the reader's real world. There may of course be other, crass objectives, such as filling up the length of the three-volume novel that publishers expected, or economically using up material left over from or unsuitable as newspaper and magazine work. By changing his material from antiquarian to journalistic, Gaspey – if he was the author of *Richmond* – may have been drawing on his profession rather than on his hobby and changing his compositional method less than his subject matter. If the author of *Richmond* was not Gaspey, there is good reason, from both its content and form, to believe that its author was someone in or close to the world of journalism.

In short, the fact that all but one of the novels known to be by Gaspey are historical romances, whereas *Richmond* is a novel of contemporary life, does not alter the issue of *Richmond*'s form. As shown here and in the general introduction to Gaspey's novels, both these and *Richmond* incorporate important issues in the news. At this time, both the historical romance and the novel of contemporary life dealt with issues current at the time of the romance's or novel's composition and publication, though they do so in different ways and usually obliquely. In both kinds of fiction, drawing explicit connections between the situations of the story and issues in contemporary reality was usually done lightly if at all, though not so much from overriding concern with artistry. Rather, most readers and authors seem to have considered that a novel's being too explicit about such connections jarred or interfered with the novel's effectiveness as a novel and thus with its rhetorical and ideological persuasiveness about real world issues and concerns. Historical romances 'find' such issues in the past and there are few if any novels that are entirely antiquarian in the sense of representing a past period or moment for its own sake. Moreover, historiographical and antiquarian works themselves can usually be demonstrated to address issues and concerns current at the time they were researched and published. Similarly, novels of contemporary life usually avoid much 'editorializing' – to use a later term from journalism – about issues from contemporary life depicted in the novel. The important point is that the cultural and ideological work of both historical romances and novels of contemporary life – indeed, all kinds of the novel – is to illustrate or dramatize the operation and effect of such real-life issues in individual, domestic, local, everyday life but shaped and given a closure that such issues seldom have in the real, ongoing experience and lives of readers. Such present-centredness was and is a large part of what interested the novels' readers, in the sense of addressing those readers' real material interests and their understanding of the world they returned to when they set down a novel they had been reading. The relationship between historical romance, novel of contemporary life, journalism and the real world and its larger issues may, then, be understood in this way: the first two are different methods of fictionalizing or representing the real world and its larger issues, as these are also reported or represented in journalism. Put another way, novels and newspapers are different discourses related to the same real world and its larger issues. The question that remains is the relationship between *Richmond*, specifically as a novel of contemporary life, and its use of novelistic and journalistic discourse.

Richmond may be seen as a journalistic novel in terms of its form as well as its content, or topics from the news; it attempts to converge or fuse these otherwise different discourses. A 'journalistic novel' in this formal sense may be regarded as one that appropriates, adapts or incorporates the overall structure of a journal or newspaper as well as the compositional and stylistic practices characteristic of journalism. It is true that as a whole *Richmond* seems like two different novels crudely joined together – a first volume of picaresque road adventures and a further two volumes of disparate tales of crime and detection. The first volume looks like the opening of a novel of bohemian adventure, or genteel vagrancy, though unlike some earlier picaresque novels it is predominantly comic rather than satiric in tone. The second and third volumes look like a folder of police detective cases. It is possible that the author of *Richmond* set out to write one kind of novel and then decided to change it to another. Nevertheless, both parts of *Richmond* may be seen to be informed by journalism and journalistic discourse. As illustrated earlier, both parts of *Richmond* represent issues in the news, sometimes the same issues, and ones that were reported according to conventions of journalism in the kind of newspapers that Thomas Gaspey worked for. Further, both parts of *Richmond* may be seen to have underlying connections with journalistic method and the discourse of journalism, or its assumptions, practices and conventions, as these were developing in the 1820s. Gaspey began his career in journalism when newspapers were still developing their newsgathering practices and increasing staff reporters, and investigative journalism was relatively undeveloped. The idea was only beginning to be established of the newspaper press as a 'fourth estate', in addition to the three constitutional and political estates or powers of monarch, aristocracy, and commoners (sometimes varied to mean aristocracy, clergy, and commoners). In this 'estates' model, journalism was seen to have a particular responsibility to inquire into and, if appropriate, to expose and challenge the activities of government and the other estates that controlled and dominated the government. In the 1820s, the notion of the press as the fourth estate was associated by some specifically with the parliamentary reporters, of whom Gaspey was one. Others in the 1820s went further and associated the 'fourth estate' not with the kind of newspapers Gaspey worked for but rather with those produced by reformist journalists such as William Cobbett,[18] precursors of what would now be considered investigative journalism, who professed to detect and expose the hidden crimes and secret conspiracies of the privileged classes and the established order. In this understanding of a 'fourth estate', the kind of newspapers Gaspey worked for were assumed, often correctly, to support either the government or the parliamentary opposition, to receive payment for doing so, and thus to condone or collude with the established system to a greater or lesser extent.

Nevertheless, Gaspey's novelization of the news in his early works of fiction indicates that he understood the political role of journalism and may have seen himself as a member of an emergent 'fourth estate'. Gaspey's early professional years were spent as a parliamentary reporter, a relatively settled and regular job in journalism, and he went on to become a newspaper editor, around the time *Richmond* was published. As such, his responsibility would have been to have a sense of the overall and fairly regular structure of kinds of news presented in the newspapers of his day, as described here in the introduction to Gaspey's life and career. As a journalist and even more as editor, Gaspey or someone in a similar position would likely develop an understanding of the contemporary world in terms of both the overview and the particular instance – the general structure of relationships between economy, politics and society developing over time, and the individual events that formed the news, classified according to a newspaper's way of ordering such events. These related understandings of the profession of the journalist and the structure of the world and of the journalist's role in mediating or reporting that world to the reading public, day by day and event by event, may be seen as informing the structure and form of *Richmond* in four particular ways.

Tom Richmond, both as genteel vagrant and especially as Bow Street officer, occupies a position analogous to that of the journalist in several respects: he is a voluntary social outsider, he is thereby able to observe and investigate society from the outside and reveal its 'truth', he sustains an identity that is independent of the obligations and responsibilities that trammel the lives and actions of most people, and as the narrator of his own story he reports his findings to the reading public. Further, as a detector of crime, Richmond resembles the emergent investigative journalist of the 'fourth estate'. It is true that, as a Bow Street officer, Richmond is part of a hierarchical organization and an arm of the state but, like the detectives of the much later 'private eye' and 'hard-boiled' popular fiction, the Bow Street officers were famous for the degree of independence they enjoyed and initiative they showed in pursuing and preventing crimes – certainly this is the way the Bow Street officers are portrayed in *Richmond*. Though investigative journalism or the glamorous crusading journalist-hero hardly existed at that time, journalism, and especially parliamentary reporting, was emerging as a distinct professional identity with a sense of having a particular calling and esprit-de-corps, and of being somewhat apart from and perhaps at times opposed to other professions more obviously implicated in the prevailing systems of hierarchy, power and privilege – professions satirized in Gaspey's *George Godfrey*. The same situation prevailed for the police detective, the precursor of which was the Bow Street officer. At the same time, in the 1820s both the journalist and the police officer retained associations with earlier identities as mere unprincipled 'hacks', willing to serve whoever paid them. The analogy between police detective and journalist is not made explicit in *Richmond* and recognition of such an analogy does not seem necessary to understanding the novel's purpose. This purpose was an explicit if muted critical representation of society as systemic exploitation of the weak by the powerful, unaffected or even exacerbated by unreformed state institutions and agencies, and disrupted or corrected only by the efforts of upstanding individuals such as Richmond, the naval officer Frampton and the magistrate W—m M—d.

A journalistic perspective and practice, with their underlying ideological assumptions, may also be seen as informing the structure of *Richmond*. This structure seems highly episodic, comprising an assemblage of stories more than a connected series of incidents, and united mainly through being brought together in one place and reported by a single observer. Critics have seen the structure of *Richmond* as crude, but rather than being inept and casual it may have its own aesthetic and ideological purpose and meaning. It can be argued that, like the apparently unconnected or loosely connected sections of a newspaper, the sections of *Richmond* may have an underlying principle and coherence. For one thing, *Richmond*'s episodic structure resembles that of earlier picaresque novels such as the Spanish *El Buscón* or Defoe's novels. Such novels were once seen as formally inartistic, especially when compared to nineteenth- and twentieth-century literary fiction, but they are now credited with having certain kinds of thematic unity and critical social purpose, such as exposing systemic social injustice, institutional abuses, or human self-interestedness. Similarly, the lack of connectedness in *Richmond* is only apparent. As discussed earlier, there are important contemporary themes that emerge in and align episodes otherwise apparently disparate, such as abuses of love and marriage, vagrancy and its causes, and the pervasiveness of fraud and deception in society. Even these different topics may be gathered under the broad concern over reform in the 1820s.

It may be, too, that the seemingly weak or disjunct structure of earlier picaresque fiction and of *Richmond* has its own purpose as an anti-structure, implicitly set against and critiquing certain kinds of structuring. Much nineteenth- and twentieth-century fiction that distinguished itself or was later distinguished as 'literary', or motivated by 'high' artistic standards and 'serious' moral and intellectual purpose, did so in part by manifesting unity of plot, connectedness of episodes, a causal or dialectical relationship between character and action, and a distinct closure or resolution. A social and cultural function of this form is to represent a middle-class ideology according to which the individual life and the development of society as a whole are, in a general sense, formable and hence reformable by human agency. The individual life and society as a whole can be fashioned by knowledgeable and self-disciplined persons according to a pattern that is 'progressive', in a structured sequence of foreseeable cause and effect characterized by continuous 'improvement' or betterment. Detective fiction, as a more 'popular' form developed later in the nineteenth and in the twentieth century, was often based specifically on the assumption that the 'truth', or relation of such cause and effect, can be uncovered. By contrast, a purposeful lack of such connectedness in a fiction may suggest that life and social relations are more subject to chance, coincidence, and 'fate', or social and other forces that are usually unforeseeable, mostly unknowable and ultimately uncontrollable. In short, differences in novelistic form may express ideological and political differences.

A 'logical' and 'unified' novelistic structure was pursued vigorously by certain reformists of the 1790s, such as those in the circle of William Godwin and Mary Wollstonecraft – in fact, Godwin's *Things As They Are; or, The Adventures of Caleb Williams* (1794), which is based on this formal principle, is also cited frequently as the first detective novel. Opposing these reformist novelists were conservative writers who denied that the individual and society were formed by discoverable causes or could be subjected to any 'system' of reform or general 'improvement', and their novels reflected this denial both formally and thematically, being highly episodic, foregrounding chance and the circumstantial, and burlesquing the definitive closure. By the time *Richmond* was published, the idea that the principles of individual and social development can be known and directed in certain 'progressive' ways, however defined, was also associated with a variety of reformists, from humanitarians and religious Evangelicals through 'political economists' and socialists to utilitarians to 'Newgate novelists' such as Edward Bulwer. *Richmond*, like Thomas Gaspey's early novels, rejects the idea of systematic and systemic reform for belief in the ethical conduct of moral individuals, at times acting in concert. In general, such a view seems more characteristic of the professional and predominantly conservative newspaper journalism of the time than of the crusading reformist journalist such as William Cobbett. Like Thomas Gaspey's early novels, *Richmond* is not lacking in reformist sympathies and attitudes, but it may be considered mutedly or conservatively reformist.

The moderately reformist as well as journalistic rather than literary structure of *Richmond* as a whole is reinforced by its journalistic handling of individual episodes. This is perhaps the most innovative and experimental feature of the novel. Richmond's accounts of his adventures as genteel vagrant and of his investigations as police officer often resemble newspaper or magazine reportage in pace and tone. The episodes are reported with a journalistic immediacy, and most episodes resemble newspaper stories, rather than literary stories, in lacking a distinct closure, or indeed any closure, and some incidents are related as situations rather than finished and completed stories, as in the case of the minister of Duckenhurst and the case of the husband re-enacting *The Taming of the Shrew*. Even when episodes, storylines, or crimes are wound up, as with Richmond's courtship of Maria, his capture of Jones, or the story of Percy, the closing seems muted or even indeterminate. As noted earlier, the novel as a whole stops rather than concludes. These features seem more characteristic of a newspaper story or magazine piece than a work of literary fiction. This is in contrast to Thomas Gaspey's early novels, which seem determinedly, if sometimes awkwardly, literary. Such a departure need not indicate that Gaspey was not the novel's author, but rather indicates that Gaspey, or someone with his journalistic background, was attempting an innovative approach to novel-writing by introducing features of journalism. The episodes have these journalistic qualities throughout the novel, in both Richmond's genteel vagrancy and his police detective work. If not altogether characteristic of a newspaper report, the handling of episodes seems somewhere between such reports and the more literary magazine pieces that Thomas Gaspey produced over several decades of his career. The consistency of this journalistic handling throughout the novel also suggests that it was deliberate, and not an effect of ineptness in or indifference to novelistic conventions and literary quality. Gaspey's early novels introduced the news in certain ways, as themes and aspects of character and setting, while remaining conventionally, and even formulaically novelistic in other respects. *Richmond* introduces the news in similar ways; but it also goes further in attempting to fuse the novel with journalism – to inform the novel, or shape it formally, with journalistic discourse. Such an attempt would be consistent with, though an innovation in, the known novelistic practice of the journalist Thomas Gaspey. The point here is not to establish the authorship of *Richmond*, however, but to specify its distinctive character as a journalistic novel, in form as well as content. Even if *Richmond* turned out not to be by Gaspey, it could or should have been by someone like him, with his experience and engagement in journalism and the news of the day.

In what ways, then, is *Richmond* a Newgate narrative, and what kind of Newgate narrative is it? Most obviously, though it does not mention Newgate prison, *Richmond* is a work that deals in large part and directly with policing and crime in the heyday of Newgate as a major, if infamous, institution within the judicial and penal systems, as a symbol of state power and its limits and as a focus for, and recurring topic in, the continuing debate over reform generally. Like most other Newgate narratives of its time, whether fictional or non-fictional, *Richmond* considers Newgate prison less, if at all, as a material actuality than as a symbol or synecdoche for a complex discourse, or set of ideas, beliefs, practices and cultural objects, including novels. This discourse was concerned with important issues in real contemporary private and public life, such as moral and ethical

conduct, economic relations highlighted by property and theft, social relationships of trust and power, and the political relationship between the individual
and the state and how these should and could be made better. *Richmond*, or any
Newgate narrative, does not have to mention Newgate prison for Newgate and
especially what it represents to be a presence in the text. The often represented
realities of Newgate prison and the constantly discussed and debated issues that
Newgate stood for were familiar enough to the reading public to enable them
to understand the novel's distinctive contribution to Newgate discourse. As
demonstrated earlier, though it is a novel, *Richmond* incorporates themes and
methods from other media, including polemical and controversial writing and
especially newspaper journalism, that also engaged in the social, economic and
political discourse around Newgate and what it represented at the time. Like
other kinds of non-fiction writing that incorporates Newgate discourse, such as
social reportage, reform polemics and parliamentary reports, *Richmond* represents Newgate discourse through a narrative form – in this case, the novel.

As a novel, *Richmond* engages with Newgate discourse in ways appropriate
to that form – representing in individual cases and everyday life the nature and
consequences of the same wide social and political issues that are treated otherwise in other forms, such as historiography, legal discussion, religious writing,
statistical analysis, 'true crime' pamphlets and compilations such as the *Newgate
Calendar*, newspaper journalism, parliamentary reports and legislation and so on.
Despite its engagement, as a novel, with Newgate discourse, however, *Richmond*
was not considered a 'Newgate novel'. The controversy over so-called 'Newgate
novels' emerged in the 1830s as a debate over a kind of fiction, represented by
such novels as Edward Lytton Bulwer's *Paul Clifford* (1830) and *Eugene Aram*
(1832) and William Harrison Ainsworth's *Rookwood* (1834), supposedly glam-
orizing crime and criminals and using them to promote reform (see the general
introduction to this series). At that time *Richmond* was overlooked and was not
considered among such fiction until Keith Hollingsworth's 1963 critical and
historical study, *The Newgate Novel 1830–1847: Bulwer, Ainsworth, Dickens,
and Thackeray*. Even here, *Richmond* was discussed only briefly and it is often
not included among 'Newgate novels' in standard reference works today. Nevertheless, *Richmond* is a Newgate narrative in the sense just outlined; and it is a
Newgate novel in the sense that, like other Newgate novels recognized as such,
it develops Newgate discourse in particular ways. It draws on and evokes a long
tradition of fictional representation of crime, criminals and social underworlds,
going back to early picaresque fiction, at least; it reworks that tradition and its
themes and formal techniques and conventions and does so in order to portray
critically certain social injustices and institutional abuses of the time. In summary, *Richmond* participates in Newgate narrative as a novel dealing with issues

of crime and punishment, with other but related issues in the news at the time of its composition and publication, and with the issue of reform more broadly.

It is *Richmond*'s treatment of Newgate discourse in the particular aspect of policing and crime detection that connects it to the later development of the detective novel. This connection is the reason for *Richmond*'s survival into the twentieth and twenty-first centuries. This introduction has argued that *Richmond*'s major innovation was to incorporate news and journalistic method in the novel form, but today its innovation is usually seen as being one of the first novels to feature a police detective and to portray cases of crime detection, and its place in literary history is as a precursor of the detective novel. The *Oxford Companion to Crime and Mystery Writing* (1999), for example, mentions *Richmond* in the section 'Precursors of the Genre (to 1840)'.[19] The other 'precursor' often mentioned is William Godwin's reformist novel, *Things As They Are; or, The Adventures of Caleb Williams* (1794). In this novel, the narrator-protagonist is a servant who recounts his uncovering of a murder committed out of injured 'honour' by the gentleman employer whom he reveres, but who then relentlessly persecutes Williams to prevent him from disclosing the crime, and the dishonour. Godwin's narrative of crime and detection was designed as a fable of the exposure of the 'crime' that Godwin saw as inherent in upper-class culture and identity, and the dangerous consequences of allowing such exposure to provoke social confrontation and conflict. More broadly, Godwin's novel may be seen as an early but characteristic instance of what the French crime writers known as Boileau-Narcéjac have identified as a central myth of the detective novel. This is the belief, originating in eighteenth-century Enlightenment rationalism and carried into the rationale of social, political and economic modernization, in the power of reason to discover chains of cause and effect and uncover the 'truth'.[20] *Richmond* may be generally and distantly indebted to Godwin's novel, but it is a work of a different kind and purpose.

Though much of *Richmond* deals specifically with the detection of crimes of various kinds, many eighteenth- and early-nineteenth-century novels also do so, though in a less concentrated way. In these novels, the 'crime' may or may not be so defined by law, but it is nevertheless treated as a 'wrong'. Often this crime involves concealment, theft or usurpation of the protagonist's identity and property by 'enemies', and solution of the crime results in disclosure of the protagonist's 'true' identity and family relationships, thereby enabling restoration of the character's social status and property and marriage to an appropriate partner. The myth underlying this kind of crime fiction is the belief of the middle-class reading public that their class 'enemies' have unjustly deprived them of their 'rightful' status and property. Examples would be Samuel Richardson's *Pamela; or, Virtue Rewarded* (1740–1) and Henry Fielding's *Tom Jones* (1749). In the late eighteenth and early nineteenth century an important variant of this 'crime' plot developed, in which the main character's social status and property were not lost or concealed, but rather undervalued or degraded, perhaps maliciously, in relation to the character's 'true' worth – his or her subjective, moral and intellectual merit. Such novels narrate the discovery or revelation of the character's 'true' or inner worth and show that such worth is appropriate or even superior to his or her ascribed social status and property. The myth underlying these fictions appealed strongly to a middle-class reading public concerned to establish their subjective merit in a society still largely based on and run according to ascribed social status. Examples would be the novels of Frances Burney and Jane Austen. Thomas Gaspey's novels participate in this kind of 'crime' fiction and in fact often involve murder and theft of identity and property. There is significant continuity, then, between *Richmond* and these other kinds of crime and detection fiction.

The relationship between *Richmond* and later detective fiction seems to be of another kind.[21] Histories of detective fiction, which began to appear in the twentieth century, usually date the beginning of the genre to Edgar Allan Poe's 'The Murders in the Rue Morgue', published in 1841, and treat earlier instances such as Godwin's *Caleb Williams* and *Richmond* as 'precursors'. Such an approach is 'Whig history', or a historical narrative based on a plot of progress toward some perfected form of the genre, in this case, and depending on the historian-critic, Arthur Conan Doyle's 'Sherlock Holmes' tales, or the novels of Agatha Christie, Dashiel Hammett, Georges Simenon and others. Further, Whig histories of a genre often collaborate with a typological or taxonomical approach to it, which seeks to specify or prescribe the genre's distinguishing traits or necessary conventions, evident in early forms but fully developed in works of the later golden age. In this case, taxonomists often distinguish detective fiction from crime fiction: the former focuses on the detective and the puzzle presented to him or her by the crime; the latter focuses on the crime and the criminal and often the punishment. Taxonomists also distinguish detective fiction from police detective or 'police procedural' fiction: the former features the solitary detective, often an amateur or private professional, working principally or exclusively alone, and usually choosing which cases to solve; the latter features the detective as part of a team dealing with whatever cases come up according to procedures imposed at least partly from without. A more recent development has been in psychological or psychoanalytical approaches to detective fiction, which see the form as reenacting intense curiosity, desire to know, or drive for intellectual mastery, generated by kinds of psychological repression. Finally, informing the historical, taxonomical and psychoanalytic approaches to the genre is usually an aesthetic or technical argument which designates certain works as exemplars or 'masterpieces' of the genre as an art or craft, based on certain, though not necessarily compatible, formal-aesthetic criteria, such as economy, simplicity, complexity, innovation based on convention, purity of form and matter and absence of 'extraneous' elements. An aspect of form, artistry and craft closely associated with detective and crime fiction, though not exclusive to it, is suspense, or techniques of generating feelings of uncertainty, anxiety and expectation in the reader, which are usually dispelled by the disclosures and resolution of the plot. In all cases, historians, taxonomists and theorists place the realization and golden age of detective fiction after the publication of *Richmond*, usually – with the exception of Poe's stories – long after, leaving a work such as *Richmond* as at best a 'precursor'.

In recent years the Whig-historical and formalist approaches to detective fiction have been challenged by post-structuralist, historicist and cultural studies approaches. The first understands a genre as part of a discursive continuum, related to other genres, and as a constantly changing interpretative and creative code used by readers and writers, rather than an ideal form to which individual texts aspire. Historicist and cultural studies approaches see genre in a similar way and understand the particular instance of a genre in its own right, in its cultural and social context and in terms of its possible ideological implications for historically and socially specific groups of readers, rather than as an approximation of an unchanging, transhistorical ideal or as an unrealized and flawed version of some perfected instance. From these more recent perspectives, *Richmond* may be seen as a detective or police detective novel, for what that is worth: its protagonist is a police detective who attempts, usually with success, to solve more or less serious crimes through methodical investigation and mental and physical effort. More important for understanding *Richmond* in its time and place, however, are the features discussed earlier – *Richmond*'s adaptation of the forms and traditions of picaresque fiction and fictitious autobiography, together with its incorporation of news and journalistic ways of writing. The result is an open-endedness in individual episodes and the novel as a whole that is at odds with the kinds of resounding and definitive closure found in much fiction of its day as well as in most later detective and crime fiction. From the perspective of Whig history and formalist poetics of detective fiction, such open-endedness may seem to be the effect of artistic incompetence or indifference, rather than an attempt to use the novel form in a new way, for a particular ideological and political purpose. Here it has been argued that *Richmond*'s open-endedness served a particular political ideology, a cautious reformism or progressive conservatism; but in other novels this form could serve other purposes: in post-structuralist, historicist and contextual readings, formal elements, structures and techniques do not have absolute or fixed meanings.

In light of such readings, it may seem that the potential of *Richmond*'s innovativeness remains to be developed. This is despite the fact that several novelists have recently taken up the figure of the Bow Street runner developed in *Richmond*. The American mystery writer Kate Ross has a runner named Peter Vance appear in *Whom the Gods Love* (1998) to help the protagonist, dandy-detective Julian Kestrel, solve a murder. The Canadian writing duo of Sean Russell and Ian Dennis, known as 'T. F. Banks', has produced two novels, *Thief-Taker* (2001) and *The Emperor's Assassin* (2003), in what is evidently designed as a series featuring a fictitious Bow Street officer named Henry Morton. In 2002 the American school teacher and writer Suzanne K. Rizzolo launched a series featuring a Bow Street runner appropriately named John Chase, with her novel *The Rose in the Wheel*, followed a year later by *Blood for Blood*. In 2004 Kathryn Smith, writer of 'Vampire romances', 'Nightmare romances', and 'Regency Historicals', published *In Your Arms Again*, one of the Regency Historicals, featuring the runner North Sheffield. In 2005 the American historical romance writer Kimberley Logan published *A Kiss before Dawn*, featuring a Bow Street runner who is also an accomplished lover. The English writer known as 'James McGee' (Glen Moy) has produced two novels featuring a 'runner' named Matthew Hawkwood, entitled *Ratcatcher* (2006) and *The Resurrectionist* (2007). The American romance writer Lisa Kleypas has published a 'Bow Street trilogy' of novels: *Someone to Watch Over Me* (1999), featuring the 'runner' Grant Morgan; *Lady Sophia's Lover* (2002), featuring the 'sexy' Bow Street magistrate Sir Ross Cannon; and *Worth Any Price* (2003), featuring the former 'crime lord' turned Bow Street runner, Nick Gentry. The erotic glamour of the earlier twentieth-century 'hard-boiled' detective is appropriated to the runners in these novels, and given a sharper twist in the story 'Fallen Angel' by Jess Michaels, in the historical erotica collection *Parlor Games* (2006). All of these novels deploy the established conventions of the contemporary police detective novel, here set in Regency London. This novelistic activity was probably due more to the reemergence of the figure of the Bow Street runner in academic social history and popular culture than to *Richmond*, though the appearance of the 1976 paperback reprint edition of the novel perhaps played some role.

Meanwhile, the Bow Street runner had continued to circulate in fact and fiction, though, again, probably owing little to *Richmond*. In 1837, only eight years after the Bow Street officers were replaced by the metropolitan police service, the *Penny Magazine*, in an article on 'The Municipal Government of the Metropolis', spoke of the Bow Street officers as a romantic but outdated and already almost forgotten body:

> ... we need not regret that the good old Bow Street officer is no more. We have fallen on better times, when it has been proved to be unnecessary to maintain a system of police espionage and acquaintance with theives, and to uphold a practice of compounding felonies, in order to check crime. These things are going out; and it is to be hoped that they will be soon as completely numbered with the tings that were as is the mounted highwaymen.[22]

In 1838, Charles Dickens had two ineffective runners, named Duff and Blathers, appear in his 'Newgate novel', *Oliver Twist*. The Bow Street runner was introduced in the United States, where in 1884 the prolific dime novelist Gilbert Jerome published *Dominick Squeek, the Bow Street Runner; or, An English Detective in America*. In 1888 Percy Fitzgerald published a collection of factual anecdotes entitled *Chronicle of Bow Street Police Office: with an Account of the Magistrates, 'Runners', and Police, and a Selection of the Most Interesting Cases* (2 vols, London: Chapman and Hall). In the 1920s the popular and prolific novelist Jeffrey Farnol (1878–1952), one of the founders of the popular 'Regency romance' genre, created a runner named Jasper Shrig who appeared in *The Loring Mystery* (1925), *The Jade of Destiny* (1936), and *Murder by Nail* (1942). In 1930 Gilbert Armitage published a factual *History of the Bow Street Runners 1729-1829* (London: Wishart and Co.). In 1942, Samuel Duff McCoy (1868–1964), Princeton-educated journalist, biographer and novelist, published a story entitled 'The Bow-Street Runner' in *Ellery Queen's Mystery Magazine*. In 1956 the manuscript *Memoirs* of runner Henry Goddard were published (London: Museum Press). In the 1950s and 60s the runners appeared in a number of academic studies of crime and policing, as part of a renewed movement of social history. This work may have instigated the 1976 Dover paperback reprint of *Richmond*, with an introduction by the energetic compiler, E. F. Bleiler. The figure of the academic histories was popularized for young readers with Charles Buchanan's short 1992 English publication *Bow Street Runner* for the 'Key Stage 2' educational series, designed for pupils aged seven to eleven.

These versions likely inspired a wide range of others in popular culture. There was a 1960s London rhythm and blues band called Bo Street Runners, so named for their covers of compositions by the American Bo Diddley. Jeffrey Farnol's pipe-smoking runner Jasper Shrig appeared in the 1964 BBC television series, *Detective*. There was a psychedelic rock band called Bow Street Runners from Fayetteville, North Carolina, who produced one record in 1970, which slowly garnered a small cult following. There is currently a British indie band called the Bow Street Runners, who affect a form of Edwardian dress and play music somewhat reminiscent of the 1960s band the Kinks. The 1974 British film comedy *Carry on Dick*, in the double-entendre laden 'Carry On' series, depicted Dick Turpin, perhaps England's most famous criminal, pursued by the head of the runners, Sir Roger Daley and two of his officers, Desmond Fancey and Jock Strapp. In England, the Bow Street Runner pub in Hove, another of the same name in Tamworth and the Bow Street Runners tavern in Rugeley apparently aim to recreate the louche ambience of Regency London. In 1999 a team calling themselves the Bow Street Runners competed in the Hastings, England, half-marathon. They did this only two years after they (or perhaps a team with the same name) had participated in the London, England, 'Grand Monopoly Pub

Crawl Challenge', which required teams to drink in at least one pub located in as many streets as possible found in the English version of the 'Monopoly' board game. The 2005 BBC television film *Sweeney Todd* featured a Bow Street runner named Matthew Payne. In 2006 a web-log or 'blog' appeared on the internet entitled 'Diary of a Bow Street Runner', critical of British penal policy and ostensibly written by a former United Kingdom police officer now living in Australia and working as a security officer.[23] The Bow Street runner seems to have a life of his own.

Notes

1. For an account of Colburn, see the Introduction to Gaspey's *George Godfrey* in this series. Dates of advertisements for the publication of *Richmond* are at 'British Fiction 1800–1829: A Database of Production, Circulation and Reception': http://www.british-fiction.cf.ac.uk/titleDetails.asp?title=1827A069 (accessed 17 November 2007).

2. *Richmond: Scenes in the Life of a Bow Street Runner*, introduction by E. F. Bleiler (New York, NY: Dover Publications, 1976), pp. ix–x.

3. M. Adams, 'Thomas Gaspey' in *Dictionary of Literary Biography*, vol. 116: *British Romantic Novelists, 1789–1832*, ed. B. K. Mudge, p. 120.

4. The *Memoirs of Vidocq* formed volumes 25–8 in the series; the earliest recorded French edition, titled *Mémoires de Vidocq, chef de la police de sureté*, is from 1828–9, though there may have been an earlier one.

5. For a survey of the issues of policing in this period, see L. Radzinowicz, *A History of English Criminal Law and Its Administration from 1750*, 5 vols (New York, NY: Macmillan, 1957), vol. 2: *The Clash between Private Initiative and Public Interest in the Enforcement of the Law*, parts 2–4, and vol. 3: *Cross-Currents in the Movement for the Reform of the Police*.

6. C. Emsley, *The English Police: A Political and Social History* (Hemel Hempstead: Harvester Wheatsheaf and New York, NY: St Martin's Press, 1991), pp. 19–20.

7. House of Commons, *Report from the Committee on the State of the Police of the Metropolis* (1816), pp. 137–45.

8. House of Commons, *Report from the Select Committee on the Police of the Metropolis* (1822), p. 21.

9. L. Radzinowicz, 'Trading in Police Services: An Aspect of the early 19th Century Police in England', *University of Pennsylvania Law Review*, 102:1 (November 1953), p. 30.

10. C. Emsley, *Policing and Its Context 1750–1870* (London and Basingstoke: Macmillan, 1983), pp. 62–3.

11. House of Commons, *Report from the Select Committee of Criminal Commitments and Convictions* (1827), p. 6.

12. House of Commons, *A Bill to Enable Rectors, Vicars, and Other Incumbents of Ecclesiastical Benefices and Livings, to Commute Their Tithes by Agreement with the Owners of Lands* (1827), p. 2.

13. R. Richardson, *Death, Dissection and the Destitute* (London and New York, NY: Routledge and Kegan Paul, 1987), ch. 3, 'The Corpse as Commodity'; Tim Marshall, *Murdering to Dissect: Grave-robbing, Frankenstein and the Anatomy Literature* (Man-

chester and New York, NY: Manchester University Press, 1995), ch. 1, 'The Dead Body Business'.

14. J. Gifford [A. Wellier], *Gifford's English Lawyer; or, Every Man His Own Lawyer: Containing a Summary of the Constitution of England, Its Laws and Statutes*, 11th edn (London, 1825).

15. *Newgate Monthly Magazine*, 2 (October 1825), p. 90.

16. *Economist and General Adviser*, 11 (31 July 1824), p. 171.

17. M. Clapson, *A Bit of a Flutter: Popular Gambling and English Society, c. 1823–1961* (Manchester and New York, NY: Manchester University Press, 1992), ch. 2, 'Gambling, culture and economy in England, *c*.1823–*c*.1906'.

18. See the entry in the Oxford English Dictionary for 'estate', section 'fourth estate'.

19. R. Herbert, C. Aird and J. M. Reilly (eds), *Oxford Companion to Crime and Mystery Writing*, (New York, NY: Oxford University Press, 1999).

20. Boileau-Narcéjac [P. Boileau and T. Narcéjac], *Le Roman policier* (Paris: Payot, 1964).

21. The historical, critical and theoretical literature on detective and crime fiction is extensive, but see H. Haycraft, *Murder for Pleasure: The Life and Times of the Detective Story* (New York, NY and London: D. Appleton-Century Co., 1941); G. Grella, 'Murder and Manners: The Formal Detective Novel', in *Novel: A Forum on Fiction* (autumn 1970), pp. 30–49; J. Symons, *Mortal Consequences: From the Detective Story to the Crime Novel: A History* (New York, NY: Harper and Row, 1972); G. Most and W. Stowe (eds) *The Poetics of Murder: Detective Fiction and Literary Theory*, (San Diego, CA: Harcourt Brace Jovanovich, 1983); Herbert, *et al. The Oxford Companion to Crime and Mystery Writing*.

22. *Penny Magazine*, 31 (January 1837), p. 37.

23. http://bowstreetrunner.blogspot.com/ (accessed 23 October 2007).

NOTE ON THE TEXT

The text was digitized from the copy in the British Library, London.

RICHMOND;

OR,

SCENES

IN THE

LIFE OF A BOW STREET OFFICER,

DRAWN UP FROM HIS PRIVATE MEMORANDA.

Some be'th of war, and some of woe,
And some of fun and fudge also,
Some of escapes, and guile, and death;
Also of love forsooth there be'th.
LE FRÊNE.[1]

IN THREE VOLUMES.

VOL. I.

LONDON: HENRY COLBURN.[2]
1827.

NOTICE.

I HAVE often wondered, and shall always wonder, why authors write long prefaces, which they may be certain nobody ever reads, when introductory to any narrative whether of fact or fiction. A commodity of wit or good writing may be thus unprofitably thrown away; and as I can ill spare either, for the best reason in the world, the reader must be contented, in lieu of a preface, to learn the important fact that Mr. JOHN RICHMOND, late a clerk in the Police Office, Bow Street, is not in any manner, directly or indirectly, connected with this work.

London, March 16, 1827.

CONTENTS
OF
THE FIRST VOLUME.

CHAP. X.

Green-room debut – Managerial manœuvring – The biter bit – Ale-house jollifications – Bucks and the cobbler – Mysterious elopement

CHAP. XI.

Night scenes on land and by water – Unexpected rencontre – Vocal music – A fair swain and a dark nymph – Trusted promises

CHAP. XII.

Romantic breakfast, with rural music – Liberty on the wing – Welcome and unwelcome news – An *honest* sheriff's officer, and his new method of arresting – An escape without a rescue

CHAP. XIII.

Castle-building – Despairing beside a clear stream – A gipsy lunch – Wilton's mountain flight – Marriage and no marriage – Proposed wedding at Rydal Water

CHAP. XIV.

Westmoreland hospitality – Wandering Mary – New afflictions – Wilton's chapter on church-yards – A gipsy funeral

CHAP. XV.

Morning rambles – Donkey comforts – Gipsy budget of ways and means – Game markets at Warwick and Leamington – Poaching by wholesale – A poaching battle royal – Doings of a poacher's cub

CHAP. XVI.

Scheming – The game-keeper's pepper-boxes – A lodge scene – Chimney sweeping – Carousing, brawling, and mystifications – More poachers – Grand expedition and division of forces – Triumph

CHAP. XVII.

Cambridge gipsying – Cantab credulity – Lord B—'s admiration of old women – Gipsy masquerade – Lord B—'s marvellous genius and grasp of mind – Shifts to raise the wind – Gipsy theatricals – Spectre apparitions

CHAP. XVIII.

University painters – Gipsy fêtes and rural balls – Wilton's Oxonian tale of love and jealousy – Supper on Hampstead Heath – Vestry politics – Charms of a night-storm

CHAP. XIX.

Mischief and mystification – Sylvan painting in Bishop's Wood – All snug at the Three Spaniards – Muddling of a Hampstead draper

RICHMOND.

CHAPTER I.

The first fruits of genius – Boyish method of disposing of stolen property.

I MUST certainly have been born to a stirring, random life, – at least, from my earliest remembrance, I have ever been engaged in some bustling scene of mischief.

As a boy's whim – (I was then about twelve, though I cannot be particular to a year) – I had set my heart on the nest of a pair of goldfinches, which had made choice of a pretty espalier, covered with apple blossoms, in the garden next my father's. To the great delight of the old lady to whom the garden belonged, the goldfinches had built in this same espalier for several years undisturbed.

Every day she visited her favourites; while, all day long, I was contriving how I might procure their eggs to add to my string. In daylight I dared not go, though I could easily have got over the young quickset hedge which separated the gardens; and it was not easy to escape detection if I ventured out of the house after dark: but as this was my only chance, I resolved to make the attempt.

One night, accordingly, after pretending to go to bed, I stole out unperceived, and, the better to avoid observation, took a circuit through the fields till I reached the corner of the old lady's garden farthest from my father's. This corner was enclosed by a privet hedge, which I easily got over, and the next minute was at the espalier, and secured my prize – four little eggs streaked and clouded with red – the first goldfinch's I had ever seen.

I trembled, however, when I got back to my father's, lest I should meet some one before I could get to bed; but in this respect also I was fortunate. Next morning, as I was going to add the eggs to my string, I heard the old lady, who had just discovered her loss, threatening vengeance upon the depredator. This determined me to conceal rather than show my eggs; and as it was discovered that the garden had been entered at night through the privet hedge towards the fields, I was not even suspected. The affair was forgotten for a time, and some days after I quietly placed the eggs on my string, without any body observing the addition.

Successful deception emboldens the deceiver, and prompts him on to other schemes. The old lady was doomed to feel this, when she found her finest fruit disappear in the same manner as the goldfinch's eggs; though I should not perhaps have dreamt of robbing her of her gooseberries, had not the eggs first tempted me to transgress, and taught me the way over the privet hedge.

Next summer the espalier was again rich in blossoms, and, as the season advanced, had a fine show of apples; while I looked forward with eagerness to the time when, as I intended, I should have the finest for my own use. My visits to the gooseberries, however, had put it into the old lady's head to strengthen *my* corner, as I called it, of the privet hedge with a high paling, over which I could not climb; but I was soon relieved from this difficulty by somebody, as fond of mischief as myself, carrying the best part of the pales away for firewood. This was a fortunate incident for me, as it transferred the blame of all the garden robberies to those who had carried off the paling, which offence, at any rate, I could never be suspected of. The espalier apples I now looked upon as already mine.

The old lady, who was a widow, had a son several years older than I; and I discovered by accident, that he also had a design upon the same apples, which were indeed very fine ones, and just beginning to show tempting shades of red and golden yellow when the sun shone upon them. He was old enough to have a sweetheart – a very pretty girl – I remember her blue eyes and laughing face as if it were yesterday!

Young as I was, I had a liking for Anne, which, though it could not perhaps at my age be called love, yet had very similar effects, and made me feel towards the youth all the enmity of a rival. I was determined to deprive him of the apples, for I could not bear to think that he should have the pleasure of presenting them to Anne. My great distress was in the idea, that, if I robbed the espalier, Anne could not have the fruit, as I dared not give it to her, and indeed dreaded lest she should know that I was capable of doing such a thing. Love is sometimes, though not always, an excellent moralist.

No time was to be lost however, for the apples became every day more ruddy and ripe, and the old lady herself might take a fancy to anticipate me by gathering them. Night came, and I was resolved to make the attempt. My heart beat violently when I reached the privet hedge, the paling of which was still unrepaired. I got over, but had only time to hurry two apples into my pocket, when I saw, or fancied I saw, a light passing rapidly from window to window in my father's house, and instantly imagined they had missed me. I therefore, with great reluctance, quitted the espalier, hastened home, and listened with all caution at the windows, but could hear nothing that indicated a search for me.

Having been thus scared, however, for that night, I did not venture back to the garden; neither durst I go in to bed, lest I should encounter the person with the light, whoever it might be. To avoid observation till I should contrive what to do, I crossed the road and got into a field, which, as it happened, was behind the house where Anne lived with her uncle – her parents being both dead.

Now, thought I, if I could but put my two apples into her pretty hand, I should be so happy! This was impossible, for I had stolen them; and as they were a peculiar sort, and easily recognised, I could not have made any story about them plausible enough to pass muster. I could not then have the pleasure of giving them to her, but I was resolved that she alone should have them. I accordingly tied their stems together, slipt with the caution of a cat up to the window, and hung them on a peg which I found there. Having succeeded beyond my expectations in this boyish enterprise, I watched my opportunity, got snug into bed undisturbed, and dreamt all night of Anne and the apples.

The following morning I got up betimes, and ran to the field to watch if Anne herself would discover the apples. I had indeed the gratification to see her find them, and I enjoyed her puzzled looks. She knew, I daresay, they were intended for her; but could not suspect whence they came.

I was so taken up with this affair, that I wandered about, and almost forgot to go home to breakfast. The old lady did not miss her apples, I suppose; at least the paling at the privet hedge was not repaired, and I meditated all day on a more thorough spoliation of the espalier, the proceeds of which I had now found a safe way to dispose of according to my fondest wishes: it was not now, as formerly, that I cared so much for the indulgence of my own appetite as to disappoint the old lady's son and to favour Anne. The passions, indeed, of a boy are the same in kind, and as violent, if not so lasting, as those of a man: – a fact which the recollections of every one will testify.

CHAPTER II.

What is love? – Springes to catch woodcocks – New method of setting houses on fire without injury – Melting moments.

I PURSUED my scheme with great ardour; and the very next night succeeded in cramming all my pockets, as well as my hat and handkerchief, with the finest apples of the espalier. I selected some of the largest for Anne, – it was too dark for me to choose the prettiest – and proceeded to hang them up by the window, as I had done the first, with the greatest caution and secrecy, as I thought; but whether I had made more bustle than I ought, or whether Anne was watching, I know not; at all events, she discovered me, and gave me a pat on the shoulder. I was in the utmost terror. Not knowing who it was, I imagined the worst, and immediately thought of my father! I dared not look round, though luckily I did not cry out, but hung down my head as a boy will do when detected in a fault. I have no doubt that she had a shrewd guess of my motive; for girls, even when young, are very quick-sighted in such matters. She pretended, however, not to understand the mystery of the apples, and said to me in a low whisper – her hand resting still upon my shoulder,

'Tom! What are you doing here at this time of night?'

'Nothing,' I said; for I was quite puzzled what to answer.

'What apples then are those?' she continued to whisper.

I thought my heart would have sunk within me at this question, and I could only mutter out,

'They are for you, Anne!'

'And where did you get them, Tom? – but come farther off from the window, or my uncle may hear us and come out, and it would look so strange.'

She pulled my arm very gently, and I followed her to a short distance from the window; but she still continued her cautious whisper.

'Now tell me, Tom, what *is* the meaning of all this?'

'I don't know,' was all I could sheepishly answer; but I have no doubt, as she was some years older than I, that she understood my feelings better than I did myself. She urged me very much to tell her where I got the apples, but I struggled hard for my reputation, and would rather have suffered any punishment than confessed myself a robber to her – though orchard-robbing is somehow, like poaching or smuggling, always considered as a kind of pardonable crime.

By one hint and another, however, she soon came to understand the whole affair; but said it was 'so *very strange*' that I should do such a thing for her. I could only reply that it was because she had always been so good and kind to me, and because I hated the old lady's son.

'You are indeed a most strange boy,' she whispered; 'but you must promise me never to do such a thing again. I will forgive you this time, and I shall not tell anybody. Good night! we must away, or we shall be missed.'

I could hear by the tone of her voice, and see by the starlight that glanced on her face (for it was now quite dark), that she was more pleased than offended, and I left her with my heart beating in a flutter of exultation, which banished all fear of detection.

Next morning there was a hue and cry set up about the robbery of the espalier, though nobody suspected me except my father, who did not, however, question me about it, but went with a sorrowful look, and quietly examined all the places where he thought it was likely I might have hid the apples. I daresay my disturbed countenance gave him the first hint, for I had slept little all night, not from fear but from joy, to think that I had not offended Anne. How she concealed her apples from the general scrutiny set on foot, I do not know. My father looked very hard at me, but when he could find no trace of what he was seeking among my things, he seemed to be satisfied, and did not say a word, nor hinted that he suspected me, and I was cunning enough not to volunteer a denial.

Anne was faithful, and did not betray me. I enjoyed the disappointed looks of the old lady's son, and exulted in my heart that I had outwitted him, though I had many a bitter reflection when I thought that Anne could not fail to consider me guilty of robbery. When we met by accident, however, (and this happened by some means or other more frequently than before) she was kinder to me than ever, and I imagined she endeavoured to shun my rival, at least I seldom saw her speaking to him, as she was wont to do; but this I daresay was only a fancy.

From the time that Anne came to take up so much of my thoughts, I had less leisure to plan mischief; but my mind was too active to be long quiet, and I soon began to invent other contrivances for annoying the widow's son.

I had observed that, since the loss of his espalier apples, he often took solitary walks in the garden; that he was particularly partial to a turf seat near the privet hedge; and the following summer he began to train up some straggling honeysuckles to arch over the seat, and shade it from the sun. This spot I accordingly selected as the scene of mischief. I had some time before found an old rat-trap in a neglected corner, and for want of something else to do I had set about brushing it up for use. This trap I considered as an instrument just made for my purpose, and the better to disguise it, I procured some green paint, and with the greatest secrecy painted it all over.

It was, I think, in the month of June that I hid the trap thus prepared among the grass close by his favourite turf seat, so that if he ventured to set his foot there, he was certain to be caught. I was eagerly on the watch next day, to see the consequences of my plot. He did not fail to make his usual visit to the place, but I waited long and in vain for his setting a foot upon the treacherous engine. At last, his knife fell among the grass, and in stooping to lift it he thrust his hand directly into the trap, which caused him to spring up like a frightened hare, and roar out murder. In an instant doors and windows flew open, and the whole neighbourhood was alarmed by his cries, while he stood in pitiful plight beside his honeysuckles, with the green trap hanging from his wrist, and the old lady running, or rather hobbling along in great trouble, crying out,

'What is it, Johnny, my dear? What can be the matter with my Johnny?'

I could with the utmost difficulty restrain myself from bursting out into a loud laugh; and, indeed, all that saw the poor fellow were more disposed to laugh at than to pity him; but I was much afraid lest I should betray myself, and judged it best to make off with all convenient speed from the scene of action. I did not get away, however, before encountering a very knowing, and, as I thought, reproachful look from Anne, who had come as a spectator of the trap affair. I was particularly delighted that she had seen the ludicrous plight of 'my dear Johnny;' but I did not at all like that she should suspect it was a prank of my contrivance, as her knowing look at me seemed to intimate.

This time also I was fortunate enough to escape detection by my father; for the trap, being painted, could not be identified with the old rusty one, and even the existence of that had been forgotten. Anne, however, was not so easily deceived. She knew I could get into the garden, and she knew also that I detested 'Johnny,' as his mother called him at the time he was caught in the unlucky trap, though at other times 'John' was deemed a more respectable name for the heir apparent of a snug house and garden, and a couple of good farms. All day I took care to be out of the way, for I was afraid to meet Anne; and as soon as quiet was restored in the garden, and *Johnny* had his hand released from durance and the wound bandaged, I set off to visit a relation who lived about a mile distant. Anne had observed my motions, and just as I was crossing a stile a few fields onward, there was she prepared to waylay me. I was greatly embarrassed, and knew not how to look or what to say: Anne seemed to be little less so, though she was the first to speak.

'Tom, Tom!' she said, 'you will never leave off your pranks till you are found out. What could tempt you to set a trap for John?'

'And how do you know it was I that did it?'

'Come,' said she, 'none of your denials: – there is nobody else that could or would do it, and I know where you had some green paint last week.'

'Well!' I replied, 'I would not tell you a falsehood for the world;' (and this was indeed the truth;) 'I confess I did do it, and you must forgive me once more. – I did it because I hate him.'

'And why do you hate him, Tom?'

'Because I don't like to see such a sheepish fellow speaking to you, Anne.'

'Tom, you are a very, very strange boy. I do not know what to think of you. I must not pardon you *this* time' (though she was smiling, and not angry, when she said so); 'but I shall give you my hand, if you will not play any more such wicked pranks, that I will forgive you some *other* time.'

I trembled all over when I took her pretty hand in mine, and blushed up to the eyes. I dared not look whether *her* cheek had also become more rosy, I was so fluttered and bashful; but her little hand certainly did tremble. As we stood hard by the stile, I leant my back upon it, still holding her hand, but scarcely daring to look up, and I imagined that I felt her warm breath upon my face. Girls are more alive to fear of exposure in such cases than we are, and Anne was particularly so.

'Tom,' she said, 'I fear we may be observed. I must go. Remember to behave yourself properly, and *I will love you*, but I will not forgive you just yet – some other time' (added she, playfully,) 'will do as well.'

I wished to have said a thousand things to her, but my heart was too full; I could not speak, and she bounded over the stile and left me before I could utter a word. I scarcely knew where I was, or what had happened to me; but a certain indescribable joy, mingled with pride and exultation, was uppermost in my mind. I now felt certain that I was on good terms with Anne; and though I was not altogether ignorant of the meaning of love, as young people are always in books most erroneously represented to be, yet I could not dream that Anne meant any more when she said she would love me, than that she would be good friends with me notwithstanding all my pranks. I often thought of the expression, 'I will love you;' but, turn it about as I would, I always came to the same conclusion. The whole scene at the stile was so pleasing to my fancy, that I thought of it by day and by night. It was, indeed, a realization of many a waking dream I had indulged in of meeting Anne alone at a distance from the prying eyes of the village gossips, when, as I thought, I would tell her all my little feelings undisturbed. My fondest wish had been fulfilled, and yet after all how little had I said!

I had almost forgotten the affair of the trap when I was told, some months after, that Anne had taunted Johnny with it; and, to resent some recriminations of his, had visited him with the nickname of 'Rat-trap,' by which he was long after known. The poor fellow, who was a spoiled child and very sensitive, actually took to his bed upon this, overpowered with vexation and shame, and was said to refuse to eat. It was, however, reported at the same time (though I cannot answer for the truth of it,) that he took advantage of his mother's occasional absence in the garden and elsewhere, to rise by stealth and supply the more immediate cravings of his appetite.

This story was a powerful stimulus to my love of mischief; and notwithstanding my promise to Anne, I could not resist my desire for being *at* him again. Indeed I was pretty certain that Anne would enjoy it as much as I, though she might pretend otherwise. Johnny's bed was in an attic adjoining to that where I myself slept; and I could with some difficulty, and at the risk perhaps of a good fall, reach his window. I accordingly procured some assafœtida[3] from the apothecary's apprentice, who was a comrade of mine, and fixed it in a bit of hollowed elder with some tow at both ends, introducing a scrap of match paper at a hole in the side of the apparatus.

Thus prepared, I sallied out after midnight on the roof, – reached his window, – heard him snoring like a hedge-hog, – lighted my match paper, – introduced one end of my elder-stick through a hole in the side of his window, which was rather a crazy one, as I well knew, – and, putting my mouth to the other end of the tube, soon filled his chamber with a cloud of smoke and fumes enough to suffocate a salamander.[4] I could soon hear him tossing about in bed, and grumbling in his sleep; and at length the execrable stench of the assafœtida operating on his nostrils, he gave a loud sneeze: this awakened him, and finding the chamber full of smoke and unsavoury smells, he did not know what to make of it, but was palpably in great alarm, for I heard him muttering to himself,

'Lord! what is this? – I shall certainly be smothered: – the house must be on fire!'

I listened no longer, but, deeming it high time to make good my retreat, extinguished the combustibles, thrust the whole into a chink of the roof, and clambered back to my own chamber. I was just in time, for as I was getting in at the window, I could hear Johnny running down stairs, forgetful that he was bedridden, and shouting, 'Fire! fire! the house is on fire!' I then got into bed, where I could hear the bustle that soon began from the alarm which Johnny had given. My father had been roused to give his assistance, and had coolly examined the premises instead of standing and making idle exclamations and more idle conjectures, as the rest of the neighbours did. He soon understood the nature of the alarm; and, from the quarter in which the smoke and fumes abounded, though they were now diffused all over the house, he strongly suspected that I was in the secret. I could soon after hear him ascending the stair to my chamber door, which he opened cautiously, and crossed over to the window on tiptoe, expecting, no doubt, to find it open and me on the roof. He then turned towards my bed, and seeing me apparently in a quiet sleep, I could hear him say,

'Thank God, my suspicions are not true! – Tom is fast asleep.'

The savoury fumigation which Johnny had suffered was next morning the general topic of conversation, and I was as generally blamed as the contriver. Nothing, it is true, could be directly brought home to me respecting it, nor indeed respecting many other pranks which I had executed; chiefly, perhaps, because I never trusted a confederate with what I could accomplish myself – a good maxim in all secret enterprises.

It is impossible, however, to go on long in such practices, how secretly soever they may be conducted, without exciting suspicions of the real author. I had gradually been earning for myself a bad name, and was often in consequence blamed for mischief in which I had no hand. Several of these unfounded reports reached my father's ears; and though in such cases, I denied most firmly and justly, yet he was by no means satisfied in every instance of my innocence. What was singular enough, his suspicions of me were for the most part strongest in cases where I was least concerned. At last he resolved to send me to an academy at a distance from home, under pretence of finishing my education, though the real motive was to *bring* me *in*,[5] as it is called; but schools in general, and this was not an exception, are more adapted for teaching boys mischief than for bringing them in.

My greatest grief in going away was parting with Anne, whom I saw every day, though I had had no private talk with her since the stile scene. I was very anxious, however, to obtain her full pardon for the prank of the trap before I went, or rather to make that an excuse for a private interview: – I did not know whether or not she suspected me of the fumigation affair. One day, accordingly, I took an opportunity of whispering to her,

'When will you forgive me as you promised, Anne? – I am soon going away to leave you.'

'Come,' she said, 'to-morrow to the stile at the same time as before, and I will tell you.'

This, thought I, is more than I could have asked, and I will go, even if my father himself were to find it out and oppose me. I could think of nothing else all day than the stile, and what I should say, and what I should give to Anne, as a little present to remember me by when I should be away. This was a point very difficult to settle, since I had nothing by me which I could offer her, and though I had a trifle of pocket money, I neither could fix on any thing to buy, nor did I wish any one to know what I bought. I sauntered about in great uncertainty, which grew more painful as the period arrived when there would be no longer time to consider. At last I determined that a silver thimble was the thing which came nearest my wishes and my finances. I did not know the price, but I had some confused recollection or supposition of having heard they were four or five shillings a piece, and this sum, though it would exhaust my little purse, I was most willing to give.

I accordingly put on as bold a face as my errand would permit, and marched away to make my purchase. The shop-keeper luckily did not recognise me, but stared at me (at least I fancied so) with much curiosity, as it was rather an unusual purchase for a boy of my years. I was glad that I had over-rated the price, as it left me a shilling or two in my pocket, which would save appearances, should my father inquire what money I had when I went away.

I kept my appointment at the stile to the very minute, but Anne was not there, and after waiting a considerable time, pacing up and down, and thinking what I should say to her, – she still did not come. I was sadly vexed, and even began to accuse her in my mind of intentionally disappointing me, as a good joke at my expense. I could not endure to be laughed at, and much less in such a case as this; but after I had fretted myself into a passion, and had just resolved to wait no longer, Anne started up behind me as if she had sprung out of the earth, and tapped me on the shoulder in a manner which I recollected well since the night of the espalier apples. She had, in fact, been there before me, and had slily concealed herself to watch how I should behave; and I daresay she was well pleased to observe how much I had felt disappointed. I did not presume to blame her, but urged her to pardon me as she had promised, which indeed was the only subject I could venture myself to talk about, though I much wished to speak of something else.

'I suppose I must forgive you,' she said, 'since you are going to leave us; but do you think you deserve such a pretty silk purse as this which I have netted for you to hold your pocket money in?'

This was indeed what I had not expected, and I thanked her with all the boyish protestations I could think of; at the same time I made the best return I could by presenting her with the thimble, my whole face glowing with blushes, and my hand trembling as I gave it to her.

'Well,' she said, 'I shall keep this in remembrance of the stile; and now we must shake hands and part.'

We locked our hands together, and leaning forward as if to whisper something, she kissed my burning cheek.

'Farewell, Tom!' she said, 'you must not forget the stile.'

A thrill ran through my blood at this painful yet delightful parting, such as I have rarely felt since; and I urged her to stay as I had many things to say to her, but she would not, and we parted.

CHAPTER III.

Frolics at School – Fish and Sauce – Inkle and Yarico – Philosophical Gesticulation.

THE novelties that started up at every turn of the road in my journey to this detested school, did much to banish the regret I felt in leaving home, and, what was worse, in going far from Anne. Indeed, long before I arrived at its termination, I had begun to enjoy the journey, and to ask a thousand questions about what I saw.

I had formed, as boys usually do, a very gloomy notion of the master of the Academy or *Establishment*, as I think he called his school, wherein I was to be imprisoned. I pictured to myself an old, gruff, crabbed sort of man, who would be ready to snarl and scold at whatever I should do. I was strongly impressed with the notion, however, that I was no longer a boy, and too old to go to school; and I did not, on this account, care so much about the master.

Contrary to my foreboding, I found Mr. Figgens, or rather, as we used to call him, *Figends,*[6] to be a little dapper, rickety personage with a hump-back, a short neck, and long spindle-legs. Instead of being afraid of him, I could scarcely keep from laughing as he bowed and grimaced to my father; for he looked upon ceremony to be the very perfection of what he called 'genteel politeness;' and of this, of course, he considered himself to be a faultless model. I was very much disposed to pay him in his own coin, by caricaturing his stiff-necked bow; but luckily possessed sufficient self-command to refrain, as it would only have given pain to my father.

For the first week or two I applied very hard to my lessons and delayed making much acquaintance with my fellow-boarders, until I should once discover their dispositions. After school-hours, I sometimes took a solitary stroll to the side of a stream which the master dignified, as he thought, by calling 'The River,' though it had no pretensions to be more than a brook. In these walks I often thought of my pretty Anne; and it was, indeed, partly from a vague fancy that it would raise me in her opinion, and partly from an ambition of excelling, that I kept so hard to my books.

I wrote a letter to my father, – the first I had ever written; and, as I considered this an extraordinary feat, I took several evenings to finish it. I wished very much to write to Anne also, but as I could not send to her with sufficient secrecy, and had a horror of any body knowing it, I reluctantly gave up the idea for the present. I did, however, begin a letter to her, though without the hopes of sending it; but it was only a beginning, or I may say twenty beginnings, for I could neither please myself with the words, nor the forms of the letters. Either my pen was bad, or the ink was thick, or the paper greasy; and when none of these obstacles were in the way, I could not find words pretty enough for my purpose.

My studious fit, however, which was caused perhaps by want of acquaintance with my school-fellows, soon yielded to boyish volatility and the spirit of mischief. I thought less often of Anne; for though my pretty purse reminded me of her every time I took it out, I got other objects to engross my attention.

In my visits to 'The River,' I became acquainted with a young man who was passionately fond of angling, and might be seen there morning, noon, and night, eager at his sport, and forgetful of all things else. He undertook to instruct me in his art; but, except on holydays, the school-hours suited ill with the time requisite for angling, which I soon abandoned for the night-line – a method of fishing more suited to my convenience, and indeed to my genius.

My night-lines were made with several fathoms of strong packthread or twine, along which a number of hooks were tied and baited. My method was, to steal out alone a little before dusk, and set my lines in the pools of the brook, and to rise betimes next morning to draw them, and be home with my booty, when there was any, before school-hours.

I was by no means a successful fisher; but to make amends for my want of sport in this way, I began to play off a few pranks in my old style, – my nightly fishing excursions furnishing a good excuse for my absence; and as I never neglected my lessons, I had become rather a favourite with Mr. Figgens, and particularly in the essential matter of attending to all his nick-nack ceremonials of 'genteel politeness.' I had, however, an irresistible propensity to take off[7] his grimaces, and once or twice incurred his displeasure by overdoing my part.

Among other persons that I liked to annoy in my night-line rambles, was an old crabbed miser, who had a garden that ran down to the brook. Crusty,[8] as we called him, was always on the alert, lest, while setting my lines on the other side, I might cross over and make free with his fruit. Many a time he had held out threats to me, in case I ever again set my lines near his premises! but I treated these warnings with due contempt, and went the more frequently for the very purpose of putting him in a fidget. He was a very early riser, and usually at his post in the morning when I went to draw my lines. At last he threatened to take up my whole tackle and 'impound it,' as he termed it; but I took care to throw a few obstacles in his way to prevent him.

He had his garden so strongly and closely fenced, that a mouse could scarcely get into it. Towards the water, however, there was a door through which I supposed he would come to seize my lines. To secure this door, I procured a very large pole: – it was, in fact, a portion of the trunk of a young oak-tree, about as thick as my thigh, and of a proportional length. This I fixed across the middle of the door with a piece of strong cord, which was likewise bound to the handle of the latch and twisted tight. When I had fastened this, I ventured to the front door of the house – the only other exit he had to the brook, – and secured it in the same manner. Now, thought I, he will find some trouble in getting at my lines.

I rose betimes next morning to see the sport; and, as I expected, old Crusty had started before me to make his threatened seizure; but as he could not obtain an outlet, I had the pleasure of seeing him ranging about his garden like a tyger in a cage. When he perceived me quietly drawing my lines, he attempted, in his wrath, to get over the fence, but to my great amusement fell back into the garden. At last, he bethought him of the parlour window, which I had not secured, and came out upon me, with his eyes glaring and his mouth open, as if he meant to devour both my trouts and myself.

Having the brook between me and him, I was not much afraid, thinking I should easily escape; but just as I had packed up my tackle, he reached the side where I stood, brandishing over his shoulder one of my oak poles which he had untwisted from the door. To get away from him was impossible, as there was a high bank fenced with plashed[9] quickset between me and the field, and a stone wall crossing the bank and running into the brook behind me. I was therefore compelled to face him, and determining to stand my ground in as cool a manner as I could assume, I went on to sort my things without saying a word or even looking up, though I took a sly peep now and then from under my hat to observe his motions. Enraged as Crusty was, he looked rather non-plussed and crestfallen when he saw me thus undaunted; and instead therefore of annihilating me with the oak, as his attitude betokened, he vented his wrath in farther threatenings of imprisonment, or the pillory, or the stocks, for my daring attack upon his doors.

I was glad to get so easily off, as I cared not for his talking. I was not, however, so much at my ease, when I saw him, about noon, coming to my master's with a countenance that foreboded nothing good – his indeed seldom did. He accordingly lodged a complaint against me in form, and Mr. Figgens, as in duty bound, reprimanded me, but in no very severe terms, for he and my accuser were not the best friends in the world. Mr. Figgens, indeed, looked upon old Crusty as a rude savage, who was and ever would be entirely ignorant of 'genteel politeness;' whilst Crusty, on the other hand, considered Figgens to be little more than a faggot of nick-nacks, holding in supreme contempt all his best bows, and the smirks he had picked up at second-hand, as we shall see anon, from Mrs. Figgens. These peculiar opinions, also, were duly conveyed by gossiping whispers to the parties concerned, and produced the usual effect of all such good-natured communications.

Mrs. Figgens took care to exaggerate my offence, however; not on account of Crusty, but to disgrace me. She had taken a dislike to me from the first, because I had made a wry face at and refused to eat some potted herrings of her own curing, and which she declared to be the finest that were ever seen: in reality, they were a part of her economy to save butcher-meat. This good lady, as I suppose I must call her, was in person a complete contrast to her little husband. She was more than the head taller than he; and as his shoulders were bent forwards by disease, so hers were as ludicrously bent backwards by art, according to the true boarding-school angle now so much in fashion. She was besides scraggy and awkward, and her grey eyes, her shrivelled and sallow skin, and her hook-nose, made her look very cross and disagreeable. The only point in which she agreed with Mr. Figgens was the ceremonials. In many of these, indeed, she had first instructed him, as in her former capacity of lady's maid to the Hon. Mrs. Hitchcock she had enjoyed more opportunities than he for studying the science of 'genteel politeness;' and her countenance exhibited a continual struggle between ceremonial smirks, in imitation of Mrs. Hitchcock, and cross wrinkles and sour looks natural to herself.

To fall under the displeasure of such a dame was no joke, as I came to find by experience; and as I had uniformly persisted in refusing her potted herrings, on which she had set her heart as a great saving, I had no hopes of ever conciliating her. We were therefore not exactly at open, but at concealed, war; and I could trace many unfounded insinuations against me to her private malice.

One morning I was summoned with a mysterious air into my little master's study, to answer, as I could anticipate, some weighty charge.

'Richmond!' said Mr. Figgens, with a sort of grin meant to be expressive of stern authority: 'this is a very serious business, – not so much on account of the loss, – that is but a trifle – a mere trifle, – as the wicked example it inculcates.'

As I looked nothing daunted, being unconscious of having done any thing very wrong or serious, and having no idea what was meant, Figgens paused with a disappointed air, expecting, I suppose, that I should have been awed by his looks, while I asked boldly what was the matter.

'Matter?' said he: 'so you pretend not to know it? That is the very strongest corroborative evidence that you do. You shall be condignly punished, sir!'

'For what?' I said, still more boldly. As I said this, I heard the door creak, and looking round, saw the grey eyes and long lank face of Mrs. Figgens peeping in. She had been, as it appeared, listening to what was going forward; and not liking my master's mode of proceeding, she burst into the room, her sallow cheeks puffed up with rage – flew at me with her skinny hands, and seized me furiously by the collar, crying out,

'You wicked rascal! I'll teach you to play your devil's pranks in my house!'

She then, with a most ferocious look, attempted to shake me, aiming at no less, I suppose, than dislocating every bone in my body. Being stout-made, however, and strong for my age, I not only kept firm, but untwisted myself from her grasp in a moment, and stood fiercely at bay; while neither of the two, thus foiled by my boldness, knew what to do.

'Tell me,' said I triumphantly, 'what I have done to deserve this usage, or I shall leave the house on the instant, and go home to my father.'

'Done? you rascal!' said the virago, 'I knew from the first what it would come to, when you turned up your nose at my beautiful herrings. I said you would never come to no good.'

'But what have I done just now?' I repeated: 'tell me that.'

'I tell you, jackanapes!' she continued, 'that the Honourable Mrs. Hitchcock declared as them were the most beautifullest potted herrings she ever see'd. Set you up, indeed! I hear say his Majesty himself have potted herrings every day, and a pug like you to think of throwing *my* potted herrings into the pig-stye – but I'll be revenged of you, you rascal!'

'I know nothing of your herrings,' said I firmly, and I spoke the truth; 'but I confess I detest them.'

'D'ye hear that, Mr. Figgens?' exclaimed she, addressing humpback. 'I wonder how you can stand by and see me insulted in my own house by such a sniff of a boy: – out with you, sir!' she continued, turning to me, 'and pack up! – you sha'nt bide another night in my house.'

'Good bye, then, Ma'am,' said I, caricaturing at the same time one of humpback's bows; 'but I tell you again, I know nothing about your rascally herrings.'

On going out to prepare for my sudden and unexpected departure, I soon learnt the mystery of the potted herrings. Young Hitchcock, who was one of the boarders, disliking to imitate the example of his Majesty in the article of eating herrings every day, as Mrs. Figgens asserted, and equally disregarding his Honourable Mamma's opinion of the excellence of those cured by Mrs. Figgens, had some time been meditating a plot against them. He was stimulated in his design by Snells, another of the boarders, who had discovered in his Geography that pickled herrings were a principal part of the food of the negro slaves in the West Indies; and though Mrs. Figgens was always very particular in pointing out the difference between *pickled* and *potted* herrings, and repeated almost every day her marks of distinction, Snells kept to his belief about the negroes, and Hitchcock was strongly inclined to agree with him. I confess that I did lend them a remark or two not in favour of the herrings, but took no farther concern in the affair.

A plot was, however, contrived by them, of which I was kept in ignorance, to rob Mrs. Figgens of her whole stock of *beautiful* potted herrings. By what means they obtained possession of the firkin[10] containing them I do not know; but on the morning, the events of which I have just celebrated, the entire contents were found deposited in a pig-stye; and, surely, no one can blame Mrs. Figgens for being in a great rage, when she saw the fruits of her careful economy so unceremoniously dealt with.

Mrs. Figgens had to endure a farther mortification in being informed that the real delinquents were her favourite young Hitchcock, and Snells, the son of a rich alderman, through whose influence she sanguinely hoped to increase the respectability of their 'Establishment for Young Gentlemen;' while, under a gross mistake, she had attacked me who was innocent; and had strong reasons for not altering her opinion even on conviction, had not the evidence in my favour been clear and incontestible. Accordingly, to smooth over the affair, she prevailed on Figgens to come to my room, where I was busy packing up my things, to offer an apology and make it up again.

As a sort of salvo to efface any unfavourable impression I might have retained against Mrs. Figgens for her attack upon my person, I was kindly invited to accompany her and Mr. Figgens to see a company of strolling[11] actors, who had set up their temporary stage in the great room of the village inn. Mr. Figgens, indeed, entertained a very high opinion of the stage – not as a school for morals, but as affording a standard for correct pronunciation and gesture, and an admirable auxiliary to his two great authorities, Walker's Dictionary, and Enfield's Speaker.[12] The latter work, indeed, was beginning to lose ground in his opinion, in consequence of his having lately procured Austin's Chironomia;[13] the figured positions in which he was privately practising, before he ventured to teach them to his pupils by personal exemplification. Mrs. Figgens was also a great admirer of the stage ever since she had been to Drury Lane, when the Hitchcock's were in London, and had on that occasion been charmed with the *most elegantest manners* there exhibited.

To me it promised to be a high treat, and we set off in great expectations. The play, I think, was Inkle and Yarico,[14] and badly as it must have been mangled in the performance, of which of course I could be no judge, I was quite spellbound with interest and delight. I could not get the scenery and the singular dresses out of my head for several days, and the songs rang in my ears even when I was asleep. Mrs. Figgens, however, presuming on her taste, and absurdly comparing it to Drury Lane,[15] pronounced the whole execrable; and I should have pleaded in vain for leave to go again, had it not been for the false accusation about the herrings, on the merits of which I was allowed great liberties.

I contrived, indeed, to get away every evening when the strollers performed. I soon became acquainted with them, and was delighted with their facetious manners and witty conversation, interlarded with numerous quotations from plays and poems. It increased my interest also intensely, to observe, in the love scenes, how finely the actors expressed some of the feelings which had affected my own mind for my pretty Anne; and this revived my remembrance of our innocent parting at the stile, and all the incidents connected with it.

I was eager, in a word, to become myself an actor, and with this was interwoven a strong desire to have Anne to accompany me. I never once thought of my father's consent, nor of the objections which Anne's uncle would undoubtedly make to such a mad proposal: I was too sanguine to conjure up obstacles. I even went so far as to sound Mr. Bucks,[16] one of the strollers, about my project, and he gave me every encouragement; but as the company was soon compelled to remove their quarters in consequence of want of support, I could not mature any plan for immediately accompanying them, though it occupied my thoughts by day and by night.

The holydays were at hand, however; and I could not rest, so eager was I to communicate my schemes to Anne, never doubting of her entire concurrence. But enthusiastic as I was, I thought there was no necessity for hurry, and the schemes I planned were more for future than immediate execution. I had never communicated my intentions to any one except to my strolling acquaintance, Bucks; for I considered the subject too noble to be committed to vulgar ears. I reserved a full disclosure of my plans for Anne alone, when I should go home during the holydays.

The day arrived, and I took leave of the Figgenses in a very different manner from what I had anticipated the morning of the affair of the herrings. Mrs. Figgens, indeed, was all smirks and courtesy, and Mr. Figgens returned my farewell bow with a stiff-necked flexion, meant to be unusually condescending and kind; and both, in a breath, told me I should find my room improved in comfort on my return.

CHAPTER IV.

Peep behind the Scenes at Liverpool, with a Bird's-eye View out of doors – Lucky Moonlight.

THE liberty which is allowed at home during the holydays I took full advantage of, to see and talk with Anne as often as I could. I found her still the same spirited girl I had left her; and though her advance towards womanhood had improved her looks and obtained her many admirers, she seemed, I fondly thought, to prefer me – boy as I still was – to them all. It might be that she could use more freedom with me on account of my age, but I cannot say positively.

By reading some of Mrs. Radcliffe's wild stories,[17] Anne had imbibed a desire for adventure on which I calculated much; but she knew a little better than I did the value of money, and the difficulty of procuring it; and on this score I could not satisfy her scruples, as I had never once thought of money matters in my original plan of going on the stage. I was fascinated by the notion of always 'living and loving,'[18] – of being applauded by numerous spectators, – and of meeting with romantic adventures. I calculated not on making money, nor thought of how I was to live, though this was the first question which Anne asked. I was pleased, however, to perceive that otherwise she took as deep an interest in the scheme as myself.

My father, from whom the project was carefully concealed, soon remarked my intimacy with Anne; and our stolen interviews had often been observed and watched, and had indeed become the talk of every gossip in the place. Boyish frolics, or romping,[19] would not perhaps have attracted his attention; but quiet meetings with a girl older than myself could not fail to excite suspicion, and I was most unexpectedly and severely interrogated on the subject. I may say, *unexpectedly;* for I was foolish enough to imagine we had always been so secret, that nobody knew of our meetings besides ourselves. Love is blind in more respects than one, but it is also fearless of all things except the object beloved; and I was altogether indifferent, now it was known, what might be said by others of my attachment to Anne.

I made, however, no confession of any thing to my father, but remained obstinately silent, though I was naturally the very reverse of obstinate. My silence was, as usual, construed into delinquency of some sort or other; though my father was slow to believe the true cause, and had formed vague conjectures about my being employed as a go-between by some of my elder companions. At all events he was resolved to put an end to it, and accordingly gave me orders to prepare for my departure – not for school, as I expected, but to begin the world in a merchant's counting-house[20] in Liverpool.[21] I was well aware that a plan of this kind had been long proposed for me, though I did not think much about the matter, as I looked upon it as a thing still at a distance; but when I thought of it seriously, and compared an inglorious drudgery at the desk with the delightful life of an actor, my heart sank at the prospect.

In spite of my father's strict injunctions, I was determined to see Anne to inform her of my unfortunate destination. We met by moonlight at the well-known stile. My late dramatic studies and her romance reading rendered us both much more aware of our situation, and also furnished us with words more expressive of our feelings than when we first met there. It was, in truth, a finished love scene, in which a dash of the book language of passion was thrown in to express genuine and natural feelings. We vowed to remain true to each other for ever, in spite of all opposition. I would have promised her any, even the most impossible thing, as her beautiful eyes and the smile that played on her cheek never looked so heavenly, as when illuminated by that summer moon. I was indeed completely bewitched and giddy while I gazed on her sweet face. Her whispers were music, and her sighs quite unmanned me.

She did not now, however, offer to renew her former farewell token; but I was emboldened by the vows we had exchanged to press my lips to her glowing cheek. It was a moment too absorbing for words, for we were now to part for ever, and our hearts were too full to speak. Tears came to her relief, but I could not weep. Our parting was indeed a trial, but such exquisite feelings as we then experienced, both pleasing and painful, seldom occur twice in human life. They can only be felt by the young and the innocent in their first impassioned breathings of affection.

I had no choice but to obey my father, and reluctantly consented to go to Liverpool. I had indeed determined to take the earliest possible opportunity to give the counting-house the slip, and had even mentioned it to Anne at our parting interview; but she was against any rash step, unless a good prospect of emolument offered.

No place could be imagined more at variance with romantic notions than the town of Liverpool, with its docks and wharfs and prison-looking warehouses. Even had I had leisure for walking, there was no place but the flat sandy beach, the barren north bank of the Mersey, or the dusty public road. The theatre was my only attraction, and I had now sufficient pocket-money to indulge in going there; though my fellow-clerks warned me that my master would not permit me, if he knew it, to spend my time and money in such an unprofitable and frivolous amusement. I soon found means to elude his knowing this by making acquaintance among the actors, and instead of appearing in the pit, getting behind the scenes, where I took my regular station every night of performance.

As a matter almost of course, I became acquainted with some young men of similar inclinations with myself, who had formed a spouting club[22] for the recitation of favourite speeches and scenes: they had not yet aspired to the performance of an entire piece. It was here that I first made trial of my powers; but I soon found that I was much inferior both in voice and action to all the others, and I laboured most assiduously to improve myself. I attended, indeed, the regular hours in the counting-house, and did what I was required to do mechanically, while my whole thoughts were bent upon the pieces I was to recite at the club.

In the mean-while, my old strolling acquaintance, Bucks, came to Liverpool in quest of an engagement, and I introduced him to our club with great eclat. He did not however succeed in his main object, as the theatre was about to close, and he was obliged to seek out another company. This was a great temptation to me. I saw Bucks ranging about the country at liberty, while I was chained to the desk like a galley-slave to the oar: such was my comparison. I execrated the very names of invoices, ledgers, and bills of lading, and longed to escape from their dry and revolting details. Markle, or, as we used to call him, *Mark-all*, one of my desk companions, was indeed the only young man in the counting-house who seemed to have a liking to business, and he often gave me grave advice upon the subject; but I only laughed at him, and considered him a plodding blockhead. Markle, however, by keeping steadily to business, ultimately realised a fortune, and is now retired to enjoy it, while I pursued a random, rambling life, and have saved nothing.

Bucks was a man much more to my mind, and I resolved to follow his warm advice to prepare myself for the stage, agreeing as it did with my own inclination – the only sort of advice, indeed, which is ever attended to or relished. His going from Liverpool in quest of an engagement was precisely the opportunity which I had so long wished for, and I resolved to embrace it and accompany him. I accordingly, by Bucks's directions, procured a large knapsack into which I packed all the things that I judged necessary, left my trunk to be forwarded to my father's, and after leaving a letter for my master, set off one evening, with my knapsack at my back, by Scotland Road for Ormskirk,[23] Bucks having gone on to Preston,[24] where we had appointed to meet.

It was a beautiful moonlight summer night, without a breath of air stirring; and I hurried along at a rapid pace, while a thousand fancies floated through my agitated mind. I did not exactly repent of the step I had taken, but all my thoughts were gloomy and perturbed. I felt as if I were alone in the world, and looked forward with a sort of vague apprehension – it could not be called actual fear – with respect to what was about to happen to me. If Anne had been the companion of my adventure, then, O then! I should have exulted; but a solitary journey, or rather flight in the dark, on a road with which I was little acquainted, was far from cheering. I was no coward, and had small personal fear of danger; yet I was rather doubtful on passing any shaded corner, and more than once started back when the bushes in the hedge made any unusual rustle, or when the white trunk of a tree looked suspicious.

The first sparkling of the sun, as the morning broke, soon wore off the depression of my spirits, and I began to put on once more an air of exultation, and to dream of the glorious career upon which I imagined I was now entering. I found Bucks according to appointment; and, after breakfasting together, we steered our course for Lancaster,[25] where he had learnt that the company he wanted were then playing. Bucks was a fellow whom no misfortune could depress, and he talked, joked, laughed, sang, and kept me in high spirits all the way. He suffered nobody to pass us without some humorous remark or witticism, and, with only a few shillings in his pocket, was quite happy and unconcerned for the future. He had seen a good deal of the world, having been at sea, taken prisoner by the French, and escaped with two others across the channel in an open boat. After this he had been in the employ of the proprietor of a travelling collection of wild beasts, whom he left for the more bustling life of a troop of show-folks that usually kept company with the menagerie at fairs and assizes;[26] and, as a still higher step, had sought promotion in the strolling company where I first knew him. I listened to the stories he told of his adventures with the utmost avidity, and my highest ambition was to follow a similar career. I absolutely longed to get to some place where we could begin life, deeming all the time I had hitherto lived as blank, and utterly lost – always excepting my stolen meetings with Anne. My longing for adventure was sooner gratified than I expected.

CHAPTER V.

Game at bo-peep with two constables – Debut in public life.

As we were thus travelling on towards Lancaster, beguiling the way with stories of adventures, and anticipating others which we might meet with, we perceived two men on horseback advancing at a round trot behind us. When they came near, they stopped for a moment, looked hard at us, and, taking out a paper, scrutinized us in a manner which I by no means liked. I at once imagined they had been dispatched by my master in pursuit of me (the guilty are always suspicious); but I was soon undeceived, when one of them, giving the bridle to his companion, sprang from his horse, seized Bucks by the collar, and producing a constable's staff, told him he was his prisoner.

Bucks, having had some rather bitter experience in the matter of jails, had no notion of being made a prisoner so quickly; and, being a strong muscular fellow, he wrenched himself from the constable's grasp in a moment, darted through the hedge-row, and ran off across the fields with the swiftness of a greyhound. The man on horseback galloped to the nearest gate to pursue, but his horse, not being blood,[27] refused to put his legs in danger by attempting to clear the gate, and mean-while Bucks had got more than one cross-hedge between him and his pursuers.

'He bees off, Tim!' said the dismounted constable; 'clear off. – But who bees you, master?' addressing me: 'soome desarter, I d'resay. You must come with me, sir.'

I had a strong desire to follow the example of Bucks by darting through the hedge; but my knapsack was too heavy for running with, and I had no chance of escaping from the constable, who, while I was hesitating, laid hold of me, and without farther ceremony was proceeding to handcuff me with his *derbies*,[28] as he called them. This was horrible – to be hand-cuffed on mere suspicion! – and I resisted with all my strength.

'Why,' said I, 'do you use me thus? I am no deserter, and am innocent of any crime.'

'We'll see that by-and-bye,' said he, continuing to fix the handcuffs. 'I daresay you knows soom'at of that there chap as was with you. There is room enough for both on you in Lancaster Castle.'[29]

I had no choice but to go with them, in order to be examined before a magistrate; but, as soon as we reached the next public-house, they deemed, and not unwisely, that their morning's exertions required a glass of ale. The ale, as it happened, proved good, and one glass was the prelude to another, till my rascally guardians became very talkative, and from talking went on to loud betting.

'I maintain, Tim,' said the one, 'it was all your fault as let the chap escape; for, d'ye see, when I had a hold on 'im you should ha' coome to my assistance.'

'I'll bet you fifty of it, you bees wrong,' said the other, his whole face glistening with the fumes of the ale. 'This here yoong 'un seed it all.'

'So your prisoner escaped you, did he?' said a grim looking man in the corner of the room. 'A pretty pair you are to be entrusted with prisoners! – Why,' turning to me, 'do you not escape also?'

The two ale-drinkers looked first at the door, and then at the derbies, to see whether all was secure. I said nothing; and in the mean-time the bar-maid, who was a Lancashire beauty with staring eyes and puffy red cheeks, entered with a fresh supply of ale.

'Hark ye, Sooky!' said Tim: 'if you let this here yoong 'un, as has got the derbies, out of the house, we'll pull you oop to the Castle.' And so saying, he laughed, and chucked her under the chin as an old acquaintance.

'Ho!' cried the grim-looking man, stretching his neck, and looking out at the window as a man was seen to run past – 'your escaped prisoner, I'll be bound! After him, you flats![30] and secure him!' – and up started the constables in pursuit of the fugitive, as they supposed.

'Now is your time, master!' said my grim companion to me. 'I love to see such flats be-fooled.'

'But I am not guilty of any offence,' said I, 'and an attempt to escape will be a confession that I am.'

'Pooh!' said he, 'you will not find it so very easy to prove your innocence as to escape now.'

'But these horrid handcuffs!' said I, casting a despairing look at them.

'Oh! true! – but we shall soon dispose of them;' and taking an instrument from his pocket, he set me free in an instant. 'Now,' said he, 'make all haste across the fields till you are out of danger. I will take care to amuse the ruffian dogs if they come back soon.'

'Thank you most kindly, Sir!' whispered I, as I stole away through the back door of the house into the garden, without being observed even by Sooky, who was gone to see the constables' chace. While I was cautiously creeping along by the hedge, to avoid observation, I could hear the two wiseacres at high words about the identity of the man who had run past.

'I don't think as it were him at all,' said Tim.

'I'll take my Bible oath on't,' said the other, 'and bet you a pot of ale to the bargain.'

'Hark you!' said Tim. 'I've a notion that's a bad-looking chap as sits in the corner of the room; and mayhap, for all as is coome and gone, is the 'dentical man we be a-seeking.'

'Aye, and there he goes,' said the other, 'off for Garstang.'[31]

I listened no longer: I was too anxious for my own safety, and steered my course, under cover of the hedge-rows, as much as possible in the direction which Bucks had taken. As soon as my distance allowed me time to breathe, I began to think that this was a pretty fair beginning of my so long anticipated adventures, though I did not much relish the turn which it had been likely to take, and half wished myself safe back again to my desk in the counting-house. I was embarked, however, and must now sail on, whether through sunshine or storm. I was pretty much of opinion that the constables were right concerning the grim man who had released me – perhaps for the purpose of keeping them in play till he got clear off from observation.

I kept on at a good pace across the fields, hoping to overtake Bucks, for without him I did not well know how to proceed. I was convinced that the constables had been quite mistaken in apprehending him; at least I was not aware of any offence he had committed. When I had proceeded several miles, I took a cross path, which I was told led to the turnpike road to Lancaster, whither I thought it best to go as my only chance of finding Bucks; and to be sure, just as I got within sight of the Castle, there was Bucks trudging it along at a snail's pace, and humming a song. We took up our lodgings in a small ale-house kept by a buxom widow, who might well have passed for the mother of Sookey the bar-maid. Indeed, all the women in Lancaster and its vicinity seemed to me to belong to one family, with their great rosy cheeks, and pert piercing eyes.

We found that the players we expected had not yet arrived at Lancaster, but were making the best of their time at Penrith and Kendal[32] till the approaching assizes; and were accordingly compelled to begin our journey afresh. We took leave of our rosy landlady, and pushed on to Kendal without meeting with any thing worthy of record; and here we found the company we were in search of. Bucks was at once admitted into the corps at a very small salary, but which was to be increased at Lancaster. It was with the greatest difficulty, however, that I could obtain any sort of engagement at all. They were quite full, the manager said (a standing reason for refusals), and could not spare a penny on any additional performer. I pressed hard for a trial, which I offered gratuitously, having saved a few pounds on which I could live the while. This was precisely the point he wished to gain, but he made a show of yielding with great reluctance. When the business was settled, however, he appeared to take great interest in me, and instructed me himself in the parts I was to undertake.

At first, I tried a few minor parts, but the manager's plan was not to bring me out to the public till he had perfected me in the part of Young Norval, in Douglas,[33] when he intended to produce me as a London performer – a trick often practised by small provincial companies and strollers.

The night arrived when I was to appear; and every exertion was made to get up the piece, which is a great favourite with country audiences, and is well adapted to a small company from comprising but few characters. I was very much agitated, and my knees felt feeble as I took my station at the side scene to be ready to appear. In spite of some brandy and water which I had swallowed, when it came to the trying moment I was quite disheartened; but the first applause of the audience when I made my bow, at once dissipated my agitation and my fears. I got through my part with considerable spirit, and, what was more, was loudly cheered. The tragedy of Douglas was accordingly given out for repetition the following week, the part of Young Norval by a London performer.

In the interim, the manager urged me to study hard; though, intoxicated as I was with success, I scarcely required any spur: but this kind of thing did not so well agree with the notions of my companion Bucks, who was too fond of rambling to think of study, and indeed had all his parts, which were chiefly in the comic line, ready at a moment's notice. He accordingly devised some frolic every day to withdraw my attention. One of these is strongly impressed on my memory; but the relation of it will require a new chapter.

CHAPTER VI.

Pastorals among the Westmoreland Mountains – Pic-nic with a highway-man – The Devil among the shepherds of Shap-Fells.

WE had all heard from our companions who had lately been at Penrith, what a wild place Shap[34] was; and indeed the mountains and their hollow defiles, in that direction, as viewed from Kendal, appeared like an impassable wilderness. Bucks had not much relish for scenery, but he was always alive to fun and frolic; and he had a notion that he might play off some of his humorous pranks among the mountain shepherds. I was less eager to see pastoral manners than to enjoy the wild scenery, which accorded so well with the romantic[35] life I had just chosen, and was so different from the forest of masts and the barren sandy shore of Liverpool, which I had lately quitted. Such were the motives that determined Bucks and myself to make an excursion to Shap.

Accordingly, as early as our habit of a long morning nap would permit us, that is, about noon, we bent our steps towards the mountain-pass which leads, on the south-west of Lowther Castle,[36] towards Shap. Bucks looked around him in vain for adventure. The mountains stood in solitary grandeur, and their sides were at intervals covered with straggling flocks of sheep; but we saw no shepherds nor pretty shepherdesses for many hours.

At last we descried a man whom we supposed to be a shepherd, stalking along the side of a deep gully at a considerable distance. Bucks immediately hailed him by hallooing at the very stretch of his voice, but he did not, or would not, recognize the signal; and Bucks, to make sure of his game, set off to overtake him. The man, who had been deaf to his crying, soon observed his motions, and seemed resolved to try my friend's speed; for he took to his heels immediately, and made for a large patch of brushwood which lined the sides of the gully farther up the mountain.

Bucks seemed equally resolved not to be balked, and increased his haste, hallooing all the while as if he had been cheering on a pack of fox-hounds. I got upon an eminence to view the sport; but when I saw the man still hurry on, then disappear among the rocks and brushwood at the head of the gully, and Bucks pursuing him with unabated speed, I began to think he might carry the joke too far, as he did not know what he was about, or whom he was following in this wild-goose chace. I soon lost sight of Bucks also, who had now got among the rocks; and soon after I heard the report, and saw the smoke, of a pistol arise from a clump of bushes at some distance beyond where they had first disappeared.

I knew Bucks was unarmed, and became very anxious for his safety, as the horrid supposition darted into my mind that he had been fired at by the stranger, and probably shot. I had only one course to pursue. I hastened to the spot, fearless of any personal danger, and determined to do my best to assist Bucks if he were still alive, and to revenge him if he were dead. The place was indeed well fitted for deeds of darkness; for the rocks, and the bushes that grew amongst them, on either side of the gully, nearly met, and excluded the sun from the deep channel of the stream, which I could hear gurgling over the stones far below. I reached the edge of this steep precipice in great agitation for the fate of Bucks, but could hear nothing except the hollow sound of the stream, and could see no possible descent by which I might explore the channel below. But on passing farther up, – and it was no easy matter, the huge fragments of rocks were so thickly strewed about, – I perceived the bushes agitated, and heard their branches crashing, with other evidences of a violent struggle going on.

I rushed towards the spot, and made my way down the steep by clambering from bush to bush. When I reached the channel, I was thunderstruck to find Bucks with his knee on the stranger's breast, and holding him fast by the throat, and hard by them a horseman's pistol lying on the stones.

'What does this mean, Bucks?' said I. 'Are you mad?'

'Not quite mad,' replied Bucks, breathing violently, though endeavouring to appear cool and careless; 'but I did not relish being murdered by a ruffian, as I have nearly been.'

Upon this, the vanquished stranger, nettled probably by the appellation of ruffian, made a desperate struggle to free himself from the grasp of Bucks, and upon his turning round his face, I at once recognized the features of the grim man who had released me from the inglorious handcuffs; and the opinion of the constables respecting him, which I had overheard, at once came into my mind. But whatever the stranger might be – innocent or a felon – I felt grateful to him for my escape; and I said,

'Here must be some mistake. This is a friend of mine, Bucks; and I cannot imagine how he could have any design upon your life.'

Bucks, however, did not release him, for he had experienced how desperate a fellow he was, and did not think it safe to trust him till a mutual explanation had ensued, when it was discovered that Bucks had actually been apprehended instead of him by a mistake of the constables, who were indeed a pair of flats; and that Bucks's escape, and still more my own, had given him an opportunity to elude observation and get away. He had been hard pursued, however, and was forced at last to leave the level country and take refuge in these wilds; and in this same gully he had subsisted for several weeks in a very precarious manner. He had reason to think that his retreat was still undiscovered, a circumstance which had emboldened him to venture forth to reconnoitre his position, when Bucks's frolic alarmed him, and led to the consequences that had just ensued.

The name of this desperado was Blore.[37] He was a regular highway-man and house-breaker, and had committed so many extensive depredations, that large rewards had been offered for his apprehension; but hitherto he had, by the most ingenious artifices and disguises, baffled every attempt to take him. I felt interested for the poor fellow, felon as he was; for he looked haggard and emaciated, and was so weakened by his struggle with Bucks, partly, as he told us, from want of food, that he could hardly stand. Bucks was now also interested for him, and said,

'It will go hard with us, indeed, if you perish of hunger, my brave fellow. We also must have something for dinner, as we cannot now reach Shap, I take it, before night. I know how to manage. You two keep snug here till I come back!'

I was not over-pleased with this arrangement, for I did not know what Blore might do; and though I was tough for my years, I was by no means a match for him, weak as he was, or perhaps, as I fancied, he only pretended to be. Blore also, on his part, seemed to suspect some plot to surprise him in his hiding-place; but Bucks joked him out of it, and set off to procure provisions: where or how he was to find them, I had no guess.

Bucks having been away, it might be, about two hours or more, returned, bringing with him a quantity of oaten cakes, such as are common in those parts, and what looked to be a side of lamb or mutton, but sadly mangled.

'Now,' said he with a joyous air, 'prepare your fire, and you shall have as fine a lamb-chop as you could see in a summer's day.'

We removed, therefore, to Blore's dining-room, as he termed it, which was a piece of large flat rock, a little raised above the channel of the stream, and thickly overhung with hazels. He had also a place for making a fire hard by with dry leaves and sticks; so that we were not at so much loss for conveniences as I had anticipated.

Bucks told us that, when running up the hill in the first pursuit, he had descried a house, to which he went and with some difficulty had procured the oaten bread – the only eatable which they said they had. This he justly considered as too dry and meagre to dine upon, but he had, it seemed, no choice. On leaving the house, disappointed and in no good-humour, he took a circuit round the hills to prevent his being traced. His good fortune, however, did not desert him; for as he was making his way across a piece of marshy ground, he observed a lamb stuck fast in a corner of it, and a large raven perched on its head and tearing out its eyes, while its poor mother stood at some distance bleating most pitifully. Bucks soon scared off the raven, and dragging out the lamb – which was quite dead, but still warm – to the dry side of the hill, he made no ceremony of dividing it for our behoof in the best manner that he could.

Our chops relished excellently, and our oaten bread, though not quite to my taste – (in Derbyshire we make it very differently) – was by no means unacceptable, the mountain air having sharpened my appetite, whilst the romantic situation in which we were placed rendered even the dark brown water of the gully-stream very palatable.

The day was now wearing on, and we were still a good distance from Shap. We had not, indeed, seen much of pastoral life, but could not well have met with a more stirring adventure than that with Blore. I was for returning to Kendal forthwith; but Bucks said he had set out to go to Shap, and to Shap he would go before he slept.

Blore took leave of us in a very melancholy mood; for he was too well known, he said, to venture to Shap, and he intended besides to set out, that same night, for some of the midland counties, where he had never yet been, and would be more safe from surprisal. He was evidently tired, for the time, of his hazardous mode of life; though he would probably not have kept free from some depredation or other for a month together, even if he had been secured in pardon and independence: – so strong is the influence of habit when once established.

Blore pointed out to us a mountain path to Shap, nearer than the road we had been going; and Bucks and I accordingly departed for our destination. We travelled on over mountain and moor, sometimes following what appeared to be a foot-path, and at other times losing every trace of it. We encountered in those solitary mountains but very few sheep, and not a single shepherd to direct us. Bucks, however, was in high spirits, and detailed with triumph all the particulars of his struggle with Blore, – singing at intervals snatches of songs, and repeating scraps of comic speeches from farces. On my part, I admired the purple bloom of the heath, which was altogether new to me, at least in such extent; and I felt the highest enjoyment in the romance of our almost aimless expedition.

Evening was now rapidly advancing, and still no appearance of Shap, but one endless range of mountains, and gullies intersecting them, was seen wherever we turned. We rarely saw a house; and when a solitary cottage was descried, it was generally so far out of our road, or we had already passed it so far without perceiving it, that we did not think of going thither.

'I see nothing for us now,' said I, 'except lying down for the night among the heath, or wandering about at random till morning.'

It was, indeed, already dusk, though some of the very high hills still exhibited upon their summits the fading rays of the sun; but this also passed, and 'all was grey.'[38] We were standing in hesitation how to proceed, when Bucks ascended an eminence near us, humming, as he went,

> Faint and wearily the way-worn traveller
>   Plods uncheerily, afraid to stop,
> Wandering drearily, a sad unraveller
>   Of the mazes tow'rds the mountain's top.
>   Doubting, fearing,
>   While his course he's steering,
>   Cottages appearing – .[39]

'Ho!' he shouted as he reached the top, 'Shap for a ducat!'[40] and pointed to a stream of light which was glancing, as we supposed, from some of the houses of the village, at the apparent distance of half a mile or so. This was a prospect as cheering as if we had actually arrived, for we were both getting disheartened, and blaming ourselves for leaving the main road at the instance of such a fellow as Blore, who, for aught we knew, might betray us into some ambuscade of his confederates.

As we hastened on towards the light, other doubts started into the mind of Bucks. He had often heard of travellers being led into quagmires by following a will-o-wisp,[41] and he became half persuaded that the light which now attracted us was this very same mischievous sprite, come abroad to lead us a dance, and terminate our career in a morass.

'Poh! Poh!' said I jeeringly, 'I don't believe in the existence of your will-o-wisp – it is all nonsense to frighten children.'

'I am of a different opinion, however,' said he, 'and am inclined to say with Goldsmith's Hermit, that

> Yonder Phantom only flies
> To lure *us* to *our* doom – [42]

though I wish I may be deceived for once; but we shall soon see.'

'Aye, my lad!' said I in a theatrical style, 'and feel too, when you get snug beside the chimney-corner, and a glass of good ale in your hand.'

We rapidly neared the light, and if it were a will-o-wisp it was a merry one, for we heard the sounds of mirth and revelry loud and continued, and Bucks was all on the fidgets[43] to mingle in the frolic – whether it were sprites or shepherds he was quite reckless, at least he pretended to be so, though his sea trips had in reality made him as superstitious as an old woman about apparitions and diablerie.

We had now reached the spot from which the rays proceeded, though we found it was not Shap, as we had supposed, but a large irregularly built farmhouse of one story, and covered with thatch. Bucks without ceremony bolted into the room where the fun was going forward, and made a low theatrical bow at the entrance, saying,

'Hail! all hail! my merry masters! Fun, I say, is the life of man, and I always make free wherever I meet with it by night or by day. What say you, master?' addressing a brisk old fellow who held a brimming glass of ale in his hand, and wore on his face the remains of a hearty laugh at one of his own jokes, which he had just ended as Bucks entered.

Seeing us rather odd-looking fellows for these parts, he gave a particularly sly wink to the man next him, but said nothing, and waited, as it appeared, for us to proceed, naturally imagining that it was a prank of some of those who had met at his house for a merry-making, to disguise themselves and come upon him in this odd manner. Accordingly, to keep up the humour of the thing, I interrupted the pause with

> Pity the sorrows of a youth forlorn,
>   Whose wandering steps have led him to your home,
> Whose night, at least, of every hope is shorn,
>   O grant relief – and he no more will roam!⁴⁴

I said this in the highest tone I could assume of theatrical delivery, and with the most extravagant gestures.

The numerous group of merry-makers who crowded the apartment seemed quite mystified what to make of us, and well they might. Some of the wags laughed loud; others seemed to be in a passion at having the current of their mirth interrupted; and the women looked at us pryingly, as if they could have read our history in our dress, which indeed had that air of rakishness so characteristic of strolling players and gentlemen adventurers.

One whispered that we had been set on by Jack Richardson for a frolic, as he was never out of such things; another said, 'Nay, indeed! it is the mad chapman⁴⁵ of Carlisle and his companion Billy;' and a third averred that we were robbers on the look-out for spoil – one of us perhaps 'the notorious Blore himself, who was reported to be lurking among the mountains thereabouts.'

'To cut the matter short,' said Bucks, 'for I always like a short story if it is good – don't you, master?' addressing the old gentleman with the ale glass, which during the bustle had remained untasted: – 'To cut the matter short, I'll tell you who we be. – This chap is Tom Richmond, fresh from college, an't you, Tom? and up to all sorts of devilment; and I am Jem Bucks, at your service, ready to sing a song, join in a catch, tell a story, or dance a jig with any pretty maiden who now hears me.'

'Nay,' said the old gentleman, who was master of the revels, 'if that be so, make room for 'em; they seem glib o' the toongue, however, and we'll ha' soome

foon o' them an they had a coop of ale. D'ye know the old song, masters? that
goes,

> Not drunk nor yet sober, but brother to both,
> I met a young man upon Aylesberry vale;
>> And I saw by his face
>> That he was in good case
> To come and shake hands with a tankard of ale.
> Tara la lay, Tara la lay, Tara la, Tara la,
>> Tara la lay,[46]
> So come and shake hands with a tankard of ale.'

Without pausing, indeed, he sang the song, which is none of the shortest, to
the end; and filling up two bumpers of his October[47] for Bucks and me, we were
not backward in pledging him.

'Ah!' said the old chap, as we went on to praise his ale, 'that is the prime
stoof! D'ye know I have seen a coople o' glasses of my October set my old neighbour Kirby here to begin his favourite catch without bidding, and I can now see
his toongue quivering to be at it – Eh, Ralph! how does it go again?'

Ralph Kirby, a sly humorous looking farmer, thus appealed to, peered round
the apartment as if he wanted assistance from some individual, and at last fixing
on a tall awkward fellow who was sitting silently between two buxom lasses, and
did not seem to dare open his mouth, he suddenly pointed to him, and attacked
him with the words of the old catch,[48]

> 'Twas you, Sir! 'Twas you, Sir!
> I tell you nothing new, Sir!
> 'Twas you that kissed the pretty girl,
> 'Twas you, Sir, you![49]

The tall fellow blushed up to the eyes, and wriggled on his seat as if it had
been cushioned upon nettles; while the two lasses, or shepherdesses, if you will,
held down their heads indeed, but more to conceal their laughter than their
blushes. Ralph continued his catch at the expense of the blushing youth, and to
the great amusement of the company, still pointing to him:

> 'Tis true, Sir! 'Tis true, Sir!
> You look so very blue, Sir?
> 'Tis true you kissed the pretty girl,
> 'Tis true, Sir, true!

He knew his trade better, however, than to harp too long on one string; and
turning round the circle while he was repeating the last two lines, he accused
every man present, but had no sooner concluded than a dozen voices bawled
out,

Oh, Sir! No, Sir!
O no, no, no, no, Sir!
How can you use me so, Sir!
I did not kiss the pretty girl,
But I know who.

And the catch went round, followed by another brimmer of the October; to both of which Bucks and I lent most willing assistance.

Here then we were, seated in the midst of a pastoral group of merry-makers in the wilds of Westmoreland; and Bucks, just in his element, cracking his jokes and trolling his songs as if he had been acquainted with every individual of the goodly company from his childhood. When he had been with the show-folks going the round of fairs and assizes, he had also picked up several slight-of-hand tricks, which, as he became more familiar with the good folks, he began to play off, to their great amusement in the first place, but some of them they could only explain by his having formed a connection with the devil, and soon began to look upon him very suspiciously; and as I had occasionally assisted him, I was evidently, for the rest of the night, considered as one of Satan's agents.

The story, by exaggeration, afterwards went, that the devil himself had come in amongst the merry-makers at Beckston in form of a square-built man, with an attendant (meaning me) who had sold himself to him, soul and body. A thousand lies also were gossipped about of the wonderful exploits which we had performed.

These odd suspicions produced one effect in our favour. We were most kindly treated, out of a dread of our supposed power to work mischief and trouble. The frolic was continued till very late, or rather early, when the greater number of the revellers took leave and departed for their several homes. Bucks and I would have gone off also in as mysterious a manner as we could, the more to astonish those simple and superstitious people; but as we knew not whither to go in the dark, we were compelled to petition for accommodation during the night.

The old dame who claimed the management of the household concerns of Beckston was evidently very averse to this measure, dreading some awful catastrophe to herself or her establishment as the sure consequence; but she took care to wear the looks of civility, which, being forced, appeared like a caricature of good manners. Thanks to a comfortable bed and the potations of Beckston October, we slept most soundly; took leave of our hospitable friends next morning with many thanks, and returned through Shap, (which we had passed in the night) by the main road to Kendal, without any farther adventure worth relating; except that Bucks frightened from the road an innocent mountain nymph, whom we met, by swaggering up to her and singing,

Molly! Molly! my dearest honey!
My lovely jewel! my only life![50]

The girl, whom Bucks pronounced to be a Westmoreland shepherdess, ran off to the hills, and he in a feigned pursuit followed; but when the poor thing began to cry for assistance, he halted; for he meant no harm, and only wanted to have a joke and a laugh at her expense, to help to digest the October he had drunk at Beckston.

CHAPTER VII.

Love and madness – An old woman clothed in grey – Moonlight musings.

THE manager now offered me a regular engagement during the Lancaster Assizes, at a salary somewhat higher than that of Bucks. During all the bustle and agitation in which I had lately lived, I often thought of my pretty Anne, and my highest desire was to have her as the companion of my adventures. Now also, as I could maintain her on the proceeds of my engagement, I became more anxious for her society than ever. Still I could not devise any probable plan to accomplish my wish; for she was now distant from me more than a hundred miles, and could not travel unprotected, even if she should, upon my writing to her, consent to come, of which I was by no means certain. I could not, on the other hand, leave my engagement to go for her, which was the mode I greatly preferred. I was relieved from my embarrassment by the manager complaining to me of his great want of a young female performer; for his wife, who took the leading parts, was in bad health, and frequently unable to perform; and another lady being none of the handsomest, even with all the aids of rouge and pearl-white,[51] could not appear as Juliet or Belvidera[52] without being laughed at and hissed, and was only fit for hoydens and housemaids. I eagerly told him of Anne, whom I described in terms that made him as desirous of having her with us, as I was myself.

It was arranged that I should immediately set out from Kendal for Derbyshire, in order to be back in time for the Lancaster Assizes. I had, indeed, some painful misgivings about the libertine principles and manners of my associates, and I shuddered to think of Anne, innocent and pure as she was, being brought within a contaminated atmosphere; but I quieted my conscience in some measure by relying on my own principles being still uncorrupted by libertinism, and trusting to my own spirit to be able to protect her from insult.

To save time, I travelled as far as Castleton[53] by the stage, though I should have preferred footing it with my knapsack for the sake of adventure, my appetite for which having been of late keenly whetted by associating with Bucks. He would willingly have accompanied me, but as this was an expedition in which I had so much personal interest, I did not like to share it with any one. I had engaged in it, indeed, with great alacrity, but was still sadly puzzled how to execute my plans.

I had never written to my father since I left Liverpool: – to confess the truth, I was ashamed to write; for though I exulted in my emancipation from the ordinary trammels of life and business, I was perfectly aware of the bad opinion entertained by the world of actors and adventurers, and I felt a sort of secret impression on my mind that it was too true. This impression, of course, I strove hard to get rid of in the same manner as one tries to forget a painful dream, but the more I strove, the more deeply was it rivetted in my mind; and, in short, I could not write to my father, as I had no doubt he would give me up for lost, and discard me for ever. As I had resolved not to write, I determined for the same reasons not to go home, though I was so near, and thought it the best way to apprize Anne of my coming by letter, trusting to the post, and hoping it might not be pried into in the village. My letter was sufficiently laconic, and ran thus: –

My Dear Anne,
    Meet me on Wednesday night, at the old time and place. I wish most particularly to see you without any one knowing of my coming.
    Your's,[54]
      Most faithfully and affectionately,
        T. R.

Should this chance to fall into any other hands than hers, it would be unintelligible; and on the faith of this, upon the night appointed, I hastened to the place of meeting, across fields which I well knew, avoiding all the roads wherein I might be recognised by any village acquaintance. I had also slouched my hat over my face, and buttoned up my frock coat close to my chin, the better to conceal my features if I did chance to meet any one who knew me. It was a little after dusk when I got to the field where the well-remembered stile was, and which I had entered on the side farthest from the village. I went forward in high glee and spirits, as I should, within a few minutes, meet my beloved Anne, and what was all the world besides to me if I had her!

Such were my feelings as I approached the scene of our last parting, when we exchanged our vows of mutual affection; and I looked as if my eye could have pierced the darkness to see her true to the appointment, and waiting to receive me. I did imagine I saw a figure moving between me and the hedge-row, but as I eagerly rushed forward, it disappeared, and I found myself alone close by the stile. As Anne had tried my patience once before by concealing herself, I imagined that this was some prank of the same kind; but was soon undeceived when a tall dark person came up behind me and seized me rudely by the collar.

'So, you vagabond scoundrel!' said the man, 'you are not contented with running away yourself, and breaking the hearts of your parents, but wish to entice others with you! We shall take good care to prevent that, however, clever as you may think yourself in plotting mischief.'

I at once recognised the voice of Anne's uncle; and the next minute my father appeared at the other side of the stile, with a most melancholy and downcast air which it went to my very heart to see.

'O! Tom, Tom!' he said to me in a broken voice, 'I never thought it would have come to this. O that I should have brought you up to disgrace yourself in such a manner, and bring my grey hairs with sorrow to the grave!'

I could not bear to see my father so grieved, and the tears started into my eyes when I heard him sigh over my conduct. What a change of feelings a few moments had produced! I was but just exulting in the anticipation of carrying off my beloved Anne in triumph to Lancaster, and now I was actually in sorrow for ever having gone thither myself. I spoke not a word, either to resist their interference, or in confession of having done wrong; for the latter was the feeling uppermost in my heart.

Without attempting to refuse, I went home with my father in no very comfortable mood, but continued obstinately silent respecting my adventures or my intentions. Grief, and not anger, seemed to pervade our whole family respecting me, and I was most kindly treated. This affected me much more than recrimination or threatening could have done, and I fairly began to regret that I had ever thought of adventure.

The night was spent in sleepless musing on what I should now do. Were I to remain at home and resign my Lancaster engagement, my old companions and acquaintance would jeer me and look down upon me: this I could not support; and what would Bucks not think and say, if I renounced the free life I was but yet commencing, for sober business and moping at home?

> The world's dread laugh,
> Which scarce the firm philosopher can scorn,[55]

has often more influence upon our conduct than we are willing to believe – at least, I have felt it so in my own experience; and now, when I had to decide on an important step in life, it overbalanced every other consideration of filial duty, and even the stronger feelings of grief and sorrow for the affliction of my parents.

I need not say, also, that love had a great share in directing my plans. I had not seen Anne; and her uncle, I doubted not, would prevent our meeting if he could. This was the very thing which would have stimulated me to accomplish my original design, if I had had no other motive than that of balking his vigilance. It is, indeed, a vain attempt to shackle such a powerful and sleepless passion as love, and the Scripture saith well, that, 'many waters cannot quench love, neither can the floods drown it.'[56]

I was forced, however, to have recourse to artifice to gain my point, and accordingly pretended that I should at least stay at home for some weeks. But how I was to proceed, I knew not; for Anne, I was certain, would be strictly watched, and without trusting a confederate (and that I detested), how was I to communicate with her, much less see her? I was not even sure that she knew of my arrival; for I thought it most probable that her uncle had never let her see my letter, but had learned from village gossiping where we were wont to meet, and had by this means surprised me.

I was taking a solitary walk in my father's garden, meditating on these various obstacles, and casting an occasional glance of recognition, by no means unpleasing, over to a certain espalier in the next garden, and also to the privet hedge in the corner of the same, when I observed a girl, in the field beyond, making signs to me with her hand. I was not long in obeying the signal, and was delighted to find that it was Anne's favourite companion, who put a pretty little note into my hand, saying,

'You know, I daresay, who this is from; but you must be both quick and cautious, or you'll spoil all.'

I need not say that the note was from Anne, telling me that her uncle had, on my account, treated her with great harshness, and had come home last night in a great rage, threatening to lock her up, feed her on bread and water, and subject her to other similar severities, if she dared to hold any correspondence with me. She had never, I found, received my letter from Castleton; but she was so harassed by her uncle's harsh usage, that she was resolved to leave the house at all hazards, and if I would meet her at the farther end of the bridge a little after dusk, she would go with me wherever I chose.

How she was to contrive to escape her uncle's vigilance she did not inform me; and how, on the other hand, I was to tear myself away from my sorrowing parents, I as little knew. It must be done, however; Anne's claims upon my protection, sealed with our mutual vows of faithful love, were paramount to every other consideration, and I resolved.

Under pretence of making some calls, I left home early in the afternoon, and tried to look as composed as I could when I parted with my parents, who nothing doubted that I should return in the evening. I had no desire for exposing myself to observation by paying any visit, and concealed myself in a wood near the bridge till the appointed time; when I hastened to the spot, making use of the same precautions as before of slouching my hat, buttoning up my coat, and walking with an assumed swagger. I was recognised, however, by more than one person who passed, for I heard them whispering,

'That's Tom Richmond, as came home t'other day! I wonder what he bees after tonight.'

At length I perceived an old woman come creeping along, supported by a staff; who, frail as she looked, seemed determined to keep up with me, though I walked quicker and quicker, and crossed the road more than once to avoid her. Nothing is more vexing than a stranger thus coming in your way, when you wish to be private and secure from observation. I got quite irritated at this old woman's intruding herself upon my walk, and, determining to lead her a dance, went off at a pace which she could not keep up with; but to my utter surprise, after turning a corner and regaining my post by another way, I found my persecutor stationed to waylay me again. There must be something in this, thought I; perhaps she has a message from Anne that she cannot come. With the expectation, therefore, of having my hopes once more disappointed, I approached the crone, who caught me softly by the hand, and whispered in an accent I well knew,

'Tom! it is I – your own Anne. – What shall we do?'

'Anne!' said I, 'and in such a disguise – but we must not lose a moment.'

'And whither can we go?' whispered she, in her own sweet accents.

'I can tell you better when we are out of danger; in the mean-time we must speed.'

Anne thought it better to continue for a little her character of the old woman, by assuming which she had eluded her uncle, who supposed her safe in her own chamber, and would not probably discover her escape till next morning. By walking at a smart pace we soon got out of the vicinity of the village, and the moon fortunately rose to light us on our way. It was a most memorable and interesting night for us both. I was still but a youth, and here I was, with a beautiful girl who trusted to my love and protection, casting myself on the varying and uncertain chances of the wide world. Anne, however, gave me little leisure to moralize, for she was eager to hear the history of my late adventures, which I began to relate, to beguile the way. She was quite delighted with my narrative, declaring it to be more interesting than any romance she had ever read; and no doubt to her it was so, for she was now about to share my fortunes and take a part in my adventures.

We had hurried on so fast that Anne, unaccustomed as she was to travelling, soon felt fatigued, and we sat down by the road-side, on a grassy bank, to rest ourselves. I intended that we should get to the inn, where I had left my things, to breakfast, and then proceed till we should reach a convenient stage to take us on by Manchester to Lancaster. Our situation was now however somewhat equivocal; and it puzzled us not a little how to manage.

'O!' said Anne, 'I'll tell you what, Tom! – I shall pass for your sister, till we be lawfully married.'

'But, my dear!' said I, 'it will be very hard for me not to betray our secret by some fond word or action. It will be better to say at once that we are married, which we really have been, you know, love, ever since we exchanged vows at the stile.'

On this point, nevertheless, I found her inflexible, romantic though she was; and I am persuaded that more girls would, in similar cases, act in the prudent manner she did, than the world is apt to suppose. I confess, however, that I did not feel pleased to see her so obstinate about this; and though she spoke to me as fondly as ever, and the moonlight showed the same pretty smile, and the same soft and loving eyes which had once before so enchanted and unmanned me, I imagined that she was become more cold and reserved, and, in a word, I did not experience the same overpowering feelings as I had done the last time I had seen her lovely face by moonlight. I was, in fact, half inclined to quarrel with her; and, had I not been so much fascinated by the novel situation in which we were placed, and by the poor girl just at that moment clinging to me for protection from a bull which had broken from his inclosure, and was roaring along the road whereby we sat, – I daresay I should have chid her for her obstinate scruples about our mode of travelling.

The bull having passed without observing us, we resumed our journey, and arrived at my inn without again mentioning the disputed subject; and as we were not to sleep at this inn, we said nothing whatever of our relationship, though, from the whisperings and prying looks of the bar-maid, I could perceive that our affairs were better understood than we imagined. We remained here, however, only till we had breakfasted, as I was fearful of being pursued by some of our people. To put them on a wrong scent, if any body did come here after us, I was cautious enough to go out in a direction quite opposite to that we meant to travel in, and regained the road by a cross-path.

CHAPTER VIII.

Trip to Buxton – Romance of real life, still life, and stirring life – Twilight music in Monsal-Dale – Rock robbers at the Lover's Leap.

Our way lay through Bakewell,[57] where we had tea; and we intended to reach Buxton,[58] and put up there at night. We travelled in high spirits, as the evening sun was shining on the rocks and woods that began to skirt the road, and the thrush was making every echo ring with his vesper song. The river Wye, here but a small stream, accompanied us part of the way, and added to the beauty of the scenery of Monsal-Dale, which is the name of this romantic road, or rather defile; for the rocks on each side of us, as we advanced, became steep and lofty, with little more than space between them for the road, and the river, and a few narrow slips of green meadow ground.

Towards their summits the cliffs were naked and grey; but half way down they were thickly clothed with bushes, which became more luxuriant where they hung over the road, and threw upon it a deep gloomy shadow.

Anne would have enjoyed this fine scene, stored as her mind was with the high-coloured pictures of romance; but the darkening and narrowing road, which had no appearance of termination, alarmed her with a sort of fear she could not account for; and she drew closer to my side, and looked with apprehension into every bush.

Anon, we heard a loud shouting; and, as fear is contagious, I also was thrown off my guard, and fancied that it was some horrid deed of murder and robbery committing. I was obliged, however, to assume courage, and listened and looked more attentively, when I soon discovered that it was only some shepherds washing their flock in a pool of the Wye.

As soon as we found that our fears in this case were groundless, we proceeded on to the very gorge of the defile, when we heard the noise of a carriage coming up behind, which gave us additional spirits, though the rapid advance of the twilight, and the narrowing of the rocks and bushes on each side the road, were much more gloomy than gay. In a solitary place like this, even the sound of running water is cheerful; but the Wye had also deserted us, its course being through another rocky pass towards the right.

The carriage was slowly advancing, though we could not yet see it for the windings of the road among the high rocks; but as it was an object of great interest, particularly to Anne, who considered it as a sort of protection from apprehended violence, we listened with eagerness to its approach. On a sudden we heard it stop, and a loud shriek, seemingly from a female voice, came from the same direction. Anne clung to my arm, and looked the very picture of terror, saying in an agitated tone,

'O Tom! what can have happened? The carriage, I fear, has broken down, and the lady must have been killed!'

'Shall I go then,' said I, 'to see whether I can render any assistance?'

'We must both go,' said Anne, looking round at the dark woods, as if afraid to trust herself from my side.

We accordingly hastened back to see what had happened; but as soon as I got a glimpse of the carriage, which was a phaeton, I saw that no accident had occurred, for a lady and gentleman occupied the seat, while a middle-sized but strong-built man, whose back was towards us, held the bridle of the horse in one hand, and a pistol in the other, levelled at the travellers, while he muttered in a low growling accent, –

'One word, and I draw the trigger! – Your money, instantly! – I have no time to parley.'

When I heard this, I hesitated what to do. I was instinctively about to dart upon the robber, dash the pistol out of his hand, and rescue the travellers; but Anne, who strongly grasped my arm, pulled me back, while she trembled like an aspen-leaf. I was so agitated, indeed, that for a moment I forgot Anne was with me; but when she appeared thus alarmed, and when I reflected that she too might be endangered, I paused, and we withdrew behind one of the dark bushes that skirted the road, to await the event in silence.

As the travellers were slow in parting with their money, the patience of the robber became exhausted; and, as he appeared to take a fresh aim, with the same hoarse accent he said,

'Here goes, then, master! – your blood be on your own head!'

'Hold! hold! for the love of God, and you shall have all!' screamed the lady; while the robber, now secure, as he imagined, of his prey, lowered his pistol, and stood impatient to receive the purse.

'Now is my time,' I whispered to Anne: 'keep close here till I come back.'

She tried to hold me, but I sprang forward in a moment, and before the robber was aware of my presence, I was master of his pistol, which I now levelled at his head, saying,

'Villain! you are for once disappointed; and if you do not take yourself off on the instant, I shall make your quietus with your own weapon.'

'Softly! softly!' replied the fellow, coming close up to me, and looking me keenly in the face; 'you would not shoot an old friend, Tom!'

It was Blore, whom I had not recognised in the dusky shadow which the bushes threw over the road; and he had also disguised his voice.

'Mercy on us!' I could hear the lady whisper. 'This is another on 'em! O dear! what *shall* we do?'

I looked up to reconnoitre the travellers I had saved from the fangs of Blore, and to my utter surprise discovered that the scraggy awkward figure, which represented the lady, was no other than my old friend Mrs. Figgens; and beyond her, little Hump-back, whom terror had nearly deprived of speech, was sitting with his head shrunk in between his shoulders, – his little short neck having almost disappeared. From the first, he had made no effort to defend himself either by word or action, and would have quietly resigned himself, I have no doubt, coiled up like a hedge-hog, to be either robbed or murdered, or both. Neither of them at first recognised me, and I was anxious to get Blore out of the way.

'Ah!' said I to him, 'still at the old trade! you will not cease till you are taken. You are safe, however, for the present. I shall lodge no information, and for my sake my friends in the phaeton I know will be silent; but be off speedily, if you value your own safety! for others may come up who will not deal with you so gently, and I think I can hear the prance of horses coming this way.'

Accordingly Blore, bidding me a hasty farewell, dived into the thickest part of the wood and disappeared; while Mrs. Figgens, having got a little courage when she saw the danger over, stretched up her long skinny neck, and exclaimed, –

'Tom Richmond! as I do live by bread! – our own Tom, as we used to call him. How lucky – wasn't it? – that you were here! O how I tremble! Look for my smelling salts, Mr. Figgens, in that reticule beside you! O dear! I shall certainly faint!'

'Faint! – fiddlesticks!' said the little man, his neck having become a full inch longer; 'why should you faint when the danger is over, and when I and Master Richmond are here to protect you?'

This speech was a great effort on the part of Figgens, and he could add no more till he had taken breath. Mrs. Figgens went on panting, and sighing, and twisting herself about, in what she imagined to be a proper lady-like mode of action, exclaiming all the while against the rudeness of Figgens, who would not look for her smelling salts, which she had to find for herself. As little Hump-back was giving no attention to her fine airs, she began to think it useless to carry on the farce, till I unluckily said,

'Compose yourself, my dear Madam! – You are terribly flurried, but I hope you will soon get better.'

This was a tone of sympathy which seemed to vibrate through every nerve of her body, and it produced a shock little less violent than the menacing voice of the robber.

'Oh! Mr. Richmond!' she said in a low tremulous voice, 'I shall never recover it. I shall go into a swoon, I know – I always thought I should die in a swoon.'

We had no time for this nonsense, as the twilight was waning fast, and we had still a considerable distance to travel; and I bethought me, that it would be the best restorative for the fainting fit of Mrs. Figgens to hint that Blore might return with his confederates and overpower us all. This, as I expected, speedily put her swooning to flight.

During the whole of this scene Anne had remained concealed, experiencing of course the most intense feelings so long as there was any doubt of the issue; but as soon as she perceived that I was amongst my friends, she ventured forth and took her place by my side. I had therefore to invent on the instant an explanation of my own circumstances, and how Anne came to be with me.

Presuming that my late adventures were unknown to my friends in the phaeton, and that they supposed me to be still engaged at Liverpool, I told them I was now going thither, on my return from a visit to my father, and that Anne was a girl of our village, who had taken advantage of my protection to go to Manchester. This story passed as satisfactory; and we had only to bid our friends good bye, and let them proceed on their journey to Buxton, to which place we should follow them.

The restorative hint, however, which I had given to Mrs. Figgens, of the possibility of Blore's returning with a strong party of his gang, made her protest against leaving us, for she had no faith in the courage of her husband; and as there was only room for two in the phaeton, it was proposed that Figgens should resign his place to Anne, and join me as a foot-guard against all attack. Figgens had no relish for such an arrangement, and disliked the notion of acting in the dangerous capacity of a foot-guard as much as he did foot travelling; yet, as he disliked still more having his gallantry called in question at the same time with his bravery, he complied with the best grace he could assume.

The night was fine, but the darkening woods which rose above us, and left only a narrow stripe of the twilight sky visible, made the whole too gloomy and dismal to be enjoyed, especially after the adventure we had just met with; and we proceeded up the ascent in silence. At length we descried a light from the window of the little turnpike-house,[59] the inhabitants of which, we found, were well aware of their dangerous neighbourhood, for they had their windows defended with strong iron bars.

'Late travelling, Master!' said the turnpike-man to me as he came out to survey us. 'Any thing stirring in the Dale to-night?'

'Not a mouse,' said I; for I remembered my promise not to betray Blore, though I doubt not, the turnpike-man already knew as much of the transaction as I did, – at least I fancied that I could see beyond one side of his big lazy belly, which filled the door-way, a grim person, very like Blore, seated in the chimney-corner with a glass in his hand. In this fancy I might, indeed, be mistaken.

We soon emerged into the open country, where, under the canopy of a wider sky, we got time to breathe from our fears of robbers, and arrived safe at Buxton; though, when we passed the high rock called the Lover's Leap, Figgens looked fearfully up to the cliffs, and fancied, I suppose, that every dark shadow in their crevices was a robber, ready to sally forth and try his courage as a foot-guard to the ladies in the phaeton.

CHAPTER IX.

Resistible temptations – House-breaking extraordinary – Scholastic discipline
– Apparition of a candle – The punisher punished.

ON our arrival at Buxton, Figgens procured us accommodation for the night
in the lodging-house where they put up; and, what was no less acceptable, a good
supper and excellent wine. It was amusing enough to hear the little man recount,
with great ostentation, what he *had intended* to do in the case of Blore's attack. I
do not know that I can justly accuse Figgens of actual falsehood; but had we not
been eye-witnesses of his terrified behaviour in the transaction, he would have
made it appear that he was the most courageous person present. Like all dwarfs
and deformed people, indeed, he was peculiarly afraid of any loss of dignity, and
was always jealously on the watch to defend this from every encroachment. Mrs.
Figgens, however, who held the reins of authority, would not in this instance
allow him the least credit for his magnanimous intentions, seeing he had not
manifested the same by any visible sign.

In proportion as the courage of Figgens had fallen in the opinion of his
beloved spouse, my own seemed to have risen; and she lavished all her rhetoric
upon the bravery which I had displayed, to the evident annoyance of Hump-
back, who thought every epithet bestowed on me was at his own personal
expense. On my part, I liked, as most persons do, a little due praise well enough;
but whether it were that Mrs. Figgens had on this momentous occasion indulged
in an extra glass of wine, I cannot say – her praises became as disagreeable as they
were fulsome and endless, and, in fact, she began to look at me in a manner I was
by no means willing to understand. She took my hand and pressed it warmly,
uttering rhapsodical protestations in her own vulgar way, that she was indebted
to me for her life, and could never repay me; and that I might command her to
the utmost of her ability. This was followed by what she meant to be a very tender squeeze of the hand.

Figgens by this time had dropped asleep in the arm-chair, and Anne had
retired some time before; so that I was left at the mercy of this female anatomy[60]
of skin and dry bones, whose leering looks, glazed with the fumes of the wine,

were enough to wither me; and I meditated an escape as soon as possible, though this I found to be no easy matter. It was now far in their night, and the candles were burning low in the sockets. I was also becoming drowsy, and, I believe, should have soon followed the example of little Hump-back, had I not been so unpleasantly besieged. I was just about to rise and make good my retreat, when she pretended to hear a noise at the door, and clung around me in great apparent alarm. Even at this distance of time, the remembrance of the grasp of her skinny fingers, like the coil of a snake, makes me shudder and sicken to very loathing.

'O! Mr. Richmond!' she said in a sort of cracked sentimental whine, meant to be tenderly pathetic; 'you must protect us again! – won't you? There be robbers below, breaking into the house!' And she pulled me towards the window, where, indeed, I heard a suspicious sound, as if some one were working about the lock. I was going to throw up the sash, and demand who was at the door, but she eagerly prevented me and said, –

'For heaven's sake, Mr. Richmond, don't expose yourself! you don't know but they mayn't fire upon you. – O! what shall we do if they get in? – Let me bolt this door however!' and she went and shot the bolt of the door to secure *me* at all events, if not to protect herself from hostile ingress.

While she was doing this, I threw up the sash, reckless of the danger of being fired upon, and challenged the person at the door, whom I found was only the servant securing it for the night, and I shrewdly suspected that Mrs. Figgens knew as much. The bustle we made broke in upon the dreams of Figgens, who began to toss himself, muttering and grunting through his teeth, as if under the horrors of nightmare. His brain, indeed, and no wonder, had been quite unsettled by the events of the night, as well as by the wine he had despatched to warm his heart, and uphold his courage; while his dreams, no doubt, partook of his troubles, rendering 'confusion worse confounded,'[61] till he could bear the turmoil of this inward distraction no longer, and started up from the arm-chair like Richard the Third from his camp-couch,[62] with his hair on end, his eyes glaring, and his little visage the very caricature of a ghost.

This apparition of Humpy was to me a very lucky occurrence; for her device of the housebreakers having entirely failed, Mrs. Figgens, who still held me fast in her shrivelled claws, had just at the moment begun to throw off the veil of delicacy (thin enough in all conscience) which she had hitherto preserved, and to make a more open attack on my good nature. But when she saw the form of her husband start up so ghastly, she was seized with terror of the discovery of her meditated infidelity, and performed a screech that would have done honour to a donkey. Upon the disturbed senses of Figgens, this operated like a spell; and to make amends for his former cowardice, as his courage was now screwed to the sticking-place with wine, dreams, and the impending danger of which the scream advertised him, – he armed himself with a hearth-broom that stood in the chimney-corner, straddled towards the window where we still stood, over-turned and extinguished the lights in his confusion, and pounced in the dark upon his affrighted spouse, (under the delusion, I suppose, that she was a robber) seizing her by the throat and crying out,

'Ah! I've caught you at last! Death to me, but you shall suffer in the flesh!'

The terrified dame, perhaps from her conscience being justly smitten, made no resistance, and spoke not a word – her usual prerogative of supremacy having wholly merged in her fear of detection; whilst, for my part, I had enough to do to repress a burst of laughter.

'I shall be avenged of you!' Humpy went on. 'You shall be punished if there's a bit of birch[63] in Derbyshire!'

I could not, in the absence of the lights, see what he was about; but I fancied he was proceeding to inflict the only punishment with which he was familiar in his scholastic profession, by substituting the hearth-broom for the birch. The first application of this barbarous instrument to the person of Mrs. Figgens produced another alarming screech; and immediately afterwards I heard the servants hur-rying up stairs to see what was the matter with the *lady*.

The door soon flew open, and a candle was the first object which appeared, suspended forward in mid air, by way of shield no doubt against all evil to the holder, whose mystified countenance was seen peering beneath it in the door-way. The light manifested the correctness of my fancy with respect to the scholastic proceedings of little Hump-back, who held the hearth-broom ready poised at a due elevation for a second infliction, just as the light flashed in upon him. The singular position, however, of the loving couple was not long exposed to rude and menial gaze; for the house-maid, in her hurry to get a peep at what was going on, came in collision with a dumb-waiter which stood in the passage with the supper-tray, and upsetting the whole, and herself besides, smash upon the hinder portion of the candle-bearer, he was upset likewise, and the light along with him, so that darkness again spread her blanket over poor Mrs. Figgens and her fundamental disgrace.

The *lady* having had a moment to recover from her surprise, rage and resentment soon quashed all her compunctious visitings[64] of conscience for her meditated wickedness. She flew upon little Humpy like a cat, assailing his ears with scolding, and his countenance with scratches, till another light was brought, which exhibited the poor man perked up in a corner, and in great bod-ily fear, – his face clouded with red and yellow, like a ham-and-egg handkerchief, and his *lady* brandishing the hearth-broom of which she had disarmed him. The re-entrance of the servants with the lights had no effect in quieting the violence of her passion; for she had already got beyond the boundaries of shame, and was going to commence another attack on the devoted head of Figgens, had I not stepped in and interfered on his behalf. Indeed, I should perhaps have interfered sooner; but I was quite taken by surprise at the whole scene, and more disposed to laugh than to look upon it as a matter of wounding and maiming.

It was no easy affair, however, to pacify the enraged dame; and if I had not taken advantage of the presence of the servants, who were collecting the fragments of glass, stone-ware, and eatables of all sorts, scattered about from the upset dumb-waiter, I should have had, I believe, to employ main force for the protection of poor Figgens, as he had no notion of remonstrance or resistance himself – now that he was fully awake to his danger – and bore all with a Job-like patience.[65] My protection, however, would only, I foresaw, be a temporary respite, as Mrs. Figgens would no doubt take her opportunity of repaying him an hundredfold for the scholastic chastisement she had suffered at his hands.

As soon as I had effected a sort of reconciliation between them, I thought it best to withdraw, and leave them to 'chew the cud of sweet and bitter fancy.'[66] Getting up betimes next morning, Anne and I determined to begin our journey before the Figgenses were stirring, as it could be little pleasure to them to see me after the affray of the night. I had also some fears that I should not be able to restrain my mirth on the occasion, and might bring, by its indulgence, lasting discredit on Mr. Figgens's former instructions in the science of 'genteel politeness.'

CHAPTER X.

Green-room debut – Managerial manœuvring – The biter bit – Ale-house jollifications – Bucks and the cobbler – Mysterious elopement.

THE morning was calm and cloudless, and the round hills of the Peak[67] looked
green and fresh in the early sunshine – a bright image of our youthful hopes as
we hastened onwards, bidding adieu to our native Derbyshire, to commit ourselves to the chances of a world which, alas! we little knew, or we should not, I
daresay, have been so light-hearted and eager for the journey. The adventures of
the preceding night furnished us with ample topics for remark and chit-chat;
and the varying prospects of the way were more interesting to Anne than to me,
as it was the first long journey she had ever made.

When we approached Lancaster, she was sadly disappointed at the sight of
the Castle, filled as her mind was with the sublime solitude of Udolpho[68] and its
gloomy turrets – 'bosom'd high in tufted trees.'[69] The word *Castle* had made her
form a similar notion of the county-prison of Lancashire; but when she saw it
rising like a naked pyramid on the sea-shore, and surrounded by common-place
comfortable houses, her romantic day-dream was at once dissolved. She was
more struck with the sea, which she had never before seen; and her enthusiasm
was boundless at the sight of the distant range of the Westmoreland mountains,
which compensated fully for her disappointment respecting the Castle, by giving her a sublimer picture of the dark ridges of the Appennines in Udolpho,
than the smooth green hills of Derbyshire had done. The view of the mountains
revived the recollection of my pastoral excursion to Shap along with Bucks; and
Anne never tired of hearing me recount the adventures we then met with. Her
enthusiastic fancy was so excited, that I believe she would have thought it no
hardship to be siezed[70] by banditti, and carried into the wilds of Westmoreland.

All this, however, was mad romance; and we had mean-time to think of the
commonplaces of real life, by finding accommodation for the night. The buxom
widow's was the only house I knew in Lancaster, and thither we repaired till
I should learn something of our company; for I was too much jaded with the
journey to make much inquiry that night.

We had resolved to get married as soon as I could procure a licence, or, more properly, in the first place, money to purchase it; for my purse was nearly exhausted by our travelling expenses, and my only dependence for a supply was on the manager. I accordingly waited upon him next morning and introduced Anne, who soon found, to her cost, that though she might be treated as a lady or a princess on the stage, she was not, when off it, to expect much courtesy from him. He received her very coolly, and after eyeing her with a contemptuous look from head to foot, like a horse-jockey about to make a purchase, he said, in an affected whimper of pity, –

'I'm very sorry, Mr. Richmond, to give you my opinion of this young person; but she won't do for me, Sir, that's flat! – wants dignity for high parts: – a hoydenish figure, you know, won't do – a dull, sleepy sort of eye, too, I perceive – no fire in it for the passionate parts – and as for voice – if I may judge – those thin wiry tones may do for love-whispers in Derbyshire, but would not be heard beyond the orchestra. – Sorry for your trouble and expense, but can't help it – she won't do for me, by Jupiter, that's flat!'

'Nor shall I either, Sir, since it is so,' said I, endeavouring, as much as I could, to suppress my outraged feelings, which strongly prompted me to interrupt his harangue by knocking him down.

'O! as you please!' he said, with cool indifference. 'No compulsion in my company! none! Actors are now as plenty as blackberries!'

The more cool he seemed, the more I was enraged at his contemptuous and unfeeling conduct towards me. Anne, also, heroine as she had fancied herself, could not stand his cruel remarks, and became pale and faintish; whilst my blood boiled at the sight. The endeavour to suppress my passion almost deprived me of utterance, and indeed I had no wish to wrangle with a fellow who had so unfeelingly blasted my hopes. I therefore drew Anne's arm within mine, and was about to leave him without another word, when he resumed, –

'One word, Mr. Richmond, before you go. You remember, I presume, certain monies which I advanced for your Derbyshire trip. Money is very scarce at present – and in short, Sir, you must repay me, that's flat!'

'You unfeeling monster!' I replied, giving way to the passion I could no longer master; 'I neither can nor will pay you one farthing! – you don't deserve it, and have no claim upon me – the journey was made on your account.'

'We shall soon see that, young man!' he said, with the same imperturbable coolness. 'I don't wish to do any thing unpleasant, though there is such a thing as law, you know; but I am anxious to befriend you, and will give you leave to perform in my company till the debt is paid. As for the young lady you are so hot about, I shall consider if any thing can be done for her in minor parts. – Aye, now I think of it, perhaps the old nurse in Romeo and Juliet would suit her voice and figure as well as any other character – and it would be well if she studied the part of Juliet at the same time: – young performers, you know, can never be too well acquainted with the pieces they appear in.'

During this speech, a thousand conflicting passions agitated my mind. I saw I was completely in his power, having only a few shillings left for our immediate support; and though my spirit would have impelled me to leave him as I had at first determined, I perceived at once that in my circumstances it would be impossible.

'What shall we do? what can we do?' I whispered to Anne; but all her romancing had now given way to dejection, and she answered me only by a pitiful look, and a sigh that went to my very soul.

'Well, Sir!' I said to him, 'we shall consider of it,' and I hurried Anne away to condole over our disappointed hopes.

I was fully resolved to be avenged on the manager for his insults, which I took care, however, to say nothing about till an opportunity might occur for paying him in kind. I advised Anne to study the parts he had mentioned, particularly Juliet, as I suspected that he meant, notwithstanding his pretended contempt for her voice and figure, to try her in that character, – his design in depreciating her being to get her services at a low rate, or for nothing.

As I had conjectured, so it turned out; for at the rehearsal of the piece, his wife, who was to play Juliet, was *taken suddenly ill*, and Anne was requested to continue the part, – merely, as he said, to fill up the piece, while her own part of the nurse, being less important, was read by the prompter. Anne acquitted herself to the admiration of all, as she did not barely recite, – her resentment at the manager having excited her to do her utmost, in order to belie his pretended ill opinion of her powers.

The manager took care to conceal the impression which the universal applause of the company had produced in the young candidate's favour, and remarked to me with indifference, that he hoped his wife would be sufficiently recovered before the night to play Juliet. He made this remark, I have no doubt, in order to prevent our supposing that he had any wish for Anne to play the part.

Before evening arrived, however, we were honoured by a visit from the manager in person, who informed us that his lady would not be able to appear; and though it would be a great disadvantage to the company, and a loss to himself, he should be under the necessity of trusting the part of Juliet to Anne; and he had, accordingly, he told us, announced this in a bill which he had got printed for the occasion at half-an-hour's notice.

'The devil you have!' said I, who had foreseen and was prepared for this low manœuvre. 'Then you have reckoned without your host, for I tell you she will not, and shall not, play Juliet!'

'Softly! softly!' said he, dissembling his surprise at my unexpected refusal. 'Let there be no fracas about it, and I shall make all right. You see how I am placed: – the bills are already in circulation – we may count on a full house – and without a Juliet what can we do?'

'Aye, friend! but you forget her hoydenish figure, – want of dignity – dull sleepy eye – and thin wiry voice that will not be heard beyond the orchestra!'

'I beg a thousand pardons, my dear Sir! and I pray the lady to forgive me for my hasty opinion and strong expressions – I intended no offence – none in the world, I give you my word.'

'Then, Mr. Manager, since it is so,' said I, 'we can only consent on condition of your signing a release for the money you say I owe you, and of your making the lady a present *now* of a handsome sum, for the unwarrantable liberty you have taken, in announcing her for Juliet in your bills without her knowledge or consent.'

In making this demand I had an eye to our marriage expences, but at such unexpected terms he looked quite aghast, – muttered something about 'impossible' – seemed lost in thought – drummed on the floor with his foot – cast his eyes up to the ceiling – and finished by proposing that I should be content with the release, as he really could not at present advance any money. I was inflexible. He had insulted and injured me deeply; and I thought I had him now in my power for revenge – exactly of the sort I had wished for.

He pleaded with great earnestness for mitigation, but the more he intreated, the less was I inclined to make any concession; and when he saw he could do no better, he complied, and reluctantly emptied his purse into Anne's lap. He was wholly unprepared for the spirit with which I had received him, and now showed as much mean fawning as he had before exhibited low cunning.

While Anne was revising her part, I went in quest of Bucks, whom I had not seen since my arrival, to exult with him over my triumph in managing the manager. I found him in all his glory at an ale-house, in the midst of a group of mechanics,[71] who were listening with open mouths to his wonderful stories, at the same time that he helped them most willingly to drink their home-brewed. The moment he saw me, he started up, crying out, "Tis Tom himself, by jingo!' and taking me by the hand with a hearty slap, and shaking it till all the bones in my arm cracked again, he seized a jorum[72] of ale that stood before one of his pot companions, whose apron betokened him of the gentle craft,[73] and sung up,

> Here's to thee, Tom Brown!
> To thee, my jolly lad!
> With thee I'll drink a crown,[74]
> While money's to be had.
> Here's to thee, Tom Brown![75]

and he did ample justice to his toast, by scarcely leaving a drop of the ale for his aproned friend to follow his example withal. The cobbler, – who was, like all ale-drinkers, a good-natured jolly soul – had his jorum instantly replenished, and handed it to me with the wink of good-fellowship as a token of welcome.

The health and the toast went round; and I sat down and willingly joined in the revelry, to dissipate for a time the anxieties which had lately harassed me. The potent ale, and the high spirits which my victory over the manager had put me in, were not long in 'ascending me into the brain,'[76] like Falstaff's sherris-sack;[77] and with bright anticipations of Anne's success in her approaching *debut,* I gave myself up to the boisterous mirth of the minute, – laughing, joking, singing, and swaggering, till I was more tipsy with joy than with ale.

I could have spent an age, I thought, in this mad ebullition of mirth; while my companions, though with less cause perhaps, seemed equally inexhaustible in the spirit of jollification and love of fun. I was compelled, however, to put some method into my madness, as I had both a part to play and to take care of Anne. I had accordingly to season some of the best passing jokes with a wistful look at the clock in the corner of the room, which told me the unpleasant tidings that my hour was at hand. Bucks, who had only to appear in the farce, cared not how the time sped; and I confess I was quite infected with the fun, and reluctant to leave the merry ale-drinkers even for the higher enjoyment of the theatrical applause which I made no doubt would fall to my share in a double portion, as I was sanguinely confident of Anne's success, while my own was of course beyond all doubt. Then, in such parts as Romeo and Juliet, we should be quite at home in recalling all the doubts, and fears, and sweet hopes, of love; and acting over again our stolen meetings and painful partings.

The clock at last struck the hour of my departure, and I started up to go; but every voice protested against this, asserting it was too fast by a full half-hour. My own watch I had left with Anne, and my boon companions were too poor to muster one among them all, to appeal to. An appeal, indeed, would have served little purpose, for they were resolved to detain me by main force; and as I was no less determined to go, a tipsy altercation and struggle ensued, which prolonged my exit a full quarter of an hour.

At length I got away by sheer force, and to my utter consternation perceived by the church clock that I had mistaken the time by a whole hour – in consequence, no doubt, of the laudable practices exercised by all publicans upon clocks and time-pieces. It was already, indeed, past the time when the performance at the theatre was to begin. I ran through the streets like a madman, but, in my haste, took a wrong turning which increased my flurry by adding to the delay.

I got home, at last, and hurried into the house to find Anne; but she had gone, I was told, without me. I was partly rejoiced at this, since I had not been in time to escort and introduce her, for I was more anxious on her account than my own; and if she were in readiness for her part, short as the time now was, I hoped by expedition to recover my ground. Consoling myself in this manner, and meditating on an apology to Anne for disappointing her, I made all haste to the theatre, which was luckily at no great distance. The people were thronging into the entrance, and my heart beat violently at the thoughts of Anne having to appear before a crowded house. On going forward I met the manager, who seemed to be in a great passion.

'Good God! Richmond!' said he, 'why have you not brought your Juliet? The time is already expired.'

'She is here,' said I: 'she must be here: she left home, nearly an hour ago, to come hither.'

'Then she has *not* come, I can tell you – and the house is waiting. I believe, indeed, it is all a trick, Sir! I know it is – but you shall repent it! I'll not be swindled out of my money, and the character of my company damned for your whims, by Jupiter!'

Saying this, he pushed by me and ran to his own lodgings, leaving me in a state of mind more easily conceived than described. What had become of Anne I could not conjecture; though I was somewhat incredulous of his assertion, and went to make myself sure that she was not in the house; but nobody had seen her, nor seemed to care about her or me, – every one being in busy preparation for the performance, and not inclined to take the trouble of answering my inquiries. It was my duty to prepare also, but unless I knew what was become of her, it was impossible I could perform; and I stood hesitating and distracted, not knowing what to do, when my attention was caught by one of the actors already dressed as Romeo; and immediately after the manager entered with his pretended sick spouse, ready to play Juliet – whilst he sneeringly said to me, –

'You see, *Master* Richmond, I was prepared for your trick! – mustn't think to humbug me, Sir! – too old, by Jupiter!'

I did not deign to reply to this, but instantly left the theatre, indignant at his unjust suspicions of me, and anxious to go in search of Anne, who had so unaccountably disappeared.

CHAPTER XI.

Night scenes on land and by water – Unexpected rencontre – Vocal music – A
fair swain and a dark nymph – Trusted promises.

It was scarcely possible, in so small a town as Lancaster, that Anne should
have lost her way; or, if she had, that she would not have been soon put right:
any other case than this I could not conjecture. I again hurried home to make
further inquiries, which were equally fruitless. All I could learn was, that she had
waited impatiently for my return till the time for the performance approached,
and then had gone out alone in the direction of the theatre, leaving a message for
me that she had proceeded thither. I ran out into the street, and made inquiry
of every body I met; but from the stare of surprise which was upon every face, I
little doubt they took me for a madman. In this way I ran through all the streets
of the town, and pried into every lane and by-path, but all to no purpose.

I, at length, began to conjecture that the agitation of making a first appearance might have caused her to be taken ill on her way to the theatre, and that
she might perhaps have been carried into some of the houses in the vicinity. I
inquired at every house; but meeting with no better success, again went home
in the hope that she might have returned, and again had to suffer the misery of
disappointment. To the theatre it would serve but little purpose to go back, as
she could not, under all the circumstances, remain there long.

I therefore threw myself down on the sofa, disconsolate and sorrowful, racking my thoughts with conjectures – this minute entertaining hopes, and the
next, abandoning them, till it was past midnight. The streets were now comparatively deserted and quiet; for though I greedily listened to every noise, I
could hear nothing but the heavy step of a chance passenger, or the occasional
song of a tipsy mechanic reeling homewards to bed. The sound of her knock,
which I so much wished to hear, came not – she was gone – quite gone! and I
was distracted!

At length it came into my mind that her heart had perhaps failed her when
the time arrived for her appearance, and that the shame of meeting me might
have caused her to conceal herself. The morning, I thought, would at all events

bring her back, or some intelligence where she was; and upon the faith of this I should rest in hope. Alas! this resolution was more easily made than followed; for the more I tried to persuade myself that I would wait with patience, the more impatient and restless did I become.

I once more sallied forth into the street, thinking I might perhaps meet her wandering about; but the echo of every distant footstep, which I keenly listened to, raised hopes only to disappoint them: my fancy even made me picture a white plank, which stood by the gate of a wood-yard, to be a female – perhaps Anne herself. Imagination has often played me such tricks when my mind was strongly excited. I passed the ale-house where I had left Bucks, and could still hear some of the tipplers there, carousing and boisterous; but this only made me more melancholy; for had I not foolishly gone thither, I should not have lost my poor girl, and I was ready, for the moment, to curse both their ale and their tipsy merriment, which a few hours before I had so highly enjoyed. Indeed, I have found, by sad experience, that most of our vivid pleasures terminate in a similar manner.

As a final conjecture, I imagined that if fear or reluctance had prevented her from appearing upon the stage, her romantic habits might perhaps have led her to the sea-shore; yet, even if she had gone there, it was not probable I should discover her while it remained dark. Vague as my hopes were, they induced me to go in the direction of the beach, where at least I might walk unmolested, and indulge my feelings in solitude. The time had been, when I could enjoy such a walk, and take delight in hearing the tide ripple upon the sands, while along the surface of the water broken rays of star-light glanced from wave to wave, like myriads of floating diamonds. Now I was too sad to enjoy the beauties of the night, though the freshness of the air, the serene calm of the sky, and the deep solitude around me, did more to quiet my mind than all the conjectures I had harassed myself in forming and abandoning. I traversed the beach hour after hour, sometimes expecting to find my lost Anne, and again rejecting all hope, till it was near morning.

My spirits became quite exhausted, and I was ready to sink with dejection, when, at some distance before me, I heard a female voice singing a brisk lively air. For a moment I thought it might be Anne, as I readily made every circumstance agree with my anxious wishes; but, on reflection, it appeared more probable that it was some girl early abroad to take advantage of the ebb-tide for gathering shell-fish, and if it were so, she might perhaps be able to give me the intelligence I wanted. As it was too dark to see the singer, I went towards the spot the voice came from; but as I drew nearer, she finished her song, and I now indistinctly saw two persons walking along the sands in close conversation. I was just about to accost them, when the girl's companion began also, in a clear youthful voice, to sing a wild air to verses seemingly inspired by the very scene before him. This song (of which I afterwards procured a copy) ran thus:

> The stars are all burning, cheerily, cheerily,
>   O, my Mary, dear! turn to me!
> The sea-mew is mourning, drearily, drearily,
>   O, my Mary, dear! turn to me!
> High up is his home on the cliff's naked breast,
> But warm is her plumage that blesseth his nest.
> The ice-winds ne'er blow there,
> And soft falls the snow there,
> O, my Mary, dear! turn to me!
>
> O! once smiled my dwelling, cheerily, cheerily,
>   O, my Mary, dear! turn to me!
> Though the wild waves were swelling, drearily, drearily,
>   O, my Mary, dear! turn to me!
> In the rock-girdled bay as I anchored my skiff,
> A sweet voice would sing from the top of the cliff.
> Ere the last notes were over
> She sprang to her lover,
> O, my Mary, dear! turn to me!
>
> The waters are sounding, drearily, drearily,
>   O, my Mary, dear! turn to me!
> But the red deer is bounding, cheerily, cheerily,
>   O, my Mary, dear! turn to me!
> Away to his lair in the forest so deep,
> Where his hind with her fair fawns is lying asleep,
> On green mossy pillow,
> Like summer sea-billow.
> O, my Mary, dear! turn to me!
>
> O! green rose our shealing,[78] cheerily, cheerily,
>   O, my Mary, dear! turn to me!
> Through trees half concealing, dreamily, dreamily,
>   O, my Mary, dear! turn to me!
> At night like a deer through the forest I flew,
> Till I saw the tall smoke wreathe in heaven so blue,
> On the soft tender lawn there,
> My sweet hind and fawn there.
> O, my Mary, dear! turn to me![79]

I could not tell what to make of this singular couple. They seemed to be lovers, but had certainly chosen a strange time and place for their merry, musical courtship. As it was, I trusted in their sympathy, and had no hesitation in interrupting the song, and making the inquiries which so much interested me. I told them my story. The young man took a keen interest in it, and, on hearing the particulars – which I related as briefly as I could, – to my utter astonishment he clapped his hands, and exclaimed,

'Glorious! A romance, as I live! – a glorious romance! Now, Mary, we shall have something worth doing – the recovery of a stray damsel! glorious! glorious! By the beard of Ariosto,[80] the best thing I ever met with!'

'I'm at a loss to understand you,' said I; 'it is neither good nor glorious to me, I can tell you.'

'Ah! my friend,' replied this singular youth, changing his raptures to a tone of deep sympathy, 'you know not the joy of grief – the sublime pleasure of love sorrows. – I could sing you, by the hour, of lost damsels and mad lovers. Don't you know the old ditty?

> Despairing beside a clear stream,
> A shepherd forsaken was laid.'[81]

'But, Wilton!'[82] said the girl, 'you know songs won't bring back her that's gone.'

'No! I said not so, Mary! Leave that to me. I only wished to instruct my friend here how to enjoy his sorrow, and draw pleasure from despair.'

'I should have much more pleasure,' I replied, 'in recovering Anne, than in learning such a strange lesson.'

'You shall have both, man!' said he; 'both, I tell you; but as you cannot perhaps get back the strayed fair one on the very instant, you may indulge the joy of grief till she returns. Have her you shall, I promise you, if she is alive and still loves you; for otherwise we cannot and will not interfere.'

'Then you know where she is?' said I, with intense anxiety.

'Not so fast, my friend! I said not so; but if we do not know, we shall, I promise you. It is just the thing for me! – a glorious romance, indeed! – Not quite so wild as mine, though; but good – excellent in its way. You brought her from Derbyshire, I think you said? Think you either of her relations has traced her?'

'It is scarcely possible,' said I, 'the time is so short, and we took every precaution.'

This was, indeed, a point of view in which I had never thought of her disappearance; though now it was suggested to me, I knew not what her uncle might have done to follow us.

'It matters not,' said Wilton; 'we shall find her if she is above ground.'

'You talk it well, however,' said I, in theatrical phrase; 'but, if I may be so bold, in God's name who are you that speak of her so confidently?'

'All in good time, friend! You may come to the knowledge of that and many other things; – for the nonce, be assured you are in safe company.'

I doubt, however, if I should have put much trust in this assurance, had not the grey light of the morning begun to give me a more definite notion of the singular beings I had encountered, than I could at first make out by star-light. From the dress of Wilton, it was hard to tell what he might be. It was more like a theatrical than an every-day garb, and corresponded well with all that I had seen of his behaviour.

His fur cap was of an uncommon shape; and his other habiliments were partly concealed under a large grey cloak, which he had wrapped around him similar to what I have seen worn by Northern cattle-drovers. His boots also smacked of the stage, being buskin-shaped, and of thick shamoy[83] or buff, instead of black leather; and what I could see of his other garments seemed to be of the same materials. The wild song, and the romantic language of the youth – for he was apparently not more than eighteen, but might be two or three years older, – confirmed me in my opinion that he was an actor, which was still farther strengthened by what he said concerning Anne, of whom I was persuaded he knew more than he had yet told me; and without some connection with our people, I could not divine what he could have learned of her. The thought, indeed, had at first passed through my mind, that the girl who was with him might possibly be Anne herself; but day-light soon showed me how much I was mistaken.

The girl, whom he called Mary, seemed to be about his own age, or younger, and was also dressed in an uncommon manner. She was certainly not a peasant girl, that is, not one of the great rosy-cheeked Lancashire witches; but though she was too meanly attired to be much better, her costume was quite unlike that commonly worn in the country, and had a foreign air not easy to describe. Her hair, long and black, was not curled, but knotted up in separate locks, which, being parted, hung down not ungracefully from her forehead. Her eyes were dark, and her complexion that, which gives a woman the title of a deep brunette.

I should, indeed, have taken her for a gipsy rather than an actress, had she not been accompanied by the youth Wilton, whose fair skin, light hair, and blue eyes, were sufficient witnesses that he had no Egyptian[84] blood in his veins. The girl had also a good carriage, and a manner certainly superior to this proscribed race of wanderers. I once thought she might be a Savoyard;[85] but in the little I had heard her say, she spoke better English than could be expected from a foreigner.

I have been the more minute in describing my first interview with these singular persons, as it had so much influence on some of my subsequent movements, and perhaps gave a colour to my whole after-life. The history of Wilton, as I ultimately learned, was as romantic as his appearance; but I must not, for the present at least, interrupt my own narrative with an account of his eccentric rambles. I may only remark that he was of good family, and had had an education suitable to his prospects of independence.

Whether Wilton and his female companion were players or not, I was induced, by the confident tone in which he spoke, to trust to him for retrieving Anne, believing that he well knew where she was. I therefore accepted his request to accompany them whither they were going, though the supposition was strong in my mind that Anne must be already returned; and I could not help casting a misgiving look back to Lancaster, particularly as it appeared at a greater distance than I imagined possible from the time I had spent in walking.

CHAPTER XII.

Romantic breakfast, with rural music – Liberty on the wing – Welcome and unwelcome news – An *honest* sheriff's officer, and his new method of arresting – An escape without a rescue.

My companions soon left the beach, and we proceeded across the open field till we reached a small brook, along the bank of which we went for a considerable space, continuing the conversation as we had begun it – each of us endeavouring to decipher the character and views of the other. Wilton seemed to take deeper and deeper interest in my affairs the more he knew of them, and this would have awakened in me a more friendly feeling towards him, had not his wild look and strange expressions made me doubtful whether he was not half crazed; and well he might have inferred the same of me. Mary said little, though she did not appear to have any of the awkward bashfulness and false shame, common to girls of her age in the presence of strangers. As we were ascending a small rising ground where the brook made a circuit, Wilton said to me,

'Now, my good fellow, we shall soon see what can be done for you; but we modern romancers cannot perform our exploits without eating, as I daresay you know, and we must first have some breakfast to spirit us up.'

The truth of this remark I began to feel – not so much, indeed, from hunger as from exhaustion, in consequence of wandering about all night in a state of agitation; but as there was no house to be seen near us, I could not perceive any chance of speedy refreshment. When we got to the top of the rising ground, however, and when I saw in the hollow beyond, by the side of the brook, a gipsy encampment consisting of two tents, and a couple of donkeys feeding beside them, the mysterious character of Wilton and his companion was at once unravelled. I was, indeed, not a little surprised, and Wilton soon saw and enjoyed my puzzled looks, as I compared his fair complexion and polite bearing with his brunette companion, and looked in alternate wonder at him and the tents before us.

'Aye! look you there!' he said; 'that is a still more romantic life than yours of the stage, you must allow. No hours to keep here – no parts to learn – no managers to fume at you – and with the blue sky above, the green earth around, and the summer music of the brook, what more could be wished for on this side heaven!'

On saying this, he looked at Mary with an expression that showed me he had other reasons for his eulogy – other ties that bound him – besides flowery meads and tinkling rills. I expected to see Mary blush; but as this was not gipsy etiquette, I was disappointed, and she returned him a look as loving as his own.

'Yes!' he went on, 'this is freedom – glorious freedom! to wander where we will through the wild woodlands – over the red mountain heaths – by the sunny lake – the broad river – or the deep sea! It is the only life worth living for; – it is the liberty of the young world when the fields were unpeopled, and cities were not – the liberty of the eagle, soaring unfettered through the trackless blue of the firmament!

> O give me liberty!
> For were even paradise itself my prison,
> Still I should long to leap the crystal wall!'[86]

I had my own romantic dreams of life, but in these Wilton soared as far above me as the eagle he was talking of; and I could not appropriate to myself his rapturous and wild expressions – or, perhaps I might say, ravings, without much injustice; for the small confined hollow, the bepatched tents, and the two donkeys, contrasted strangely with his soaring eagle. Yet there was a wild charm in the scene, with the colouring which his enthusiasm gave it, that in other circumstances would have made me an immediate disciple of his fantastic creed. But my mind was not then enough at ease, to catch enthusiasm by sympathy.

As we approached the tents, a dog, prettily marked with black and white, his bushy tail arched up over his back, came bounding along to the side of the brook to meet us; but on seeing me, a stranger, he all at once changed his frolicking leap into a grave pace, at which he returned; and, taking his station at the tents, set up a bark of defiance.

'There is our faithful guardian,' said Wilton, 'who will defend his trust to the death. I have known Rover keep watch for days, when nobody was by, without deserting his post for a minute. He once saved Mary's life from – but I cannot tell you just now. I would not take a hundred guineas[87] for him.'

This is, indeed, bravado, thought I, from the apparent possessor of about five pounds worth of goods and chattels, with the donkeys included; and I considered it to be little else than tedious impertinence, as most persons do such matters as concern not what is uppermost in their own minds. I almost thought that Wilton began to get indifferent about my affairs, though he had taken so much interest at first; and half repented that I had not left him, and returned to Lancaster. It seems, indeed, a propensity of our nature never to be satisfied. At

all events I could be none the worse, but should move the brisker, after breakfast; which Mary was preparing with all haste, having lighted her fire with wood,
swung her kettle to the trivet over it, and spread out the rest of her equipage on
the smooth grass, which served for both table and table-cloth.

'There! mark that!' said Wilton. 'The wealthiest nabob[88] that ever came from
India could not procure a richer table than this green sod with its pretty daisies;
and his perfumed chambers could not give him so keen an appetite as this morning air, freshened by the passing stream. And we can have music too, if we wish
it, finer than all that art can pretend to; for the sky-lark, you hear, is mounting
through the falling dew to pipe his morning song to the sun; and Mary, my dear,
sing us one of our matin hymns till your kettle boils.'

Mary, at his bidding, began a song of liberty suited to their wandering life,
which ran thus: –

> Through forests deep we love to roam;
> The shade of green leaves is our home,
> Where nought is viewed but boundless green,
> And spots of far blue sky between.
> The wanderer needs no costly dome;
> Where'er he rests to him is home.
> A weary head soft pillow finds,
> Where leaves fall green in summer winds.
> From men and cities far exiled,
> With beasts joint tenants of the wild,
> Enough for them – enough for me,
> To live at large with liberty.
> With her to wend through forest free,
> Is better far than bend the knee.
> She glads the wild fox in his den,
> Her temple's in the mountain glen.[89]

The breakfast, which was then introduced, was exquisite – at least to me,
who was so jaded and exhausted, it was so; and I did not fail to do justice to
Mary's excellent tea, seasoned as it was with some fine ham and a cold roast fowl.
These gave me a much better opinion of gipsying than the patched tents and the
donkeys; though I had my misgivings as to how they procured so much good
cheer. Wilton, who seemed to divine my very thoughts, pressed me to make free,
assuring me that all was honestly come by; and I could not mistrust his frank and
unsought declaration.

'And now for business!' he said, as he finished his last jug of tea – for there
were no tea-cups. 'We must see what can be done to regain this stray damsel of
yours.'

From the moment I found out the character of my companions, I had grown
into more confidence in their assistance; as from their wandering life, and their

almost universal connections over the kingdom, I knew they had extraordinary means of procuring intelligence.

I had remarked that we had breakfasted by the side of the newest of the two tents, which Rover seemed to have under his particular guardianship. The other, which was much patched and weather-beaten, stood at a short distance apart, and I had not yet seen any of its occupants. Gipsies, indeed, as I have since found, are by no means early risers, except when business presses them. Wilton, however, deemed it requisite to interrupt the morning slumber of his neighbours on this occasion, and sent Mary to call them to a consultation.

A man and a woman, at her summons, shot out their heads almost at the same instant, to see what was going on; and their toilette, as may be supposed, requiring little care, they quickly joined us. There was nothing very singular or extraordinary in the appearance of either; and, except for their dark complexion and keen shrewd looks, they might have been taken for ordinary peasants. They were both about middle life, and the resemblance between them and Mary told me that she was their daughter.

Wilton briefly acquainted them with my story, and asked them what was best to be done, professing that he himself was ready to undertake any journey, or any enterprise, which might accomplish the recovery of the *damsel*, as he took delight in calling her.

'Did she wear a light-coloured dress and a cottage bonnet?' inquired the female gipsy.

'The same!' said I, anxiously. 'Where did you see her?'

'Blue eyes,' continued the woman, without taking any notice of my question, – 'a prettyish face, and a tripping genteelish walk.'

'It is she!' I cried out, 'it is she herself! Tell me where she is, and I'll give you all I have.'

'Mayhap,' said the gipsy, 'all you have won't do to get her out o' where she is by this time.'

'For the love of heaven tell me what has befallen her! Is she – tell me – is she – dead?' exclaimed I, with breathless agitation.

'Indeed, young man, I can't tell you positively if she be dead or not since yesternight; but she was in ugly hands, I know, as my own eyes witnessed, though I daresay they did not kill her however: – pretty girls are too precious to be murdered in cold blood.'

This speech made me quite distracted – the more so as I could not understand from it what had happened to her. Wilton, on the contrary, perceived at once how the matter stood, and cried,

'We'll have a rescue! – a glorious rescue! I saw from the first that the thing was a fine romance! But do tell us plump down[90] all about it, for we must be stirring without delay.'

To come to the point, however, was a mode of narration which the gipsy did not understand, as her practice of fortune-telling had made her more dextrous at putting her auditors on the rack, than at satisfying their inquiries. I had, there-fore, to suffer much tormenting suspense, and Wilton had his patience well tried before we gathered from her, – that having been in Lancaster on the previous evening, she had seen a girl, answering to the description I gave of Anne, arrested in the street, and carried she knew not whither. She knew the officer, she said, though not to his advantage; but she did not know a sour-visaged old fellow who was with him, and of whom the girl was more afraid than of the officer.

As this portrait seemed to me to belong to nobody so likely as Anne's uncle, I thought I could perceive the whole extent of the evil that had happened to us. Yet I could not imagine under what pretence he had arrested her; for, so far as my slender knowledge of the law went, her running away with me was no serious crime. The gipsy, – who had pried into the affair from a wish, as is usual with her craft, of fishing out something that might be turned to advantage, – soon resolved my doubts by telling me she was arrested for debt! and the sum, she understood, was very considerable.

'I thought,' said Wilton, 'her relations would be in it; but we'll have a rescue, be it as it may! – the thing is too good not to hazard something! We must to Lancaster in the first place – on by that foot-path, my good friend! – Lose no time! – I'll be up with you in a trice!'

On the word, I set out in all haste; while Wilton, I perceived, jumped into his tent, and disappeared. I proceeded at a quick pace across the fields till I reached the main road, pausing sometimes to look back for Wilton; though, had I known that he piqued himself on being the swiftest runner in England, I should not have paused a step for him. I was close upon the town, indeed, before he came up with me, skimming as smoothly along as if he did not touch the ground. He had changed his wild dress for a handsome suit of blue, which, with a smart, new, fashionable hat instead of his romantic fur cap, gave him all the air of a gentleman.

I stared in wonder at this transformation; and, indeed, could hardly credit the testimony of my own eyes. He seemed to feel the change almost as much as I did, if I might judge from the complaisant glances he frequently cast at his dress, as youths may often be seen to do at their holiday clothes. I did not then know any part of his history; but my previous impressions, that he was not a gipsy, were now confirmed beyond all doubt; and from this time forth I looked upon him to be, – as he really was – a gentleman eccentric.

Wilton told me that the rest of the gipsy party were following for the pur-pose of giving their assistance, should it prove necessary. For my part, I saw not what any of us could do. If Anne was arrested by her uncle for money, which we were unable to raise, her release was out of the question. I was determined, at all events, to see her, and give her what consolation I could; though I had little for myself, and could think of no means to extricate her from her difficulties.

Wilton, however, was in high glee, and resolved, he said, upon the enterprise. The more difficult or hazardous it was, the better for him, as a love for romance and adventure was his ruling foible. Compared with his mad flights of fancy, and his expressions of fearless daring, I felt myself and my little adventures as nothing; but I was an apt scholar, and my enthusiasm kindled into a warmer glow, while he talked with the utmost confidence of performing absolute impossibilities.

'We'll have her,' he said, 'if we should bind every officer and jailer in Lancaster – aye, or blow up the castle itself from its foundation! Such things have been done for damsels in durance;[91] and why may not we try our hand at the game, were it for nothing more than the fun of the thing?'

It was this 'fun of the thing,' indeed, that, with Wilton, as I began to suspect, was at the bottom of all; but my feelings were too serious and painful for fun, and I did not altogether like his wild talking, since I still doubted that his head was none of the soundest, and that he might involve us in some mischief with his madness. In spite of my doubts, however, I was obliged to trust the affair wholly to his management; for he evidently knew much more of the nature of an arrest, and of the persons we had to deal with, than I could pretend to.

By the mother-gipsy's directions, we found the house of the officer who had arrested Anne, and were ushered in with great ceremony and politeness by a woman whom we took to be his helpmate, and who supposed, perhaps, that we were come to request her spouse's services in the way of his profession. The *gentleman* himself, the moment he saw me, was of a very different opinion from his wife; for he knew me at once; told me he had been expecting this visit since last night; said he had business of importance with me; and expressed his satisfaction that I had brought a friend whose assistance might be useful.

Upon this, he took Wilton aside in a mysterious and confidential manner; pulled a paper cautiously out of his pocket; and whispered so low in his ear, that I could not distinguish what he said. Wilton, I could perceive, looked much surprised and displeased; while the officer continued to whisper earnestly, as if trying to persuade him to something of moment. At length Wilton's countenance began to brighten up a little, though there was still much uncertainty in his eye, – very different from his recent lofty expressions of determination. Their whispers then became louder, and Wilton at last said, –

'Since it is so, I must consult himself.'

'Dangerous!' said the other. 'I couldn't think of such a thing.'

'Then I can't stir in it: – you must take your course.'

'It is very dangerous though, by G—; it might cost me my place if he nose.'

'I'll answer for that,' said Wilton. 'We'll tell nothing, I promise you.'

'Ah! but what security have I for 'un?'

'My word of honour! If that don't satisfy you, you may be – '

The officer looked very incredulous at this intangible sort of security; but seeing he could carry his point no farther, he yielded with the best, or rather with the worst, grace he could. Wilton then stept towards me, and told me that the officer had shown him a writ against me at the suit of Anne's uncle, who had resolved upon immediately proceeding legally against me for the loss of her services by her seduction and elopement. I protested my innocence as to the charge of seduction;[92] but Wilton told me I should not be believed by any body, even on my oath, in the face of so many circumstances; and a moment's consideration convinced me he was right.

Here, then, was another difficulty to encounter; and they were accumulating around me so rapidly, as it appeared, that my head was in no small danger of being turned. Wilton told me in a whisper, there was one way of escaping which the *honest* and *upright* officer had hinted at – namely, that if he were paid down a certain sum in the way of hush-money, he would keep the writ in his pocket while I escaped by his back passage, – pretend to his employer that I could not be found, and afterwards it would be my own fault if I were many hours in Lancashire. The only difficulty in this scheme was the sum necessary for the bribe, – Wilton not having much money about him, and the officer having mentioned something considerable. I had, in my purse, the present made to Anne by the manager, but could not think of using it to procure my own liberty while she was left a prisoner.

'Leave that to me,' said Wilton. 'It will go hard if we don't set her free before long. Have I not said it, man? and I say again I will bring her to you if they should carry her to a vault in the centre of the earth. The sum the fellow hints at, however,' he continued in a lower whisper, 'is unconscionable. We must get off with less, if we can: I hate to see such scoundrels getting money.'

On the faith of Wilton's confident promises to obtain Anne's liberation, I consented; and handed him my purse to make the best bargain he could with the *honest* officer, who, like many others of his class whom I have known, tried to make the most of his opportunities in the way of business: – foul or fair was not the question, so that he could add a few guineas to his purse.

Wilton manifested his zeal in my service by driving a hard bargain, and making the fellow take about one-fourth less than he had at first proposed. I saw with joy the ominous paper consigned to his pocket, while Wilton and I made the best of our way through a back passage into a lane which led out of the town, and lost not a moment in getting to the fields in the direction of the encampment; for we could not trust the assurances of the officer, that he would not secure another bonus for himself by an immediate pursuit. We had not gone far before we encountered the two female gipsies, who expressed great surprise at our haste; but Wilton would not permit me to stop a moment to explain.

'Carry your heels off the ground,' he said; 'point your toes well, and run for liberty. If you think the tents unsafe, there are some snug hollow banks higher up the brook. I'll be with you in a few hours; and, if I can, I'll bring your damsel to dine with us. Aye, by the way, I must borrow your purse again – a golden key opens every lock.'

I threw him my all; and, following his advice as to my manner of running, I got to the tents breathless and panting, and with my thoughts so confused, that I knew not distinctly what had happened, or what I had been doing, except that my liberty had been in danger, and that now I was, at least for the present, free.

CHAPTER XIII.

Castle-building – Despairing beside a clear stream – A gipsy lunch – Wilton's mountain flight – Marriage and no marriage – Proposed wedding at Rydal Water.

THE gipsy man, whose name I understood to be Marshall, was still at the encampment, though he was preparing to follow the rest to the town. When I told him of my escape, he judged that I should be safest, as Wilton had mentioned, at some distance from their establishment, which might be searched if I had been pursued in that direction. I accordingly got into the channel of the brook, and proceeded upwards over the gravel about a quarter of a mile or more, at which point I found several parts of the bank undermined by the water, and formed into a sort of over-hanging arch of green sod. The brow I made choice of was surmounted by an old willow tree, grey with moss, and ready to fall across the brook, which had washed away the soil from its roots, and left a space well adapted for temporary concealment.

Here, then, with the roots of the willow for a canopy, and the brook eddying round in a little pool beside me, I had leisure to reflect on the singular circumstances in which I was placed, and to rack my fancy as to how I was to proceed in future. I now began to see, however, that it was not of much use to form plans, as some unlucky accident was ever occurring to frustrate them.

In spite of this inference, I soon went from one step to another, till I found myself in the midst of as wild a scheme of castle-building[93] as had ever before engaged a day-dreamer's fancy. This habit, indeed, was now become too strong in me to yield either to disappointments or to moral maxims; and the recent conversation and singularities of Wilton had certainly tended nothing to abridge the range of my thoughts, or bring them nearer to the sobrieties of common life.

I perceived that the stage, at least with the Lancaster party, must be given up. Still the recollection of the applauses I had received at Kendal – the free and easy companions I had lived amongst – the Shap excursion, and other frolics, – gave a charm to strolling which no other life seemed to afford. I thought not, indeed, in this my waking vision, of rascally managers, and all the other disagreeables which the itinerant actor must submit to and endure. In castle-building, nobody thinks of accidents and difficulties: all is fairy-work, performed at the fiat of fancy – perfect and faultless.

I dreamed away the hours in this manner under the shelter of the brow, sometimes venturing to peep out cautiously to see if any one approached, and longing at intervals for the appearance of Wilton, to bring me intelligence of Anne; till the shadow of the tree on the pool indicated, by its increasing length, that the sun was now considerably past his meridian. I had nearly exhausted my patience; for my air-built castles were vanishing as fast as they had been created, and were leaving me to the sole company of the eddy and the willow roots: – the motions of the one, and the forms of the other, I had already gazed on to weariness; when I heard the bark of a dog, approaching in my direction. Immediately after I recognised the welcome voice of Wilton, crying,

'Seek him out, Rover! seek him out!'

Upon hearing these joyful sounds, I ventured out of my hiding place, when I perceived Wilton coming up, accompanied, as I supposed, by Mary, and preceded by Rover, who gambolled along and thrust his nose into every corner, in obedience to the commands of his master. The instant Wilton got his eye upon me, he exclaimed,

'Ah! there he is, sconced like a hunted otter, and, I swear by the wig of Theocritus,[94] under a willow tree, as I live! A prophecy, by all that's sacred! I am indeed become a genuine prophet in these days of wonder, and my prophecy fulfilled too within twenty-four hours! Don't you recollect, friend, how I recommended to your study the old ballad? –

> Despairing, beside a clear stream
> A shepherd forsaken was laid,
> And while a fair nymph was his theme,
> A willow wept over his head.[95]

And there you are! Do tell me what you now think of the joy of grief, with the pretty accompaniment of the willow and the crystal stream – something better, I take it, than the naked and narrow walls of a prison-cell in Lancaster Castle.'

He went on so volubly that I could not edge in a word in reply; while his female companion kept in the back ground, as if afraid to come near me. But as soon as I had got out from my den, and stood upright in the channel, I saw it was not Mary; and the next minute found me in the arms of Anne herself, who could restrain no longer, but ran down the brow to meet me. It was little wonder I had not recognised her, for she was dressed in the very garments which I had seen Mary wear that morning; and even her hair was completely muffled up in a cap, so that there was nothing to betray the Derbyshire girl but the laughing blue eye, and the clear carnation of the cheek. My joy was unbounded; and Wilton himself confessed, that with all his Ossianic[96] flourishes about the joy of grief, there was more exquisite and intense feeling in such a happy meeting, than could ever arise while the spirits were depressed and the soul in sorrow.

'But come,' said he; 'we must not lose time in idle parley. Neither of you are safe while you remain in Lancashire; you must be off on the instant for Yorkshire or Westmoreland. In the mean-time let us see what provisions are in this basket, which I picked up as we passed the tent; it is bad travelling, and worse flying, with an empty stomach – that is my creed – eat, drink, and be strong – merry, if you will, – but strength is indispensable for all sorts of exploit. A hungry soul is always feeble and cowardly; and an empty stomach is the deuce for begetting a faint heart.'

Wilton's basket contained, besides the remains of the ham and other break-fast viands, a cut of excellent cold salmon, with bread to match; and, what was no less acceptable, a bottle of fine Hollands[97] – smuggled, I have no doubt, *viâ* Ramsay,[98] like the tea we had had in the morning; for I afterwards found that a little encroachment on the revenue dues did not enter into Wilton's ideas of dishonesty.

'A nice bit of salmon, that,' Wilton remarked. 'I had some fine sport in taking him yesterday morning – played him along the stream for an hour – good tackle or I should have lost him.'

While we were thus laying in provisions for our flight, out of the basket, the contents of which we rapidly diminished, Wilton told me how he had managed to deliver Anne from the fangs of the law.

'I learned,' he said, 'whilst negotiating your affair, that she was still in the officer's house, and that her uncle only wished to terrify her for the purpose of inducing her to go quietly home with him. From the rapacity of the man I saw he might be easily tampered with; and upon this I contrived the plan of introducing Mary, by means of your little golden key, you know, to speak with the impris-oned damsel, exchange clothes with her, and remain in her stead.'

'Good God!' I exclaimed, 'and is Mary there now?'

'To be sure she is,' said Wilton, 'and what of that? When she tells who she is, they cannot detain her; and the fellow knows too well what he should earn for himself if he dared to maltreat her. Gipsy revenge is too terrible for a sneaking scoundrel like him to provoke. Besides I owed him a grudge for the guineas I gave him in the morning – he deserves to have the escape of a prisoner laid at his door, and the uncle is not the man I suppose him to be, if he do not make the fellow pay down every farthing of the alledged debt, for which the damsel's escape renders him responsible. I had the precaution also not to be seen with Mary; as, the moment you were gone, we got behind a hedge, where I lay in wait till Mother Bunch,[99] as I call her, brought me the disguised damsel in distress to protect on her way hither. It was well I thought of changing my clothes before I set out.'

'The young gentleman,' said Anne to me, 'knows more of adventure than we do, you see.'

'Aye, indeed!' said Wilton, 'you are green in the business; but you are in a hopeful way to learn. You will have to commence your travels again immediately, and here are the little savings of your purse to help you onwards.'

With this he handed me the purse, which had proved so useful to us, and which I found only diminished a few shillings, as Mary had taken care not to offer too liberal a bribe for her admission, since this might have raised suspicions of her object.

'I must not part with you, however,' continued Wilton, 'without a rendez-vous. We must meet soon again, and plan some other romance with a little more seasoning in it than your Lancaster theatricals. The deuce take regular hours, say I, and conning over parts, and all that! Liberty for me – merry liberty! – dancing on the daisied green – skipping through the forest, – or wandering among the mountain breezes, and singing with the poet,

> I wander as free as the wind on the mountain,
> Save love's willing fetters, – the chains of my dear.[100]

I have a right to know something of these things – a little experience in wander-ing and in love too, i'faith; for if, as the song goes, I had not "lov'd a lass and lov'd a glass,"[101] I should not have been here now to aid your escape by telling you, that across that field, and along by the beach for some miles, will lead you to liberty and Westmoreland.'

Anne's countenance brightened up at the sound of Westmoreland, which, from my description, was identified in her fancy with wild mountains and pas-toral adventures.

'And shall we go to Shap?' she inquired, with keen interest.

'Let me see,' said Wilton, stroking his chin, and glancing his eye to the moun-tain range in the distance, to consider of his answer. 'Yes, to Shap, if you will: but in that case I cannot so soon see you, and the Lake road is finer and greener – wood and water in rich variety – valleys running up into the clifts of the moun-tains, – cascades leaping down into them, and gleaming in the sunshine. Did you ever see a cataract, my fair damsel? There's none in Derbyshire, I think. O! a cataract is the very symbol of freedom, whirling and rushing on through rocky barriers, and dashing over precipices, foaming and fearless like a patriot tram-pling on tyrants! But you must see Scale Force[102] in all the glory of a thunder flood, to understand me. Often have I gazed and gazed for hours at the sweep of the torrent, till I have wished to become a river god, – mingle in the strife of waters, and stream with them down to the sunny lake or the broad ocean!'

Wilton had got into one of his flights, and went on rhapsodizing in this strain; while Anne stood fixed in wonder and admiration, and would, I believe, have thought little of falling down to worship him as the very deity of romance.

'Then if you love mountains,' he continued, 'there are Langley Pikes, and Helvellyn,[103] and all the fine groups around them, with their embosomed lakes and hanging woods. I have loved mountains since my childhood, and if you take the direction of Lowood and Ambleside, I'll meet you on the banks of Rydal Water[104] on Saturday next, at noon, to the minute: –

> Then hie we to the mountains. O! once more
> I long to swathe me in the streaming mist,
> That wreathes its tresses beautifully hoar
> Upon the crested mountain – to be blessed
> With still sweet solitude, where the stream is kiss'd
> By woods that bend them o'er it lovingly;
> And free to rhyme and ramble as I list,
> To wander mid the thousand thoughts that lie
> Slumbering by lonely lake, or vision'd in the sky.

Away then! – away with you for life and liberty!'[105]

Our enthusiast, however, with all his fanciful flights, had much good sense at bottom; and lowering his lofty tone, he said,

'But avoid the turnpike road, and all villages and inns. Lodge in the peasant's cottage; or in the gipsy's tent, if you meet with one, my name will be your passport to hospitality. Think not of to-morrow while your money lasts – nor of the stage again, till you see me. I have a scheme worth two of that. Away then! speed, and farewell!'

'Had we been but married,' Anne whispered to me, lingering and hesitating to depart.

This was the old dilemma again conjured up to harass us; but on mentioning our scruples to Wilton, he broke out into a loud laugh at our simplicity, as he called it.

'Think you,' said he, 'that Mary and I would submit to have our warmest feelings chilled and withered by the church ceremony? No, no! – "love's *willing* fetters,"[106] or none, for me!'

And he launched out into a rhapsody on the superior strength of the ties of genuine love to the cold and feeble bonds of legal matrimony – seasoning, as he was wont, all the usual commonplaces on the subject with his own extravagant imagery and scraps of poetry between, in which he did not forget Pope's favourite and insidious lines –

> Love, free as air, at sight of human ties
> Claps his glad wings, and in a moment flies![107]

which have furnished so many seducers with an irresistible spell. Anne listened to these questionable doctrines with less pleasure than to his bursts of rapture about mountains and cataracts; but she was without remedy: – she must either go with me or return to prison; and it was not hard to see which alternative she would choose.

'Cheer up!' Wilton cried to her, as we parted, 'and we'll make a gipsy wedding for you at Rydal Water.'

CHAPTER XIV.

Westmoreland hospitality – Wandering Mary – New afflictions – Wilton's chapter on church-yards – A gipsy funeral.

WE accordingly left Wilton, who went back to await the return of his Mary from her successful exploit, while we took the way of the beach in the direction of Westmoreland. We travelled on without meeting with any thing worth record, till we reached the banks of Windermere; when, in consequence of fatigue, anxiety, and exposure to cold and wet (for the weather had changed from sunshine to showers), Anne was taken ill, and could proceed no further.

In the full glow of youth and health, when we were revelling in fancy about adventures and romancing, we had never thought nor calculated on the possibility of illness, and the difference, in such a case, between the quiet comforts of home, and the unwilling and uncertain accommodation which may be obtained from strangers. We had now to feel all this by bitter experience; for on reaching a pretty cottage, the sight of whose white-washed walls and curling smoke cheered us with the hope of rest, I hastened to request a temporary shelter from the rain, which was now pouring down in torrents, and was rudely refused admission; for even though I offered money – my all – I could only obtain for answer, that no vagrants nor gipsies should ever pollute the threshold of that cottage. Gipsies, indeed! thought I; but Anne's dress, which was what she had exchanged with Mary, sufficiently accounted for our being taken for gipsies, and at the same time for our inhospitable reception, which galled me to the very soul, and roused my indignation so far, that I began to threaten a forcible entrance if it were not granted peaceably.

'Not a step farther at your peril!' said a gruff old man, who had not hitherto made his appearance, but had now advanced to the doorway to reconnoitre us. 'Nay, indeed, fellow! I'll *enter* you, if I had my goon!' and on saying this he ran in, and instantly returned with a rusty fowling-piece in his hand, – ready, as he professed, to make us acquainted with its contents, if we did not speedily beat a retreat from his premises.

Faint and drooping as she was, Anne was glad to escape from the presence of this fellow, who perhaps, although he was so inhuman to us, might have acted very differently, had her gipsy dress not prejudiced him so strongly against us. We travelled on in the rain, not knowing whither to turn; till at last Anne could proceed no farther, and we were forced to sit down under the imperfect shelter of a rude stone fence, with our clothes soaked in the cold rain, and our spirits depressed and sinking.

Under such circumstances Wilton himself, I imagine, with all his buoyancy, could not have found much joy or consolation; and though I tried to cheer her with hopes, I felt nothing in my own breast but blank despair. His poetical flights, perhaps, if he had had any spirit left for them, might have drawn off the mind for a moment; but they would soon have been felt to be as impertinent and out of place, as a merry-andrew[108] at a funeral. Could we have looked forward to a snug cottage and a blazing hearth, we might have braved the blast at least with fortitude; though, as it was, with no home but the cold wet field, and no hope either of shelter or fire to warm us, we were too miserable for consolation.

The place where we had sat down was a cross bridle-road, and but little frequented, as the long grass indicated; so that for ought I could see to the contrary, we might remain here all night, and Anne, now ill and exhausted, might perish, without my being able to afford her any relief. To our great comfort, however, the clouds began to clear away, and the rain to abate. We tried again to hope. I got upon the stone wall to see whether we were near any cottage, or if I could discover any peasant who might assist us.

At this very time, a man came whistling along the road as gaily as if it had been a sunshine holiday, and driving an ass before him laden with panniers. I perceived at once that he was a gipsy; and as I could now, on the influence of Wilton's name and Anne's dress, in some degree claim confraternity with the tribe, I rejoiced at the event, expecting at least more civility than we had just experienced. Our story was soon told; and we had not to appeal twice to the wanderer's humanity. Anne was immediately seated between the panniers, while the gipsy and I jogged on behind; and in a short time we arrived at a small encampment in a dell, not far from the lake of Windermere.

The kind reception we met with showed that hospitality and humanity were not every-where extinct in this vicinity, though our rebuff from the white-washed cottage had led us naturally enough to infer as much. We found that our kind conductor was nearly related to Wilton's friends, the Marshalls; and when we told him of our late adventures and escape, he good-humouredly professed his readiness to adopt Anne as his niece, till her natural, or rather unnatural, uncle should learn to treat her in a more Christian spirit.

The comforts which the gipsies had to bestow were scanty enough, as the rain had partly soaked through their tents; but what was wanting in accommodation, was fully made up by kindness; and Anne, though she continued indisposed, was greatly revived by the warm reception accorded by our new friends. Wilton's name, I found to be, as we would have said at Liverpool, an excellent 'letter of credit;'[109] and they were loud in their praises of him, for his warm heart, his merry humour, and his pretty songs.

'Ah! hark! there now!' said our conductor; 'listen, and you may hear that poor girl singing her baby asleep with a song Wilton taught her last time he was in Westmoreland. It is a melancholy thing, to be sure; but she is very melancholy herself ever since Harry went. I think she'll never cheer up again at all.'

I listened accordingly, and heard, in the adjoining tent, a female voice, in a plaintive, sorrowful tune, singing the following verses to a very pathetic air: –

> Bleak blows the storm upon that breast
>   Whose guest is life-consuming sorrow!
> Oh! take me to some place of rest,
>   Where I may slumber till to-morrow!
> You view my face – it once was fair –
>   At least, so said my charming Harry;
> Now he is gone, and black despair
>   Is all that's left for wandering Mary.
>
> No thief am I, as some allege,
>   Though oft has cold and hunger tried me:
> I pluck the hawberry from the hedge,
>   When human aid is oft denied me.
> Then hush, my babe! though large the load
>   Of woes that we are doom'd to carry,
> Within the cold grave's dark abode
>   Thou'lt sweetly sleep with wandering Mary.[110]

Our troubles were not, however, terminated. Anne continued to grow worse during the night, and before morning was in a high fever, and could not raise her head from the pillow. Our only solace in this new affliction was, that we were now in Westmoreland, and beyond the power of the Lancaster officer and his writs; but this I looked upon as nothing, when she was confined to a sick bed, from which, perhaps, she might never rise. This thought was madness; for my conscience accused me as the cause, in bringing her from home, and exposing her to hardships she had not been used to, and was unfit to bear.

But regret and reflection could not amend or cure the disease, which increased in a rapid and alarming manner in spite of the remedies that her gipsy attendants had recommended as infallible. Before night she became at times delirious, and talked with wild incoherence of the incidents of her childhood; on which her ideas seemed wholly to run, for she made no allusion to any recent event. But when she had any interval of quiet, she spoke more than once of the wedding which Wilton had joked us about at Rydal Water, – a matter that appeared to have taken a deep hold of her fancy, though I began to fear she would never live to reach this place of rendezvous.

I was anxious to go for an apothecary or a physician, as I had still money enough left to pay for advice; but all the gipsies protested against this as a thing unheard of in their community: at the same time, they gave so many instances of the efficacy of their own simples, that I yielded, though with reluctance and doubt, to trust her recovery to their care. I shall regret having done so, as long as I live; for she grew hourly worse, and was evidently sinking in strength; while the delirium became also more permanent and alarming.

For two or three days she struggled in great suffering under the violence of the fever, till it was apparent to us all that she could not survive, as death was already marked in her countenance. I was inconsolable, and little less distracted and delirious with self-reproaches than she was from the fatal disorder, which soon, alas! numbered my lovely and betrothed Anne with the dead.

This fatal stroke deprived me, for the time, of all thought and all energy. I gave myself up to bitter sorrow and remorse. She had fallen a victim to my rash romancing; and I was now punished, by her irretrievable loss, for my wild folly. O! had I but betaken myself, I thought, to some steady, sober, every-day sort of life, she might yet have been alive to brighten my hopes: now I had hastened her end, and I was left a solitary wanderer, without a home and without an aim – lonely, helpless, and hopeless.

In the midst of my distress I was surprised by the unexpected arrival of Wilton, on his way to join us at Rydal Water. In any other mood I should have rejoiced at this meeting; but as I expected that he would again assail me with his mock consolations, I looked upon his arrival as an unwelcome intrusion. I had strangely mistaken the character of Wilton. Instead of showing any heartless frivolity, he seemed little less affected than myself; and said every thing that kind-hearted interest could suggest, to soothe my grief.

To save my feelings, Wilton offered to take upon himself the funeral arrangements, which it would be necessary to proceed with immediately. The nearest churchyard was at some distance; but he thought that immaterial, he said; and, if I had no unconquerable predilection in favour of consecrated ground, he should himself prefer to have her buried at the head of the dell.

'And think you not,' said he, breaking out into one of his rhapsodies, 'that the redbreast will sing a sweeter dirge from his thorn, than the artificial toll of the church bells? – and that the grass will spring fresher and greener under the dew of the weeping birches, than among the rank graves of every boor and beggar? Instead, also, of the lurid night-shade, hemlock, henbane, and thickets of nettles, here will the early violet woo the winds of March with beauty; and the rath[111] primrose, blooming on the mossy bank, will charm away the lingering chills of

winter, light the budding copse with its sunny smile, and welcome the nightin-
gale's return to his native woods. Here is wild nature unhedged and free – there
is art with her paltry enclosure, her rude grave-stories, and ruder epitaphs. O!
how I should hate to be buried in a rank churchyard! Old father Abraham made
choice of the field of the Hittite[112] with its trees; and I should like to follow his
patriarchal example, and rest my bones in such a pretty dell as this, with the
mountains above, the lake below, and the fresh winds playing over my grave. I
would sing with the Northern Minstrel,[113]

> Mine be the breezy hill that skirts the down,
>   Where a green grassy turf is all I crave,
> With here and there a violet bestrown,
>   Fast by a brook, or fountain's bubbling wave;
> And many an evening sun shine sweetly on my grave.

I was quite carried away by his enthusiastic raptures. It was a subject, indeed,
I had never thought of; but as this doctrine of his raving fancy was such as would
have accorded well with the notions of the deceased, after some hesitation I gave
my assent.

The day arrived. I could have wished it a gloomy one; but, on the contrary,
the weather had cleared up, and the sun shone brightly. I was almost angry with
the blithe aspect of the fields, and the clear blue of the firmament, so little in
unison with my hopeless sorrow; though the general calm of nature, as it always
does, threw a quiet over my mind, such as I had not hoped to experience. I was,
indeed, sad; but had the comfort of seeing all those around me sympathising for
my irreparable loss.

The last offices were performed with as much solemnity, according to the
simple customs of the gipsies, as if they had been honoured with the full service
of a cathedral. But I cannot dwell on this sad event: it recalls feelings too painful.
I shall therefore proceed to subsequent adventures, in which, perhaps, the reader
may take greater interest.

CHAPTER XV.

Morning rambles – Donkey comforts – Gipsy budget of ways and means – Game markets at Warwick and Leamington – Poaching by wholesale – A poaching battle royal – Doings of a poacher's cub.

I HAD now, as I have said, neither hope nor aim, and could form no plan for my future life. I had become sick of adventure, as may readily be conceived; but had plunged too deep to get easily back, and must now either swim with the tide, or sink. I had no middle course. Home I could not go, as I had so cruelly deceived my parents; and even if I could have hoped for their forgiveness, I could never again appear in the village with the imputation of Anne's death upon my head: – had it not been also upon my conscience, I should have cared the less. I had seen enough of the stage to be heartily disgusted with a strolling life, particularly as I was desirous of freeing myself from the stings of conscience by throwing the chief blame of Anne's misfortunes on the rascally manager.

The only thing that was within my reach was to join my gipsy companions, if they would accept of my fellowship. I did not, indeed, know well what would be required of me. I had seen them do little else than idle about for the short time I had been with them; and yet they lived well – better, indeed, a great deal than the players. Wilton had assured me that all he had treated me to was honestly come by. I could not distrust him, but had my doubts if it were so with the set I was now among; for I had been prepossessed from my very boyhood that all gipsies were thieves by trade, and lived by plunder.

Whilst I was walking up and down the little dell, and turning these things over in my mind in every point of view I could think of, Wilton came opportunely to resolve my doubts by inviting me, in the warmest manner, to accompany him in an excursion which he intended to make towards the south. He had procured, he said, a supply of money which would more than suffice for us both, and therefore he should not again require to borrow my little purse, which he well knew was my all – as I had been compelled to abandon even my clothes, and other necessaries, on my escape from Lancaster. Nothing, however, appeared difficult or impossible to Wilton, who undertook to recover the whole by despatching Marshall, with a seasonable bonus, to the buxom widow, our quondam[114] landlady.

As our southern journey was to be wholly performed in the gipsy style, I had to doff my theatrical garb; which, though it had, I daresay, enough of a rakish look, was too fine for my new profession; and I got myself equipped in more humble garments – not quite so suitable, indeed, as Wilton's, but passable for ordinary occasions and every-day wear. My better suit I carefully reserved for future use, if I were ever obliged to resume it. Several days were passed in preparing, for we had no particular motive to hurry our movements; and gipsies are constitutionally indolent and lazy, when they are not roused to exertion by something of moment.

On the morning of our departure, Wilton called me up at day-break to take a farewell stroll on the banks of the Windermere. I expected to be entertained with instructions for the road, and for my new sort of life; but Wilton was in one of his flighty moods, and being, as usual, rapturous in admiration of the natural beauties around us, would talk of nothing else.

'Mark,' said he, 'the far off sound of waters on the hill side! – how soft it swells, and sinks again as the breeze flits by! And look up to the glorious garniture of the eastern sky beyond the outline of the mountains, where the streaks of golden light wreathe the brow of the firmament, and fringe the dark clouds with their sunny splendour. O! it is rapturous to gaze on those bright fore-runners of the sun! – but alas! while we gaze, they fade – melt – and pass away, like a morning vision, before the full blaze of the coming monarch. There! The rosy clouds lose their blushes and grow grey – silvery – white – and, indeed, I may well say –

> Morn wakes in beauty; but her eyes are pale,
>   As, pillow'd downy in aerial snow,
> She bids from off the lake the dull mists sail,
>   And watches, with her mild and sunny brow,
>   Till slowly up the green hill's side they go
> To cling around the cliffs their glistering wreathes.
>   There! Moving forth in smiles, her foot-steps glow
> With dewy radiance o'er the purple heaths,
> And fresh through all the air, her rapturous spirit breathes.'[115]

Such was the usual strain of Wilton's conversation when walking in the fields; and it certainly formed a singular contrast with his present gipsy life, and with many of his habits. This morning we could not, however, indulge long in flights of fancy, as we had to return to the tents, and prepare for our southern excursion.

When every thing was ready, we commenced our journey, – the donkeys, of course, coming in for their usual share of heavy burdens; and sometimes, though seldom, for a precarious supply of provender. In the latter respect, indeed, the gipsy's ass generally fares better than his brethren owned by wealthier masters; inasmuch as the road sides not only abound more in his favourite thistles, but he frequently also has a feed of good corn, that cannot fail to put him in better condition than the finest thistles in England. The question here will naturally occur, – where does the gipsy, if he does not steal them, get these feeds of corn for his ass? Upon the faith of my own experience I answer, that the ass's corn is got in the same way as he gets bread, beef, and other good things for himself – from those who require his services, and pay him well in money or in kind.

In our own case, so long as Wilton's fund lasted, – and it must have been considerable, – very little was done for the budget of ways and means. What little our people did was in the way of fortune-telling, and interpreting dreams – a deception I confess; but the contributions thus levied were all voluntary on the part of the donors, and the gipsies could scarcely be considered as parties to the deceit, for they all firmly believed their own predictions. In several instances, also, we were concerned in aiding escapes similar to mine. The gipsies were always particularly interested in lending their assistance to poachers, who, in turn, supplied them with game; and when they were not in a neighbourhood where they could dispose of this to advantage, they regaled themselves with hare soup and roast pheasant.

We had one rather stirring affair, on account of a poacher whom we were anxious to protect. We had pitched our tents for a day or two near Warwick,[116] on the banks of the Avon, and were soon visited by a very blackguard-looking man, whom Marshall familiarly accosted by the name of Dick, and whom I learned to be a notorious poacher. He did not come empty-handed; as he left, I understood, a brace of fine fat partridges, which, for the general use of the party, were soon exchanged at Warwick, by one of our women, for a comfortable supply of beef and mutton, which was more to our liking than dry game.

Early next morning, while it was still dusk, the same man came again, loaded with as much game of various sorts as he could stagger under. These, however, were not, it may be supposed, meant, as the former were, for our sole behoof, – the poacher being desirous of reaping something more substantial for his perilous risk than empty thanks or uncertain gratitude. He was generous enough, indeed, to make no bargain. The price of the articles he left entirely to our liberality, and to the success we might have in disposing of them at a proper market. All the female part of our establishment were accordingly put in requisition with baskets, capacious pockets, and cloaks, to conceal the spoil, and despatched to Warwick and Leamington[117] as the best markets within reach – Coventry and Birmingham being voted too distant. Their success, particularly at Leamington, was even beyond their hopes; and Dick shared a sum sufficient to keep him in ale, brandy, and Irish-blackguard, (which was his favourite snuff) for more than a month to come.

Dick thought himself in high luck, and repeated his visit on the following morning with another load, though not quite so much as the former; for while good fortune (as is usually the case) attended the contraband sale of his game, the game themselves became scarce and shy – his gins and springes[118] went out of order – his powder was damp – and his flints bad. He was strongly stimulated, however, to redouble his exertions by his second cargo fetching a still higher price, with orders for more on his own terms. He accordingly purchased a fresh lot of ammunition – refitted his gins – and with a glass or two of hot brandy and water, to season I know not how many pints of ale he had drunk – and a waist-coat-pocket filled with blackguard Irish, to save the trouble of a snuff-box – out he sallied for another field-day, to which the greater part of the night was to be added, if the sport were good.

Whether Dick's late expeditions had been too frequent, or too daringly incautious, I cannot say; but something had awakened suspicions among the keepers of the game-preserves wherein his depredations had been chiefly committed. On this particular night, accordingly, three of them had associated themselves to watch for the suspected intruder. The commotion in his brain, arising from the strife between the fumes of the ale and the brandy, had, however, put him beyond all fear; and, of course, his wonted caution was out of the question. He went to work, indeed, (he told me himself,) as if he had been squire of the property he was poaching upon, and sporting under the protection of the law with a regular licence in his pocket.

Hitherto he had never been detected; for he had put forth all the cunning and caution which are so indispensable to success in this hazardous trade. Suspicions of him, he knew, were entertained; and he had got more than one hint from those who had a greater interest in saving the game than in benefiting him, that he would do well to take care. This night, he was to prove by experience the soundness of this advice, whatever might be the motive it had been given with.

Dick was in the very act of taking a hare from one of his gins, when the three keepers all at once sprang upon him and collared him. All the resistance he could make, was a desperate struggle to free his arm so as to reach a sheath-knife, which he always wore about him in anticipation of a mischance of this kind. The three keepers, however, were too powerful to be shaken off from their hold; though Dick considered his own strength equal to that of any two of them. It is probable that their superior numbers made them too secure of their prize; and as security most commonly ends with incaution, they began to relax the fast hold they had taken of him.

Dick seized this opportunity – wrenched his right arm out of their grasp – in one moment unsheathed his knife, and made a plunge at the groin of one of the keepers, who was so stunned with the stroke that he staggered and fell, crying out he was murdered. The two others were so taken by surprise and consternation, that instead of trying to re-master Dick by their united strength, they flew to their firelocks, which they had thrown down when they first seized him. Dick was no less alert than they in picking up his trusty rifle, which he had laid down beside his hare-gin; and though the odds were still against him, he was resolved to sell his life as dearly as he could, since it had come to this pass, and immediately levelled his piece, saying,

'Now, d— ye! here goes for one on ye!'

He was just in the act of pulling the trigger when, as his ill-luck would have it, the wounded man – whom he supposed to be *hors de combat*,[119] as they say in the newspapers – having recovered from his surprise and his fall, came up behind Dick, beat down his rifle, and collared him a second time. He was now defenceless, for he had flung away his sheath-knife on picking up the rifle, and it was useless to contend against three men, when he had no weapons, even though one of them was partially disabled, as he supposed, by his wound. The wound, however, was but a mere scratch; and Dick was soon pinioned and conducted to the nearest keeper's lodge, till he could be more securely disposed of.

It was about midnight, when Rover's loud bark announced the approach of some intruder upon our little encampment. All of us were sound asleep; but the continued barking of our trusty watch awakened me. The intruder turned out to be a stout, shapeless, shock-headed boy, who had advanced upon Rover without fear, and, when the dog sprang at him, had dextrously parried his attack, and, with a short knotty cudgel, had become assailant in his turn. The noise of this combat was not long in bringing out several of our people to see what was ado; when the urchin was recognised to be Dick's son, whom he was faithfully training up to his own desperate trade by taking him out on his excursions as a watch.

We learned from this imp of mischief, that he had been as usual on the look-out for the keepers while his father was doing business; but like a true chip of the old block, he had also, before setting out, treated himself to a pint of beer and a glass of gin. This had probably muddled his head, thrown him off his guard, and prevented him from seeing the keepers till too late. He had no fear himself, and would not have hesitated to rush into the fray and lend his assistance; but before he could come up, he perceived that his father was already pinioned; and it came into his shaggy head to think it more expedient 'to hover about the enemy,'[120] and watch a more favourable opportunity. Even when he saw his father fairly housed at the lodge, like a true poacher, he did not despair; but set out for our encampment to give the alarm, and, if possible, procure our assistance.

CHAPTER XVI.

Scheming – The game-keeper's pepper-boxes – A lodge scene – Chimney sweeping – Carousing, brawling, and mystifications – More poachers – Grand expedition and division of forces – Triumph.

THE gipsies did not like intermeddling in the business, as, on their part, there was so much to risk and so little to gain. They would have to venture, probably, in the face of fire-arms, and encounter death itself, if they openly attempted to rescue Dick; and no other plan seemed practicable. Wilton was of a different opinion. The more the risk and the greater the danger, the more did the enterprise charm him; and, in the present case, I entirely agreed with him, as I had had little of late to stir my blood up to its natural flow, and longed to be once more in the midst of adventure.

I therefore proposed a scheme which I fancied might be successfully executed; namely, that Wilton and I should lay aside our gipsy garments, and go to the keeper's lodge as two young gentlemen who had lost their way; obtain admittance under that or any other pretence; and amuse Dick's sentinels, who would doubtless watch all night, till the gipsies, with the aid of the urchin, might fall upon some contrivance to liberate the prisoner. Wilton liked the notion; the gipsies, who never refused obedience to his will, consented; and we set out forthwith on our expedition, with young Dick for a guide.

The night was very dark, and the woods we had to pass through made it appear still darker; but just as we got to the ridge of the sloping ground, the moon rose, and showed us a house at a short distance, which the boy pointed out as the lodge where the poacher was now, of course, at his midnight meditations, instead of going the accustomed round of his gins and springes.

This house stood, solitary, on the brow of a slope overlooking the park and pleasure-grounds of the manor on the one side, and the thick wood we had just quitted, on the other. It was a fantastic sort of building; intended perhaps to be Gothic, if one might judge from two little pepper-box-looking turrets with loop-holes to them, and narrow slips of windows with pointed arches. Altogether, indeed, it was more like a couple of pigeon-houses joined together, than a human habitation: such fancies some whimsical gentlemen love to indulge, in the buildings near their mansion-houses. In one of the aforesaid pepper-boxes, – which was used to serve the double purpose of a lumber-room and a spare bed-chamber, – the boy had ascertained, by eves-dropping, that Dick was confined for the night, and designed of course to take his trial at the assizes for repeated acts of poaching.

Wilton and I, according to our device, now separated from the rest, and proceeded to insinuate ourselves into the chimney-corner and good graces of the keeper. As we announced ourselves gentlemen, we had less difficulty in this than we had anticipated; for the three heroes had left their prisoner securely pinioned as they fancied, and were assembled around a blazing fire, making themselves comfortable over the contents of a black-jack,[121] (which by the way was flanked by their loaded fowling-pieces); and, being in high spirits at the capture of the redoubted Dick, they were by no means suspicious, and looked upon our arrival as a fortunate chance, since they could not only better pass off their bravadoes to strangers, but we might be witnesses to their hearty zeal in performing the most dangerous part of their duty.

We were soon made acquainted with three several versions of the exploit, – each of the keepers having a different one. The wounded man, in particular, was very desirous to shield himself from the imputation of carelessness and cowardice, though he did not seem averse to cast similar imputations on his companions. Wilton and I, in the true spirit of mischief, did our best to promote these differences of opinion, and warmly took opposite sides, to stir up the rising ferment of discord to an actual brawl, in order thus to withdraw their attention from any suspicious noises our party out of doors might make.

We had left them to frame their own devices; but as the house was not high, every thing was now in a fair train for success. I afterwards learned that young Dick, with the assistance of Marshall, clambered up to the top of the turret, where he knew there was a chimney; and, at the risk of sticking fast in its throat, (since he was much too stout for a climbing boy,[122]) he dropped down the flue, and without accident reached the chamber where Dick lay. This apparition no doubt astonished the poacher; for the boy was all begrimed with soot, and the very picture of a young devil, – as he in some degree really was, since a more wicked, desperate, and fearless boy I never saw.

The urchin, it may be conceived, made great despatch in releasing Dick from his bonds of affliction, and in informing him of the assistance at hand to aid his escape. There were only two ways of egress from the chamber; the one, that through which young Dick had just entered, namely, the chimney; and the other through the door. The chimney, as the boy averred, was not high, and it was wide enough to admit the fat inn-keeper of Warwick[123] himself, let alone his father; but the poacher did not like this upward path to liberty at all. He would have preferred leaping from the window, had there been one; but the pigeon-hole, or loop-hole, or whatever it might be called, which was meant to represent a window, was scarcely wide enough to admit his arm, much less his body.

The door, again, – although, as is common in such houses, it had no security but the latch – was safely fastened outside; somewhat, probably, in the manner in which I had done up old Crusty's doors when I was at Humpback's school. The only chance of getting it open was by pulling till the latch-handle – if they had strength enough to effect it – should give way; and, in this case, there was the danger of making too much noise, and alarming the keepers.

In this dilemma, Dick was forced to try the chimney; but after he had got his head fairly into the region of soot, he bolted back, and protested that he could not proceed, except with the certainty of being suffocated, – a thing probable enough, as he had already blocked up one passage to his lungs with enormous pinches of snuff, and the soot had taken possession of the better half of the other.

There was no resource, therefore, but trying the door, whatever noise it might occasion; and to it they now began to apply their united strength. Wilton and I, whose ears, from expectation, were much quicker than those of the keepers, soon hearing what was going forward, redoubled our efforts to engage our heroes in actual combat, and at length succeeded just in time; for they had already risen, begun to drive about the chairs, and make passes at one another, when, in the turmoil, crash went the table with the black-jack and the muskets, and almost at the same instant Dick and his devil's cub showed their sooty phizzes in their descent by the stair, which landed at the entrance of the apartment where we were. Our heroes were too eager in their quarrel to perceive this apparition; and we started up and took our positions so as effectually to cover Dick's retreat, pretending the while to be very busy in reconciling the disputants. Dick speedily undid the bolts of the outer door, and got clear off without exciting the least suspicion in his brawling and tipsy guardians.

It was now our turn to effect our retreat as quietly as we could, though we foresaw it would be somewhat harder to get out than it had been to get in; for as we had pretended we had lost our way, we could not consistently pretend we could find it again in the dark. A device struck me, which, though rather far-fetched and doubtful in its result, I determined to try. I knew that one of the gipsies was armed with a horseman's pistol; and as I was pretty sure he would not be far off before we made our appearance, I shammed occasion to go out, and, to prevent suspicion, told them to keep a good look-out upon the door. I soon found the gipsy, despatched him to a short distance with instructions to fire off his pistol, and went back to my seat at the chimney-corner, where I found peace restored, and the black-jack again in requisition. The report of the gipsy's pistol operated on our heroes like a thunder-clap.

'More poachers, by the dickens!'[124] said one.

'And devilish venturesome, too,' said another, 'to come so near the lodge.'

'Let's have at 'em, however!' said the third.

'Rare sport to-night, chaps! an't there?'

My plan, I perceived, had taken effect; and, winking to Wilton, I encouraged them strongly to pursue, and volunteered my poor services in assisting them. Wilton did the same; and I, being furnished with Dick's rifle which they had just been exhibiting as a trophy, went forth to set them fairly on the wild-goose chace I had devised. Of course I took care to lead them in an opposite direction to where the gipsy was, who, as soon as he saw us at a sufficient distance, loaded and fired again; then taking a cut across the park under cover of a thick row of trees, he fired a third time, which so distracted the fellows, muddled and half tipsy as they were, that they knew not well what to do.

'By the dickens!' said one, 'if all the poachers out o' purgatory an't in this here park to-night; thof we ha' one on 'em snug, however.'

This was precisely what I wished them to believe; and Wilton and I immediately proposed a division of our forces, in order to secure as many of the supposed poachers as possible. They all argued against this, having, I suppose, some rather unpleasant recollections of the mortal dangers they had run in securing Dick; but, by a few seasonable insinuations that cowardice was at the bottom of their objections, we soon gained our point. Wilton and I, as friends, were of course not to be separated; and we contrived to get off with the best grace imaginable, leaving the three mystified heroes to cool their blood by hunting down shadows at their leisure.

We found all our friends, including Dick and the urchin boy, assembled in the wood; and the women having brought our clothes in case of need, we thought it best to lay aside our genteeler habiliments on the spot, as a precaution against accidents on our return. We also took separate roads home; while Dick, with his recovered rifle, which I took care to restore, set off with the boy to examine his gins as if nothing had happened.

It may readily be supposed that we did not sleep much more that night; and, about his usual time at the dawn of the morning, Dick again came with what spoil he had secured, having escaped a second encounter with the keepers. It was necessary for him, however, in consequence of what had happened, to decamp from Warwickshire; and on receiving a small sum of money for his present cargo, he took his leave.

On our part we did not apprehend much danger; since the keepers, as we thought, would for their own sakes make no mention either of the capture or the escape of Dick, and would far less dream of looking out for their two gentlemen visitors in the gipsy encampment. Notwithstanding, I was scarcely at my ease about the affair, which would have brought us into an awkward scrape enough, had we been suspected; and I urged Wilton to use his influence in hastening our departure, which was accordingly fixed for the following morning.

CHAPTER XVII.

Cambridge gipsying – Cantab credulity – Lord B—'s admiration of old women – Gipsy masquerade – Lord B—'s marvellous genius and grasp of mind – Shifts to raise the wind – Gipsy theatricals – Spectre apparitions.

From Warwick we crossed the country in an easterly direction, through Northamptonshire and part of Bedford, by easy journeys and with several haltings, not devoid of curious incidents; but these, for the present, I shall not stop to record, as I only wish to give one or two scenes more from my earlier days – or what I call the period of my education for my future duties at Bow-street.[125]

We designed to make some stay in the vicinity of Cambridge,[126] as the gipsies are partial to the young gentlemen of the Universities, who in their frolics resort to them to have their fortunes told, – not so much out of credulity in most cases, as from sheer fun. We had avoided Oxford,[127] though more in our way, out of deference to Wilton, who was himself of that University, and did not wish to be recognised among his present companions by his former associates; while he did not know any body at Cambridge for whose opinion of his eccentricities he in the least cared. So, indeed, Wilton pretended to say; and, I doubt not, tried to persuade himself into indifference; but he began by degrees to change his mind, and in the end resolved to wear his dress suit whenever there was any chance of college visitors, and assume the air of a gentleman visitor himself. Had I been in his circumstances, I daresay I should have done the same; as it was, I enjoyed the fun better in my gipsy garb than I should have done in my theatricals.

We made choice, for our encampment, of a green lane[128] which was sheltered by tall elms, and which led, at the distance of about a quarter of a mile or less, to the banks of the Cam. The lane widened considerably in front of the tents, and was almost as smooth and level as a bowling-green. It was, indeed, with the exception of the dell at Windermere, the prettiest rural spot we had yet encamped in; though it might be its resemblance to a lane near my native village which made me like it so much, or perhaps the returning cheerfulness of my mind. My sorrow for Anne, indeed, began to wear gradually away, except when anything occurred to awaken painful recollections; and then I was vexed with myself that I could not grieve so much as I had formerly done. The mind cannot be ever on the rack of grief nor any other violent passion, as I have often experienced; and at this time, particularly, I could join in the laugh or the frolic as heartily as my companions.

It was not long before we were found out by the University *men*, as they call themselves, on the assumption, I suppose, that when they leave school they are no longer *boys*. The greater number of them, in truth, are neither men nor boys, but, as Shakespeare has it, 'like an after-dinner's sleep, dreaming on both.'[129] They were very liberal with their money, provided they got what they considered its worth; and our people reaped a good harvest by their prophecies, at all which the Cantabs[130] made a point of laughing; though some I perceived were credulous enough to believe most of the dreams and nonsense which they were told.

I remember one of these youths who was deep in credulity – 'steeped,' indeed, if I may use a theatrical expression, 'to the very lips.'[131] One evening about dusk, this *man* came galloping down the lane on a fine blood horse,[132] and asked for our chief priestess of prophecy, whom he wished to consult on business, he said, of great importance. Mary's mother presented herself as the person he inquired for; but when he saw her, he looked quite disappointed, and protested with a thundering oath that she was too young by half a century to have experience enough for his purpose. She was, indeed, a fresh and rather good-looking woman of about forty or thereabout, though she did not appear to be so old by several years.

Whence the opinion has arisen and gained ground, I know not, that ugly and decrepid old women are endowed with the exclusive power of seeing into futurity in proportion as their eyes have become dim and lustreless; but so it is and has been. The college *man*, indeed, was so fully prepossessed with this opinion, that he would not intrust his momentous case to a woman who had no wrinkles on her face, and who still preserved some of the fire of youth in her eyes.

Wilton and I, who heard what was going on from behind the curtain of the tent where we were lying, devised, on the moment, a scheme for gulling this admirer of old hags and their faculties of foreknowledge. We accordingly sent Mary to inform him that there was a very old woman belonging to our party, but that it would not be convenient for him to see her before midnight, when, if he could visit us, it might probably be to his advantage. Our bait took, and he promised to return at the time appointed.

In the mean time, Wilton, who undertook to play the part of the aged prophetess, prepared by my assistance to dress for the character. We fashioned a quantity of tow[133] into the rude form of a wig, which we bound round his head with a handkerchief in the Irish fashion: the same article furnished a pair of capital eyebrows – shaggy and sulphurous. With such materials as we had, we gave the requisite shades of sallow and iron-grey to his cheeks; but as the imitation of wrinkles and dim eyes was beyond our art, he was to muffle up his face as much as he could, and keep his eyes closed; for which purpose also it was contrived that he should receive the *man* in bed,[134] under the pretence of exhausted frailty. The trembling and feeble voice of age he would find no difficulty in assuming.

'Punctual as lovers to the moment sworn,'[135] the credulous youth returned at midnight on the same handsome steed as before. The light showed, however, that his face was paler, and he appeared much agitated. It is not unlikely that he had endured a hard struggle in consequence of the superstitious dread of visiting a gipsy hag at midnight, and that his agitation arose more from this fear than from anxiety to learn his fate; but he had been spurred on, by the importance of his business, to face the danger, whatever it might be. To him, of course, the business was important, though to others it might appear rather ludicrous: to us, at least, as we had anticipated, it afforded some little sport.

On being introduced into the tent, which was only illumined by the glimmer of a rushlight,[136] he chose to approve of Wilton's hag-ship as having the requisite marks of antiquity and decrepitude. He was about to begin his story, but Wilton refused to hear it till he told his name. To this he was extremely averse, as he dreaded exposure among his companions; but when he was told it was indispensable, and assured of secrecy, he announced himself as Lord —. I suppress the name out of deference to his family, as well as on the faith of Wilton's promise. By report, Lord Blank was well known to us all as one of the most notorious, dashing, drinking, sporting, *rowing*,[137] young noblemen of Trinity;[138] though, having never seen him before, we were all unacquainted with his person.

From his own confessions, it appeared that his Lordship's sporting extravagances had been, according to the common current of University dissipation, carried so much beyond his means of supporting them, that he was now reduced to his last guinea, which, as a fee, he tendered to Wilton; and he could not raise another shilling from the Jews by begging, borrowing, or post-obiting.[139] His gambling chums also had smoked[140] this, and would no longer bet or play[141] with him; so that he had no means of recruiting his finances, for paying several debts of honour[142] which *must* be paid; for supporting his favourite mistress, who had threatened to leave him; or, (what went to his heart worst of all) for purchasing a celebrated hunter,[143] together with the genuine identical saddle Buonaparte had used at Marengo,[144] at less than half its real value, which was estimated by good judges at four thousand pounds.[145]

The only two means which had occurred to Lord Blank for getting out of these terrible difficulties, were suicide, or – a lottery ticket.[146] The latter, if he were lucky (and he had often had devilish good luck at *rouge et noir*[147]) would bring him thirty thousand smack,[148] with which he could outbid his chum, Sir

Byam Finch,[149] for the favours of Miss Cherry,* and in that case he would dismiss his present mistress; or he might send his valet, who had a good eye in such matters, to Paris, to bring over the handsomest opera girl he could select, at any price. He could then also purchase a racer to sport at Newmarket;[150] and perhaps a smallish pack of foxers[151] might be no bad move for an occasional hunt.

In this manner did his Lordship open up his views and wishes to the ears of Wilton, who, to his credit be it spoken, maintained a proper gravity in listening to the detail. The momentous business required of Wilton was, to discover whether the number of Lord Blank's ticket was a lucky one; and, in a word, whether it would come up the thirty thousand. He had been put to all sorts of shifts to obtain the money for purchasing it: he had even condescended to ask his tailor for the loan of twenty guineas[152] for a week or so; but the scurvy rascal pretended he had not twenty shillings in the house. Sir Byam Finch, whom he next tried, was *expecting* a remittance, but could not *then* muster *the trifle*. In short, he was obliged at last to dispose of his gold repeater,[153] to raise the sum. If, after all this, his number came up a blank,[154] he was undone – plucked – ruined – and must take to his pistols or a dose of laudanum;[155] neither of which he had much mind to, if the gipsy could assure him of the thirty thousand.

It appeared to Wilton, who led him on to disclose all his dissipated follies, that his notion was not so much to ascertain the luck of his number, as to have some incantation tried to *make* it fortunate in spite of the fates. In such a matter, however, Wilton would not interfere; at the same time he assured him the number was in itself the luckiest he could have chosen.

'But I must know,' continued Wilton, 'the very day of the month and week, and also the hour and minute at which your Lordship purchased it: much will depend on that!'

'On Friday, the 15th, at one o'clock precisely,' said Lord Blank.

'Ah! how very unfortunate! Friday, of all days, is bad, – the 15th is worse, – and one o'clock – my stars! your Lordship could not have chosen a more unlucky hour!'

'It is all over with me, then!' sighed his Lordship, in a most lugubrious tone.

'Perhaps so, my Lord; but if you could purchase another to-morrow at ten o'clock!' Lord Blank shook his head; – 'or you have still one chance left: if no disaster befal you before next noon-tide, I venture my credit on your success. All will depend on this, and I am sorry I cannot satisfy you on this point. Danger I foresee threatens; but the storm may blow over.'

With this doubtful assurance, Lord Blank mounted his horse and departed, no wiser than he came. We had not, however, yet done with him; for Wilton's menace of danger before next noon-tide was suggested by another design we

---

* The story and the fate of this interesting young lady will appear in the next volume.

had on his Lordship's credulity. The moment he departed, Wilton sprang up from the bed; and he and I, furnished with a blanket apiece, to wrap ourselves in (sheets would have done better, but we had none), and a bit of chalk to whiten our faces, ran across the fields by a near cut, so as to reach the head of the lane before his Lordship. We had also brought with us a dark lantern,[156] and a quantity of theatrical lightning.[157]

Thus prepared, we placed ourselves in line across the lane, and just as he rode slowly up – musing gloomily, no doubt, on the ticklish state of his affairs, – I saluted him with a tremendous flash of my lightning, and Wilton followed it up with another; while we stood with our blankets, like shrouded spectres, in the blaze. The horse at once stood trembling and snorting as if the devil had crossed him: indeed I have always found horses, contrary to the vulgar belief, by no means knowing in the difference between real and counterfeit apparitions. Lord Blank actually screamed with fright; for though we did not exactly take him for a coward, yet his fancy, as we knew, had just been excited by his gipsy expedition; while the aspect of the dark and solitary lane at the witching time of night, the ominous lightning, and the apparition of two spectres, were altogether enough to appal a stouter heart than his.

'Lord — !' Wilton called out in a hollow sepulchral voice, 'we are sent to warn you to repent of your horrid deeds of iniquity, – your mad prodigality – your dissipation – your whoredoms – your debaucheries – and, particularly, your abominable crime of pursuing games of chance, – impiously worshipping fortune, and seeking after witchcraft! Repent! Reform your wicked life, and betake you to other courses! Cast from you that abomination – that accursed ticket on which you have set your heart! – Forth with it from your pocket, and trample it under your feet, or

PREPARE!

instantly for your fate!'

Upon this I greeted his Lordship with another flash, and echoed the word,

'PREPARE!!'

in a deep hollow tone. Wilton re-echoed,

'PREPARE!!!'

while I sent another flash streaming through the darkness. All this time his Lordship sat speechless upon his restive and trembling steed, terrified, I doubt not, and expecting instant death. The last flash of our lightning, however, exhibited him in the act of reluctantly unpocketing his ticket, and committing it to the winds.

Our object being thus attained, we instantly vanished behind the trees of the lane till he got the affrighted animal to move onwards, in which he had no little difficulty; and he then rode slowly away to digest his misfortune. When he was fairly gone, we produced our lantern, and after some search found the ticket on which so many wondrous and vain hopes had been built. We easily quieted our conscience from considering this prank a robbery; for we did not mean to keep his Lordship's ticket, far less participate in any chance benefit which might arise therefrom. We only retained it, indeed, till it was drawn a blank; when we enclosed it under a cover addressed to his Lordship, and despatched it by post.

I never could learn how he represented this affair, if he ever spoke of it at all, or how he extricated himself from his embarrassments. We saw no more of his Lordship at this time.

CHAPTER XVIII.

University painters – Gipsy fêtes and rural balls – Wilton's Oxonian tale of love and jealousy – Supper on Hampstead Heath – Vestry politics – Charms of a night-storm.

It was not the object of all our college visitors to have their fortunes told: many of them, who were fond of drawing, brought their portfolios, and would have spent whole days in sketching our tents, and our donkeys, or in taking portraits of such individuals among us as struck their fancy. Others came to admire the dark eyes and raven hair of our girls; and Wilton's Mary was in this respect a general favourite. The latter order of visitors frequently got up a rural entertainment, or, as it might be called, a fête,[158] with great life and spirit; for they not only brought with them wine and brandy, but frequently a profusion of cold provisions, with dainties of every description; and to keep the spirit of fun alive, they always either had a hired musician, or some one of themselves played the violin or the flute; and a dance was struck up on the green, to assist in the digestion of the good things that had been devoured there.

On these occasions, I remarked that Wilton was in a fever of anxiety when Mary danced with any other than himself, and had recourse to every possible shift to prevent such arrangements. His romantic love and his poetical fancy had rendered him jealous; and his plan of appearing only as a gentleman stranger, who was amongst us by mere chance, prevented him from assuming any open right to protect her. On her part, Mary evidently saw into the state of his feelings; but though I had no good reason to suspect her real affection for him, I perceived that she by no means liked his apparent distrust of her fidelity. She appeared, on the contrary, to take delight in thwarting his little manœuvring to retain exclusive possession of her hand for our rural dances. The torture which this often gave him was too great to be concealed; and he had more than once got rather warm in asserting a claim of priority, since he had resolved to acknowledge no other right. To me he unbosomed himself without reserve, as one who could sympathise with his feelings on this subject.

'Ah! Richmond!' he would say, 'you know not what I have suffered for that girl since I first saw her. Loss of friends, – but let them go! – the scorn and scoffs of my college chums – sentence of rustication[159] passed against me – scurvy doggrel ballads, about my supposed adventures, sung to vile tunes by common beggars in the streets. It crept through my blood like poison to hear myself (and I *have* heard it) thus turned into mockery, and made the butt of vulgar laughter. Yet all this I endured for her, though now, you see, she makes light of it, and dances and smiles on every booby that comes hither. You cannot feel, Richmond, how it galls me – how it rankles in my heart's blood! I feel the sting the more deeply that this green lane recalls the day I first saw her near Oxford; I was then as mad, – aye, more mad and merry than you have ever seen me. We made a party to have a frolic among the gipsies who were encamped as we now are. Mary was there. I need not say I was at once struck with — but *love* is too feeble a word to express my emotion! – it was the delicious whirl of admiration! Madness – insanity you may call it! I was overpowered. I gave myself up to the sweep of the torrent within me – abandoned all for her – and here I am, galled and tortured at the pleasure of every brainless idiot who writes himself Cantab! Richmond, I'll tell you what; do you stand by me, and I'll fell to the earth the first beardless fool that presumes to — '

'Hold!' said I, interrupting him. 'Be advised by me, and do nothing rashly! Your Mary is still true to you – and will be, I could swear. You take her merriness too seriously – indeed you do. Beware, if I may advise you, of any broil with the Cantabs; and rather use your influence to get away from them as soon as possible, by breaking up our encampment for London.'

By urging these and all the other arguments I could think of, I succeeded in quieting Wilton's perturbed spirits for the time, and in reconciling him to himself; for I perceived that the appearance of the University *men*, in all their gaiety and light-hearted frolic, had produced unpleasant reflections, and made him think with regret (which was natural enough) of all the comforts he had given up for the many privations inseparable from his present wanderings. It was all very well to rhapsodize about liberty in the warm sunshine of summer; but the lengthening nights, raw mornings, and chill rains of October, were a very different matter, – with the prospect also before us of the still more dreary season of winter, of which these were the unwelcome forerunners.

The gipsies, who had been trained to all this from infancy, and never knew any thing better, could bear cold and wet without a murmur; but Wilton and I had been used to comfortable shelter, and were not sufficiently inured and hardy to relish the reverse. Sometimes, however, we contrived to enjoy even the inclemency of stormy weather, which had a certain wild charm to us, – with nothing to shield us but the tent and the hedge-bank, – very different from that which sometimes arises in the warm parlour, and at the snug chimney-corner. Sometimes we had not even the shelter of a tent.

One stormy night of this kind I particularly remember. We had dined at Hornsey Wood, and had arrived in the afternoon on Hampstead Heath,[160] the first station we had pitched upon since leaving Cambridge; but here we unexpectedly encountered a large board, put up by order of the vestry,[161] prohibiting and warning away from the parish all 'beggars, gipsies, and other vagrants.'[162] With the fear of this before our eyes, we did not venture to set up our tents, but lighted our supper fire in one of the sand-pits on the north side of the Heath, intending, early next morning, to remove to Norwood or Wimbledon.[163]

The vestry prohibition, I perceived, rankled deeply in Wilton's mind. He considered it an insult to his freedom, and talked in a lofty tone, as he was wont, of the liberty of wandering over the country at will. In this mood we walked out upon the Heath, leaving the gipsies around the fire in the sand-pit to drink perdition to the Hampstead Vestry, in some hot punch they had made to drive away cold and care, and make merry withal. Wilton did not usually absent himself, more than I, when good liquor was circulating; but to night he was too moody for mirth.

The wind blew strong and gusty, and accorded well with the tone of his thoughts, which by turns sank into deep depression from the sad conviction that he had lost his rank, and was now justly designated by the vile terms on the vestry-board, and by turns rose again to indignant contempt for the paltry conclave which constituted the parish authorities. He was, as it appeared to me, altogether tired of his gipsy life, yet tried to persuade both himself and me that he was the same enthusiastic worshipper of wandering liberty as when I had first met him on the beach at Lancaster. I saw the struggle which was going on in his mind, but could not interfere without adding to his inquietude, and therefore listened in silence to his strong and often rhapsodical expressions of feeling.

The wind increased to a storm; but we walked about the Heath for several hours, listening to the roar of the blast among the tall firs, and observing the dark ocean of clouds driving along the firmament. I was myself charmed with the wildness of the scene; but, forgetting his grievances for the time, Wilton became absolutely enchanted with visionary ecstacy.[164]

'O! how I could wish,' he said, 'to be wrapt in those viewless winds, and dash along from mountain to mountain, and from cloud to cloud! I feel as if I could spurn the earth from under my feet – spring aloft into the dark air, – and companion me with the spirit of the storm! Richmond! you may call this dreaming madness, but it is a dream I like to indulge in. I like to let my fancy go with the blast, and revel among the clouds; and a night-storm is so grand – so sublime – so darkly beautiful! – the very music of magnificent sound – the very poetry of resistless motion! Do you remember the lines I once repeated to you on this glorious subject?

> The midnight winds are forth, with high career,
>   Urging their cloudy chariots rapidly,
> As if they rush'd to war, or fled in fear
>   Along the champain azure of the sky!
>   The heavens are all in motion; and the eye
> Beholds the wonted visions of its search –
>   Moon, star, and cloud – all hurrying rapidly
> Away, as if upon their final march, –
> As if the Archangel's trump had peal'd along that arch.
>
> So when the hand of mighty seraphim
>   This pictur'd volume from our eyes shall roll,
> Unfolding to all eyes the face of HIM
>   Who sits enthron'd behind it; O my soul!
>   How wilt thou shrink to see, in funeral stole,
> Nature, distracted, in convulsions lie
>   On flaming pyre; and at his destin'd goal
> TIME, worn and weary, lay him down to die
> On the paternal breast of hoar ETERNITY!'[165]

The tone which Wilton's mind was now in, and which I also had partly caught, banished all thoughts of the vestry insult; and, returning to our party in the sand-pit, we helped them to finish their hot punch; and, wrapping ourselves in our blankets and tent furniture, lay down to sleep under the canopy of the driving clouds.

CHAPTER XIX.

Mischief and mystification – Sylvan painting in Bishop's Wood – All snug at the Three Spaniards – Muddling of a Hampstead draper.

WE started before day-break next morning, to avoid any unpleasant rencontre with the parish men. But I was very reluctant to be thus turned out of my quarters the very first night, without bestowing some merited recompence upon those who had taken the trouble of posting up the 'notice to quit.'[166]

Wilton, to whom I communicated my thoughts, was no less willing than myself to present the vestry with something whereby to remember us; though we could hit upon no device which pleased us. Pulling down the notice was a matter easily accomplished; but another could as easily be put up, or, what was worse, the old one could be acted upon to persecute our people, even after it had vanished.

Wilton suggested the idea of a counter-notice, nailed over the other, ordering the vestry men, by authority of the gipsies, under severe pains and penalties to quit the parish within twenty-four hours. I thought this was excellent; and we accordingly agreed to procure a board for the purpose forthwith. Wilton undertook to paint it; so that we might keep our own secret by not intrusting the job to an artisan. For the execution of this design, we deemed it best to doff our gipsy garments, and resume our other suits; and we left our friends to pursue their route southward of London, while we set off for Highgate to bespeak our board.

We were not long in accommodating ourselves with an article suited to our purpose; but were rather annoyed by the carpenter pumping us very closely as to its intended use. We joked and bantered with him, to lead him from the subject; but his thirst for knowledge was not to be so quenched: he returned again and again to the charge, and tried us, though vainly, upon all the points his ingenuity could suggest. When he saw that direct questions were useless, he attempted to surprise us into indirect admissions, with all the dexterity of a barrister cross-examining a witness. We were, however, too many for[167] him, and got off in triumph with our board, without the carpenter having the slightest guess, so far as we could perceive, for what it was intended.

The next thing was the painting, which it was necessary to execute with the utmost privacy, as we did not know what might be the consequences of discovery. We at length agreed that I should carry the board to Bishop's Wood,[168] in the thickets of which it would be easy to conceal ourselves; and that Wilton should procure the proper materials for his work in some of the village shops.

In about an hour afterwards (for enthusiasm quickened our motions most marvellously,) we were seated in the bosom of a clump of hazels in Bishop's Wood, hard at work. I held every thing in readiness, while Wilton proceeded with his task in as workman-like a manner as if he had served an apprenticeship to the trade. His versatility, indeed, was one of the most extraordinary things about him. He tried every thing, and seldom failed of success; though I was sometimes led to ascribe this more to accident, arising from a certain fearless forwardness, than to uniform cleverness or skill. This opinion, perhaps, might spring from lurking jealousy, of which at the time I was not conscious; though now, when I reflect on the circumstances, I think I have some cause for self-accusation.

With all the expedition he could use, however, it was impossible to finish the work in one day; and as the weather was now raw, and the nights rather long, it could not be got dry enough to be carried to its destination in less than two days more. What, then, were we to do with our nights in the interim? Walking about in the darkness, and rhapsodising about the winds and the clouds, was all well enough for once in a way; but a repetition of this sort of romancing was overmuch for my taste; and Wilton himself, who was too fickle to be long in the same humour, had now changed his vein, and the spirit of rhapsody had, for the moment, been vanquished by the spirit of mischief.

It occurred to me that, as Hampstead was within reach, we might, in furtherance of our grand object, endeavour to practise upon[169] some of our vestry enemies, if we could find out any of those sage enactors of parish laws. We again, therefore, took our way across the Heath towards the village, without any definite plan of operation – trusting to the fertility of our wits for taking advantage of whatever circumstances might occur. On coming to the Three Spaniards,[170] we went in and had some hot brandy and water to keep our stomachs warm, and our brains stirring. While drinking this, we entered into a little chat with an old codger, who was enjoying his pot and his pipe by the parlour fire.

He was just the sort of person whom we wanted – a house-holder in Hampstead, and fond of talking to digest his liquor, and give additional zest to the tobacco smoke, whose piquancy he enjoyed with peculiar relish, if we might judge from the motions of his cheeks, where 'every muscle quivered with delight,'[171] as he rolled the fragrant steam about, previous to puffing it off into the thankless air. One of the standing topics of this smoking toper was the taxes, or public impositions, as he loved to term them; and, above all, the parish rates imposed by the vestry.

'Gentlemen!' he said to us, 'you are young in the world yet. You know little of the tricks which are played under the mask of "general utility."[172] Why, there's my neighbour Hawkins, the smith and bell-hanger, has had God knows how many good pounds for repairing this and the other trumpery about the chimes. Never a week passes, but some one of the bells is discovered to be badly hung, or not well fixed; and Hawkins must be at it to give it a proper set, and, as the cream of the thing, to send in his bill. Many a shilling and pound too, I believe, it has cost me for their jobbing[173] and their guzzling.'

'But why do you submit to such extortion?' said Wilton, who wished for nothing better than a continuance of the subject.

'Lord love ye! young gentleman,' replied the smoker, 'we *must* submit. The vestry has the law of us; we have no choice; and if it please them to dine together once a week, why, we must pay for it, that's all. 'Tis robbery – bare-faced robbery and plunder, I say, and a shame to the parish!'

'Yet,' said I, 'your vestry seems to be very circumspect in guarding the good parish of Hampstead from vagrant plunderers, if I may judge from the notice I have seen posted up at the entrance of the village.'

'Aye, aye, friend!' said he, 'the old saying of "set a thief to catch a thief."[174] Did you ever hear of Justice Thorpe – old Justice Thorpe, as we used to call him in Berkshire, who helped himself to as much of the common[175] as made a pretty paddock for a couple of cows to graze in, besides a good kitchen-garden, and thought it no crime; but when a poor fellow, on the same principle, helped him-self to one of the Justice's turkeys that fed on the common, Thorpe consigned him to the stocks for petty larceny!'

'That was good, i'faith!' said Wilton.

'It is just the same,' continued the smoker, 'with our Hampstead vestry and the gipsies. They won't spare a bit of the Heath for the poor creatures to cook their dinner upon; but they will rack and draw every purse in the parish rather than be stinted in their own guzzling dinners. Things can't go on in this way, I know. There will be a change, and soon too, or my name's not Higglesworth.[176] Hawkins sha'n't job[177] much longer about the chimes, that I can tell him.'

'This Hawkins, I suppose,' said Wilton, 'is one of the vestry men himself?'

'That you may swear to safely,' replied Higglesworth. 'He and Josh Swale rule the roast; and a pretty pair of jack-asses they are as you would wish to see of a summer's day. Swale, however, has lately backed out of the firm: Hawkins and he have declared open war against each other, and have actually unmasked batteries of mutual accusation.'

How long we might have been entertained with similar parish gossip by our friend Higglesworth I cannot say; for an idea struck me which I was impatient to consult Wilton upon, and I gave him a hint to empty his glass and let us be off. We therefore left Higglesworth to fume out his spleen along with his tobacco smoke, and proceeded towards Hampstead.

'I have it now!' cried I to Wilton as soon as we got out. 'I have it all pat and plain, if we can but go cleverly through with it! We shall have some rare fun, I promise you, if you approve my scheme.'

'Which is — ?'

'O! a capital prank! – quite first rate you will allow when you hear it!'

'I doubt that, Tom! I hate all jokes which are prefaced with a puff.'

'Mine, perhaps, may turn out to be an exception. I propose that we play off a hoax upon those two vestry sages, Hawkins and Swale, taking the bells of the chime for a subject.'

'How? I don't understand you.'

'Why, persuade Hawkins, who it seems is the guardian of the parish bells, that they have been carried off by the gipsies; and, on the other hand, persuade Swale that Hawkins himself has robbed the belfry.'

'I thought, Tom, it would prove to be all a mare's nest![178] I can't for my life imagine how such an absurdity ever entered your brain. Why, man, you will never persuade the greatest ass that ever sat in a vestry that the bells are stolen, when he can so easily detect the hoax by stepping to the belfry itself.'

'No, Wilton, I'll bet you two to one that none of them will ever dream of looking into the belfry, if we play our cards well enough. It is the very last place which they will search if we can once get them to believe in the robbery. If the bells *were* stolen, it would be no joke at all; but if we can once get the old fools to set up a hue and cry, it will make them the laughing-stock of the parish.'

'Then, Tom, let us try at all events. It will be an excellent hoax as you say, if we can get them to bite; though I much fear we shall be detected.'

Having agreed about this weighty matter, we next planned our operations in more detail; when it was resolved that Wilton should call on Hawkins at the same time that I called upon Swale, and trump up to each the best story we could invent, – agreeing, however, to send them both to the sand-pit on the Heath, where we had slept, to look for the bells.

Upon inquiry, I understood Swale to be a draper in the general line; that is to say, a dealer not only in linen and broad-cloth, but in silks, ribbands, tape, and other soft goods, including in that phrase, muffs, comforters, and Witney blankets. I found him in his shop, alone, and busy with his ledger. He looked a sleek, prim, quakerish sort of man, with a smooth shining face that did not belie the good cheer of the vestry dinners; but under all this saintly appearance, I thought I could see a dash of the rogue in his eye, or it might be a gloss of hypocrisy overdone – I will not take upon me to determine which.

He received me with all the simpering and bowing affectation of affability which grow to so much perfection behind a draper's counter; and, in a soft measured tone of voice approaching to a whisper, asked me what I was pleased to want. I told him, with a grave face, that I came to give him information of a circumstance with which

I had accidentally become acquainted, and which I considered might be of importance to the parish. At the mention of this, his simper was turned into a Sunday look
of solemnity. He took his pen from behind his ear – shut his ledger – and opening
the swing door of his counter for me, asked me into the back parlour.

'Of importance to the parish you said, if I understood you aright?'

'Yes, Mr. Swale! and I was told, that from your interesting yourself so warmly
in such matters, you were the fittest person to come to.'

'Why, yes, I have spent a world of time on the parish concerns, as I may say;
though its all spilt porridge. I get no thanks for my pains; but blame – blame
– blame, all the year round.'

'That's very hard, Mr. Swale.'

'True, though! I can't move out o' doors but I'm attacked with "Pray, Mr.
Swale, do speak to the vestry about that sewer; it's a nuisance and a shame to have
it flooding every thing about." Or, "Mr. Swale, I suppose we may thank you for
the additional rate[179] this quarter, mayn't we?" I'm not even safe in my own shop,
Sir, from such attacks. Thus it comes of being a public man, as you see.'

'I was told also,' said I, 'it might be necessary to speak with one Hawkins.'

'No use! no use, at all, I tell you!' speaking quick; 'for between you and me
this Hawkins, who sets himself up as somebody, is, under the rose,[180] no better
than he should be.'

'So I had a hint,' said I, pretending to hesitate. 'Something about the bells of
the chime, I hear; though I don't pretend to understand your parish concerns.'

'Yes, Sir! This man, as I say – but it must go no farther – is no better than he
should be; and in this very case of the bells, he has jobbed away a world of money
from the funds. But all things have an end, and so has a pike-staff. I say nothing,
but you'll see.'

'Hawkins, then,' I continued, improving upon his hints, 'won't be employed
about the belfry again, I suppose?'

'No, that I promise you; but I say nothing. The chap himself understands
well enough that his nose is out of joint[181] in that quarter.'

'Then,' said I, brightening up as if a new light had flashed upon me, 'perhaps
it has been all a trick of his contrivance?'

'What? What trick do ye mean?' said Swale, looking like a puzzled cob[182] at
a cross-road.

'Why, this accident of the chimes, you know;' assuming the fact to be within
his knowledge, the better to get round him.

'Accident of the chimes! I've heard nothing on't yet! What is it, pray?'

'Lord, Sir! I thought you must have known all about the robbery; and I came
on purpose to inform you where I accidentally discovered that the scamps had
concealed the bells.'

I looked with keen anxiety to see how my story went down the gizzard of the sleek draper; but I could make out little from his meaningless face. He paused for a second or so, as a good general will always do before he ventures upon a plan of operations; and at last, to my great delight, said, –

'A most serious matter, truly, Sir! – both burglary and sacrilege; and if Hawkins is concerned, – though I hope not, upon my sincerity, – why it will ruin him out and out,[183] which may God forbid! I don't like the man; no more don't he like me. He has used me very ill – very ill indeed; but what of that? Such a fall as this would be too much for the poor fellow! – Sacrilege and burglary! Good God!'

'I said nothing, Mr. Swale, if you recollect, against this Hawkins; but I know where the bells are now. He may be concerned or not, – that is no affair of mine; though if you have any desire to save him in a quiet way from disgrace and ruin, I should advise you to get some trusty person to accompany you, bring the bells back, and nobody will be the wiser.'

'As you say, it would be worth thinking of this.'

'Yes, it would be an awful thing to be sure,' continued I, 'if your neighbour were to be found guilty of such crimes. I am happy, my dear sir, to find that the world has not over-rated your good heart.'

'Why, indeed, I am rather too good many times, as my Missis tells me. It is a failing I have, and I shouldn't like this to come so very hard upon poor Hawkins, though he has used me very ill. But if I could contrive to do the thing in a private way,' (chuckling at the notion,) 'it would give me such a power over him, don't you see? It would be the very thing, to the nines!'[184]

When I had got my scheme to work well so far, I had less difficulty in arranging the subsequent operations. I told Swale a long cock-and-bull[185] story – which the reader will readily excuse – of having been crossing the Heath from Highgate after night-fall; of meeting with some suspicious fellows loaded with booty; of my dogging them, from curiosity, till they deposited their burdens; and finally, of my learning, from their conversation, that it was no less than the bells of Hampstead chimes which they had daringly carried off. To strengthen Swale's suspicions on the subject, I told him that I did hear them mention the name of Hawkins more than once; but whether it were his neighbour or not, I could not tell.

I offered to conduct him to the very spot on the Heath where I had seen the bells deposited. He accepted my offer, and accompanied by a constable, who was a stout fellow and a trusty friend of his, we set out on our expedition – Swale in a great quandary how he should act so as to add to his reputation for vigilance towards the parish interests, and at the same time to acquire an influence over his rural vestry man, Hawkins, which should make him his humble servant to all succeeding time.

CHAPTER XX.

Lachrymal fate of the vestry men – Wrestliana[186] at Mother Red-Cap's – Gipsy
law proclaimed on the Heath – Higglesworth's Carmen Triumphale.[187]

I FELT some anxiety lest Wilton might not have succeeded so well as I had done; but I had provided for his failure, if fortune should not smile on him. I had resolved, be the case as it might, to lead Swale and his assistant to the gipsies' sand-pit, as the traces of the fire and the straw that lay about would be evidence good enough for them that a breach of the vestry laws had been there made; while at the same time I should regret, with assumed sorrow, the non-discovery of the lost bells, and leave them to lament their disappointment.

Wilton, however, though he had a very different sort of man to deal with, had been dextrous enough to beguile him into the snare. Hawkins, at the time in question, was enjoying the contents of a pot of beer at a neighbouring ale-house; and Wilton prudently allowed him to swig the last drop before he broached his errand; when he took him aside, to avoid any cross-questioning from third parties, which might have defeated his purpose.

Hawkins, I have said, was a very different person from the sleek draper, being a straightforward, rough, burly, savage-looking man; and, though neither very tall nor very powerful, he was more likely to enforce his wishes with a blow than to gain them by cunning or conciliation. He was, indeed, implicated most deeply in the parish jobbing aforesaid; though it did not arise through any scheming of his own, but was part of the machinery played off by Swale to gain over his consent to other jobs; and when he was found to be mulish and refractory in cases where his vote had been counted upon as purchased by his belfry bills, Swale veered about, threw him off, and saddled him with all the odium of the chime jobs, besides throwing out inuendos, of mysterious import, of his secret traffic with the gipsies in articles belonging to his trade, – a hint which the draper readily took from the strong opposition which Hawkins had made in the vestry to the notice on the board. He had, indeed, been argued or rather shamed down in this affair, and had at length given a tardy vote for the measure; but he had said enough in favour of the gipsies to furnish Swale with a weapon for his annoyance, which the draper was not slow in using.

All these particulars Wilton soon discovered from Hawkins himself; for, as has been said, be was a straight-forward man, and took a pleasure in relating his vestry grievances. After hearing enough to understand the trim[188] of the man, Wilton began his play by remarking, –

'From what you have just now said, Mr. Hawkins, I fear this will be rather an awkward business I have to inform you of, as I foresee it may give your enemy, Swale, a handle to accuse you of something unpleasant.'

'What the devil do you mean?' said he, in some alarm, though his countenance would have indicated him a stranger to fear.

'Why, about the bells of the chimes, which have been carried off by the gipsies!'

'The devil they have! Then, by the waunds,[189] I'm in for it smack![190] Swale will take care to make it a hair in my neck[191] by hook or by crook.[192] A deuced[193] unlucky thing it is, just at this moment, I know!'

When he thus saw his game all fair, Wilton proceeded, as had been concerted between us, to tell him the same story as I had done to Swale about the bells being concealed in a sand-pit on the Heath, and to offer himself as a guide for their recovery. Hawkins was not sufficiently shrewd (supposing the story to have been true,) to turn the circumstance to his own advantage; but Wilton readily suggested that it would save all disagreeables to bring the bells quietly back, replace them in the belfry, and say nothing about it.

If the gipsies were still at the sand-pit, it would not, as Hawkins knew, be very easy to make them part with their sacrilegious plunder. The straight-forward man did not much like this; but the fear of being implicated in so serious a charge as sacrilege, and his consciousness of having, in former cases, fingered so much of the parish money on account of these very bells, made him give a reluctant consent to be guided by Wilton to the Heath.

Wilton had gained his point sooner than I, who had had to listen to the prosing[194] of Swale about his vestry exploits. As I had rightly anticipated, neither of the sages had ever dreamt of visiting the belfry to ascertain the reality of the loss, before they commenced their search. The catastrophe, or rather the *denouement*,[195] was at hand; and Wilton and I were prepared for the worst, if our plot should be prematurely blown, by securing our retreat, under the colour of the night, either to Highgate or towards Finchley.[196]

As I was drawing near with Swale and the constable to the sand-pit, – which the reader may recollect was on the east of the Heath, near the group of tall firs behind the Three Spaniards – I thought I could distinguish voices in that direction, and I was all on tiptoe to know whether it could be Wilton and Hawkins.

'What if we should take your friend in the very act of colleaguing with the fellows?' I whispered to Swale.

'Nothing more likely!' said the draper; 'only I don't much like the job. Hawkins is a very devil of a fellow, and has a pique at me besides. Lud!197 Sir! he wouldn't stand a jot to murder me outright!'

'Do you really think so?' said I, in a tone of mock sympathy.

I perceived that the draper was under grievous bodily fear, and very unwilling to advance upon the unknown persons before us. The constable had more mettle in him, and paced it proudly; of which Swale took immediate advantage by falling cautiously into his rear.

'Who comes?' said a hard voice from the bottom of the sand-pit.

'Gad-a-mercy!'198 gasped out the draper in a sort of stifled cry. 'It is the very man by all that's gracious! What shall I do? He will murder me, to a dead certainty!'

'Hark!' I heard Wilton say; 'the gipsies, I daresay, coming back for their booty! But you know how to manage them, Mr. Hawkins!'

'Seize him!' whispered Swale, in a great flurry, to the constable. 'Seize him, and we'll help you to secure him!' – meaning after he was secured.

'Yes, do!' said I, 'and we can then make our own terms with him.'

The constable, who considered himself more than a match for Hawkins, sprang upon him and collared him; while Wilton and I could scarcely restrain ourselves from bursting out into a loud laugh. At the commencement of the onslaught, the draper had got behind me for protection, trembling at every joint with the fears of death, and wishing, I have no doubt, that the whole chime of bells was at the bottom of the Red Sea, and himself safe in his back parlour. Hawkins was not a man to yield without a struggle. He stood fiercely up to the constable, and lent him such a blow as put him in great danger of losing his perpendicular.199

'Gad-a-mercy!' muttered the draper; 'he will certainly murder us all!'

The constable, however, recovered his balance, made himself known, produced his staff, and told Hawkins that he felt it to be his painful duty to take him into custody for a matter which he must know too well to require any explanation of it from him. Hawkins surrendered without farther resistance; and as soon as the draper saw that the danger of death had passed away, he came out from behind me, pretended the utmost pity for the misfortune of Hawkins, and offered his services to assist him.

'Assist me, indeed!' said Hawkins. 'By the waunds, it is all a deep-laid plot to ruin me! My name's John Hawkins, and I want none of your pity!'

'Only tell us where you have hid the bells, and we'll hush up the matter for good,' said Swale.

'Bell me no bells, I tell you, neighbour Sneak! I know nothing on[200] 'em – you know I don't; though by the waunds I'll swear you do!'

While this and similar altercation was going on in the bottom of the sand-pit, Wilton and I stole off unperceived till we got to the edge of the high bank above them; when, bursting out into a loud laugh, we cried –

'O you crazy, crack-witted fools! The bells are all safe and untouched in the belfry! O you precious pair of ninny-hammers![201] You'll be the laughing-stock of the whole parish!'

And herewith we took to our heels along the Heath, with some fear of the constable, who was really a powerful man, in our hearts, but with more delight at having succeeded in hoaxing our enemies the vestry men.

We had not yet done with them. The hoax was only known to themselves, and they would take care to keep it quiet. Were any of us, on the other hand, to repeat the story, we might not gain credit; but if we actually procured a cloud of witnesses[202] from the village, the scene would be capital. Away, then, we ran, accosting every body we could meet, to tell them the story of the wild-goose chace after the parish bells; and in a very short time we had the pleasure of seeing a crowd of ragamuffin boys and idle blackguards assembling to celebrate the return of the bell-hunters. We only waited to hear the first shout of laughter that greeted them; for it might have been dangerous to expose ourselves after playing off a hoax of this kind.

We again crossed the Heath; and, on coming to the Three Spaniards, thought it would be no harm to drop in upon Higglesworth, if he were still there, and give him a veritable history, with embellishments to match, of the marvellous adventures of Hawkins and Swale in their bell expedition – concealing, of course, our own share in the business.

We found the old boy as we had left him – at his third pot and his sixth pipe, at the very least; but the heat of the parlour fire, as he averred, but which we understood to mean the fumes of the beer and tobacco, had rendered him quite stupid and lumpish. His eyes were glimmering and flickering like a lamp about to expire; his volubility of tongue was reduced to a sort of half intelligible grunt; and it was a question whether his ears were now of any more use than that of proclaiming him an ass.[203]

As we could make nothing of Higglesworth in this his blessed state of oblivis-cence, we proceeded to Highgate, and procured lodgings for the night, as we both voted a bivouac among the hazel-bushes in Bishop's Wood to be a bore not to be thought of; so much had a single day's separation from our gipsy compan-ions brought us back to former habits.

By day-break we were again at our board, which we found safe among the bushes; and Wilton worked with the more alacrity, that it would now tell much better since the hoax than before; though, as we had become known to so many persons, it would not be so very safe to put it up. We were determined, however, to stand all hazards in accomplishing what we had set our minds upon; but the painting would not be sufficiently dry till the following night, and accordingly, as soon as we could no longer see to work, we set out again in quest of more adventures.

As we dared not well venture back to Hampstead, we took the road towards Holloway,[204] and went into the parlour of an ale-house by the road-side – the Mother Red-Cap,[205] if I rightly remember. We there found the chimney-corners monopolized by two men, who seemed to be horse-jockeys, from their dress and the subjects of their conversation; as they were talking eagerly about 'fine condition,' 'good wind,' 'broad chest,' and other things which I inferred to apply to the horse whose points they were discussing.

I soon found I was mistaken, and that they were talking of pugilists,[206] a class of men of which I knew little more than by vague report; but upon this subject Wilton was quite at home, and at once entered into deep discourse with the men, though from ignorance of the slang which they used, I could not make out half of what was said. I was not of course ignorant of gipsy slang; but the flash[207] of the prize ring was an entirely different dialect, which to this hour I have never made much progress in studying.

We learned, in course, that our parlour companions were themselves high in pugilistic fame, and had gained laurels at Moulsey Hurst[208] and other places of celebrity. They were delighted with Wilton's complete knowledge of their art, or, as they called it, *science*, and at once volunteered to introduce him to their London friends.

As the men professed to be so great admirers of athletic sports, and as I could not follow their slang, I thought that I might try to give the conversation a little turn by asking their opinion of wrestling,[209] of which I was a better judge, and which I could not help considering as a more elegant and no less manly sport. The pugilists looked as much out of sorts at me as I had previously done at them; and if I had been alone, and the two against me, I should have had to yield my opinions without a struggle; but Wilton, who was in a rich vein for talking, took up the theme, and discoursed as profoundly of *hipping, back-hold,* and *outside* and *inside striking*,[210] as he had just been doing of *stopping hits, left-handers,* and *second wind.*

'I look upon wrestling,' he went on, 'to be the finest manly sport ever invented. It is quite an angelic and heavenly exercise – witness the instance of the angel wrestling with Jacob – whereas boxing is much more rude and boorish.'

'What, Sir!' said one of the pugilists. 'Do you mean to insult us? By jingo,[211] you had as well take care what you say!'

'Not so, friend!' said Wilton. 'I meant no insult. If you prefer pugilism, I give you leave to do so, while you will allow me, in the same way, to give the preference to wrestling.'

'Don't you be saucy, Sir, I tell you!' retorted the pugilist. 'A pretty pup,[212] you, to tell me *you will give me leave* to do any thing! You deserve to be twisted into inches for such a piece of impudence; don't he, Bill?'

'Goles![213] Jack, how do I know?' said Bill; 'only I'd like to see 'un wrestle a fall or two, if so be he's so main prime[214] on't.'

I was somewhat afraid of a quarrel when I saw things take this turn; and, from the apparent weight of the men, Wilton, strong as he was, would have had little chance; but I was glad to see the difference proposed to be settled by wrestling, as, from what I had seen him do, I had great confidence in Wilton's skill in the art, which is of much more importance than strength. Wilton said he was ready for either of them, who chose to try his mettle, for any stake they liked to name.

The mention of a stake operated like a spell upon the first speaker. He apologised to Wilton for his hasty language, applauded his spirit, and, as the highest eulogium in his vocabulary, pronounced that he had no doubt of his being real *game*.[215] All the while I remarked that he was measuring Wilton with his eye, to form an estimate, I suppose, of his capabilities; and having satisfied himself perhaps that a stripling like him could have no chance against his own well-strung thews and sinews, whatever might be his skill, he resolved to make up a match of it, as he termed it.

'What say you, Bill, to fifty or a hundred a-side? I think Lord — ' (naming our Cambridge friend) 'would tip the blunt[216] to back me.'

'Goles! Jack, how do I know?' said Bill. 'But if so be, who is to come it for this here chip?'[217]

'I'll sport fifty on the chance, for my own stake!' said Wilton.

I gazed at him in astonishment. I thought he was absolutely mad. Fifty pounds! I had never been master of half the sum in my life. I did not know that Wilton was worth ten, nor even five; and if he had fifty pounds, to throw it away thus on the chance of a wrestling match appeared to me to be the very summit of folly and madness.

It was looked upon in a very different light by the pugilists, with whom Wilton had in a few minutes risen prodigiously into favour. They took up the subject as warmly as if their existence had depended on it; and instead of proceeding, as I expected, to decide the contest on the spot, they began to talk of putting it off for a week, or even for a month; and of meetings to make good the stakes, make up purses, and I know not what besides.

It was finally arranged that Wilton, accompanied by me, should meet them at Belcher's, Castle Tavern, Holborn,[218] to settle all these matters, and fix the time and place. In the meantime we all joined in a brisk carouse of good fellowship till an early hour next morning; when Wilton and I tumbled into bed for an hour or two, and after breakfast returned to Bishop's Wood to give a few finishing touches to our vestry board. The inscription ran thus: –

NOTICE.

To all and sundry: – The Vestry men of the Parish of HAMPSTEAD *for the time being, and all and every who advised or caused a former wicked and illegal board to be posted up in this place, and more particularly* JOSHUA SWALE, *Draper, and* JOHN HAWKINS, *Bell-Hanger, are hereby denounced and forewarned, by authority of the Gipsies encamping on this Heath, to quit the said Parish within twenty-four hours, under penalty of their severe displeasure and the utmost rigour of law.*

(Signed)　*J. W. Clk. pro temp.*[219]

As we had to use great caution in putting up this board, we did not approach the scene of operation till about midnight, when all would be quiet, and we could go leisurely to work undisturbed. We did not pull down the vestry notice, but placed ours directly over it, so as to cover its obnoxious announcement. Just as I was driving the last nail, we were startled by what seemed to be the sound of voices approaching us from the direction of the Three Spaniards; and in a little we could plainly distinguish something like singing, but of a very cracked or very tipsy description. By-and-bye, I could make out the words of the song, from behind the tree where we had squatted to conceal ourselves. One of the verses ran thus, to the tune of the Jolly Miller:[220] –

> There was a dapper draper once,
> 　And a vestry man was he;
> He bolted his beef and guzzled his ale,
> 　And scrubb'd the poor, perdie.[221]
>
> And aye the chorus of his song,
> 　So merrily chaunted he;
> A slice of the brown, and ale to wash 't down,
> 　I pray you give to me.

There could be no mistaking the tipsy voice of the singer, much less the burden of his song: it was Higglesworth reeling home from the Three Spaniards, as merry as Sir John Barleycorn[222] could make him, and venting his humour on his absent friend Swale, – a man for whom he had a particular affection of a certain kind; that is, he liked him as a draper, but disliked him as a vestry man, and so on to an interminable series of paralleled contrasts (if that be not an Hibernianism[223]), which I shall not take the trouble to enumerate.

At first we resolved to let Higglesworth pass on without speaking to him; but Wilton suggested the propriety of reading, or rather repeating, our 'Notice' in his hearing; and in order to make it appear the more singular, Wilton repeated it slowly in a loud and clear voice, whilst I followed him like a church clerk at the Litany,[224] or Dr. Slop in Tristram Shandy,[225] with his volume of curses, humming a bass to my uncle Toby's Lillibullero.[226]

'Who the dickens[227] are you?' shouted Higglesworth.

It was no part of our plan, however, to discover ourselves. We therefore treated him, for answer, with a second edition of our 'Notice;' in which we took care to introduce his own name, designating him 'Toper of the Three Spaniards;' and then we made off, and left him to explain the occurrence as well as his tipsy brain would enable him. We could hear him, as we retreated, ejaculating –

'A queer concern, isn't it? A mighty queer concern!'

We were desirous enough to see the sequel of our devices for the annoyance of the sages of the Hampstead Vestry; but we were more desirous of keeping ourselves out of their clutches, as it was hard to tell what construction the law might put upon our pranks. We therefore set out to join our gipsy friends at Norwood, where we arrived early next morning.

CHAPTER XXI.

The witch of Chorley – Congress at Belcher's – Black-leg speculations – At it again on Wimbledon Common – Bivouac at Norwood – Wanderings ended – Jem Bucks and the Author at Bow Street.

THE day drew near for our meeting the pugilists at Belcher's, to arrange the wrestling match. Wilton was in the highest spirits about it, and talked of his victory over the braggadocio,[228] as if it had been already gained. I confess I was rather doubtful of the day, when I considered the superior weight and muscle of his antagonist; and yet I trusted much to Wilton's skill.

I recollected well a proof of this, which I had myself experienced at Chorley in Lancashire, on our journey southwards. We had left our companions, and gone into the town on a frolic. The appearance of a blooming bar-maid bouncing about at the door of one of the inns, caught Wilton's eye; and we went in to have a glass of something from the little *witch* with the rosy cheeks. A coarse print, which was hanging in the parlour, led us to talk of wrestling; and as I was aware from what I had heard Wilton say that he was skilled in the art, I asked him what he considered the best manœuvres.

'O!' said he, 'the *palsy-touch* and the *fank*[229] against the world. I'll undertake by these to put you down, Tom, if you choose to risk it, without taking hold of you at all.'

'Done!' replied I. 'You will find it harder than you think.'

I accordingly stood up, quite confident that he would fail; but down I went in the twinkling of an eye, though I could not for my life tell how, as I scarcely felt him touch me. It was rather a serious tumble, however; for I struck the sharp corner of a table with my back, and was so much hurt that I could not rise. The pretty bar-maid came running to see what was the matter, and to console me; but I was ungrateful enough to wish her in purgatory, because, if it had not been for the charms of her chubby Lancashire face, I might have escaped my back-bruise, which was so painful as almost to prevent me from speaking, or even daring to breathe with freedom.

After this accident, I could not fail to give Wilton due credit for his skill in wrestling.

At the time appointed we repaired to Belcher's; where we found our men already assembled, waiting for us, and impatiently expecting Lord Blank to back Jack for fifty pounds, or any other stake which could be made good. Lord Blank, however, did not think fit to make his appearance, for a reason which will afterwards be seen.

When they had waited for his Lordship till it was obvious he did not intend to come, a brisk play of impressive whispers and talking aside commenced, of the import of which Wilton and I were kept in ignorance. At length the whisperers seemed to come to a comfortable understanding with each other; when a young gentleman, who was addressed by the title of Sir Byam, came forward, and, apologising for the absence of his friend Lord Blank, said he would take it upon himself to stake from fifty to a hundred on Jack.

Another youth, who had much the air of an apprentice to the driver of a mail-coach,[230] though I understood he could boast of the addition of Honourable[231] to his name, said he would back THE CHIP,[232] as they had agreed to nickname Wilton, for the round hundred.

Upon this it was agreed that Wilton should keep his own money – bet it, if he so liked, – and that Sir Byam Finch and the Hon. W. W. Wansty would make good a hundred pounds a-side – the match to take place on Wimbledon Common.[233] Wilton insisted upon having it quite a private thing, as he did not wish to set himself up for a prize-wrestler, and was unwilling to be known.

It was altogether an affair so new to me, that I knew not what to make of it. I had seen so little of public life, and had been so much in the country, that I could not comprehend how young gentlemen of family and title should be found 'hand and glove,' as the proverb has it, with pugilists and prize-fighters; nor how Mr. Wansty could think of hazarding a hundred pounds on the wrestling powers of a young man, of which and of whom he knew nothing. He seemed to me to be a thousand degrees at least more mad than Wilton himself had been in offering to stake his own fifty. I did not then know so much as I have since learned of this species of gambling; but Wilton, I found, was no stranger to it, as he had passed his noviciate at Oxford, where, I have been told, it is more deeply studied than crabbed Greek or musty Logic.

We were returning to the gipsy encampment at Norwood through St. George's Fields,[234] when a person muffled up in a Spanish cloak appeared to be dogging our steps; for he passed us more than once, and pried very inquisitively into our faces. As this was a circumstance we could not explain, we concluded he had mistaken us; though our recent frolics at Hampstead awakened unpleasant suppositions that we might be hunted after to suffer for our nonsense. The man in the Spanish cloak, at length, in order to make sure of what he was about, ventured to accost us, and asked me if my name was Wilton.

'I am the man!' said Wilton, breasting himself up with a bold air to the stranger.

I fancied I had before heard the stranger's voice, though I could not recollect where; but when he began to talk of Belcher's, we soon recognised him to be the identical Lord Blank whom we had practised on in the lane near Cambridge.

'I wished to be in it,' his Lordship went on, slanging in the swell[235] style. 'All fair and fine as a *Finch*, you know,' giving me a hard punch in the ribs with his elbow. 'Couldn't go it, though – sent Wansty to come it for Chip here. Wansty is in full feather,[236] mind ye, boys! – quite flush and all that. A prime go to do him,[237] wouldn't it? What say you, Chip? Some five thousand or so would be no bad move, and could do us no harm – not a bit! All as easy as a glove[238] to pluck[239] him – up to all that, eh? Cursedly plucked myself – most blown up.[240] Safe yet though, and Wansty must come it to plume[241] me again, that's all. But no blues[242] – hate pigeon[243] colours! An entered rook,[244] by George! – black for ever! – bravo!'

His Lordship continued for some time in this elegant and very intelligible strain of gambling slang with great volubility and eagerness, occasionally favouring my ribs with a punch, to aid my understanding, and prove that he despised Chesterfield.[245] I could not withal make out what he wanted; but Wilton soon discovered that his Lordship's intentions were far from honourable; being no less than to lead on his friend Wansty to bet as many thousands as he could be gulled to risk upon Wilton, with a previous understanding that Wilton was to allow himself to be the loser.

To me this was still more incomprehensible than all I had yet seen in these strange transactions. Notwithstanding the rambling life I had lately led, and the not very strait-laced morality which I had witnessed, I had not the remotest conception that gentlemen – much less noblemen – would have descended to such low villainy and blackguardism. I have since come to know that such transactions are by no means rare; though I should hope they are not so common as is sometimes reported.

Lord Blank was, indeed, ripe for any thing. From what we had seen and heard of him at Cambridge, we were aware of his propensities and his headlong career of dissipation. The failure of his lottery scheme, on which he had set his heart, made him turn to more desperate shifts; and, in company with Sir Byam Finch, who knew the state of his finances, and only made a tool of him to serve his own purposes, he had decamped from College without leave, and come up to Town to try his luck as a desperate *black-leg*, as titled or fashionable sharpers are usually denominated.

The wrestling match they had voted from the first to be fine – exquisite – just the thing! – if they could hook in Wansty, or any other well-feathered flat.[246] Wilton they had reckoned upon as too poor to resist temptation, if he were not, as they guessed him to be, one of their own class. The latter may account, perhaps, for the free manner in which Lord Blank had disclosed his villainous plans of plunder.

Wilton listened to his Lordship with apparent complaisance, though his whole heart was swelling with indignant rage at the thoughts of being supposed capable of such base and unprincipled doings; but he quickly – almost instinctively – determined to catch the sharpers in their own snare. He accordingly evaded giving any direct promise to Lord Blank; but though he did not commit himself, he said enough to make him proceed with his bets for the purpose of plundering Wansty.

It will be perceived that, if they had Wilton secure, they might carry on their villainy to any given amount, provided they could get other gulls besides Wansty to come forward. With this view, and regardless of the promise to Wilton of making it a private match, they set themselves to work to hook in every body on the sporting list who was supposed to have money to lose. To make their play the surer, Jack, who was of their party, was put under strict training, to prevent any accident if Wilton should desert the cause in the hour of need.

Wilton, on his part, was no less assiduous to prepare himself for defeating them. He required no training. The gipsy life he had been leading had rendered him as hardy as a mountaineer; but he justly deemed that he could not make himself too perfect in all the resources of the art of wrestling, and was at it morning, noon, and night, either with me or any of the gipsies who happened to be in the way.

In this manner he went through, in regular succession, the *half-turn*, – the *fank*, – the *sailor's twist*, – *hooking*, – *back-hold*, – *outside* and *inside striking*, – the *palsy-touch*, – the *left-bend*, – *tripping*, – *splicing*, – *hankering*, – *skying*, – *hipping*, – *lushing*, – and all the other pieces of art which make the finished wrestler. He had perfected himself so fully in all these, that he was confident of throwing any man, though double his weight and strength, to whom they were unknown; for he could manœuvre so rapidly, that the man would be down before he considered the play begun, as I myself had so severely experienced at Chorley.

The day arrived; and we set out for Wimbledon Common to meet, and, if possible, to foil this gang of titled and fashionable sharpers, who had reckoned upon reaping a rich harvest, particularly from Wansty, whose head at the best was none of the soundest; whilst the coming into possession of an enormous fortune had greatly unsettled the very little wit and prudence which he naturally inherited.

As we approached the ground, Wilton was surprised and much incensed to see crowds of horsemen and carriages of all descriptions thronging to the appointed spot. It was a gross breach of the agreement, and he could have drawn back without any impeachment of his honour: it was no more, indeed, than might have been expected from such fellows as we had to do with. He was determined, however, to proceed at all hazards, now that he had gone thus far; and if he were successful in humbling them by gaining the victory which they had offered him a bribe to lose, their lengthened faces would be the better exposed before so many spectators.

The ring was formed. Jack made his appearance in high spirits, calling vociferously for 'Chip.' A creature of Sir Byam's had detained Wilton, to ascertain whether they might still count upon him; and he answered promptly that he had not changed his mind since he saw Lord Blank on the subject. This was a cheerer, the communication of which was soon apparent among all the confederates. They offered bets in favour of Jack at any odds; and, indeed, his muscular and manly appearance made me quail for my adventurous friend.

Wilton, however, confident in his art, advanced fearlessly; and before his opponent could fix his hold, he hankered[247] his heel, and treated him with a sailor's twist that sent him reeling to the ground. Jack was not prepared for such quick play, and looked very sheepish as he gathered himself up. He had intended, indeed, to let Wilton gain the first fall to encourage the gulls[248] to bet freely: he fancied also that Wilton knew as much; but to be put down thus, when he had scarcely taken his ground, was what he had not reckoned upon.

As the match was limited to the best of five falls,[249] Jack thought it was now time to look about him, lest Wilton, after all, might back out and lurch them. It was not Wilton's plan, however, to grant him time to look about or consider what he should do; for he no sooner saw him on his feet again, and ready, than he tried him with his palsy-touch, and down he went again as if he had slipped on a sheet of ice. Sir Byam, still hoping that this was nothing but a bait for the gulls, betted higher than ever on Jack; but he had begun to have his misgivings, and looked terribly mortified. I thought I could perceive him clenching his fists from rage at suffering such an affront.

'A thousand to one on Chip!' cried Wansty.

'Done!' said Sir Byam.

'Done!' said Lord Blank, in the same breath.

Wilton's eyes flashed round the circle as if he would have annihilated the gang; and he advanced upon Jack with a look which he but too well understood. Jack saw, indeed, that their game was up; and, instead of gaining, ruin would be the consequence to many of his best friends. He therefore strung every muscle of his body for the third throw, which would be final if Wilton were successful. Wilton's fault lay in being vain of his art, and fond of displaying his skill in its resources. Instead, therefore, of repeating the manœuvres with which he had already been successful, he must needs try the left bend and striking inside; but before he could perform these, Jack had established a back-hold, and by sheer strength skyed him, and sent him down.

Wilton was a little disconcerted; but resolving, at my suggestion, to redeem his error, he tried his palsy-touch again, accompanied with a fank, which instantly put Jack upon his all-fours. Here ended all the high hopes of the gang: they were completely balked of the booty they had made sure of; and instead of pillaging Wansty, he had pillaged them. The scene was sadly changed. Instead of the eager looks and bright faces which had a moment before been seen all around, there appeared gloom and despair; while curses were muttered, and revenge threatened in tones not to be misunderstood. Had it not been that we possessed evidence of Lord Blank's tampering with Wilton's honour, I have no doubt that the gang would have accused Jack of being in the pay of Wansty; but conscious of their own blackness, I suppose, they were afraid of bringing the accusation.

The fifth fall was now a matter of no moment; but Wilton won it as cleverly as he had done the other three, and was accordingly proclaimed victor. Flushed with his success, and eager to vindicate his prowess, he said he was ready to try any man on the ground, the best of three falls for any stake not below fifty. But nobody answered his challenge, at which I was just as well pleased; for I was thoroughly disgusted with the base knavery of the gang, and wished to have nothing more to do with such unprincipled fellows, titled and *noble* as some of them were.

Wilton had betted his fifty upon himself, which was taken; and he consequently left the ground fifty pounds in pocket. He might have won much more, but he was by no means fond of gambling; though he understood it better than many who gave themselves up to its infatuating practice.

We made off as soon as we could, and left the gang to digest their well-merited disappointment, as they best might. Lord Blank, we supposed, must have been left altogether *hors de combat*,²⁵⁰ as Buonaparte's bulletins have it, for he was pennyless at Cambridge when he conceived the grand scheme of the lottery ticket; he was no better, by his own confession, when we met him in St. George's Fields; and this day he had accumulated debts of honour to the amount of some thousands, under the notion that he was certain to win. That such a man (or rather boy-man) should employ desperate shifts – honourable or dishonourable – was no wonder.

At night we returned *incog.*²⁵¹ to the gipsy encampment at Norwood; and I at least slept sounder, wrapt in my coarse blanket, and my head pillowed on straw, than Sir Byam or Lord Blank on their beds of down at Mivart's Hotel.²⁵²

I now leave the reader to conceive that I spent more than a year among the gipsies, and several more in subsequent wandering and adventure; till, becoming

sick of the uncertainty of a precarious livelihood, I resolved to obtain some settled occupation, which would place me above the necessity of the shifts which
I was often compelled to make by the pressure of want. My restless habits, however, were ill fitted for any of the avocations which suggested themselves to me.

I could not submit again to imprison myself at the irksome desk of a counting-house; I had neglected my books too much to think of becoming an usher[253]
in a school; I could not degrade myself by wearing a badge of servitude in the
form of a livery,[254] – death would be preferable to this; I had also forgotten
Hump-back's lessons of 'genteel politeness,' so that I was quite disqualified to
become a waiter at an inn; and nothing occurred to me that I could endure, but
the situation of a game-keeper, in which, from the specimen I had seen, I should
at once have a settled home and an occasional brush with poachers to keep my
blood moving. Unfortunately, I was no marksman; and this was a hopeless dis-
qualification for such a calling.

I was one day musing on these various prospects in St. James's Park,[255] when,
to my great surprise, my old friend Jem Bucks came up to me, dressed in a spruce
blue coat and scarlet waistcoat. I had not seen him since we parted in the ale-
house at Lancaster, and we agreed to adjourn to the nearest tap – both, of course,
having much to tell – in order to learn each other's story with more spirits.
Bucks, like myself, had soon left the players; had been again to sea in a Manks[256]
smuggler; had afterwards been guard to the Exeter[257] Mail; and was now on the
establishment at Bow Street.[258]

On mentioning my present difficulties, he proposed that I should become
one of them. This was precisely what accorded with the views I had been forming
of a life, partly regular and partly adventurous. It was well suited to my habits, to
what I may call the *education* I had been lately receiving, to my connexion with
the gipsies, with whom I continued to keep up a good understanding; and I at
once embraced his proposal. My only objection was the scarlet waistcoat; which,
although not quite so bad and low as a livery, was still a badge I could have gladly
dispensed with.

Through the influence of Wilton, I obtained a recommendation which was
accepted; and I was admitted, sworn in, and commenced my duties among the
law-breakers, as I shall record in the next volume.

END OF VOL. I.

RICHMOND;

OR,

SCENES

IN THE

LIFE OF A BOW STREET OFFICER,

DRAWN UP FROM HIS PRIVATE MEMORANDA.

Some be'th of war, and some of woe,
And some of fun and fudge also,
Some of escapes, and guile, and death;
Also of love forsooth there be'th.

LE FRÊNE.

IN THREE VOLUMES.

VOL. II.

LONDON: HENRY COLBURN.
1827.

CONTENTS
OF
THE SECOND VOLUME.

CHAP. X.

Church-yard scenes – Sepulchral conclave of ruffians – Night researches in a family vault

CHAP. XI.

Night scenes in a ruined barn – The exiles of Erin in full chorus

CHAP. XII.

Forest scenes – Castle Malwood and the deer-stealer – Sir Byam Finch and Lord Blank at Lyndhurst

CHAP. XIII.

Vision of a forest nymph – Female sorrows – Intriguing and counter-working

CHAP. XIV.

Greek speculations upon a gentleman eccentric – Jones at Lyndhurst

CHAP. XV.

Wild horse-race on Lyndhurst lawn – The pigeon and the rooks – Irish method of doctoring a lame horse

CHAP. XVI.

All for love, and a fig for the world

CHAP. XVII.

Puzzled, not pleased

CHAP. XVIII.

Irish hopes and cottage pictures – The Hampshire magistrates and Mr. M—d – Smuggling arrangements

RICHMOND.

CHAPTER I.

The pains of office – Jem Bucks in haste – Mysterious affair at Roehampton – Maternal solicitude.

My first adventure in my new capacity gave me a strong interest in the sort of life I had now adopted, and compensated for many of the awkward and disagreeable feelings which I had to undergo. I was by this time tolerably well acquainted with London; but was personally a stranger to police transactions, and every thing at Bow Street was new to me.

At first, I had an indescribable notion that I was now degraded and shut out from all society, as every body has a dislike and horror at the very sight of an officer – caused, no doubt, by the very general prevalence of private unfair dealing and villainy, and the secret dread of unexpected detection which these must always produce. I found the officers themselves, however, a jovial set of fellows, – free, careless, merry, and full of anecdotes of their different exploits, which exhibited a more varied picture of human life than I had hitherto met with in all my wanderings.

Our tap-room parties were accordingly enlivened and interested with many a singular story of personal adventure, which took keen hold of my fancy, and made me desirous of signalising myself in similar exploits, – a desire which did not long remain ungratified.

The same spirit, indeed, which drove me at first from the inglorious drudgery of the Liverpool counting-house still haunted me, and will continue (it should appear) to accompany me to the grave; for though I often picture to myself a quiet cottage retreat for the remainder of my life in my native Derbyshire, and from year to year look forward to this as the summit of my hopes; yet, new adventures are always springing up and leading me, as at first, into unforeseen difficulties which must be encountered, or business which must be performed. My desire also for mingling in the bustle of the world and the eccentricities of life, remains unsatiated and insatiable.

At the period of which I am now speaking, namely, that immediately succeeding my enrollment at Bow Street, I was one night sitting alone in my little chamber, ruminating on the difference between its neat carpet, its cane-bottomed chairs, and the order and cleanliness of every thing about me, as compared with the litter of straw and all sorts of rubbish with which I had long been familiar in the gipsies' tents. I had ordered something hot for supper; and, alone as I was, intended to regale myself over a rummer[1] of mulled ale, with a glass of brandy therein. I was not, however, destined to enjoy any of these good things; for just as I was about to send a despatch for my ale, I heard Jem Bucks on the stairs below, with all the impress of haste which he usually assumed, calling out, –

'Tom! I say, Tom, my boy! you're wanted at the shop[2] in no time. Quick, I say!'

And in he bustled, panting and blowing; for in his haste he had outrun his wind.

'What is all this?' said I. 'What is the matter?'

'Some great affair I take it,' said Jem. 'There is such a to-do, you've no notion. First came a horseman, galloping as if he were going to the devil; and soon after a lady in a post-chaise and four, flying like Jehu.[3] Some extraordinary concern, it must be; and quality[4] people in it too. You may perhaps make your fortune on't.'

'How so, Jem? I'm but raw yet, you know. What can I do? A fortune! Ah, ha, ha! that's a good joke, upon my word!'

'I don't know, Tom; but you're to be in it, that's all; and I was despatched express to find you. Then come, my boy! and do your best for your debut.'

Jem knew nothing more of the circumstances; but I was on tiptoe[5] to learn why I was so particularly wanted, considering my inexperience in police business. I soon forgot my hot supper and my mulled ale, and hurried off with Bucks to the office, or *shop*, as he called it; when I was immediately introduced into the private room.

Here I found one of the magistrates with a lady who was in great agitation, walking about, wringing her hands, and at times sitting down, but immediately starting up again; while a gentleman stood by, making vain endeavours to console her distress.

'Oh! I shall never, never see him more!' she sobbed out. 'My darling little boy! He is gone – lost! I am sure, and I shall never see him again!'

The magistrate told her not to despair: every thing he could do should be tried; and, 'Here,' added he, 'comes the young man who will be most likely to assist us. Richmond!' he continued, addressing me, 'here is a very distressing case, in which your knowledge may prove of essential service; and if you are active, you shall be well rewarded.'

'O, yes!' cried the lady most impressively, 'any sum you please to name, if you bring me my little William once again! Any sum you please! I would give all I have to see him once more!'

I learned by degrees (for you never can get a straight-forward story in such cases,) that the little boy, whose disappearance had caused all this distress, had been riding on a pony, with a maid attending him, in the neighbourhood of Roehampton;[6] and the maid's curiosity having been taken up with a gipsy fortune-teller, the boy rode onwards, and had not been since heard of.

The pony had been found grazing on the farther side of the Heath, at the distance of two or three miles from where the maid had last seen him. The saddle and bridle, though new and handsome, were untouched; so that it was pretty evident, the boy, if he really were stolen, had been carried away by those who cared not for other plunder.

The disconsolate mother, and the gentleman who accompanied her, were both of opinion that the boy had been stolen by the gipsies, and that the fortune-teller purposely engaged the attention of the maid till they had accomplished their wicked design.

I could not help being of a different opinion; and hesitated not to tell them that I had been long acquainted with many tribes of this wandering race, but had never known nor heard of a crime of this kind being committed by them. It might be possible – I could not answer for the whole race of wanderers; but it was most unlikely, as there appeared to be no motive to induce them to the deed.

Beggars have been known to carry off genteel children, in order to strip them for the sake of their clothes; but here was the pony left with a saddle and bridle worth more than the boy's whole suit. Children have also been stolen to beg with, for the purpose of exciting more compassion; but the gipsies never beg at all: and besides, the boy, who was between three and four years of age, was rather too old to be effectively employed in this way.

The fortune-teller, however, appeared, from the description given, to be certainly a gipsy. She was said to be rather handsome, and apparently turned of twenty years of age. The account given of her dress, and the description altogether, led me to suppose that it was Wilton's Mary; and if it were, I was almost certain she could have no collusion in carrying off the little boy. The maid had observed no other gipsy near them, and had seen nobody speak to the boy: the imputation of the crime to the gipsies, therefore, appeared to me to be gratuitous and ill-founded.

This reasoning, which I urged with some eagerness, produced on the agitated mother an effect very different from what I intended or had foreseen; for, instead of weighing the probabilities of the case, (nobody, indeed, can reason or think when distracted, as she was,) she formed the notion that I wished to advocate the cause of my former friends, and screen them from blame. She did not, indeed, say so; but I soon perceived that some such notion had taken possession of her fancy.

The magistrate saw this as well as I did; but in order to divert her from it, he said, that as the circumstance was a very distressing one, for the purpose of making a thorough search and inquiry he would despatch the chief officer of the establishment along with me, as I was but young in the business; and he would answer on our parts for the utmost exertion being used.

It was now near ten o'clock at night, and it was proposed to put off our expedition till morning; but, to show my zeal in the cause, I urged the importance of losing no time and setting out instantly. It was favourable for this purpose that it was now the middle of summer, the weather being warm and fine. The gentleman, whom I understood to be the lady's brother, again told us to spare no expense, but procure whatever horses or carriages we might require in furthering our pursuit. A chaise and four was accordingly ordered at his suggestion, and we intended to drive to Putney Heath;[7] where I purposed to pay a midnight visit to such of my old friends as might have pitched their tents in that vicinity. I need scarcely say that I took care to have a brace of good pistols in my side pockets; without which, indeed, I never go out at night.

The poor mother insisted on accompanying us; but it was evidently beyond her strength, which had been much exhausted by the dreadful agitation she had suffered: yet her brother had the utmost difficulty in dissuading her. She would listen to nothing but the suggestions of her own distracted thoughts. In these, her little boy seemed to be uppermost; and she fancied that, by going with us, she should sooner see him. At last she was, partly by argument, and partly by gentle force, detained till we had departed.

I felt much for this lady, who appeared to be an uncommonly fine woman, and about thirty years of age, if I might judge; the period, when the bloom of youth begins to ripen into the graces of the matron, and the charm of intelligence to take the place of giddy though fascinating folly. She was very elegantly dressed; and from their style altogether, I was certain both were people of great wealth, if not of rank.[8] The chief officer, who knew something of the family by report, told me that the lady's name was Mrs. Manson; that she had brought her husband a very handsome fortune, though he did not want it, as he was immensely rich before his marriage. From the officer's account of him, however, he did not seem to deserve either a handsome wife or a good fortune, as he was reported to be exceedingly narrow and penurious, and would not part with a penny except with the utmost grudge.

Mrs. Manson's father had had some hints of this before the marriage; and as she was a favourite with him (she was likely to be a favourite, I thought, with every body who saw her), he had settled upon her something considerable, independent of the fortune which passed into the hands of Manson.[9] This money, it seems, proved to be a source of endless contention and ill-nature on his part; for spend it in what manner she would, he characterised it by the name of foolish extravagance.

It was said that Mrs. Manson had more than once come to the resolution of giving him up the whole of this annuity in order to keep peace; but her father strongly dissuaded her from the measure. The money was not Manson's: he had no claim upon it. He had received every shilling of the fortune promised him; and she might, if she pleased, chuck this into the Thames without being questioned by any body.

I had thought it singular that the boy's father did not appear in the business we were engaged upon; but when I learned these particulars, the circumstance ceased to appear so strange: for a narrow and avaricious disposition is seldom warmed by any of the finer affections of humanity. I pitied the lady much, who seemed to have thrown away her beauty and fine sensibility on a cold-blooded curmudgeon. Such matches, indeed, I have remarked, oftener occur among the wealthy and the noble than in the middle ranks; so fairly does Providence seem to balance the blessings of human nature.

CHAPTER II.

Night adventures on Putney Heath – A singular discovery.

I CONFESS I had not much hope of succeeding in our expedition; though I was certain, if my friends the gipsies had any hand in the business, I should not have much difficulty in recovering little William. I was by no means pleased, however, to be under the control of a superior, to whom all the merit would (as is usually the case) be given, while all the trouble would fall to my share.

I had submitted, indeed, in former days to be led – *once* by Jem Bucks, and *again* by Wilton; but those days were over. My apprenticeship was out. I had now begun to feel myself of more consequence, and was inclined to stand on my own ground. I had, therefore, to fall upon some device whereby I might get rid of my companion the chief officer, or at least detach myself from him as much as possible.

I therefore told him, what indeed was no more than the truth, that it would not be advisable for us to go both together amongst the gipsies, particularly as he had every chance of being recognised by them; and that they all had a mortal aversion to any sort of officer. The consequence would be, that if they could lend any assistance, we should lose their co-operation; which, as I was not yet known to them as an officer, I might effectually secure if I were to go alone, and make cautious inquiry. The time of the night, too, would naturally give them more cause for alarm, were we to come both at once upon any of the tents; for they were particularly alive to intrusions of this kind since the parish authorities had begun so keen a persecution against them.

They had good reason, indeed, to be in fear for themselves, and to keep a watchful look-out; since it was by no means an unfrequent occurrence for them to be taken up on suspicion of committing depredations which they never dreamed of, and to suffer imprisonment, and even condemnation, in consequence merely of their vagabond character, though altogether innocent of the charges against them.

These were satisfactory reasons why the chief officer should keep aloof, at least till I had smoothed the way a little. A rendezvous was accordingly agreed upon, while I crossed the common in search of the tents. As I knew all their usual haunts, I had no difficulty in finding the encampment of my old friends the Marshalls, faithfully guarded by Rover; who, as soon as he recognised me, changed his bark of defiance into a whirr of kindly greeting.

I found that Mary was not at home, having gone the day before to Norwood. I confess I did not like this. It created a suspicion that she might be concerned in carrying off the boy, as she had gone away on the very day he had disappeared, – most probably, as I now conjectured, to avoid disagreeable inquiries.

Marshall himself confessed to having seen a boy, answering the description of William, ride across the Heath on a pony; but he did not remark whither he had gone. At that time there was no maid with him; but a man, who was walking about, came up to him, patted the pony, and led it onwards along the turnpike-road. Marshall naturally supposed it was the boy's father, and took no farther notice of him.

Ha! thought I, there is some mystery here, – some deeper game than we at first supposed, – something more than running off with the little fellow for the sake of his clothes. But could Mary have lent herself to aid such a transaction?

Marshall assured me in the most positive manner, that it was impossible Mary could have then been on the Heath, or near it; for she had gone away early in the morning, having had an appointment at Battersea[10] with a girl who wanted her assistance in some love frolic (the nature of which will appear in the sequel), and she was afterwards to proceed to Norwood to visit some friends lately arrived there. Mary could not consequently have been the fortune-teller who cunningly withdrew the maid from her duty; and I was, therefore, entirely thrown out of my course at the very time when the track began to appear visible; for this love frolic could not possibly, I thought, have any connection with the loss of the boy.

Marshall showed every disposition to assist me in the inquiry. I took care, indeed, not to let him know what authority I now possessed, nor to give him any hint of my official situation; otherwise he might have been shy of renewing our old acquaintance. I merely told him I was interested for the family, and would therefore do my utmost to recover the boy. He proposed to accompany me to another encampment at the distance of about a mile from his; where, perhaps, we might learn something more satisfactory.

It may be thought that this was superfluous, as the boy's relatives would already have searched every corner of the Heath, and thoroughly examined every gipsy they could meet with. Yet, strange as it may seem, none of the gipsies had been asked a single question; nor had any body been near their tents on the search. The mother, indeed, in her distraction for her loss, had made up her mind that the crime had been committed by the gipsies, and consequently that it would serve no purpose to inquire of them, while it might put them on their guard to conceal him the more completely.

Mrs. Manson was also in great trouble about the circumstance being publicly known, and dreaded I know not what future evils, (even if she could recover him,) were it noised abroad that he had been stolen by gipsies. We had, therefore, been strongly cautioned to conceal, as much as possible, whose child it was we were in search of; for Mrs. Manson would be almost as much vexed at her loss being published as at the loss itself. It might be that she was afraid of the boy acquiring a nick-name, which, trifling as it appears, is often very annoying.

By Marshall's advice, then, we went towards the neighbouring encampment, which was nearer also to the place where the pony had been found grazing. As it was summer, the night was not dark, though there was no moon; and a field of thick white clouds spread over the face of the sky. We accordingly hastened across the Heath through the furze, without troubling ourselves to look for the smoother tracks which intersect it, as our business admitted of no delay.

Our speed was soon interrupted by a hollow, which we could readily have cleared, had not its declivity been so marshy that we sunk, at every step, in mud and water. We had both been aware of this pass, and had endeavoured to avoid it; but had not kept high enough to the left. As we were considering whether it would be better to go round by the head of the hollow, or try to dash right through at the expense of being well bemired in the slough, Rover, who had stolen away from his watch-post to follow us, began a low growling as if somebody were near, and finally set up a loud bark.

It must be the chief officer, thought I. He distrusts me, as the lady did, and is sneaking after me to watch. If it be so, he shall not watch for nothing, – confound his impertinence!

We listened, and looked around us and into the hollow below, but could descry nobody; though Rover continued to repeat his signal-bark, and ran forward for a short distance in the direction of a pond lower down the hollow. Upon looking very intently, I at last fancied I saw a figure moving on the brow opposite the pond, as if it were coming towards us; and I thought that, if it were indeed my superior officer acting the spy upon me, he deserved to be soundly ducked for his mean cunning.

Whoever the person might be, he was palpably afraid; for I could perceive him crouching to conceal himself. Marshall could not conjecture, and did not care, who it was; but I was determined to hail him at all events, as I did not relish the notion of having a spy upon my proceedings, when I was conscious of doing my duty to the utmost of my ability. I therefore called out, 'Who goes there?' but instead of answering me, the man, who by this time was close to the edge of the pond, made something heavy splash into the water, and ran off with the utmost speed.

'Answer me, or I'll fire upon you!' I cried after him, and Rover made a run to overtake him; but he continued his speed and was soon out of sight.

Marshall, who could not have any guess of my suspicions, expressed his own, that it was no other than the notorious highwayman, Blore. This fellow had been lately skulking about the Heath; and what we had heard splash in the pond was probably some article of plunder, which he had no readier means of concealing than by putting it under water.

This was plausible enough; but I was so prepossessed with the notion that it was my spy, that I considered the splash of the water either accidental, or a feint to make us search the pond instead of pursuing the fugitive. I had a strong inclination, indeed, to pursue him, whether it were the officer or Blore; but I was overruled by Marshall, who was more anxious to see whether we could make any thing of what had been thrown into the pond. As it afterwards turned out, I was extremely vexed we did not pursue the fellow.

The mention of Blore, for whom I had a sort of romantic liking from his accidental connection with my earlier adventures, made me very desirous of meeting with him, particularly as it came into my mind he might know more of the disappearance of the boy than the gipsies did; and though I had not seen him since the affair with Hump-back and his spouse in Monsal-Dale,[11] I imagined I might still count something upon our former connection, slight as it was.

In the mean-time we descended the brow a little farther to the right, where we found it more dry and solid, and came to the brink of the pond, as near to the place as we could conjecture from which we had heard the splash proceed. The pond was neither very broad nor deep; and though it was dark, we could see distinctly the whole white surface of the water, and nothing appeared to be floating there; so that whatever had been thrown into it had sunk to the bottom.

Being unprovided with implements, we could make no farther search; besides, my time was precious, and not to be wasted in this way; while Marshall, on the other hand, could return at his leisure as soon as the day dawned, if he wished to search for the supposed booty.

Rover still kept barking and running about on the scent where the person had passed; and just as we were leaving the pond to proceed on our way, he came bouncing up to Marshall with something in his teeth. Upon examining this, we found, to our surprise, that it was a boy's cap, of elegant make and fine materials. The colour we could not make out in the dark; but my instructions bore that little William had a dark-blue cloth cap of this very fashion, with his name written on the silk lining. I had little doubt, indeed, that this was the identical cap; and if it were so, I began to dread that he had met with a still worse fate than that of being kidnapped.

'Good God!' I cried to Marshall, 'is it possible it could be the poor little fellow's body which we heard plunge in the water?'

'Very likely,' said he: 'and if it bees, I can't think of nobody here, if it an't Blore, as would commit such a wicked crime.'

'No, no!' said I, 'it is impossible. I know something of Blore: he is indeed a hardened desperado; but he would never murder an innocent little boy who could do him no harm as a witness. The thing is quite incredible!'

'Creditable enough, as I take it,' said Marshall. 'Don't you see he might ha' some'at handsome for the job, if so be as the boy stood in any body's way, you know, in regard of an heir or so?'

'Then perdition to the infernal villain!' said I. 'If he has done this, he shall suffer the death he deserves, if I can help him to the gallows!'

'What the devil, Tom!' said Marshall, 'you wouldn't surely turn informer against your old acquaintance?'

I said nothing. I found I was entering on rather dangerous ground with the gipsy, who had an hereditary prejudice against every measure connected with legal justice; and I was anxious to conceal from him my own alliance with the guardians of the law. I had spoken, because I had felt, very strongly; for when the supposition of the boy's murder crossed my mind, I thought at the same instant of his mother despairing and wretched, – her beautiful eyes filled with tears, weeping inconsolably.

The cap rendered it highly probable that it was the body of the unfortunate little boy which had been thrown into the pond; but be that as it might, we could do nothing without light and implements; and we therefore proceeded, according to our first intention, towards the next encampment, intending to return and search the pond as soon as the dawn broke.

Bernard (or, as we called him, Barny) Allen, the chief of the other gipsy horde, could add very little information to what I had already gained. He had seen the boy riding on the pony, and recollected that a carriage was passing at the time, which startled the pony and caused it to spring aside off the road for a short distance; but he took no farther notice of the occurrence. Whether this carriage could have any connection with the ruffian Blore, or with the disappearance of the boy, I could not make out; but every circumstance, how slight soever it might be, was now made ground of suspicion. The light we procured at Allen's tent satisfied me that it was the boy's cap; for the name, 'William Granville Manson,' was inscribed upon the lining.

CHAPTER III.

Hare-hunting at day-break – A robber disturbed on his night-beat.

As the day was beginning to break, Marshall and I, accompanied by Barny Allen, the other gipsy, returned to the pond with such implements for dragging it as we could procure; being now, I thought, almost certain that the body was in the pond, in which opinion we were farther confirmed by finding a little whip by the side of it, such as he might have had for his pony.

It was not easy to conjecture how the whip came there; for if it was the child's body we had heard splash in the pond, it was evident he had been previously murdered, otherwise we should have also heard his screams; and if he held the whip in his hand after he was dead, it was not probable it could have dropped from his death-grasp. Neither did it appear for what purpose the perpetrator of the horrid deed, which was now almost beyond supposition, could have left the whip here.

We proceeded, with what things we had, to drag the pond, and were not long before we discovered something soft and heavy; but we could not succeed in getting it to the side, as it constantly slipped from us, and only rolled farther and deeper into the water at every trial we made. I was so convinced that this was the body, that I did not hesitate to strip myself and go into the water to fetch it up.

Our conjectures had been right. I brought out the body, which, so far as I could judge, answered exactly to the description that I had received. Of the cap found by Rover there could not be a doubt, since it bore the boy's name; and the clothes upon the body equally corresponded with my instructions. I could not of course judge of the features, which were much disfigured by our dragging; but the stature was that of a boy about four years old.

Here, then, it was plain, a shocking murder had been perpetrated; and, but for our being accidentally on the spot when the ruffian threw the body into the water, it might either have never been found, or it might have been supposed that the pony had run off with the boy, and cast him into the water in passing. The latter supposition would have been rendered probable, also, by the discovery of the cap and whip so near the pond.

But what could be the motives for such a deed? I could think of none except what had been suggested before by Marshall, that either Blore or some other desperate villain had been hired for the purpose. With a view to robbery it could hardly be; for none of the boy's things were missing, and we even found a watch upon the body, he having been humoured with one, young as he was, by his doting mother. There is something so amiable and lovely in such marks of maternal fondness, that I cannot help liking them even when reflection condemns them as idle. Nobody, who had ever seen Mrs. Manson pouring out her fine sensibility upon her darling boy, would, I am convinced, have dreamed of giving her pain by injuring him. Who then, for the sake of any worldly advantage, could have had the conscience to bribe a ruffian to murder in cold blood so fine a boy as William by description seemed to have been?

The gipsies were, in my opinion, as innocent of all knowledge of this deed as I was; yet, from the time, the place, and, above all, from the circumstance of the maid having been gossiping with a gipsy fortune-teller when the boy disappeared, I perceived it would not be an easy matter to make their innocence apparent to those who were generally prepossessed against their character. I knew well that it was one thing to be convinced myself of their guiltlessness, and another to convince such as were swayed by strong prejudices towards a contrary conclusion. Mrs. Manson, who would have to abide the awful disclosure, would, I was certain, remain satisfied of their criminality, unless it were disproved by the most unequivocal evidence.

The only exculpatory circumstance which I could discover for them was, that unless the fortune-teller were Wilton's Mary – a thing apparently impossible, – there was no other young woman of their tribe, so far as they knew, in that neighbourhood to whom the description would apply; at which they were sadly perplexed.

In the meanwhile it was necessary to remove the body, which we accordingly did to the Stag, I think it is called; for though Marshall's tent was nearest, I did not like to have it taken there. My mind was altogether in a state of strong excitement. My heart melted for the bereaved mother, whose distress, great as it was, would be so dreadfully increased when she came to know the worst.

At the same time I could not but feel elated at having so expeditiously succeeded in my search, it being the first time I had ever performed any of the duties of my new office; and if I should be equally successful in tracing and securing the murderer, my character would at once be stamped for activity and enterprise. This I estimated much higher than any pecuniary reward I might earn by the affair.

When the body was safely deposited, with a caution to the landlord of the Stag to keep the business private, I gave my gipsy friends something to drink, and left them, to proceed to the rendezvous at which I had appointed to meet the chief officer – now happily exculpated from the suspicion of acting the spy upon me. I found him not a little out of humour, however, at having been kept waiting so long, for it was now near five o'clock in the morning.

Upon telling him what I had discovered, he agreed with me that it would be requisite for one of us to go to town for farther instructions (Mrs. Manson and her brother not having returned to Roehampton); and particularly to inquire whether suspicions of foul play could be fixed upon any relative of the family, on account of hereditary property, or otherwise. It was prudent, however, that I should remain and make all possible inquiry after the man we had seen at the pond, who must either be the murderer, it should appear, or at least be deeply implicated.

I again directed my course, therefore, towards the gipsies' tents across the Heath, through the clumps of furze, as before. I had not gone far, when my attention was attracted by the report and the smoke of fire-arms at a short distance before me. Some sportsman, I fancied, in quest of hares; but whoever it was, I thought I should at least lose nothing by making inquiry concerning the object of my pursuit.

As I was proceeding in the direction of the place where I saw the smoke, I perceived a man run forwards as if he had killed something; but when he saw me, he crouched down, with the evident intention of concealing himself from observation.

Ha! thought I, not a legitimate sportsman, but some poacher; and if he has been long about the Heath this morning, the very sort of person I want, if I can manage him.

I therefore proceeded with all caution, as I knew it was rather a dangerous game to intrude upon such a person with loaded fire-arms in his hand. The poacher, as I had dubbed him, was instantly aware of my intentions, as I could see him skulking along from bush to bush among the furze, in order to distance me or find a hiding-place. I pushed on, however, and was rapidly gaining ground, when all at once I lost sight of him near to a clump of furze of thicker growth than the rest around it.

Here, it would appear that he had dived; and I was left *at fault*,[12] as a sportsman would say. It occurred to me at the time as odd enough that there was no dog to be seen. Perhaps the man had none, or had trained one to skulk along with him. I myself felt the want of Rover, who would soon have discovered his lair.

At all events, I resolved not to give up my search, particularly as I began to entertain some suspicions that this poacher might possibly be concerned in the fate of the little boy. I had no grounds for these, indeed, farther than his being on the Heath; but that, in the state of my mind, was enough. If it were so, I had the more need to be on my guard. I carefully and cautiously, therefore, threaded the narrow openings among the furze, and pried into every corner, as I used to do in my boyhood when bird-nesting.

At length I fancied I saw part of the skirt of a drab coat beneath a bush that was conspicuously taller than the rest. I knew that as furze grows up, the thickness of its bushy head chokes the growth of the lower branches; and as the main stems are small, a considerable space is thus left free, vacant, and well sheltered; and such have frequently afforded hiding-places on the heaths for foot-pads[13] and others. When I saw the drab skirt, therefore, I had no doubt that I had now found my man.

For my own safety, however, it was requisite that I should be guarded in venturing to rouse the lion from his lair. I hoped he had not heard my footstep; and from the position of the coat-skirt, I judged that I was behind him, and consequently that he could not see me. I advanced as cautiously as if I had been walking on glass, and dared scarcely breathe for fear of giving a premature alarm.

I was now so close to the coat-skirt that I could almost touch it, though the bush was so thick that I could not see the position in which the man lay; but on looking over it, I discerned the muzzle of some sort of fire-arms, apparently a large pistol or blunderbuss, amongst the grass, the rest of it being hidden by the overhanging furze.

My first impulse was to dart upon this and secure it, to save myself from danger; but just as I was going to do so, I perceived it moving, and heard the lock click. This 'note of preparation'[14] made me pause; but it was only for a moment, for I was now behind the man, an advantage which I might instantly lose.

I therefore made a desperate plunge at the weapon, seized the barrel as firmly as my hands could grasp, and wrenched it from him before he was aware. He sprang up from the bush, and made an effort to regain the piece; which in the struggle went off, but luckily without injuring either of us. I instantly dropt it, drew a loaded pistol from my breast-pocket, and held it to his head, saying,

'Stand! Answer me, or I shall fire!'

As I looked keenly at the man to see what sort of person I had to deal with in an affair of life or death, I thought I recognized in his grim countenance the desperado Blore. It was he, indeed, but wofully changed. His eye was now hollow, and his face ploughed with deep furrows. He had looked grim and haggard when I last saw him, some years before; but that was nothing to the expression of ruffianism now stamped so deeply on his countenance.

Blore knew me at once; and though he was rather doubtful in what capacity I appeared, he attempted no further violence or resistance till he should discover my object. On the other hand, it was important for me to conceal this, and to draw as much information from him, indirectly, as I could.

With this view I assumed a free, careless tone; told him I was an adventurer like himself, though I had not yet taken to the highway; and asked him with an indifferent and jocular air, what success he had lately met with, and what exploits he had performed. I knew this was rather a ticklish question; but I hoped, from the familiar manner which I had put on, that I should throw him partly off his guard.

I succeeded in my manœuvre. Blore was so little used to the kindly tone of friendship, that it awakened all his better feelings, (every ruffian has some of these slumbering in his bosom;) and I believe he would not have scrupled to tell me all the crimes he had ever committed. When I saw this, it gave me a painful interest in his fate, which made me tremble lest he should confess himself to be the murderer of little William, and thereby put my duty to a very severe trial.

I could not well ask him any direct question about this transaction; but I contrived to lead him on from the death of the hare which I had just seen him fire at, to the history of the previous night; and I confess I was glad to find he was not implicated in the crime which I was investigating – at least, if I could trust him; and I had no good reason for doubting his veracity, as he had no motive for concealing this from me, when I knew other circumstances to criminate him, if I had wished to inform.

I learned that Blore had been out the night before, prowling, of course, for plunder – when his attention was caught about twelve or one o'clock, by a buggy driving hard along the edge of the Heath. As this was a kind of vehicle which did not promise much in the way of booty, he stood aside and allowed it to pass without challenging the driver.

The buggy had not gone far before he heard it stop; and, as he liked not the idea of a witness so very near his *beat*, as a watchman would say, he resolved to keep an eye upon it. He was near enough to see the driver get down, tie the horse to a bush, lift out something heavy, and walk away with it into the Heath.

This made Blore conjecture, as Marshall had done, that the driver was about to secrete something of value; and he accordingly took a near cut to watch his movements, or intercept him if the spoil proved to be worth contending for. Being well used to caution in such matters, he got near enough the man, unperceived, to see that what he was carrying was the lifeless body of a boy. Hardened as he was to crime, Blore said he shuddered at this unexpected sight; and not wishing in any degree to involve himself in such an affair, he hastened away from the place without noticing what became of the man and his criminal burden.

Here, then, was another link in the chain of the hapless boy's history; but still it did not appear who the driver of the buggy could be. It was too dark for Blore to see what sort of a person he was, farther than that he wore a cap and a clumsy-looking great coat, or benjamin.

When I had procured all the information he could give me, I did not hesitate to tell him that I was interested in the boy, though I did not hint in what way; and I soon, therefore, found an excuse for bidding him adieu, and left him to cook his hare for breakfast, while I proceeded to continue my inquiries. Before leaving the desperado, however, I took care to procure from him a clue to find him by, in case I should at any time want his assistance.

CHAPTER IV.

A young lady under suspicion – Eloquence of the stable-yard – Affray with a desperado.

WITHOUT going back to the gipsies' tents, or waiting the return of the chief officer, I imagined I might be able to gain intelligence of the driver of the buggy from some of the turnpike men, though I had not much faith in this class of persons since the time I had suspected Blore to be a lodger, or at least a favoured visitor, of the fat fellow at the pass into Monsal-Dale. But as I could lose nothing by the inquiry, I resolved to try. Turnpike-keepers, for one thing, have usually very good memories respecting horses and vehicles; and if I could trace either the horse or the buggy to an owner, it would be a great point gained.

At first, I was unsuccessful. The fellows had been so drowsy and muddy, that they had no distinct recollection of any buggy passing; but at length I found a man who said he had seen one go by between eleven and twelve o'clock, which he was pretty certain belonged to Mr. Jones of Battersea; and the driver of which wore a cap and benjamin such as Blore had described.

The mention of Battersea reminded me of the remarkable coincidence of Mary having gone there; and I began to surmise, in spite of my good opinion of her, that she was at least concerned in the affair; though her father, I was certain, knew nothing of it. This was only a surmise; but it was painful even to suppose her involved in such a diabolical transaction. Who, on the other hand, was this Jones? The turnpike-man did not know what he was, and had never seen him; but he had been told 'as how the green buggy belonged to he.'

It would again be necessary, I perceived, to inquire with whom Mary was connected at Battersea; for, be the consequences to her what they might, I was determined, since I had begun, to go through with my inquiry. I accordingly set out again to find Marshall. My errand was fruitless. He had never heard the name of Jones of Battersea, and he knew not with whom Mary was connected there. Accordingly, after having made a hasty breakfast, I proceeded to Battersea to inquire about this Jones, the suspected owner of the buggy.

From what I could learn, it appeared that Jones was considered to be a man of some property; though it was whispered that he had made his money chiefly by contraband trading, and schemes which were not in the routine of fair and open business. He was, in fact, a neck-or-nothing[15] speculator in transactions where there were immense profits to cover immense risks; and he did not, of course, stickle about the illegality of his traffic, if it promised to be productive.

These things, however, were only whispered among the prying gossips of the village, where he seemed to have taken up his residence to procure that respectability of which the knowledge of his transactions might have elsewhere deprived him. Dealings of this kind can seldom be wholly concealed; and Jones himself, from having lived for some time in security, and, as he imagined, unsuspected, began to be less wary in his proceedings, and even in several instances, ventured to deposit articles belonging to his secret merchandise, in this very house.

Besides a chaise for his family, he kept the aforesaid buggy, ostensibly for bringing what family articles he wanted from London; but really, as an indispensable implement of one lucrative branch of his trade, which he had begun lately to conduct in a more regular manner at Battersea than he had at first ventured upon.

It was, indeed, the unseasonable hours at which the buggy had recently been remarked to go in and out, which first excited the suspicions of his neighbours, and led to surmises and whispered reports which impeached his respectability. Among other things, it was said that Jones, besides smuggling of perhaps a less objectionable kind, scrupled not to traffic in human bodies to a considerable extent, for the supply of the horrible dens of the London anatomists.[16]

Nobody could prove this, but all believed it; and when I connected this report with the midnight transaction on the Heath, my conjectures quickly mounted to certainty, that this Jones was either the murderer, or concerned in the murder of the hapless little boy. If he had decoyed Mary into the plot, his guilt was only the greater. That she had lent her assistance in it was highly probable, to say the least; and her story of going to Norwood must, I thought, have been all a feint to deceive her father.

The return of the chief officer might perhaps have led to the discovery of some motive for the crime; but as I had got so far into the secret, I thought it would redound more to my reputation if I were to complete the discovery without his assistance. I accordingly put forth all possible caution and cunning in the inquiries I made at Battersea; and found every body most willing to add to the infamous report alluded to about Jones, that part of whose traffic is so universally and naturally detested.

The person whom I found to be most communicative was a man who had lived some time in the employ of Jones, but had disliked his place and left him. I treated this man with a few glasses of ale, and in return ascertained from him that the report concerning the traffic in bodies was a fact, and was the chief reason of his quitting his master, who gave better wages than he could elsewhere obtain.

After much useless and desultory stuff, which I had to bear with patiently from this fellow, who, like most of his class in and about the metropolis, was as ignorant and rude as a savage, I learned that the man who had succeeded him was also going to quit his place. This was a hint not to be lost; and in order to profit by it and obtain what information I could at the first hand, I came to the singular resolution of offering myself for the situation. I should in this way, at least, have the means of seeing Jones himself, and of discovering what sort of man I had to deal with, if it should turn out to be my duty to take him into custody for the crimes of kidnapping and murder.

I lost no time in presenting myself at the house, the exterior of which was elegant and tasteful, and put me in mind of what the scriptures say of whited sepulchres.[17] The master himself was not at home; but a young lady, – finely dressed, and engaging withal, though not particularly pretty, – whom I understood to be his daughter, upon learning my errand, came out into the lobby to speak to me. She looked very much surprised that a young man of my appearance should apply for such a place; for, though I endeavoured to speak and act the boor as well as I could, I was rather respectably dressed, and had, I suppose, a manner somewhat superior to those who might be expected to apply.

The appearance of this young lady awakened a train of conjectures closely connected with my immediate business. The love frolic in which Mary was said to have been concerned, if it were not all a falsehood trumped up on purpose, related most probably to her; and both, for what I knew, might have been duped by Jones, and have unwittingly assisted him in accomplishing his wicked designs.

From what I knew of the feelings of Mary, I was certain that, on her part, it was next to impossible; and I could with difficulty bring myself to suppose that Miss Jones, mild, graceful, and polished as she appeared to be, could in any way have been concerned in the murder of an innocent child.

I resolved, however, to try her in a cautious manner; and, with this view, I told her that I had been for a long time living among the gipsies, was sick of wandering, and should like a steady comfortable service, such as I understood her father's to be. At the mention of the word 'gipsies,' I observed that she instantly coloured, and could not conceal her agitation. I had touched, as I supposed, the string which thrilled in her bosom, and called up feelings which she struggled, but vainly, to suppress.

'What gipsies do you know?' she asked me, with a sort of flurry as I thought, but in a tone which was meant to imply careless indifference.

'O well then, Miss,' said I, in assumed boorish phrase, 'I may say as how I knows the Allens, the Boswells, the Marshalls, the Stanleys, and them sort of folks.'

I particularly remarked, or at least I wished to remark – which is much the same – that the name of the Marshalls, as I had expected, made her start. I took care to introduce it among the others, to conceal from her any colour of suspicion respecting my knowledge of the loss of the boy; for this would have spoiled all.

'Is your name Wilton?' she inquired, with evident interest.

'No, Miss,' said I; 'but I knows him as you means; 'a lived, long 's the time, with them Marshalls, 'a did.'

Here she paused, and did not know what to say, though she was evidently reluctant to let me go. Perhaps she might have some vague notion of my errand, for guilt is very sharpsighted; and this may have prompted her to ask me if I had lately seen Mary. I answered,

'Not, Miss, as I may say, of a long time; but I hear say as how she be concerned in some-'at as has been done at Roehampton, – some ugly murder of a child, as I hear. The more's the pity for a young woman like she.'

While I thus continued in my assumed vulgar phrase to broach this subject, the colour of Miss Jones came and went in quick alternation; though she endeavoured to hide the cause from me by affecting to be shocked at the story, and to pity the girl, if it were true, as she hoped it was not.

For my own part, as I had now obtained evidence satisfactory to myself, that both Mary and Miss Jones had knowledge concerning the fate of the boy; and as I had certainly alarmed her fears, I also deemed it best to put on an air of indifference, and make light of the affair. I would have immediately seized Miss Jones upon suspicion, if I had had a warrant; but I was too raw to be certain whether I dared take such a step without one.

We were both relieved from our embarrassment by Jones himself coming in by the back entrance from the stable-yard, or whatever he called his dépôt of illegal articles, and making a great noise and racket, as people will do when endeavouring to hide from themselves the twinges of conscience.

'Father!' said Miss Jones, 'here is a young man —'

'A young devil!' cried he, fuming as Welshmen proverbially do. 'What the h—[18] can young men be a-doing of here, I wonder, at all hours?' Then turning round in a passion, he went again to the back door as if he had forgotten something, and called out, –

'Bob! Bob Lumby, I say, you lumbering shab!'[19]

'What a fury my father is in, to be sure!' said Miss Jones to me; 'but wait here a little, and he will soon come to you.'

She was glad to get away, and I was immediately interested in the colloquy between Jones and his man, which from the loudness of their tones was by no means difficult to hear.

'Move, blockhead! can't you?' said Jones. 'Stir yourself! Scrub up the buggy, rub down Tramper, and have 'em ready!'

'Lord bless you, sir!' said the man, 'Tramper is dead blown with last night's job; 'a cawn't stir out o' the stable this day, however.'

'Blastation! I tell you he must, and within the hour too! Let 'im 'ave corn; and if he won't go, brandy and the whip shall make 'im, that's all!'

'He'd an ugly job on't last night, however!'

'Hold your cursed jaw, Bob, and move your arms! Not much of an ugly job neither, to come from Lambeth at an ordinary trot, with only a single barrel of prime pickled pork in the buggy. Not much of a job that – was it, you pucker-faced fool?'

'You may call it prime pork, and all that,' said Bob, coolly, 'so be you likes it; thof[20] I cawn't say as I likes the hidear of it about here, however.'

'Blastation! blockhead! I tell you to hold your d—[21] jabber!'

'I an't a-going to say no more on't, only I doesn't like that sort o' article as you calls prime; and Tramper, I thinks, must ha' run woundy hard from Lambeth to be blown so. Jack Smith told me as how he seen the buggy afore twelve o'clock driving like d—[22] on the Wandsworth road. Mayhap when a-coming from Lambeth, 'a run off to Putney Heath.'

'Off to h—, you goose! Jack Smith is a dreaming noodle.'

''A seen the buggy thof; but 'a said nothing about the prime article; only 'a winked as thof 'a know'd some'at on't.'

At this home brush Jones flew into a desperate rage, and threatened to horsewhip Bob, if he gossiped about his affairs in such a manner. Bob, on the other hand, was as sober and cool as a cockney always is when in the greatest passion, and continued in a strain of similar remark; from which I suppose Jones deemed it advisable to escape, probably to concert such measures as might be necessary for his safety, since the secret which he thought was safe had so far transpired.

In this humour I met him as he again came into the house, and told him that, hearing his man was going to quit, I came to offer my services. It immediately struck him that I might be of use in some of his schemes, and he agreed, on the spot, that I should set out within the hour with the buggy, carrying two barrels of his prime pickled pork to a friend in town.

This being arranged on his own terms, as I had other views than stickling for wages, he accompanied me back to assist Bob in getting ready. When Bob learned how matters stood, not being at all daunted by the passion of Jones, he said to me in a bantering tone, –

'I say, chap, I doesn't think myself as how you'll like to sit in the buggy with them there concerns.'

'I tell you, scoundrel!' said Jones, 'to hold your — jaw, or I'll break that noodle's pate of yours!'

'If you be game enough for the go, that's all,' said Bob, quite unconcerned for the consequences; 'and more and besides, I an't a scoundrel so much as yourself, Mr. Jones, if you take on so.'

'Blastation, sir! but I'll chop you into dog's meat, if so you ben't quiet!'

'Aw! go it then!' said Bob, putting himself in a boxing attitude, 'and if I an't game for every inch o' you, why then I give you leave to pickle me in one of them there barrels of yours, as Jack Smith says you did *the boy!*'

Jones could stand this no longer; but seizing a pitchfork which stood by, he interrupted Bob's harangue by making a push at him to pink[23] him to the wall. I ran in upon him to prevent mischief, laid hold of the pitchfork, and twisted it from him in an instant. I had, indeed, just been deliberating with myself whether I ought not, independently of a warrant, to take Jones into custody; and only doubted that, if Bob should turn against me, I could not secure him single-handed; for though of small stature, like most Welshmen, he was firm-built and muscular, and desperado was written on every feature of his face.

But now, when I heard Bob's insinuation about the boy, which accorded with all my previous information; and when I actually saw him attempt murder, or something little short of it, and at the same time thought I might count on the man's assistance; I threw down the pitchfork, produced my staff,[24] and told Jones he was wanted at Bow Street for kidnapping and murder.

Jones, from being rash and passionate, was taken by surprise, and not quite prepared for so immediate a catastrophe, though he must have lived long under terror of the discovery of his various illegal deeds. The suddenness of the thing, as is usually the case, soon quieted his rage, and he began to offer me money – any sum I liked to name, if I would let him escape; but I was not to be swayed in this manner, and told him there was no help; he must go.

He then glanced his eye to Bob to see whether he looked as if he would assist him; but Bob was little less dumbfoundered than himself, and stood as if he did not well know which part to take, till his notions of boxing came to aid his doubts, and to an appeal from Jones for his assistance he answered,

'No, no, master! I ben't a-going to make a rescue on't; but if you're game, you'd 'ave a turn-up[25] for the chance, however, I know.'

'Come!' said I, 'Mr. Jones, I can't waste my time. You must go; there's no help for you.'

'An't there?' said the desperado, drawing out a pocket-pistol and presenting it at me; but I was still better prepared than he; for, on the instant, I presented a pistol in each hand. When he saw this, he shrank from the dubious trial of our skill, and surrendered.

Miss Jones, I have no doubt, was used to such noisy blustering as had been going on in the yard, and probably would have paid little attention to it, had not some words reached her of rather an ominous kind. I perceived her at first peeping out at the door-way; but when she came to understand the extent of her misfortune, she rushed out and fell at my feet, entreating – praying – beseeching me to pity her father, and allow him to go.

'O Sir!' she sobbed out, 'let him go, and he will tell you all – all he knows. Do, Sir! pity me and let him go. I will go with you myself, if you let him away.'

I sincerely pitied the young creature, and have never felt my duty more oppressively painful. If I had been assured that she herself was altogether free from blame, I doubt whether I could have stood my ground; but, from the conversation I had just held with her, I was certain she knew more of the crime than she ought to have done, and I remained firm.

The character of the person who pleads or prays for any boon, is always the most weighty circumstance for or against the cause. All the tears and sobs of woman would never influence me a jot, if I had a conviction that she was in the wrong, or was praying for what was wrong. I was not certain, indeed, whether I ought not to have taken Miss Jones into custody also. It appeared necessary, at least, that both she and Mary should undergo an examination respecting their knowledge of the affair.

All the favour which I could consistently grant was, that, in order to conceal his being taken up from his neighbours, Bob should go and order a coach to receive us at his own door. The man was not, however, over fond of the job, and was palpably much disappointed at not seeing a fair boxing match between us for the chance.

Jones gave him some money to keep his tongue quiet while he was ordering the chaise; but I suppose he had found the secret too weighty on his conscience not to ease himself a little of the load by confidential whispers to Jack Smith or somebody else, from whom, of course, it spread like a conflagration; and, by the time the coach was ready, half the rabble of the village was in attendance to honour our departure with the stare of curiosity.

CHAPTER V.

Unravelling of the mysteries – Bribery and corruption of a maid-servant – Secret confab in a cattle-shed.

WHEN we arrived at Bow Street, I found that through the inquiries of the chief officer a young man named Clarke, who was related to little William, and, failing him, was heir-at-law to considerable property, had been brought up for examination, and was then in the office. When he saw Jones enter with me, he started as if he had seen a ghost or a demon; or, what is often little less appalling in criminal cases, an unexpected witness who can clearly testify to guilt.

I did not remain to hear the examinations, but, furnished with warrants for the apprehension of Mary and also of Miss Jones, set off immediately for Norwood in quest of the former.

In the morning it would have been very hard for me to have thought of such a measure; but my successful tracing and capture of Jones had so elated me, that I believe I should have carried a warrant to apprehend my own father. I did not find Mary at Norwood. She had, indeed, been there, but was gone; and I gathered, with regard to the love frolic, that she had merely lent her clothes to serve as a disguise to somebody at Battersea; but if she really knew what had been the result of this, she had either pretended entire ignorance to her friends, or they were unwilling to tell me.

This intelligence proved a great relief to my mind, as I believed it to be the truth; and I hoped she would be able to prove her innocence, though I well foresaw that this would be no easy matter.

Who could it be that had borrowed Mary's clothes to personate a gipsy? The ostensible motive was said to be a love frolic; but it appeared evident to me that the real object had been the abduction of the luckless boy. Could it have been Miss Jones herself who had personated the fortune-teller on the Heath? The description, indeed, did not answer; for Miss Jones, being of pure Welsh descent, was very fair, with a transparent pale complexion and blue eyes; while the counterfeit gipsy was described with all the usual characteristics of the race.

Still the motive for the whole transaction was wrapt in mystery, for Jones could never certainly have murdered the poor boy for the sake of the few guineas he might receive for his body; which, indeed, he did not seem to have wanted, or he would scarcely have thrown it into a pond on the Heath.

Mr. Clarke, the young heir-at-law, on the other hand, might be concerned in the villainy, seeing that he was so much hurt by the appearance of Jones, whom he knew; and this must have arisen either out of horror at the deed, or dread of his evidence.

The whole of the day was spent in inquiries and investigations, without unravelling much of the mystery. The only other fact which came to light was, that Mr. Clarke had been, or still was, the accepted lover of Miss Jones. This was a very important circumstance; for Clarke was poor and embarrassed, though, but for little William, he would have been rolling in the wealth now in the hands of the boy's guardians.

Jones, well aware of all this, had courted, flattered, and cajoled Clarke; had advanced him money, and done every thing in his power to secure him for his daughter. These exertions were in a great degree unnecessary; for Miss Jones possessed sufficient personal attractions to win and secure the heart of the young man. Their affection was mutual; and the embarrassments and poverty of Clarke were the only bar to their marriage. Jones was wealthy, but he did not like the notion of supporting his son-in-law, any more than the latter, who had a high spirit of independence, would have agreed to be supported.

Jones had a deeper game to play than this, as it afterwards appeared. He knew the value of the property which, but for little William, Clarke would have inherited; and he of course prayed and planned day and night for his being got out of the way by some means or other. From what we have already seen of Jones, it could scarcely be supposed that he would scruple at any thing for the accomplishment of such a design. The temptation was great; for he saw that Clarke was in love with Miss Jones, and if he possessed so large an hereditary property, she might be put off without any fortune. As Clarke, besides, was young, and not accustomed to money transactions, Jones anticipated some good pickings for himself in the way of managing or arranging his accounts.

Such, I suppose, must have been some of the views of Jones in anticipation of the proposed match; but he was too shrewd a speculator to trust to futurity for the *chance* of the property coming into Clarke's possession, or think of sanctioning the marriage so long as this was in doubt.

My own opinion, therefore, supported by these facts and views, was, that Jones had, either in concert with his daughter and Clarke, or without their knowledge, contrived to carry off the boy; had turned his pony loose on the Heath; had afterwards taken away his life, thrown him into the pond, and left his cap and whip hard by, to make it appear that he had fallen therein and been drowned by accident. This was, at least, a probable account of the fate of the boy, and the motives for the deed; but the coroner's inquest[26] was to sit next day on[27] the body found by us in the pond, and something might then come out in evidence, which would clear up what was still left in the dark.

It is unnecessary for my purpose to record, in detail, the evidence which the coroner elicited. The most extraordinary circumstance was, that the body found in the pond was not identified as that of little William, though it agreed pretty much as to size, and, what was still more puzzling, was dressed in his clothes. This, independent of finding his cap and whip so near the pond, was most inexplicable and perplexing, and threw us out in all our conjectures.

The body, however, it could not be. The face, indeed, was a good deal disfigured, and could not be spoken to with certainty; but William had a birth-mark on his breast of a bunch of grapes, which his mother during her pregnancy had longed for,[28] and upon the body there was no such mark. The hair also was considerably darker in colour, and more luxuriant, than William's. The surgeon, moreover, who examined the body, gave it as his opinion that it was not recently dead; and that the cause of its death had been some lingering disorder, if he might judge from the great emaciation, particularly of the lower part of the body and limbs; whereas William was as stout, plump, and healthy a little fellow as the riding of his pony and the pure air of the Heath could make him.

The only inference that could now be drawn was, that William's clothes had been put upon this boy, who had probably died many days before; and that the whole was a deep design (now frustrated) for making his relatives believe that he had really met with his death in the pond. My search for him had consequently been all in vain, though it had given very strong cause, from the motives above-mentioned, for suspecting Jones or Clarke of being concerned in the abduction.

It farther appeared that Mary had lent her clothes to Jones's house-maid, who had absconded, or, at least, was not to be found; but from the description, it was evident this girl had acted the fortune-teller. This partly acquitted Mary; for if she had been knowingly concerned in the abduction of the boy, it would have been more in her line to act the fortune-teller herself. She had been imposed upon, then, it should seem, under pretence of the above-mentioned love frolic. These circumstances were proved by the evidence of Miss Jones, who was very much agitated the while.

My suspicions of Miss Jones herself had been also quite unfounded; and, had I known her better, would never have been entertained. She deposed that on the evening of the day on which the boy disappeared, the maid Sally, who had been out for a holiday, had come to her, trembling and flurried, to tell her that William had been stolen by the gipsies – the Marshalls she supposed, – and that his body had been found in a pond on the Heath. Now, as the girl had told her this several hours before the body which we had found had been thrown into the pond, it was plain that she was acquainted with all the secrets of the iniquitous plot.

The known connection of little William with her lover Clarke, and the story which had been told her by Sally of his singular fate, accounted for the feelings which Miss Jones had evinced when I mentioned the Marshalls, of whom she had heard much in consequence of Wilton's romantic attachment to Mary. She had, indeed, seen Mary herself more than once, and was interested about her, as most young ladies would be, from knowing that she had so long charmed a young and handsome Oxonian from the comforts of a civilized life to wander with her through the country.

Miss Jones was in great distress about the loss of the boy before she knew that her father was implicated; and this increased her feelings to agony. She had no anxiety for the fortune. She loved Clarke when he was poor, and would have married him, as I understood, if he had been a beggar. She had never known the evils of poverty, and of course could only have the pretty notions of it which are to be met with on the shelves of a circulating library.[29] Millions, I daresay, much less thousands, would not have tempted her to touch a hair of the boy's head.

Jones, I have little doubt, knew all this too well to entrust her with his design; and as Clarke was much of the same caste of principle, he did not venture to broach the subject even to him. Clarke, indeed, must have been painfully taught the importance of money by the want of it; and no doubt he knew that this would form an insuperable obstacle to his marriage. He was of a mild and yielding disposition also, and was easily persuaded; yet, though Jones might have taken advantage of all these circumstances, he was probably afraid of Clarke's not being equal to go through with any part of the villainy, and was therefore resolved to conceal it from him.

It was much against the investigation that the girl Sally could not be traced, as she had been so deeply concerned in the plot. She had absconded immediately after telling her young mistress her story about the fate of the boy.

Jones himself had been kept in custody only on strong suspicion. It could not be proved that he was the person who threw the body into the pond, nor even that it was his buggy which had passed the turnpike; for though my first informant had spoken positively to me, he would not swear to it before the coroner. The body not being identified also, rebutted any charge of murder. He was accordingly acquitted and discharged, as many a guilty wretch has been from lack of evidence.

The evidence of Mary had been much wanted during the investigation; but hitherto we had all been unsuccessful in discovering where she was. Marshall, who had naturally, from the circumstances of the case, become alarmed for her safety, set off in search of her, and returned with her just as the investigation was about to close. Jones, it may be important to remark, had been then gone a considerable time, and had taken immediate advantage of his liberty to escape the chance of a second examination.

Both Mary and her father were much afraid and agitated, the cause of which will immediately appear; and will also in part account for her being so difficult to be found. She had been terrified lest a charge of murder should be brought against her, and not without good cause.

From her account, so far as I could make it out, broken and interrupted as it was in consequence of her alarm, it appeared that she was waiting in the dusk of the evening, according to appointment, in a field near Battersea, for the return of Sally with her borrowed disguise. In the corner of the field, and at some distance from where she was, stood a large haystack, and hard by it a sort of wooden shed or stable for cattle; which, if the door were open, would afford a better place for their exchange of apparel than the back of the hedge. With this view, she approached it to examine its accommodations.

As she drew near, she heard a muttering of voices in a sort of half whisper, which excited her curiosity to listen. For this purpose she applied her ear with caution to a chink of the wooden building, when she distinctly heard a male and a female voice in close conversation; which, as it is of importance to my story, I shall report after Mary as nearly as I can recollect.

'You've done it cleverly, Sal, you little devil!' said the man, 'and earned your reward and a kiss to the bargain.'

'Go, you naughty man!' said Sal. 'It's easier a deal to kiss me than pay me the money. Did you mind to bring the stuff with you? I won't take gammon[30] this time.'

'Aye, wench, here it is. Five, wan't it? Here's five chinkers[31] for you. Many's the one ye ha' had o' me first and last, Sal, ye little cunning devil!'

'Never for nothing thof, I knows,' said the girl.

'And, Sal, if you does me another little job, I ha' some'at more o' the stuff for you.'

'Well! perhaps I ha'n't no objections in particular. I likes a bit o' money for my trouble; and all right, an't it?'

'But, Sal, this is some'at rather particular I wants o' ye.'

'Well! what be it? I was a-thinking it was only the old concern over again.'

'Sal, this is a very ticklish affair about this here boy, you knows.'

'Lud,[32] Sir! I don't know nothing on't. So be it's ticklish, that's your business.'

'Then, wench, you'll 'peach me, will you, after I kissed you and paid you the gold and all that?'

'O Lud, Sir, not I! You knows I'm as true as blue[33] is blue all the world over. Me 'peach![34] Lord save you! how ever could you think o' that?'

'But the gipsy wench as lent you them clothes may 'peach you, Sal, mayn't she? And then it will all come out how and about it.'

'Well! but she don't know nothing on't. I told her as how I was a-going to put a frolic on a girl as had beguiled my beau from me; thof God knows, for matter o' that, I be true to you, Sir, and never goes with no beau whatever since that night you promised to have me, and make me an honest woman again, and your own lawful Mrs. Jones.'

'Right, Sal! I remember what you mean; but in the mean-time —'

'Aye, you always gammon me off that way; but I likes to see a promise kept true as blue, that's what I do.'

'Well, Sal, you sha'n't ha' no reason to complain o' me, I tell you; but as I was a-saying, in the mean-time if you do as I wants you, I'll come down with some'at handsome.'

'Lud, Sir! I be ready now if you tempt me with stuff.'[35]

'Then, Sal, as I was a-saying, this is a ticklish concern, a devilish ugly concern about this here boy; and if you would *buy a brush* – cut and run, you understand me – and take yourself off to a convenient distance – why then, I don't know yet how much o' the stuff your cunning little tongue might beguile out o' me.'

Here there was a long pause; Jones, of course, waiting anxiously to mark the effect of his proposal, and the girl pondering on the unexpected nature of this job, so very different from those which he had hitherto required of her for various purposes.

'Well, Sir!' she at length said, in a melancholy tone, 'I can see how it all be. You wants to get rid o' me for good! I can see it all!'

'No, no, my dear Sally! You knows I wouldn't part with you on no account – you knows I wouldn't, ye little sly devil, with that pretty face of yours. But you see this is an ugly concern, as I was a-saying; and if it be's any ways found out, we'd both be done for. Now I was a-thinking, the Swallow, Bill's schooner, you know, is to sail to-morrow for France; and you'd just be in time to get aboard, so be as you'd no objections, with plenty o' stuff in your pocket.'

'How much, then?' said Sal, in a half hesitating tone.

'Fifty: – I say fifty down, all right and tight, and away!'

'No, Mr. Jones, I won't for fifty, by goles![36] I won't; but make it a hundred even money, and mayhap it would tempt me.'

'With the five what I gived you now, ye mean?'

'O no! no gammon! The neat[37] hundred, or no go.'

'Well, I believe I must yield to your sly little tongue for once; for really I'm devilishly afraid you might be pulled up[38] for to-day's affair. I did not tell you that the little chap is safe under hatches!'[39]

'As how d'ye mean? Ha'n't you sent him off to your friend in the New Forest,[40] as you proposed?'

'No, Sal! safer nor that! aye, safer, wench, I say; all as one when we were at it to make sure work, you know!'

'Lud, Sir! you didn't surely murd–'

'Hush, for God's sake, Sal!' and the whisper became so low, that Mary could not hear any thing except the word 'pond.' Jones, however, soon began in a louder key, and said,

'You see how it be! You may be found out, and pulled up for the death on 'im; so you'll be safer in Monseer's country[41] a bit, till all blow over; and perhaps I may have to go to the New Forest myself. Good bye, Sal, I must be off. A devilish ugly concern, if I be smoked.'[42]

'But you've forgot the money, Mr. Jones; my neat hundred, as I was to have.'

'True, Sal! but here it is in good bankers[43] – good as guineas all the world over. It's a devilish round sum, wench; but it was an ugly concern, that. You won't 'peach now, my pretty Sal, so be as you be pulled up before you get away? and you mustn't by no means bilk me and not go. You know me now, Sal; I won't stand bilking.'

'Aye, Mr. Jones, I does surely know you now, as you says, for a deceiving murderous dog!'

'How, the devil! you — — —, I'll soon teach you as how dead dogs can't bite! D'ye see that?'

Mary strained her eyes to look in at a chink in the wood, but could see nothing; though she heard the ring of some weapon, which she thought resembled that of a large knife, or perhaps a cane-spear. She trembled for the fate of the girl in the hands of such a ruffian, but was afraid of trying to give her any assistance.

'O God, Sir! don't murder me!' the poor girl cried out.

'Dead dogs, I say, can't bark, nor dead — neither; so say your prayers, and be — to ye!'

'O don't kill me! don't, Sir, for mercy's sake! I'll promise any thing – on my bare knees, I'll promise and swear never to 'peach or whisper!'

'Be off, then, and never let me see your — — face again! Mind the Swallow sails with the first tide to-morrow!'

Mary thought it time to escape from this scene of ruffianism without waiting to hear more of their parting words; and having a strong but indefinite suspicion that Sal, in her disguise, had been concerned in the crime hinted at so often in their conversation, rather than in any love frolic, she was alarmed lest it might be visited on herself. She accordingly did not keep her appointment for the exchange of dresses, but made the best of her way to Norwood, and consulted with her friends there how she might most completely conceal herself, in case a search was made for her, till something more might be learned of the affair.

My particular inquiries at Norwood, accordingly, and the noise of the loss of the boy, which, in spite of our precautions for the sake of his mother's feelings, had spread in all directions, made her very careful of letting herself be known. Sally's holiday dress, which Mary still wore, proved of considerable advantage for this purpose.

When her father, however, saw the turn which things were likely to take, he thought it would be better to find her out (he did not know where she had hid herself); and he had, with this design, eagerly and successfully exerted himself. The story of Mary was so naturally told, and her agitation, particularly at first, so great at being supposed capable of either of the crimes of kidnapping or murder, that she was unanimously acquitted, with an admonition to be more careful in future to whom she lent her clothes.

There was now universal regret that Jones had been so hastily discharged, as Mary's evidence bore so strongly against him. It was hoped he was not yet beyond the reach of being re-captured; but when a villain is once out of your sight, you cannot calculate much upon his motions. Jones had undergone a fright which he was determined he would not suffer a second time, if he could help it; and he had made such good use of his time, that, after the most active pursuit, he could neither be found, nor traced beyond Wandsworth.[44]

CHAPTER VI.

The Battersea pot-boy – The barge-maid and her barge – Stabbing in the dark
– Liberality of a miser – A mother's feelings.

WE were again at a stand in our investigations. The boy was lost, without a trace of what had become of him. Jones had failed in his scheme of palming[45] upon the relatives the body that was dressed in William's clothes; though it appeared, from the conversation which Mary had overheard, that he had made the girl Sally believe it, and that she had accordingly repeated it to Miss Jones, whom she had visited, it would appear, before her departure to embark for France, if she really did embark according to her promise.

His design in causing the girl to believe that little William was murdered, was, probably, to make her alarm for her own safety quicken her departure out of the country. To us, indeed, it did not yet appear whether the boy was murdered or not. Jones was a ruffian quite fit for the perpetration of such a deed, if the devil had prompted him to it; but probably, in this case, he might take it into his head that any marks of violence on the body would spoil his scheme of making it appear that he was accidentally drowned in the pond; but if so, why not think of drowning him at once, rather than take to the roundabout shift of dressing another in his clothes? This, I suppose, must remain one of those inexplicable pieces of cunning which are so common in the annals of crime.

The whole affair, both from its real interest, and from its being the first in which I had exercised the functions of my new office, excited me to bend my keenest attention to the means of tracing and recovering the boy, dead or alive. We had now lost all clue of him, farther than that he had fallen into the clutches of Jones.

I now bethought me of what I had heard from Bob in his altercations with his master, and supposed I might perhaps elicit something by interrogating him and his principal authority Jack Smith, who seemed to know more of Jones than he liked to hear repeated; and Bob had, indeed, plainly alluded to the night-expedition of the buggy to the Heath. I was so strongly prepossessed with the notion of obtaining important information through their means, that I wondered why I had not thought of it sooner; and I accordingly made all haste to Battersea.

I found Jack Smith to be one of those great lubberly boys, so well known in London and its vicinity by the name of *pot-boys;* a term, however, which will not be understood by provincial readers without explanation.

A pot-boy, then, is of the same genus of animal in a public-house as 'boots'[46] is in an inn. He does all the dirty work of scouring and cleaning, washing glasses, rinsing bottles, and wiping up the beer-flooded tables of the tap-room; but above all, his business in chief is to carry out pots of beer round the neighbouring houses at the hours of dinner and supper; to which he returns with his cord slung over his shoulder, (or his wheel-barrow, if his round is extensive) to collect the empty pots for the operation of washing and refilling them against the next meal. When he is unemployed, and even when he is going his rounds, he is generally carrying on low badinage with the servant girls, or blackguard gossip with the sturdy vagrants whom he encounters in the streets. In this way he comes to know all that happens in the neighbourhood, and frequently more than ever happened; as common fame is not niggard in the exercise of fancy when there are any materials to work upon.

Such was Jack Smith, the chosen companion and informant of Bob Lumby, in all that report whispered about the deeds and doings of Jones, his master.

It was the afternoon when I met Jack going homewards, and crouching under the weight of a string of porter-pots which dangled over his shoulder. During the wandering life which I had led, I had acquired some tact in getting into the good graces and confidence of all classes of people by talking as much as I could in their own way, and by giving them *line*, as a fisher would say, to talk most themselves; for every body is better at talking than listening. As soon, therefore, as I had got over the preliminary of accosting the sturdy pot-boy, and had dextrously led him to the subject of Jones, I gave him *line*, and let him play about with the bait at his will and pleasure.

His version of the loss of little William was the original one, of his having been found drowned; but when I told him the result of the inquest, though he was a little surprised at it, he soon devised a ready solution of the mystery, and gave it as his opinion that William had been carried to Windmill Street,[47] or Guy's Hospital to be dissected alive,[48] as he had known done in many other cases in which this Jones had been concerned.

This was a thing I had never heard nor dreamed of before: it was much too horrible, I said, to be thought of for a moment; but Jack was positive the thing had been done, and certain, also, that such had been the fate of little William.

By playing him about upon the subject, I soon got Jack into proper trim[49] for my purpose; and he told me such diabolical stories of Jones as were altogether incredible, though they might have some foundation for their origin. In particular, as illustrative of the fate of the boy, he told me of a pretty servant girl (not Sally) who had lived with Jones, and who had disappeared in an unaccountable manner, till it was reported on good authority, at least such as Jack took for such, that Jones had himself covered her mouth with a plaster to prevent her crying, had tumbled her into the buggy, and whirled her off to the surgeons.

My credulity in this case, however, was greatly shaken by what I knew of the disappearance of Sally, who would probably be by-and-bye reported to have shared a similar fate, merely because she was not to be found.

This hint, notwithstanding, which was the only one I could obtain from Jack, was not to be thrown away; and I determined, though shuddering with horror at the stories I had just heard, to search the places he had mentioned in spite of my revolting feelings. I was engaged in the inquiry, and resolved to go through with it at the risk of life itself; so much was my mind excited by the varying turns which the affair had taken.

I left Jack Smith, and was crossing the bridge on my way to town, musing on the disagreeable scenes I should have to go through, when I accidentally saw Bob Lumby hanging about idle, and looking at the craft passing down with the tide, which was rapidly ebbing. As soon as he saw me, he called out –

'Ah, ha! boy, master was too deep for you. A rum cove is Jones, and sly as the old 'un.[50] He bilked Bow Street, as I hear say, and the coroner and all.'

'I know all that, Bob,' said I; 'but it was no fault of mine. I took care that he did not escape from me. But have you any guess where he is skulking now?'

'I hear say, as how he took to the water like a fish, and didn't so much as wait for a boat, but leaped into the Thames and swam to a barge he keeps off and on here, for no good I'll be bound.'

'And where is this barge you talk of now, Bob?'

'It has fell down the river with the tide a good hour or two agone, as I may say.'

'Wouldn't it be possible to follow it, think you?'

'Cawn't say; but you may try to catch 'un, so be you had a good boat.'

There was no time to lose. I immediately procured a boat, and, as I should probably have a desperate game to play, I engaged Bob to go with me, under a promise of paying him well for his trouble. The waterman said he knew the barge in question for a very 'ugly piece of goods,' and would pledge his life that he would overtake her before she passed London Bridge.

Off we darted, then, in pursuit, and were rapidly borne along by the tide, aided by the ready oars of the waterman. Many a barge we passed dropping down the river; but still we saw no appearance of the one I wanted. It was useless for me to keep a look-out, as I did not know her; but Bob was eager to make the discovery, both from hopes of the promised reward, and pique at the treatment he had experienced from his old master.

Just as we shot through an arch of Westminster Bridge, the waterman, giving me a wink, pulled a-back; and Bob at the same time whispered that he saw the prize we were in pursuit of at some distance, in by the bank among the craft that are usually moored there. It was necessary now to be cautious in our proceedings; for if we rowed openly in upon him, he might escape into the labyrinth of narrow streets and courts on shore, where our search would be in vain.

I accordingly directed the waterman to pull back through the arch, and land us on the Lambeth side[51] of the bridge; in order, if Jones were in the barge, to cut off his retreat to the shore by making our own approach from that direction. With the same design also, I thought it expedient not to take the public entrance at the end of the bridge, but to go farther down amongst the narrow lanes, thereby getting as near as might be to the barge before the alarm could be given.

In one of these narrow streets, as we were passing an ale-house, I recognised the voice of Jem Bucks singing one of his merry songs at the very top of his voice, accompanied, as usual, by a noisy chorus of boon companions. In this state of things I could not reckon much upon his assistance, as he was more set upon fun than business; but yet he might be useful. I accordingly enlisted him for my enterprize of boarding the barge from the landside; and towards her we immediately proceeded, making our way over the broad pavement of coal-luggers,[52] and other craft which lay between her and the shore.

When we came to the barge, she seemed to be deserted; at least there was no indication of any body being aboard. Had Jones, then, escaped, or was he secreted in some part of the vessel? It was necessary to ascertain this; and we therefore prepared to descend into the dark hatchways, where it was possible he might lie concealed.

Our descent was opposed, however, by a person who acted as guardian of the secrets below, and who stood ready to intercept and bid us defiance. As the evening was now setting in, and the hatchway was rather gloomy of itself, I could not at first determine what sort of a person this was; but on a nearer view I perceived that it was a masculine-looking female, of Welsh origin like her master.

This virago, over a white cap trimmed with fine lace, wore a man's hat much the worse for the wear, its original black colour being weathered into a rusty brown; and a sailor's jacket glazed with oil and pitch, which hung down unbuttoned, showing under-garments more in the female style of dress. Her face was much of a colour with her hat, – tawny, weather-beaten, and betokening no acquaintance with soap or water; whilst her hair, of a carroty hue, hung tangled and uncombed from under her head-dress. She was, indeed, a true specimen of those amphibious creatures of doubtful sex, which are to be seen steering the luggers of a canal, or cooking a mess of leek-soup on the deck of a Welsh coaster.

'Tell Mr. Jones,' said I, 'to come on deck: we want to speak with him.'

The virago peered at me with her green eyes, as if to ascertain whether we were true men; and not liking our looks, I suppose, she made all haste to shut the hatchway without deigning the least reply.

'Stop, stop, dame!' said I. 'We must and *will* see Mr. Jones; so you may as well leave that alone;' and Bucks and Lumby, at the same time, seized it to make sure work.

She still returned no answer, but hastily disappeared from our view in the dark recesses below. We made all haste after her; but, as we descended, light failed us, and we had to grope about without rule or compass whereby to steer. There was a large empty space in the midst of this black hole; and as we felt our way along, we were aware of several barrels and packages ranged along the sides, but nothing like a full cargo.

All our darkling search, however, could discover nothing either of Jones or his barge-maid, as I suppose I may call her, according to the use and wont of the term *maid*.[53] Bob Lumby, who had come down with us, did not relish this part of the business at all. He was enough of a dare-devil with his fists in fair and open combat in a ring, and cared not whom he faced; but he had most particular objections to being stabbed in the dark, and pickled up in one of Jones's pork barrels; and still more to have his mouth plastered up while he was dissected alive, – the only two alternatives which occurred to his mind, if Jones should master us in the dark.

Jem Bucks had too much gin in his head to be afraid of any thing; and I myself was brave from the strong wish to succeed in my adventure. Yet it must be confessed we were in some danger, even though there should be nobody on board but the woman, considering that she knew every corner in the place, of which we were entirely ignorant.

Bob Lumby's fears were not imaginary. At the farther end of the hold I reached a partition, and in it I found a door standing a little ajar, which I resolved to open, supposing that the culprit might be concealed there; but just as I was about to enter, I heard Bucks call out behind me, –

'Help! Tom! I'm murder'd!' and the bustling noise of a violent struggle ensued.

'Come! Tom! for the love of Christ!' he continued.

I tried to reach the scene of strife, though it was not possible in the darkness to say exactly from what quarter it proceeded.

'Where are ye now, ye devil's limb?' I next heard Bucks say. 'Stay, could'nt ye, till we settled your account for ye?'

It was now my turn to be assailed. The barge-maid, for it was she, sprang upon me like a tiger, fixed her iron claws in my cravat, and made a stab at me with some weapon, but luckily missed her aim at my heart, for it only grazed my side with a slight wound. The stab of a deadly weapon, however, so near my heart stunned me considerably, though I recovered myself in a moment, and made a spring at the woman; but instead of her, I found myself grappling with the great rough head of Bob Lumby.

'O Lord! O Lord! I'm a dead man!' exclaimed the terrified fellow. 'Don't pickle – don't pickle me, dear Mr. Jones, and I'll promise any thing as you please!'

'Be quiet,' said I, 'you great oaf! I sha'n't pickle you, I give you my word.'

The woman had made off in the dark; and the sounds from the door in the partition, indicated that she was shutting and securing it. As I saw that nothing farther could be done without lights, I thought it best to get on deck again and despatch Bucks for torches; while Lumby and I watched to prevent any attempt at escape from the barge. I was almost convinced Jones was in it, and it would be strange, I thought, if he should now escape us.

Bucks returned with the torches, and we again descended with much greater chance and better hopes of success than when we had to grope our way in the dark, and run the hazard of being assassinated by a woman. We soon forced open the partition door, though we found nothing within except a sort of box-hole, with straw and blankets meant for a bed. The woman had gone somewhere else; and Jones likewise, if he had really hidden here.

I fancied there might be secret doors in a vessel belonging to such a desperado, but though we searched carefully, we found no marks of any other than the one we had entered by. What was more vexing still, we heard the voice of the woman mocking our search, and defying us to reach her.

'No use to poke in that there place, ye blood-hounds!' we heard her voice booming through the planks. 'Ye cawn't ever get to me. It's no use; and him ye're after is off to the Borough,[54] safe and sound.'

'Hurra! old pepper-box!' shouted Jem Bucks. 'We'll ha' ye out of it, if we should fire the ship. We'll teach you a better game nor stabbing in the dark!'

Bucks, indeed, had narrowly escaped her murderous weapon at the first encounter; and he was now bent upon having his revenge for the assault. She must, however, have been pretty certain of the security of her concealment before she ventured upon taunting us. She must have entered it from below also, as I had kept a strict watch on deck. We accordingly tried again all round to discover a trap-door, or a spring-door; but we had no better success than at first.

'Well then,' I called out to her, 'if you do not tell us immediately where Jones is, or, if you know, where the boy is whom he stole off the common at Roehampton, we shall burn the barge about your ears.'

Her voice came from a different quarter altogether, when she answered that Jones was positively gone to the Borough, and might be found in the little back parlour of the Bear and Ragged Staff, Tooley Street. As for the lost boy, she professed entire ignorance of any thing connected with him.

I told her that her own fate depended upon the truth of her information; for she should be well guarded till one of our number went to Tooley Street to ascertain. She again affirmed her story, and I despatched Bucks to the Bear and Ragged Staff, if there was such a house, while Lumby and I remained in the barge.

It appeared, from the circumstance of the sound of her voice coming from different parts of the vessel, that her place of concealment must be extensive, and probably was contrived by double planking round the vessel. The hollow sound it emitted when struck, confirmed this. If I had had a hatchet, I should have tried to cut my way into this secret gallery; but it now occurred to me that we had not sufficiently examined the bed. We had, indeed, sounded and pressed all around it; but we had never thought of trying under the straw.

I therefore hauled out the blankets and the straw, and, after some little trial, found that the lower end balanced down, raising the upper end, and disclosing an entrance to two narrow steps which led to a very small apartment, in which was another bed of similar construction; and, for aught I knew, there might be a dozen such in the barge communicating with one another; and if they made a circle round the hold, which was possible, the dame might well consider herself secure, even if the device were discovered.

I tried another of the bed-traps; but still there was no appearance of the virago. Yet I was resolved to go on as far as I could. In the third one I heard a noise as if somebody were hastily escaping through the secret opening. I pushed onwards, and, in the fourth, came upon the hag just as she was proceeding to raise the bed. As soon as she perceived herself caught, she hastily drew a curtain across the front of the bed; and I heard her say something in a very low whisper, as if to another person within.

Ha! thought I, here is Jones himself, I daresay, much safer and snugger than in the parlour of the Bear and Ragged Staff; but, if it be so, I shall have terrible odds against me; for I had left Lumby with his torch on deck, to guard against any escape that way.

The woman stood resolutely at bay, flourishing a hanger of outlandish shape; the weapon, probably, with which she had assailed us in the dark. I was not at all afraid of this weapon, formidable as it was, nor of the savage looks of the Welsh fury, being provided with my trusty pistols ready primed for use; and when she saw the reception she was likely to have, she did not advance upon me, as had evidently been her first intention, but stood gazing irresolutely, as if considering what to do.

'Tell me instantly,' said I, 'is Jones in that bed?'

'Suppose he be, what then?' replied she.

'Then I should send you to purgatory, you murderous hag!' said I, presenting one of my pistols, as if taking aim.

'And what if he ben't?' she continued, with the utmost coolness, and without shrinking from the death-shot she saw ready for her.

'If it is not he,' replied I, 'it is some one no less criminal, I doubt not, whom I shall feel it my duty to seize.' I conjectured, indeed, that it might possibly be the abandoned wench Sally, or some other of his confederates.

'Will you let me go if I tell you?' she resumed.

This request I peremptorily refused: I had the matter in my own hands, and was determined to do my utmost to secure as many of the gang as I could. The woman did not appear to have any fire-arms; but I knew not how the person whom I supposed to be in the bed might be provided. Indeed, I would at once have examined it without wasting time in parleying, had it not been for this apprehension, and the certainty of the virago stabbing me behind.

Be it as it might, I should have to risk my life; and as retreat was not only ignoble, but would be certain death, I went boldly up to the woman, and told her to surrender at discretion, or I should shoot her on the spot. She hesitated – I placed my finger on the trigger. The love of life prevailed; she held out the handle of her weapon, which I seized; and producing a pair of handcuffs, secured her without another word passing between us.

All the while there was no motion made from the bed for her assistance, which I thought very strange, if any of the gang were really concealed there. She saw my surprise and enjoyed it, trying to make me believe that there was nobody in it at all, and that it was wholly a fancy of my own.

This was a matter soon settled, I drew aside the curtain which she had so carefully drawn, and indeed it appeared to be as she had said; for I could see nobody, and the bed was of such small dimensions, that no grown person, at least, could be concealed there. The pillow, however, seemed to be of uncommon bulk, compared with those in the other beds; and on putting my hand upon it, I felt what appeared to be a head.

I instantly turned down the blanket, and there lay a boy stretched across the pillow, trembling with fright, and not daring to lift his eyes. It proved to be the lost boy, little William Manson. I did not at first know him, for his dress was, of course, different from the one described; but the situation in which I found him soon made me conjecture who he was, and the first question which I put confirmed my suspicions.

This was the luckiest hit I had yet made, and I was almost as much overjoyed as, no doubt, his weeping mother would be when I should have the pleasure of delivering him up to her – a pleasure which I anticipated to be as exquisite as any I had ever experienced. The poor fellow, so far as he could make out a story, had been at first cajoled into a carriage, under all the specious promises best calculated for gaining a child.

He had then been hurried away to a solitary house, and kept there till evening; when his clothes were stript off, and others given him. Flattery and cajoling were now exchanged for terrible threatenings; and he was conveyed blindfolded into the barge, and put under the superintendence of the Welsh virago, into the concealed apartment where I had discovered him. What Jones had designed to do with him did not appear; perhaps he himself had not yet decided; though possibly he had some notion of sending him off, as he had at first told Sally, to his friends in the New Forest, to be out of the way.

The woman had certainly calculated on concealing the boy, whom she had threatened with the most horrid tortures if he dared to speak or make the least noise; but when her crime was fully detected, she was agitated with stronger emotion than she had been even at her loss of freedom. This arose, probably, from her knowing the capital nature of the crime which could thus be proved against her. The agitation, however, was momentary; and she showed no reluctance to be led from the recesses, to whose security she had too confidently trusted.

When Lumby first saw her shoot her head through the hatchway, he was ready to give her a finishing stroke with an enormous barge-oar, which he had shouldered like a fire-lock, while standing sentinel with his torch; but when he perceived she was secured, and that I was following, he shouted out 'bravo!' and appeared as animated on the occasion as any of his apathetic class ever seem to be. He stared at her as he would have done at the Lord Mayor's show, or any other exhibition; but he had no notion of cutting any of the capers of exultation which an Irishman would have played off to perfection, nor any of the hand-rubbing, chuckling glee which might have been drawn from a Scotchman.

As I deemed the woman quite secure with the handcuffs, I was not so particular in keeping close by her, and was more taken up with questioning the little boy. I took no notice, therefore, of her going towards the stern of the barge. I had no fear, indeed, of a rescue, for all the craft around were apparently deserted by their crews; who were on shore, I suppose, at their usual heathenish devotions to Bacchus.[55]

While I was talking to Lumby, with the boy standing beside me, I heard something plunge into the water behind us. I seized Lumby's torch, and ran astern to look what it was. My prisoner was gone; she had actually leapt over the side, handcuffed as she was. What was more strange still, I could not see her in the water, though the torch burned brightly. She had either sunk or got behind some of the numerous barges which lay about. I stept from one to another, and flared my torch into every corner; but the hag was not to be found: I had to return disappointed, and remain content with having recovered the boy.

It was already wearing late when we got safe out of this infernal barge. I did not think it necessary to go to Bow Street to report my success, nor to wait for the return of Bucks from Tooley Street. I felt for Mrs. Manson, who had remained, I understood, in a state bordering upon distraction from the time I had first seen her, and had been carried, nearly insensible, to Roehampton. I therefore ordered a post-chaise and four, and drove thither with little William express.

On our arrival we were immediately greeted with the noisy congratulations of a crowd of servants, to whom the news had spread as if by magic. Mr. Manson, William's father, whom I had not hitherto seen, came down from the drawing-room to meet us, followed by a physician, exerting his professional coolness to prevent any premature disclosure to Mrs. Manson, on whom he was attending.

The father, for his own part, did not seem to require any hint to be cautious, as his feelings of joy appeared to be under absolute command. He said, indeed, 'my dear William, I am glad to see you again;' but the tone of his voice was measured and cool: no burst of joy escaped him – no overflowing of parental tenderness – no yearning of the heart to 'fall on his neck and weep.'[56] His very movement was regulated, and his words well weighed. He acted, indeed, more like a machine wound up to perform certain movements, than like a being endowed with flesh and blood, and moral feelings.

To my bitter disappointment, he took very little notice of me. I had anticipated a hearty, cordial, grateful reception; and the anticipation of this had been one of my strongest spurs to exertion throughout the whole affair. I had pictured Mrs. Manson, with her fine eyes beaming with joy, pouring out to me the most glowing thanks and protestations of gratitude, with unlimited offers of reward, according to her own expression of 'any sum' – confessedly the strongest stimulus which can be held forth.

Like many other pictures which hope has led me to paint, this turned out to be a 'baseless fabric of a vision'[57] – a mere empty shadow of things which were not. Mr. Manson, with cool indifference, asked William if I was the man who had brought him. The little fellow warmly replied,

'O yes, indeed, papa! It was Mr. Richmond that took me away from the naughty woman, and brought me home in the coach.'

'Then, I suppose,' said Mr. Manson to me, 'I must give you something for your trouble. A man would require to be made of money! Every thing – every body cries for money. There,' said he, 'will that satisfy you?' holding out to me a couple of half-crown pieces.

I looked at him with the most indignant contempt, and did not deign to make him any answer.

'So ho! friend! and you don't think a crown is enough? Why the boy has not been gone much more than two days, and half-a-crown a-day should pay you devilishly well, I think, when I can get as many labourers as I choose for half the money.'

I turned about on my heel to leave the cold-blooded calculator and his paltry sum, without honouring him with a single word; for his pitiful argument of the labourers merited no answer. I could see him casting after me a vacant sort of stare, while he carefully replaced his two half-crowns in a well-lined purse, pleased, I suppose, with what he would term my saucy folly. Just as I reached the hall-door, however, I heard Mrs. Manson's voice on the stairs, crying out, –

'O! where is he? Let me see him! I will not be stopped, Doctor! Stand back and let me see my lost child! my dear little boy!'

And she rushed down, and in frantic mood caught the boy in her arms, while Manson stood by like an immoveable block, wondering, of course, what could render people so foolish! This scene rivetted my attention, and I lingered at the door to see how it might end.

I now felt that I was well rewarded for all my exertions and anxieties, in the burst of pleasure I had given to this charming lady. My heart beat, and tears started into my eyes, to see her fondness for her little boy. I enjoyed her rapturous expressions far more than I should have enjoyed a handful of Manson's gold; but my delight was mingled with regret that so fine a woman, and so fond a mother, should be united with a man of so little feeling. My heart leaped up when I heard her say,

'But who brought you, William, my dear? Where is your deliverer?'

O! how I wished and longed, at that moment, to return and confess myself the man; but the freezing look of Manson fixed me to the spot till the little boy pointed me out.

'What! is not the saucy fellow gone yet?' said Manson, in a tone of pique, afraid, perhaps, that I might still claim the two half-crowns. His question was answered by Mrs. Manson running to me in the same passionate manner she had done to the boy; and falling at my feet, she grasped my knees and cried, –

'O! thank you! thank you! But I cannot thank you enough – I can never repay you!'

'Madam!' said I, 'rise, I entreat you. I don't deserve this; I only did my duty.' And I raised her gently up, my whole frame thrilling with indescribable emotion. At the same time I could hear Manson say, –

''Gad! she is mad to a dead certainty. Don't you think so, Doctor?'

'What shall I give you?' Mrs. Manson continued. 'What can I do for you? All I have is nothing to my dear little boy! But take this for the present,' holding out her purse, 'and let me know in what I can be of service to you.'

I took the purse from her agitated hand with profound obeisance; more, however, from a wish not to offend her by refusal, than from a desire for the money. The fine feelings which I had been the happy means of eliciting both towards the boy and towards myself, were an abundant reward to me. The purse, even empty, as a token of remembrance, I should have considered an ample reward. The sight of it, indeed, made Manson more alive than he had hitherto shown himself.

'Mad!' he said aloud; 'absolutely insane!' Then addressing his wife, continued, 'Why, you crazy fool! you won't give that fellow a purse-full of good gold, will you, for two days' work?'

The lady made no answer, and seemed as if she did not hear him. I was for returning her the purse, as I could not bear to see her rated about it by her unfeeling husband; but she motioned me away, and ran back to the child.

'I say, fellow!' Manson called after me as I was leaving the door, 'you don't mean, do you, to carry off that purse from my house, because it was given you by a mad woman?'

I thought it best to follow the fair example of Mrs. Manson, and feign that I did not hear his question; while I stepped into the post-chaise and drove off to Bow Street. I then had leisure to recollect that Mrs. Manson had in her own power a considerable command of money, independent of her husband. Even if this had not been the case, however, I should have resisted any attempt of the cross-grained miser to deprive me of the purse.

Bucks, I found, had returned without finding either the Bear and Ragged Staff, or the culprit Jones: the whole had been a device of the Welsh hag to gain time; and it was probable enough that Jones, through the aid of his shipping connections, was now far on his voyage to the high seas – a fact, indeed, which we ascertained next morning, and the pursuit was therefore for the present abandoned. It will afterwards appear that he had not sailed to a very great distance; and that he had only changed the scene of his operations awhile, till the affair of the boy might be forgotten.

Though I had been unsuccessful in securing Jones the second time, my activity in the whole affair was highly applauded by the magistrate, who told me it should not be overlooked when any other case of moment might require an enterprising officer. This was just the sort of stimulus which I required to spur me on; and I waited impatiently for another opportunity to signalise myself, as I took but little interest in the petty routine of the office.

CHAPTER VII.

Morning intrusion upon Souchong and Epping sausages – The rise, fall, and subsequent promotion of an attorney – Parish laurels of a D.D.

THOUGH the Mansons had endeavoured to keep the story of the boy as private as possible, it was known to too many to be concealed, and was soon circulated with innumerable embellishments and exaggerations: my fame travelled in company, waxing, like the moon, brighter and broader as it rolled on.

The consequence was, that I came to be in much request for enterprises of 'great pith and moment.'[58] Among other scenes into which this notoriety brought me, I shall take the liberty to chronicle the following, as a chapter of incidents and accidents where I had 'ample verge and scope enough'[59] for bestirring myself.

I was one morning sitting comfortably at breakfast in my little room over a cup of Twining's Souchong[60] (I had become a connoisseur of good tea among the gipsies), with a couple of Epping sausages[61] by way of relish and at the same time to provide against the possible accident of missing dinner, when I heard somebody below asking if I was at home.

Immediately after, a stranger entered with an air of impertinence which I did not much like. He was rather a little man, with a thin sharp face, small grey eyes half hid under a pair of shaggy eye-brows, but withal keen, greedy, and peering; a turn-up nose, tipped with a frost-bitten sort of red, to which there was a companion-spot of the same colour on each cheek about the breadth of a crown piece; the rest of his physiognomy being sallow, lank, and leathery, such as you might undertake to carve out of an old boot-top.

I liked neither his pertness nor his appearance. If there is such a thing as love at first sight, in which I believe most religiously, there may be such a thing as *hate* at first sight also; and I confess I was disposed to bestow a little of this latter upon the stranger, who, besides that his looks were not to my liking, seemed about (which was no better) to spoil my unfinished breakfast. As soon as he got in, he said, in a demi-official tone meant to be authoritative,

'You are Richmond, the officer, I take it – Thomas Richmond?'

I assented, but could not divine to what this preface was to lead.

'I have been instructed – '

Ha! thought I, this 'instructed' smacks of law: none of my old pranks, I hope and trust, coming aboveboard[62] to vex me.

'I have been instructed,' he went on, 'that you are the fittest person to intrust with cases requiring caution, vigilance, and activity.'

'Well, sir!' said I, my mind being freed from rising apprehensions, 'if you are pleased to say so – '

'Nay, I know it must be as my friend Gumping[63] instructs me; and the case being so very important, I have come to be advised by you thereupon.'

'I have no power, Sir, to do any thing of myself to serve you without the orders of the presiding magistrate. Why did you not apply at the office?'

'My dear Sir,' he replied, softening down his authoritative tone to something meant to be conciliatory, when he observed that I was inclined to be smart with him, 'I did not wish to trouble the magistrate till I had heard your opinion upon this very vexatious and, I may say, distressing case; and whether you would undertake the business.'

'Well! what is it?' said I, wishing to cut short his exordium.

'Why,' said he, 'every thing that is teasing, vexing, and tormenting! I have the fortune, or rather the misfortune, to be Rector of Duckenhurst, and expected to have lived in peace and comfort in the Parsonage – a pretty rural retreat – *otium cum dignitate*,[64] if you understand Latin; but I had scarcely set foot in the house when my torments began, and are not, I fear, likely to end.'

'A hard case enough, I must say.'

'A wicked conspiracy, it is, against my peace. Every thing turned topsy-turvy – every thing abused or destroyed! Can't eat a meal in comfort, nor sleep a night in peace!'

'Then if it is a conspiracy, as you say, had you not best indict the conspirators at once?'

'Don't know one of them; that is the difficulty. Suspect twenty persons – more than twenty; but no proof against either. Can't bring an action for fault of proof. I have spent a power of money to have them watched; but the watchers have all turned out as bad as, or worse than, the watched. The whole parish is leagued against me, for aught I know; and I have at last been forced to come up to London to seek protection.'

'A most singular affair, Sir, truly; but bless me! what could I do, if the whole parish, as you say, are in the conspiracy? It would take our whole posse[65] to fight your battles.'

'No, no, no! I only want one person, shrewd, cautious, vigilant, and who can be trusted. One such person will be enough to secure, in succession, two or three of the ringleaders. Get them punished, and fear will settle the rest.'

'Well,' said I, 'with permission of the magistrate, I'll try what can be done for you.'

I began, in fact, from the Rector's explanation (so far as it was an explanation) of his distresses, to perceive that his parishioners liked him no better than I had done at first sight; and that they had taken a great deal of trouble to make him acquainted with the fact.

It was a sort of thing, altogether, which would have suited my genius better as one of his flock than as an officer, for the Rector seemed just that kind of man whom I should have delighted to worry into a passion; but if I went to this Duckenhurst, I should at least, I thought, see part of the fun, if fun it was; and I must now perform my duty rather than indulge in mischief.

My duty, indeed, I was resolved to perform; but I also half entertained the feeling, that if I could in any way favour the mischief-makers, perhaps I might. I dared not, however, even whisper this circumstantially to myself; it was high treason against my office, and perjury to my oath: yet I could not banish the thought; it haunted me like a shadow. The devil had determined upon the temptation, and stuck by me as fast as a Jew,[66] to gain me by all sorts of insinuations, which, however, I manfully resisted.

Such was the humour in which I set out for Duckenhurst under the instructions of my frosty-faced friend the Rector, who answered to the name of the Rev. Dr. Cockspur.[67] He had told me none of his troubles specifically: all his complaints were couched in general terms; and I was therefore wicked enough to suppose, from what I could fancy of the case, that they were too trifling, or too ludicrous, to bear detail. The sequel will show how far my conjecture accorded with the facts.

I was not left long in the dark respecting the real state of things at Duckenhurst; for, as I went down by the stage, I found myself in company with a jolly, ale-drinking, good humoured farmer, – Flindal by name, a neighbour of Cockspur's, and well lined with beef, bacon, and small gossip. Flindal had been to town to bring home his daughter, who had been 'finishing her education'[68] at a fashionable boarding-school, and of course unfitting herself for attending to the dairy, the pantry, or any other thing connected with her station in life: such is the rage now for aping the manners of the great.[69] Miss Flindal was a soft, vacant-looking, young lady, whose whole conversation consisted in 'La,[70] papa, you don't say so!' interjected between the old gentleman's bits of gossip, or following the appeals which he made to her upon every subject – the only method he had for showing his paternal fondness, and at the same time drawing her out to exhibit her boarding-school manners. To me, however, it appeared that all she had brought away from the *finishing* boarding-school might be summed up in the aforesaid, 'La, papa, you don't say so!' with the addition of an awkward twist of the shoulders backwards, and an additional flounce to her frock.

According to my invariable practice, I took care not to let Farmer Flindal know who I was, nor what business I was upon; but led him on (it was not difficult) to tell the whole history of Duckenhurst, including the biography of the Rector and his chronicle of mishaps. Upon this authority, and what I subsequently learned, I gathered the following narrative of the events which had occurred previous to my official visit to the parish.

Cockspur, it appeared, had no sooner been inducted into his rectory as the spiritual guide of the parishioners, than he began to show tokens of being a wolf in sheep's clothing – a 'ravening wolf,'[71] moreover, seeking, not whom, but *what* he might devour. This, indeed, I could have augured from his sharp face and greedy eye; and the circumstance did not surprise me. I had been surprised, indeed, at finding him a parson at all; for he had no proud humility about him – no sleek sanctity – no quiet look of stubborn meekness – no chuckling and comfortable self-denial; in short, no one mark upon him of the possession and enjoyment of a good living.

The truth was, he had neither been educated nor intended for the church, and had not come in by the door, but had got into the fold by climbing up some other way; a fact which accounts sufficiently for his want of the proper clerical exterior, and for the discovery of this portentous want which was instantly made by the good people of Duckenhurst.

It appeared that Cockspur was the son of a dealer in old furniture, who being of a quarrelsome and litigious disposition, and having ruined himself at law, came to the wise conclusion, that the calling of an attorney was extremely lucrative, and the best to which he could bring up his son Dan; hoping in the distance, very naturally, that when Dan was up to a thing or two, he might aid him in recovering his law losses without subjecting him to the interminable columns of six-and-eightpences, the very dreams of which gave him a fit of the nightmare.

In the attorney's office Dan was precisely in his element – every thing that his master could wish, particularly when there was any quirk to be managed, or roguery to be atchieved. He had an intuitive knack at petty-fogging in all its circumvolutions, and an instinctive perception of ways and means to multiply obstacles, and to make the proper charges for every step in the process of removing them. In due course, accordingly, he made himself so indispensable, that his master was compelled to take him into partnership to avoid his commencing for himself.

Things had thus gone on prosperously for some time, the new firm of Crome[72] and Cockspur having it all their own way in the neighbourhood, without opposition or question as to their manner of doing business; but at last whispers multiplied, that Mr. Daniel Cockspur was not the thing. Old Crome, indeed, griped[73] rather hard, as all attorneys do, or are said to do; but Master Daniel griped three times harder. The old one's conscience was narrow enough; but the young one had no conscience at all – not a scrap for either man, woman, or child that came within his gripe.

The consequence was, that the business of the firm declined apace, to the great alarm of the senior partner and the vexation of Cockspur; distresses, which were nothing relieved by the arrival of a young attorney connected with the most respectable families in the vicinity, who established himself in opposition to the house of Crome and Cockspur. This was a death-blow to the hopes of Master Daniel: it was a consummation he was not prepared for, as it had never entered into his calculations; but it was necessary now to prepare for the worst, as all the practice of the place, even at the utmost stretch of racking and drawing,[74] was barely enough for two, and of course three must starve.

It usually holds, I believe, that the multiplication of lawyers increases litigation, and that an opposition-attorney proves of advantage to the one who may be first established in a village; but the present case was peculiar, inasmuch as the old firm had, step by step, lost the confidence of the people, and fallen into irreparable disrepute through the griping practices of the junior partner.

Cockspur had some credit, though little money; but he had gained no friends. He was therefore thrown into an awkward puzzle what to make of himself, and how to turn his talents to the best account. He felt conscious that he was an excellent attorney; but what of that, if nobody would employ him? He could, indeed, scrape together bread and cheese as a copying clerk; but he was not yet sunk quite so low in his own estimation as to drudge at quill-driving fourteen hours a day for a pound[75] a week.

In the midst of his distresses he happened to be professionally employed in drawing up some papers relative to the advowson[76] of Duckenhurst, for a young man who was both ignorant of its value, and withal as great a flat as a man like Cockspur could wish to meet with in time of need. The private history of this advowson transaction I could never learn; but the conclusion of the whole matter was, that our attorney was tempted by the prospects thereupon disclosed to change his profession, and secure a good thousand a-year, as Rector of Duckenhurst, in lieu of the paltry hundred or two which was the utmost of his sharings from the firm of Crome and Cockspur.

This thousand also, upon inquiry, he perceived might be easily increased to a great amount by overhauling the commutation of the tithes,[77] which could be done at his leisure when he was once fairly inducted into the Rectory. He set himself accordingly to cram his memory with the Dutch Latin of Grotius De Veritate,[78] and such other shreds and patches of learning as might pass muster with the Bishop, as a substitute for University credentials.[79] All this Cockspur got over (how, I have no means of knowing), and with all the self-gratulation of successful scheming, made his appearance at Duckenhurst to take possession of his living.

His reception was any thing but cordial; for his very look was chilly and forbidding, and so unlike the frank, warm, hospitable, and charitable kindness of his predecessor, that the rich shunned him, and the poor shrank away as he passed, and dared not accost him. Somebody persuaded him that all this arose from his being barely *Mr.* Cockspur, whereas his predecessor had had the dignified addition of DOCTOR to entitle him to the honour and respect of his flock. This difficulty Cockspur in course of time also surmounted, through a relative settled at New York, who had the influence to procure him the degree of D.D.[80] from some American university.

Amidst all the unpleasant heart-burnings, however, which Cockspur had to suffer on his first coming to the Rectory, he had been neither slack nor slow in his inquiries respecting the tithes, compared with the thousand a-year which their commutation produced; and, as the result of his researches, he had come to the determination of either doubling this sum, or receiving his tithes in kind.[81] He was somewhat averse, indeed, to press this obnoxious requisition till he had got the parish into better humour with him by means of the talismanic D.D., which he expected would smooth his way to the measures he meditated, by investing him with more clerical consequence.

Never was a man more mistaken in his hopes. The high title of DOCTOR IN DIVINITY, instead of adding a cubit[82] to his stature, actually sunk him down from 'the Rev. Daniel Cockspur' into *Daddy Dumps* – the interpretation given to the American diploma of D.D. by the wags of Duckenhurst, in allusion to what they called his *dumpish*[83] looks.

Their dislike of Cockspur had previously been manifested only by shy avoidances, and repulsion of all his advances to make acquaintance. The forebodings, however, which had spread about respecting the tithes, soon produced a ferment which began to vent itself by more intelligible tokens. The first of these tokens met the Rector's eye in the form of two great D's indented in the gravel-walk that led from the Parsonage to the church, with the vile addition, 'i. e. Daddy Dumps,' in a parallel line. This was too good a thought to be lost; and accordingly every patch of sand and every road-side was inscribed with the Rector's new nickname, besides its being chalked on the cross-bars of gates, and other conspicuous places; so that he could not move out of doors without meeting with it wherever he turned.

It must be confessed that this was very vexatious to a man who wished, as he said, to enjoy the *otium cum dignitate;* though Cockspur had for this phrase a rendering different from the common one, taking it to mean, '*leisure*' to look into his tithes '*with legal power*' to enforce the same. It was not, therefore, to be wondered at that the D.D. inscriptions should rankle in his bosom, and rouse the spirit of revenge; and as they were general, – all over the parish indeed, it was but just that his revenge should be co-extensive. The long-contemplated measure respecting the tithes was, with this feeling, to be put in immediate operation; and he lost no time in intimating his design.

His enemies, however, did not flinch, but kept pace for pace with him; and their first ebullition was, to instruct the boys who had written the inscriptions to waylay and salute the Rector, where-ever he went, by calling out 'Daddy Dumps.' This annoyed him the more that he had resolved, in addition to the increased product of his tithes, to augment his wealth and his family by marriage; the lady whom he had selected possessing the irresistible charms of an ample purse and some good broad acres, as a set-off to an indifferent figure, a still more indifferent face, and forty, or it might be fifty years of age.

Cockspur was one day showing his lady-love the improvements he meant to make about the Parsonage by clearing away an old straggling hedge, – running a serpentine walk bordered with shrubbery along the lawn, and other tasteful devices, when a ragged imp of a boy popping out from the dry ditch beyond, shouted 'Daddy Dumps!' and darted off through the next field. It may charitably be supposed that the imp had been set on to this by his seniors; though boys require but little prompting to such pranks.

Cockspur took no notice of the affront; but bit his lip, continued to talk more volubly of his improvements, and to saunter through the grounds. The boy watched his opportunity, and repeated his ditty. The Rector could not condescend to take notice of this, though he was sadly vexed and mortified. The story of his wooing soon brought the lady also to share in the blushing honours of the D.D., and the urchins took due opportunity to accost her with the names of 'Mother Dumps' and 'Goody[84] Dumps,' as if she were already Mrs. Doctor Cockspur. This was more than her maidenly pride could endure; and she could only rid herself of the annoyance by breaking off the match, and leaving the Doctor really *in the dumps*.[85]

This was a loss which the Rector could not readily retrieve, as there was not another spinster within his knowledge who was sufficiently rich to suit his matrimonial views.

CHAPTER VIII.

Tithing and teasing – Jubilee of mysterious bell-ringing – 'Get thee behind me, Satan' – Tithe ghosts – Law at fault.

'It is an ill wind that blows nobody good,' said Miss Cockspur to her brother by way of consolation for the loss of his bride, but with more particular reference to herself; for she knew well that she only held her present comfortable seat by the chimney-corner of the Parsonage parlour upon the uncertain tenure of the Rector's bachelorship. 'It is an ill wind, I say, brother Doctor, that blows nobody good; and you may think it right well that you have escaped such a cross-grained baggage,[86] who would have worried your life out of you with her tantrums. I always said so, and you see the end on't.'

'You don't understand the thing, I tell you, Dorothy! If I had once got the money and the broad acres snug, I should not have cared were she as cross as a crab. But I must make up the loss, Dorothy; I must make up the loss.'

'La! brother Doctor! you will never rest satisfied. Why cannot you be contented with my poor endeavours to make you comfortable, and all that? Wives, as I hear, are such sad plagues!'

'I tell you, Dorothy, you don't understand. I don't want a wife; I want money, and money I will have!'

'Then, brother Doctor, why not be after the tithes you are always a-talking about, and let old spinsters and their money alone?'

'That, Dorothy, is the very thing I am going to do. You don't understand; but there are my first-fruits, – the predial, personal, and mixed tithes,[87] great and small, de jure and by custom;[88] to wit: – corn, hay, hops, and hemp; fruits, roots, seeds, and weeds; wool, milk, chickens, ducklings, goslings, poults, and eggs; besides corn-rackings and pond-drawings, agistment,[89] subbois,[90] or sylva cædua;[91] all of which ought, if you understood the thing, Dorothy, to yield double the commutation at least. But you don't, as I say, understand, Dorothy!'

'No more I don't; but I understand it will be a main power of money, if you succeed.'

'Succeed! That I shall I promise you, as the fellows shall feel who have put up all the imps in the parish against me!'

This conversation was overheard, and duly reported in the gossiping circles, with the usual exaggerations, by a prying hussy who served the double office of house-maid and companion to Miss Cockspur, or, as she was now designated, Dorothy Dumps. The wags of Duckenhurst, who had taken so great a fancy to plague the Rector, were determined to treat him with a stimulus to activity in his tithing scheme, and for this purpose contrived numerous devices of annoyance.

One of these was long, inexplicable, and purported to be a jubilee of bell-ringing. At all times, but more particularly during the night, bells were heard in every quarter of the Parsonage, and even in the adjoining domestic offices. The Rector, indeed, had told me that he could not sleep in quiet; but he had given me no particulars of the disturbance. Thus, then, it was: no sooner did he get into bed, in expectation of a comfortable nap, than bells began to tinkle all about his chamber, as if a flock of bell-wethers[92] had been folded[93] beside him. Over head and around – everywhere, indeed, there was the same incessant jingle, so that the Rector was quite distracted.

His sister was worse; for she was persuaded the Parsonage was haunted by evil spirits, and every twang sounded in her ears like a death-knell. The maid harped upon the same string, and besought the Rector to try his skill in laying[94] the bell-ringing spirits. Cockspur, not being much of a scholar, (though bred to the law, and passing shrewd), was not antiquarian enough to know that the devil hates bells, and that bells were originally put up in churches expressly to *prevent* the intrusion of evil spirits.

He was at first, therefore, much inclined to coincide with the womankind of his establishment as to the spiritual nature of the annoyance; for what else could it be? Search as he would every corner of his chamber, he could see nothing; and yet he had no sooner extinguished his candle, than the bells began to tinkle on every side of him. The stable-boy made a similar complaint. He dared not venture out to feed the Rector's horse after dark, for there were 'ghosties,' he said, 'a-ringing and ringing all about and betwixt. Master might go, but he wouldn't, for no colour[95] of money.'

Rather than suffer his horse to want oats, Cockspur did go to the stables, though he was not much fonder of the job than the boy; and, to be sure, there he heard the same jingling music which had perplexed him in his own chamber. The only thing which gave him courage was, that the horse was standing as cool and quiet as if there had not been a spirit within a hundred miles of him; a thing which could not well have happened, he thought, if there had been any real visitors from the world of spirits in the stable.

This annoyance had continued, without intermission, for several days, and still no explanation of it could be found. Cockspur, indeed, had seriously resolved to abandon the Parsonage altogether, if it continued. After having spent a sleepless night, he was one morning walking out slowly, with his arms a-kimbo, towards the stable to see how his horse had got through with his oats, when he saw a strange tabby cat run out of the stable with a large rat in her teeth; and as she bounced past him, he heard the identical tinkle which seemed to be so omni-present about the Parsonage after night-fall.

The mystery was explained at once. The rat was furnished with a small bell like those used in hawking, and there could be no doubt this had been contrived to tease him; for he believed there might be at least twenty such rats in and about his premises, which had of course been caught, belled, and turned adrift by his enemies.

It now struck him that Miss Cockspur's favourite cat had been missing from the commencement of the row by these accursed rats; and, at the same time, his own terrier had been found drowned in the horse-pond – circumstances which could only be explained on the supposition of a plot for his annoyance.

When this scheme had thus wrought out its own detection, the wags, finding Cockspur to be somewhat credulous in the matter of ghosts and spirits, devised another contrivance founded on their discovery of his credulity. One of them, who was a son of my friend Farmer Flindal, rented the farm of Woodbank, about two miles or so from the Parsonage: the house, being situated hard by the remains of a forest, displayed a charming sylvan retirement in daylight and good weather, but was drear and lonely in a stormy night, when the wind roared through the trees.

This house was fixed upon, as best adapted for the plot which was next con-trived against Cockspur's peace. Young Flindal undertook to keep up a proper decorum of gravity while he waited on the Rector to inform him of the very unpleasant circumstance of Woodbank being haunted, and to take his advice as to the means necessary for laying the ghosts or spirits that had made choice of his house for the scene of their mischievous revels. It is as well to mention, that care had been taken to pave the way by having the circumstances reported more than once to the Doctor before Flindal paid his visit, so as to leave no room for doubt respecting the fact, should his Reverence be disposed to be sceptical.

Flindal told his story with a most portentous look of fear, and prayed the Rector to undertake the task of freeing his house from its unearthly visitors. The preceding Rector, young Flindal averred, had more than once prayed in haunted houses with success; and it was a service which belonged exclusively to the sacred office. Cockspur did not know well what to do about this unforeseen and unex-pected demand upon his rectorial duties. He certainly did give credence to the reality of the apparitions in Flindal's house; but he did not feel any confidence in his own powers of effecting their expulsion. He had, indeed, an unpleasant consciousness of his deficiency in piety; as out of church he never troubled himself with prayers, nor any thing else savouring of religion.

Yet he saw not how he was to escape. If he refused, he did not know whether, upon due complaint, the Bishop might not suspend him, to the certain loss of his thousand a-year for the time being; and on the other hand, if he complied, he was as much afraid of apparitions as Flindal could be for his life. The Bible, indeed, was a tried and powerful weapon in all such cases; and when at last he saw no other way of getting rid of his applicant, he determined to trust, for self-protection, to the efficacy of the sacred volume and to the Prayer-Book, for the means of laying or expelling the 'goblins damned'[96] that haunted the house of Woodbank.

As it was only at night, according to young Flindal's narrative, and indeed according to the known nature of ghosts, that the disturbances in the house took place, it behoved Cockspur to be on the spot with his spiritual armour, to fight them when they were to be found. With great reluctance, therefore, and shrinking at every step, he took the road to Woodbank; where he arrived without accident, as the wags had not yet begun their game. He afterwards admitted that he had certain wavering suspicions of some plot in the wind, and the idea of the bell-rats occurred more than once to his mind; but whatever there might be in this, he now stood committed to brave the worst.

At some distance from the house stood a large antique barn, which, from being inconvenient for the farm, had long been abandoned, and was now unroofed, ruinous, and desolate. This, according to young Flindal, was also a favourite resort of the goblins; and nobody dared to pass near it even in day-light. This, however, was near the truth, and no joke. When the Rector was about the business, therefore, at any rate he might as well make a good job of it by clearing out this strong hold of 'black spirits and grey.'[97] Cockspur himself thought this was travelling out of the record;[98] but said he would try first what he could do with those which haunted the house itself.

As soon as it was quite dark, the ghost-game began with all sorts of hideous screams and noises from the more remote parts of the house, and a villainous smell of brimstone arose and assailed the Rector's olfactories. This being proof positive, he thought, of the evil origin of these disturbers of the peace, he hastened to open the Bible where it is written, 'Get thee behind me, Satan!'[99] which words he read thrice over in a loud and solemn voice. This exorcism was followed by a long and terrible howl, in which he fancied he heard the word 'Mercy! Mercy!' indistinctly repeated, as if the fiends were afraid of him.

Hence our magnanimous doctor drew fresh courage, and began to stalk about the room with the open Bible in his hand, still repeating, 'Get thee behind me, Satan!' when his eye catching the large mirror over the mantel-piece, he started back shuddering with fear, and actually dropt the sacred volume on the floor.

The apparition which met his eyes in the mirror was no other than a very fright-ful effigy of Satan, who was represented as actually behind him, breathing flames and brimstone, and ready to devour him in defiance of his anathemas. The truth was, that a puppet had been got up for the occasion, and dextrously manœuvered by one of the wags till it produced the catastrophe recorded.

Cockspur, thus vanquished in the moment of his supposed triumph over Satan, stooped down in great terror to recover the dropt Bible, not daring to give a second look at the apparition in the mirror. This was the moment chosen to bring a lighted brimstone match in contact with his hair, which he wore long and straggling. His head was instantly all in a blaze; and the increasing smell of the brimstone, together with the apparition in the mirror, were altogether circum-stances of fiendish reality which utterly confounded his understanding.

He raised both his hands from the Bible to his hair, and then back again to the Bible, in all the flurry of terror and uncertainty. To the hair there was not much damage done – it was even improved by the singeing; but his courage had been marvellously annihilated, and he prayed in good earnest that he might soon escape from this awful Woodbank, where he had to cope so unequally with the imps of darkness.

The howlings and other noises now ceased for a space, thereby giving Cock-spur a little time to recover from the shock of the match-singeing, and the mirror-apparition of Satan. But they had not done with him. Flindal recom-mended the reading of prayers, and volunteered to act as clerk on the occasion, in order to prevent any lurking idea that the Rector might entertain of his collu-sion with the fiends, if he should become suspicious. This being at length agreed upon, Cockspur commenced the solemn service (I know not what part of it); but no sooner had he opened his mouth than it was completely filled with a nauseous red liquid, like blood, which was squirted from some concealed corner by the wags in waiting.

This was past endurance: he spit, spurted, and capered about like a maniac; while the howling, mingled with strange laughter, was renewed, and the parlour fire burned blue with brimstone which had been slily put therein.

Poor Cockspur was really in the hands of imps who had no mercy for the proprietor of the parish tithes, and seemed to care little for his weapons of spir-itual warfare. It would be endless to enumerate all the tricks which they played upon him during his memorable expedition to Woodbank; but, to his honour be it spoken, he struggled manfully to the last.

One of the few books which the Rector had ever taken the trouble to read, was Bunyan's Pilgrim's Progress;[100] and his present troubles brought vividly to his recollection some of the conflicts of Christian with the Father of Evil. When, therefore, he had wiped the squirtation from his beard, and felt whether the remains of his hair were all safe, the words of Christian came seasonably to his recollection, and he ejaculated, 'Rejoice not against me, O mine enemy! When I fall, I shall arise.'[101]

The wags, upon this, thought it a favourable time to treat him with a tremendous shock, which they had prepared by means of an electrical battery in the adjoining room; and it told so well that he went down as if he had been shot, and lay stretched for dead upon the floor. Young Flindal became alarmed in his turn, and thought the joke had gone too far; but the Rector soon began to show signs of animation, and still supposing himself enacting Bunyan's Christian, rose slowly up, sighing out, 'Though I walk through the valley of the shadow of death, yet will I fear no evil.'[102]

Several hours were spent in similar pranks against the Rector, young Flindal still maintaining a decorous gravity on the occasion, and lamenting that he could not aid him. When the 'witching time of night'[103] drew to a close, the wags became tired of their pastime; and after 'Good night!' being echoed in a lengthened howl throughout the house, quiet was restored. It may be supposed that they did not leave the Rector in any mood for venturing to the old waste barn in pursuit of them; though Flindal did make the proposal, telling him that they always went there when they departed from Woodbank.

Cockspur had a mortal reluctance not only to go to this haunted barn, but to venture out at all, even to return home; though he had no very great partiality, as may be supposed, after what had happened, to the idea of taking a bed at Woodbank: sleep was entirely out of the question for that night. It was, however, the least of the evils which beset him, and he remained with Flindal till morning.

Cockspur could only get rid of his vexations by plunging deep into the study of his tithes, and bustling about to bring his measures to bear, of which he now made no secret. His proposal was, either to have the commutation doubled, or to levy his tithes in kind; and, in the latter case, he indulged in the hopeful vision of seeing all the corn-fields in the parish studded over with green branches to mark his tithe sheaves, and his carts making their rounds to bring them home. But those dreams were ever and anon disturbed by the active invention of the wags. Among other devices, they cut a large piece of white paper into the form of a ghost, which some venturous fellow found an opportunity of sticking upon his back whilst taking a round through the village, and which bore the inscription of 'Daddy Dumps's Tithe Ghost.' The thing had been done so dextrously, that he was not aware of it till he went home, when Miss Dorothy Cockspur disencumbered him of the insulting paper.

A few days after, a cart piled high with thistles and other weeds drove into his yard, and the lad who drove it proceeded to unload them. Cockspur looked astonished, and asked him what he meant by bringing such rubbish there. The lad, who, although he had a very stupid, simple, look, was not deficient in wit, said that his master bade him take the thistles as a tithe of what grew on his farm;

'and if so be,' added the imp, 'there is ere an ass about here, he'll know what to make of them there thistles.'

Cockspur was about to strike the impudent rascal with his cane, when he cried out, –

'O Lord! Master Parson, don't take your stick to I; for I be a ghost. Run for your Bible, Master Parson!'

The Rector was exasperated into a dreadful passion; but the driver of the thistle-cart did not seem to value him a rush, and went on unloading and laughing most maliciously at his own wit. It was not till this moment that Cockspur had ever suspected the Woodbank imps to be other than what they pretended; but the sarcasm of the lad, and the late affront of the paper ghost stuck on his back, with various other little circumstances which now came to his remembrance, all combined to force upon him the conclusion that Flindal had made an ass of him. The thought was too much for poor Cockspur: first, to be written an ass; then to be made an ass, to wit, at Woodbank; and finally, to have thistles sent to him as provender.

'I'll have the law of you all, if there be law in England!' he called to the lad, as he bolted into the house to hide his shame and vexation.

Unfortunately, however, for Cockspur, all his knowledge of the law was foiled in attempting to discover any statute upon which to indict the farmer who had sent, or the lad who had brought, the thistles; and in the case of the Woodbank ghosts, which might have been actionable, inasmuch as he was assaulted, put in bodily fear of his life, and moreover had parcel of his hair burned or singed, – he had no evidence, except of a presumptive nature, that young Flindal was concerned; nor could he swear to any of the rest.

In consequence of these repeated grievances and increasing suspicions, Cockspur now had recourse to a system of espionage, by bribing several persons to be on the look-out for his tormentors. The cash, indeed, was given with a painful grudge; but what could he do? In this plan he had been no less unfortunate than in every thing else of late; for when it was once understood that money could be made of him, the very men, whom he pensioned as spies, became the chief underhand instigators of the plots against him.

His life at the Parsonage was thenceforth a series of continual distresses, many of them ludicrous, indeed, and affording good sport to his tormentors; but all preying upon his mind till he grew quite distracted with vexation; and finding all the means he tried only serve to involve him the more inextricably in the toils of his enemies, he resolved at last to go to London, and procure a tried officer from Bow Street, to assist him in discovering and punishing the delinquents. His visit to myself, and the result, I have already recorded.

CHAPTER IX.

Miss Dorothy Cockspur in mortal fear of the pit of perdition – The earthquake blown up – The sexton's brandy bottle.

WHEN I arrived at Duckenhurst, my first intention was to proceed immediately to the Parsonage and establish myself there, like a spider, ready to pounce upon whatever prey should come within reach; but Farmer Flindal's history of the Rector and his wrongs determined me to keep aloof for some time from the scene of action, till I had obtained more intelligence. I, therefore, fixed my head-quarters at the inn, and employed my time in pumping every body I could engage in gossiping, from the barber to the blacksmith; and the better to loosen their tongues, I did not spare to treat them with an occasional pot of my land-lord's home-brewed.

A considerable portion of what I have above related was derived from these sources; and it may well be imagined that I had not much liking to the job I was engaged in, of aiding the Rector against the mischievous wags, who conceived they had as good a right to vex him, as he had to screw up his tithes at their expense. Something, however, I must do for the sake of my oath and my duty, as much to save appearances as to keep up my character.

I had received a hint, among other things, that in the Rector's absence (for he had not yet returned) a plot was on foot to frighten Miss Dorothy, who was no less obnoxious than her brother, as, like most old maids, she had a very bad opinion of all her neighbours; and such opinions she was by no means slow or scrupulous in disseminating. The Rector's journey to London had left the wags without that butt for their devices; and, to keep their wit from rusting, they prepared to practise on his sister.

Advantage was accordingly taken of an account, which about that time appeared in the newspapers, of the shock of an earthquake having been felt in several parts of England, to make Miss Dorothy apprehensive of some such awful visitation coming upon the Parsonage in her brother's absence. Her companion the house-maid, who had been a party to many of the tricks, was to begin the game according to the instructions of her sweetheart, (one of the wags), by telling Miss Dorothy wonderful stories of earthquakes, and particularly of the usual catastrophe of the earth's opening and swallowing up whole cities.

Miss Dorothy, though not much given to reading, knew there had been such things; and having her fancy set a-working on the subject, she became persuaded that this dreadful earthquake, which she was told was going round the country, might come to Duckenhurst, make free with the Parsonage, and swallow up the whole house, including herself. In consequence of the continued game purposely kept up by the maid, and of her own distempered apprehensions, Dorothy had been worked into a state of restless and ridiculous fear; and trudged about from morning till night, talking of these terrible earthquakes, and more particularly of the actual yawnings of the earth to swallow up whole houses and their inhabitants.

It is probable she entertained some indefinite notion that, if an earthquake should actually swallow up the Parsonage, and lodge her in the depths of the earth, she might be there in the horrible vicinity of the bottomless pit, and the smoke of its torments; but this I can do no more than conjecture.

It was in this earthquake case that I resolved to interfere first, and to spoil, if I could, some of the intended sport of the wags; as, however much I might be disposed to laugh at Miss Dorothy's fanciful terrors, I thought it was too bad thus to take advantage of a lone woman. So far as the maid's stories went, indeed, I could not bridle her tongue; but I was determined to frustrate any manual operations which might be attempted; and such I understood were under contemplation, in order to give Dorothy an alarm of the immediate shock of the earthquake she so much dreaded. They wisely pitched upon the night for the time of their game, and as the Rector was expected every hour, were anxious to expedite the business; for he had become so suspicious of them, that they could no longer work on *his* credulity by such devices.

I thought it my duty to watch their proceedings, and, therefore, about night-fall, stationed myself near the Parsonage, so that I might observe what was transacting. I had not long taken my position in a dark corner, within sight of the parlour-window at which I had ascertained that Miss Dorothy was in the habit of seating herself for the evening, when I heard a footfall in the direction of the yard, and advancing towards the place where I stood.

It was too dark for me to see who the person was, though he was at no great distance; but I was not long left in doubt about the object, if I could not distinguish the individual; for immediately a strange rumbling noise commenced under Miss Dorothy's window, being intended, as I imagined, to imitate the prelude of the sham earthquake. At the same time, I heard an unusual bustle begin in the interior of the house. The operator without increased his noise, which, by cautiously stealing up behind him, I found he produced by rubbing a great stone hard against the rough wall in all directions.

The noise without was soon answered by a louder noise from within; seemingly as if the floors were shaken by a terrible convulsion, which tumbled every thing about in confusion. Miss Dorothy, it may be well supposed, did not, in the state of her mind, hear all this without dreading that her apprehensions were now to be awfully realised. I heard her, indeed, more than once muttering in fear; while the mischievous maid, who had been standing by her (etiquette permitted her not to sit) for company and gossip, actually screamed out with well-feigned alarm. Miss Dorothy, perhaps, thought it vulgar to scream in concert with her maid; for she contented herself with repeating, –

'O La! what shall I do? What shall I do?'

The earthquake-makers, however, were by no means timid in their operations. Success in similar tricks, particularly in the night scenes at Woodbank, had emboldened them to venture upon all sorts of measures. At the close, therefore, of one tremendous rumble, which seemed to shake the Parsonage from its foundation, I heard the glass of several of the windows shivered, and an extensive smash of what appeared to be stone-ware or china. At the same moment out rushed Miss Dorothy from the hall-door, with her thin grizzly hair streaming about her face like a possessed sybil,[104] and crying, –

'O God! be merciful to me, a sinner!'

The maid followed, offering her consolation; for she had ceased to feign fear when she once saw the scheme in operation; though she was now in her turn somewhat afraid lest poor Miss Dorothy's wits might depart amidst the hubbub. In her present plight, indeed, she had all the appearance of a maniac escaped or escaping from confinement, running about as if unconscious where she was going, and repeating –

'O mercy! mercy! Good Lord! I am a miserable sinner!'

I thought I had now allowed the game to go far enough – farther, perhaps, than I ought to have done; but I could not help enjoying a little prank, which in my earlier days I should have myself been pleased to enact. Had it been the Rector himself, I might not perhaps have been so prompt as I was; but I felt for poor Miss Dorothy, and, to put an end to the farce, I darted out of my hiding-place, and seized the operator on the wall. As Miss Dorothy stood hard by, wringing her hands to the doleful tune of 'Mercy, good Lord!' her surprise at my sudden movement put to flight, for the moment, her earthquake alarms, and she called out, –

'What's this? What's coming now? Thieves! Thieves! Robbers! Thieves!'

'No, not thieves,' said I, advancing with my prisoner, who struggled hard to get away, 'but rascals, making a villainous noise to alarm you.'

Upon procuring a light, it turned out to be the Rector's own stable-boy, who had been rumbling the stone along the wall; but he denied with the utmost assurance the whole transaction, affirming that he was returning from feeding his master's horse when I seized him, and that he knew nothing of any body making noises about the house. Miss Dorothy, however, now that her suspicions were roused, pretended to see to the bottom of the whole affair, and began to rate him with great volubility, calling him 'an incarnate imp,' 'a devil's breech-ling,'[105] and other elegant appellations from her own vocabulary.

I was most anxious in the mean-while to detect and seize those who had been intrusted with the interior operations, and who had exceeded the legitimate limits of a mere prank, by breaking the windows, china, and other valuables. When, therefore, I had ascertained the stable-boy's identity, I thought I might safely allow him to go at large, as it would probably be easy, if necessary, to apprehend him afterwards.

Being directed by Miss Dorothy, whose indignation at being duped had got the better of her fears and her shame, I proceeded to examine the several rooms where it was imagined the disturbers of the peace might be lurking. It may be remarked that the maid's anxiety to show her zeal greatly 'o'erstept the modesty of nature,'[106] and proved to me, who had got into a few of the secrets, her own connivance with the culprits.

Our search was in vain. We found nobody in any of the rooms; but fragments of ewers and basins lay scattered about the bed-chambers, and several dressing-glasses were broken to shivers, besides the demolition of a great number of window-panes.

In this state of things I considered it proper to tell Miss Dorothy who I was, and to instal myself immediately in the Parsonage, to prevent farther destruction of the Rector's property. I told her it might be as well to say nothing about my arrival, as it might prevent in a great measure my success in apprehending the delinquents. In thus discovering myself and enjoining secrecy, I had not calculated upon the gossiping propensity inherent in spinsters. I might, therefore, have saved myself the trouble of giving the cautionary hint; for she was so big with the secret, that she very soon made an excuse to leave me, and was scarcely out of my hearing before I heard her whisper to the wicked maid, –

'La! what d'ye think? He is nothing less nor a Bow Street officer, sent down by the Doctor to protect us. Only think! but you mustn't tell! Mind, it is to be a profound secret; so tell nobody, like a good girl.'

The 'good girl,' of course, would take occasion within the very minute to report this important intelligence, which would be circulated with all despatch to every corner of the parish.

Next day the Rector himself arrived; and when he heard the history of the earthquake at the Parsonage, with the bodily fears of his sister Dorothy, he flew into a most furious passion. His face changed into all manner of colours; and had the guilty stable-boy been within his reach, I doubt whether his life would have been very safe. The boy, however, was more cunning, or better advised than

I had reckoned upon, and was not to be found. The alarming report of my being a Bow Street officer had induced him to decamp without leave; and his parents pretended not to know whither he had gone.

It is inconceivable with what dread the country people of Duckenhurst looked upon me: the very children seemed to shrink from me. So many of them, indeed, were parties to the tricks which had been played off upon Cockspur, that they had some reason to be afraid. Considering all this, it was with a degree of surprise that I heard of more apparitions having made their appearance in the form of white figures, which were seen flitting about during the night in the vicinity of the Parsonage, and of the church, which was immediately adjoining.

This was a circumstance which gave Cockspur great uneasiness, and which I could not fathom. Notwithstanding his having been so much gulled at Wood-bank, I could perceive that superstitious credulity had still a strong hold of his mind; and, as the apparitions, though several times observed, had not been known to do any thing besides stalking harmlessly along, he half made up his belief that they were true ghosts, and no deception.

I had seen and heard too much of this sort of thing to believe it to be any more than a trick to serve some purpose of the contrivers; and I therefore, with Cockspur's permission, set about watching the proceedings of the ghosts. This was the only thing, indeed, in the way of business which for the present I could do; as the open warfare against the Rector, which had commenced by writing 'Daddy Dumps' on the gravel and the gate-posts, and been pursued by sending the cart-load of thistles and the like, had entirely ceased.

The church of Duckenhurst was a very ancient structure, with a picturesque tower thickly covered with ivy. It stood on a rising ground by itself, at the distance of two or three gunshots behind the Parsonage, towards the fields. A couple of fine old yew-trees grew on each side of the porch to the church-yard, which was surrounded by a low sunk stone-wall, grey with the effects of time and weather, and overhung with long grass. I am the more particular in describing the spot, as the ghosts were said to have been seen walking about this wall, and to have suddenly disappeared as if they had slunk into the hollow ditch which divided it from the surrounding field.

No explanation of these circumstances occurred to me. I could not form a satisfactory conjecture, though I was thoroughly convinced it was a trick, and might probably be connected with the system of annoyance which had been so daringly put in practice against the Rector. Or, it might be that thieves or other miscreants had taken advantage of the known reports in circulation through the parish respecting apparitions, to personate spectres in order to perpetrate their midnight deeds with more security. Yet, if it were so, depredations thus committed could not be concealed; and of these we had heard nothing.

Upon the knowledge of all these circumstances, I resolved to place myself, after dark, within the range of the church-yard wall, with the purpose of tracking the ghost or ghosts (for more than one had been seen) to some definite residence, even if it should be a tomb. I watched, however, in vain till one o'clock in the morning; when I thought I might as well go back to the Parsonage for this turn, as nothing was likely to stir in the ghost line after so late an hour.

I found Cockspur deep in the study of the tithe laws; and it was with some difficulty I could badger him to produce a bottle of wine, though I had been so long on his account exposed to the night dews. His niggard heart, however, at last softened a little; and after drinking success to his plans in a bumper or two, I went to take a preparatory sleep for the following night, being determined upon perseverance till I had made something out respecting the ghosts, if, as I began to fear, the whole report did not turn out to be a hoax.

It struck me that the sexton might know something of the matter; but I was afraid to say much to him, lest he might defeat my object, if he had an understanding with the parties, whoever they might be. I thought it proper, nevertheless, to try whether I could pick any thing out of him.

On calling upon him for this purpose, I perceived at once, from his flurry and confusion when I hinted at the subject, that there was something in it; though he was cunning enough to pretend that he himself had been almost frightened to death by the ghosts, and would not, he said, venture to the church-yard after night-fall if I were to make him 'Squire of the Duckenhurst property, which was known to be some'at to the tune of fifteen thousand[107] a-year.'

I professed to be also much afraid of ghosts, though I said I should like of all things to see one, as I had never yet had that honour; at the same time, I gave him to understand that I would not think of venturing to a church-yard for the purpose, but would prefer the meeting in a well-lighted parlour, with plenty of good liquor to keep up my courage. This doctrine seemed to tally well with his notions. He assented with a knowing wink, and went on to say, –

'Yees! Sir, a drop o' good liquor is no bad thing, as you say, and mayhap you might like to taste some'at out o' my bottle. A little prime stuff I ha' just now – right Cogniac as ever crossed the Channel, I'll swear.'

I made no objection to taste and praise the sexton's brandy, which he gave me to understand had been sent him as a present by a friend who imported it. The circumstance, however, awakened my suspicions that his friend, the importer of brandy, might be no other than one of the church-yard ghosts; for his anxiety to frighten me, and his evidently taking alarm himself when I first mentioned the apparitions, were circumstances of a very dubious kind.

CHAPTER X.

Church-yard scenes – Sepulchral conclave of ruffians – Night researches in a family vault.

WITHOUT imparting my suspicions to Cockspur – for I did not like, as the saying goes, to cut before the point,[108] nor did I wish to consult or advise with him at all when I could avoid it, – I again went, as soon as it was dark, to the church-yard; and the better to conceal myself, I leaned against the trunk of one of the old yew trees at the porch. I had not been long here, when I saw first one white figure glide past – then another – and after a little, a third. I took care to keep behind the trunk of the tree that I might not be perceived; though there was little danger, since it was very dark, and the thick shade of the yew made it still darker where I stood. I was the better able, from the white colour of their dress, to mark with my eye the direction which the figures took; and, after waiting some time till I judged they had all passed, I determined to follow them.

I confess, however, that I had some little qualms of fear and creepings of the blood, for which I hope I may be excused; as there are not many, even of those who are no cowards, who would like to be alone at night in a church-yard; and still less to see white figures there, flitting about and purporting to be spectres. Though I was strongly persuaded they were not what they seemed, and had my suspicions with respect to what they were about; yet I could not altogether banish certain boyish feelings of superstition, nor shake off the aforesaid creepings, which pervaded my whole flesh like the alarming attack of an ague.

As the figures had all taken the same direction round the tower of the church, where I lost sight of them, I went cautiously forward, with my eyes and ears attentive to every sight and sound that might occur.

After I got round the tower, I thought I distinguished voices, but could not fix upon the direction from which they proceeded. As the church stood on the gentle rising ground before-mentioned, there was a considerable declivity shelving down from the spot where I now was towards the fields. About half-way down this descent, there was a large antique tomb, the burying place of I know not what old family of distinction. After listening attentively, I thought the voices certainly proceeded from it; and on going nearer, I saw a very faint thread of light glimmering through the key-hole of the door. Here then, thought I, the spectre conclave are assembled, whatever their purpose may be.

I now went close up to the entrance, which was of large dimensions; and, indeed, the whole vault was capacious enough for 'all the Capulets.'[109] On peeping in at the key-hole, through which the light streamed, I could perceive the three white figures which had lately passed me, together with two men in dark dresses, sitting upon the coffins in earnest conversation; one of the men holding upon his knee a small lamp fixed in a horn lantern, the door of which was open probably to afford more light. One of the men in the dark dresses I imagined, upon closer inspection, to be my friend the sexton, and the sound of his voice put the matter beyond doubt; for I heard him say in the slang style, –

'I fear the trap has nosed us.[110] I tried to gammon[111] him about the ghosts, thof I don't know whyfore he kept axing me consarning 'em. I didn't like the look on't.'

'There's only one trap, you say. Are ye sure of that, Sexty?'

'Yees, sure as flint, i'faith! Daddy Dumps went to Lun'on hisself for 'un.'

'If that's all, we can take 'im on the sly – serve 'im with notice to quit[112] – and stow him right and away for Windmill Street.[113] Jones will give us four or five screens[114] for him.'

'Is the trap a leery cove,[115] Sexty?' said another of the spectres.

'Yees, main leery, I daresay. Down to[116] every thing in our line, it is to be feared.'

'Then we must gammon him on a nose, till we can tip him a scratch with a chiv on his blow-pipe.'

The reader may possibly conceive, though I cannot well describe, the feelings which I experienced on hearing this ruffian dialogue; from which I learned that I was to be decoyed into a quiet corner – my throat cut – and my body sold to Jones, at the rate of four or five pounds, for the use of the London dissecting rooms. They were not aware, perhaps, that Jones had fled.

There were five of the ruffians: I was single-handed, and knew not where I could get assistance which I could depend upon, otherwise I would have rushed upon them in their den, and secured them. I was, by good Providence, however, put upon my guard; and would not readily, I thought, be entrapped by any snare which they might lay to 'gammon' me, as they called it. I perceived the necessity, on my part, of the utmost caution, and of watching them closely; both to secure myself against their bloody designs, and to fulfil my duty by apprehending them, if I could procure assistance for that purpose.

'Sha'n't we go that there stuff this darkey?'[117] said one of the fellows, pointing to a pile of something which I could not make out. 'The kiddy[118] is waiting in Flindal's field with the fly,[119] ready to be off at a minute's notice.'

'I think,' said the sexton, 'as how it might be risky to go it to-night; for the trap may be on the nose, and blow all up out and out.'

'How, then, can we do the job, Sexty?'

'Let us see. What have we? A dozen of the one, and three of the other. Why, the fly could run 'em off, if they were stowed once and away.'

'But if we're blown, Sexty, as you say, we'll have to ding[120] 'em all. Better try what can be done now.'

'Why then,' said the sexton, looking cautiously about the while, 'mayhap it may be as well; only as I don't like to be blown in this here place, you must do the job without me, if you please.'

'No, no, Sexty! that won't do. Share and share is all fair; and the cold meat consarn[121] is all your own go, you know. We won't touch that, I promise you.'

'True!' said the sexton; 'but when is Jones a-coming with the blunt? I can't stir farther, if I don't have the ready down.'[122]

'Can't say to a minute,' replied one of the spectres. 'Jones must travel it on the sly now, since he was so devilishly blown about that boy at Lun'on. He is at present with one of our number near Lyndhurst, in the New Forest; and if you step thither, the blunt will be forthcoming I've no doubt.'

This was information in which, it may be supposed, I was keenly interested; for I inferred from it that the culprit Jones (it could be no other), instead of having gone out of the country, as had been reported and believed, had been probably landed on the coast of Hampshire, and was pursuing his old trades among the desperadoes of the New Forest; which has long been notorious as a haunt for smugglers and robbers, and the very head-quarters of poaching and deer-stealing.

Upon the whole, I found myself in very difficult circumstances, and was puzzled how to act so as to secure Jones and his associates. Had I been nearer London, I should have soon got a posse strong enough for them if they had been thrice as numerous; but in this outlandish place, eighty or ninety miles from the metropolis, with scarcely such a thing as a constable, and those who had been sworn as such not to be depended on, I really was quite nonplussed.

In the mean-time, the spectre desperadoes in the tomb were bestirring themselves in moving some large skins of liquor which were stowed there, and which I supposed to be brandy; while the sexton and the other dark-dressed man proceeded to violate one of the coffins in the vault by breaking up the lid. The coffin was new; and, from the conversation of the ruffians, I understood that it contained the remains of a young lady, which they unceremoniously stuffed into a large sack, with many a coarse jest unfit to be repeated. They then prepared to carry it off for purposes which were but too obvious.

As they were now approaching the door with their several burdens, I thought it high time to conceal myself in a recess of the tomb to watch their farther proceedings; for it would have been madness to attack them single-handed – certain death indeed, as it was by no means likely such fellows were without weapons when on a night expedition.

The three spectres I could see sally out, one after another, at brief intervals – each carrying a skin of liquor; and with these burdens they took the way of the fields. In a little while the sexton and his companion followed them with their sack; but as this was much heavier and more unwieldy than the liquor-skins, their movements were slow and staggering.

I remarked that they shut the entrance to the vault, but left the lamp burning, and the key in the door. I was half inclined to go in and examine what they had left behind them; but was afraid of alarming them prematurely, and on consideration thought it better to slip after them to see what they made of their loads. It was easy to follow the sexton and his companion, their progress being tardy, and interrupted by frequent halts for the purpose of adjusting the sack, and equalizing their share of its weight. Their liquor companions had far outstript them.

After crossing two fields, they at last came to a gate, which I recognised as one which opened upon the road; and here was standing, within the hedge, a small spring-cart with a boy attending the horse, whom I at once distinguished by his voice to be the Rector's stable-boy, who had made his escape in consequence of his concern in the farce of the earthquake. I could hear one of the fellows say to the boy, –

'Rest a bit, kiddy! one other go, and then!'

I thought that I also might 'rest a bit' behind the hedge, and wait for the opportunity of their separating, to take advantage of some of them. It was a considerable time before they returned, and I remarked that they had been broaching some of their skins; for their tongues faltered tipsily when they spoke, and they went to work much less cautiously than before. When they had stowed every thing to their mind in the cart, namely, six skins of liquor, and two of the sexton's sacks, they gave the boy instructions where to drive, but which I dared not go near enough to overhear. They then separated, the three white fellows taking the direction of the wood towards the farm of Woodbank (I thought I could give a shrewd guess at their hiding-place), and the sexton going back to the vault, where I was glad to hear him say he had yet something to do.

My plan was instantly formed. I followed the boy with his cart, till I judged he might be out of the reach of assistance from his confederates. I then walked suddenly up, and secured him before he was well aware of what had happened. It may be thought that it was rather a cowardly transaction in me to pounce upon a boy when there was better, though more dangerous, game in the field; but I was extremely anxious to have him on many accounts. He had been expressly concerned in the depredations committed at the Rector's; and if he could be induced to give evidence, we might get at the bottom of all the machinations which had

so long annoyed that worthy divine. Besides, my character for vigilance had suffered by his former escape; and this to me was as important as Cockspur had
fancied the D.D. would be to him. He had brought me from London expressly
on the faith of this character; and instead of doing any thing to support, I had,
by the boy's escape, actually contradicted it. It was hardly to be supposed that the
boy would be trusted with all the designs of the crew he was carting for; but he
knew at least (if we could get it out of him,) whither he was to carry his load, and
from that point other observations of importance might be taken. The things
which he had in the cart I considered of less moment, though I certainly should
not have objected to see one of the liquor-skins safely deposited in the corner of
my little apartment in London, for the occasional supply of an evening glass.

I had also the ulterior object in view of trying what I could do with the sexton
and his man, if I could reach the vault before they had left it. For this purpose,
however, the boy was to be disposed of; and as the Parsonage was at no great
distance, I dragged him and his cart thither, very much against his inclination,
as was natural enough, and had him securely locked up. I was like to be pestered
with questions by the Rector and his gabbling sister, Miss Dorothy; but I left
them to examine the contents of the cart, while I hurried back to the church-
yard to see what the sexton was about, if he were still there. I should have enjoyed
the terror and the screams of Miss Dorothy at the opening of the sexton's sacks,
but I had no time then to throw away upon fun.

On reaching the door of the vault, I found it a little ajar, with the lamp still
burning; but, so far as I could see, there was nobody within. This, however, was
uncertain; for there were several recesses, as is usual in old family tombs, and the
sexton might be in one of these at some of his dark jobs. Not being afraid for
the odds of two such old fellows as he and his assistant, I thought I would at all
events search; for the lamp burning there was evidence that they could not be
far off. I did not half like to stumble over coffins, or come into contact with the
horrible materials of his unlawful and disgusting traffic; but I did enter, with my
hand ready upon the butt of one of my pistols, in case it should be necessary to
use it.

I took the lamp and pried into every corner and recess, but could see nothing
except the old family coffins lying mouldering about, and two or three empty
sacks, ready, I supposed, to receive more of the sexton's merchandise, and to one
of which I was myself destined by the lawless miscreants, if they could succeed in
their design of decoying and murdering me. I shuddered at the very thought; but
it only gave me an additional spur to exert myself in defeating them.

On the opposite side of the vault, stood the new coffin which I had seen
them plunder of its inhabitant. I found that it was inscribed with the name of a
young lady, whose early and lamented death I had heard much talked of since my
arrival at the village. Her relatives, who supposed that her remains were resting

peacefully among those of her ancestors, were not, of course, aware of the lawless robbery committed by the sexton, and could never have fancied, after depositing her coffin in the vault, that she would afterwards be lugged about in a sack, and deposited at the Rector's. The distress which such a discovery would bring to her surviving relatives, was only a small part of the train of evils which the deeds of those desperadoes were calculated to produce. The sight, indeed, of this young lady's coffin, which I knew to be now empty, filled me with indignation against the hoary ruffian who had dared to violate its sanctity for unlawful gain. If he had stood before me at this moment, I should almost have been tempted to make short work with him for the sacrilegious crime.

It was not long ere the old grave-robber made his appearance at the door. I had been watchful enough to hear his approach, had placed the lamp where I found it, and lay down behind the young lady's coffin to mark his farther proceedings. He and his assistant came in with another body, stript it of the grave-clothes, and thrust it into one of the sacks.

'There!' said the miscreant, 'that fellow should bring me some'at handsome. We ha' had a toughish job o'un; but the young'un won't be so heavyish, however.'

I hesitated whether or not to rise from my ambush and try to secure them; but I thought nothing would be lost by delaying a little, and something might be gained if they should chance to separate. The sexton, however, before going for the young one, as he termed it, went to a niche at the farther end of the vault, and brought out a large black bottle; chuckled while he drew the cork; held it up to the light to ascertain its purity; poured out a bumper into a large ale glass; and, though it seemed to be strong brandy, quaffed it off as if it had been small beer. He then filled a similar bumper for his companion, and he having followed his example, they went out together.

I thought whilst such things were going, I might as well have my share; and when the two fellows were gone, I did not fail to pay the bottle a visit, but contented myself with half a glass. It proved to be brandy of the same quality as that with which the sexton had before treated me at his own house.

My plan, under the inspiration of the brandy, now was, if I could succeed in locking up one of them in the vault, to deal with the other according to our relative strength. It was necessary for this purpose to get to the outside of the door, and I therefore took leave of the coffins, and stationed myself near the entrance. As my good luck would have it, the sexton returned alone, carrying in his arms the body of a child, (the 'young one,' as I supposed, which he had talked of,) and entered the vault to deposit it as he had done the other. I looked in after him, and saw him busy with the sack. I could with very good will have fired at the old miscreant; but I bridled my indignation, and contented myself with quietly shutting the door upon him, and giving the key a double turn in the lock, cautioning him to be quiet and raise no alarm, if he did not wish me to shoot him through the head.

Here, then, was one of the crew safely lodged among his own horrible merchandise. I had managed the affair so adroitly, that I hoped I had not excited the suspicions of the other fellow, whom I now went in search of; for if he should come within sight of the vault and find the door shut, he would instantly conceive that something was wrong, and make off; in which case, aided by the darkness and a better knowledge of the place, he might escape me.

I therefore wandered about darkling among the grave-stones, till I heard the clank of what I took to be a spade grazing against a stone, or something of that sort; and following this sound, I found the fellow busy in filling up the grave which, from its small dimensions, I judged to be the one which they had robbed of the child. He had either seen me, or heard my step before I got quite close to him; for he threw down his shovel, ran off towards the fields, and, though I pursued him with all speed, succeeded in leaping the church-yard wall before I could come up to him.

A man running for his life (and almost every culprit has this motive) can always make greater exertions than a pursuer; but in this case I had the superiority in speed; for he had not run many yards after leaping the wall, when I cleared it at a spring, overtook him, and, after a violent struggle, succeeded in securing him.

It was now wearing late, and I had still to dispose of my prisoners, without having any good place of security for the purpose. The sexton, indeed, might be left in the tomb to keep company with the coffins and the black bottle; yet it was not a very safe lock-up-house after all, for the walls were old and crazy; and the cage[123] of the village, into which culprits were sometimes put, was not much better. I had, indeed, locked up the boy at the Rector's; but was not certain whether his Reverence might like to have the Parsonage turned into a general prison for the reception of all the scum of the parish.

As I was partly, however, under the direction of Cockspur, who had been at the expense of bringing me down, I thought I could not do any thing farther without his advice; and, accordingly, took my last prisoner directly to the Parsonage, leaving the sexton till I could find a place for his reception. I expected to find him, and more particularly Miss Dorothy, in a terrible quandary about the contents of the cart; and, to be sure, there was the poor woman sitting by the parlour fire as pale as a ghost, protesting that she durst not go to bed, and that she 'would not sleep another night in the Parsonage for love nor money, whilst such doings were going on.'

Cockspur was endeavouring in every possible way to calm her fears; though it may be well supposed he did not himself feel very comfortable under the notion of having such things about his house. With some difficulty I procured his consent to lock up my prisoner at the Parsonage till morning; and there was no other way to manage the sexton than by letting him remain where he was.

My task, however, was not yet finished. I thought I could give a shrewd guess at the lurking-place of the other three desperadoes, who had counselled the taking of my life and the selling of my body; and I was very much disposed to ascertain whether I was right in my conjectures. It may be recollected that they took their way through the fields in the direction of Woodbank. Now, the old barn, before mentioned as being, according to young Flindal, the scene of ghost revels, was precisely such a place as those ruffians would be likely to choose for their head-quarters. It was said to be solitary and ruinous, and it had, moreover, the convenient reputation of being haunted.

I had never been there; but, advanced as the night was, I was anxious to go, if I could get a trusty fellow or two to accompany me. This was, indeed, my chief difficulty. Nobody of the description wanted could easily be found, and more particularly at this unseasonable hour. But time pressed; and if the opportunity were lost, the delinquents (if they really were in the old barn) would to a certainty escape, the instant they heard of the capture of the sexton.

Even if I could get nobody to go with me, I was resolved therefore to try what I could do alone in the way of tracing them, if I dared not venture to attack them single-handed. The Rector knew of one stout fearless fellow, a labourer, who might probably answer my purpose if he could be prevailed upon to go. I lost no time in rousing this man; and, as I promised to reward him well, he consented.

We were still too few to cope with three desperadoes; but the labourer found a neighbour of his, a reckless, burly-looking Irishman, who undertook to knock down with his shilelah[124] half a dozen for his own share of the business, provided he were paid for the job. As soon as the men were dressed (for I found them in bed), we proceeded towards Woodbank, to discover, if we could, the strong hold of the sexton's lawless confederates.

CHAPTER XI.

Night scenes in a ruined barn – The exiles of Erin in full chorus.

THE labourer was the only person among us who had any knowledge of the way; and as it lay through the wood, and was a dark night, he more than once missed his path, and involved us in thickets. In consequence of such delays, we took a considerable time to reach young Flindal's house, though it was not very distant; and after we were there, our guide was not certain which way the old barn lay. I was exasperated beyond measure, and began to fear that the labourer himself was connected with the ruffians; in which case I was certain, I thought, to be disposed of in the summary manner that had been counselled in the vault.

On considering all the circumstances, however, as coolly as my irritation would permit, I concluded that the man was honest and true, though very stupid and stubborn. After getting to the house of Woodbank, indeed, he again led us into the wood; but when we had wandered for some time through bush and brake, we at last saw the dark gable of the old barn rising between us and the sky; and, to my great joy, a light was observable, streaming through a window or an opening in the wall.

'By the Holy Virgin!' said the Irishman, 'there the boys are, sure enough, every ha'p'orth of them, bad luck to the spalpeens!'[125]

'Hush! hush!' said I, 'we must take care to come upon them without noise.'

We drew nearer to the building, which was more solitary and desolate than I had anticipated; and I was glad I had not been so mad as to venture alone, as I had at first intended; for it would have been risking all, without gaining any good purpose. There was no use, however, in my cautions to preserve silence; for the inmates of the barn were so noisy themselves, racketing, laughing, and making merry, that I believe they would scarcely have remarked our approach, had we advanced with 'drums beating and colours flying.'[126] The brandy, I inferred, had done its office, and made them forget the dangers of their hazardous life in tipsy merriment.

I fancied also that I heard female voices mingling in the boisterous uproar, a circumstance which I could not well understand; for though I was well aware that even the wildest desperadoes are not insensible to female attractions, and commonly form attachments which make the only redeeming points in their character, yet could I not imagine how such females contrived to tenant this barn without almost immediate detection. It was desolate, indeed, and at some distance, perhaps half a mile or more, from the house of Woodbank: it also stood on the edge of the wood, which, in case of need, might be resorted to as a temporary hiding-place; but still it was much too open, and too near the daily bustle of the farm business, to be a safe retreat even for a day, much less for the residence of a female or a family, if they were desirous of concealment.

While these thoughts were passing rapidly through my mind, the Irishman ran on before us; and, not finding any crevice to peep through on the side where we were, turned round the corner and disappeared. Being still somewhat apprehensive of treachery, I did not like this movement, which was performed so quickly and without my orders. I therefore laid my hand on the butt of a pistol, to be in readiness; but dared not hint my suspicions to the labourer.

I went up to the door, but it seemed to be barricadoed on the inside, and not intended for opening at all; and there was no chink through which I could see any thing within, though I could still perceive straggling gleams of light, whilst the revelry continued loud and boisterous. As I was thus peering about the door, I was startled by a rough slap on the shoulder, which the apprehensions I had been indulging sent to my very heart. I suddenly pulled out the pistol and turned round, when my Irishman (for it was he) said in a half whisper, –

'Be asy master! No offence in life; only just len' me a houl' of one of them young fire-locks of your own, and I'll pepper the tories,[127] I'll engage, entirely.'

'No, no, Pat!' said I.

'Thady,[128] master, if you plase; 'twas Thadeus they christened me that blessed day.'

'Well, Thady, or whatever they christened you, I won't give you my pistol; and I'll have no peppering nor murder, if it can be avoided.'

'Then, by the Holy, they'll murder ourselves, every mother's son of us, I'll engage. There's a whole throop of the murderers – the blessed saints protect us!'

'Why, if so be,' said the labourer, 'it would be main best not to go on 'em.'

I judged so too, if Thady's account were to be trusted; but as I doubted this, I went round the barn myself to reconnoitre; and on looking in through one of the holes, I saw a group in the corner of the barn-floor sitting round some half-burnt embers of wood, which by fits threw up a momentary blaze. But there was besides this a steadier light, like that of a lamp or candle, I could not discern which, as it appeared to come from the side nearest me.

The group consisted not of the three spectre ruffians as I had expected. There was only one of those who now caught my eye that might be supposed to be of this class – a young man, dressed in a large, shapeless, loose coat, which, with his little round ragged hat and the carroty hair brushing out under it, bespoke him to be a countryman of Thady's.

The rest consisted of an old man, who did not seem to be much fitted for ruffianism; of a lump of a lad, very ragged; and one old and two young women, wrapped in blue cloaks. The whole party, indeed, was Irish; and Thady must have known as much when he wanted, as he said, to fire among them. I could as yet form no conjecture as to his motives for this; though, from the suspicions of treachery afloat in my mind, I had a lurking fancy that he meant to murder me to save his countrymen. I had not then seen enough of the Irish to know that their nationality, for the most part, takes the very opposite turn to mutual assistance, when they become scattered over the world.

The more closely I examined the Irish group assembled in the barn, the more I became convinced that they were not the game I had come to pursue; and were probably nothing more than a family of labourers or chance travellers, who had resorted hither for shelter, to save the expense of better accommodation. I turned about to cross-question Thady as to his opinion of the party; but the labourer, who was standing stupidly by without taking any interest in the affair, said he had gone to try the back door. Indeed, on looking through the hole again, I saw him actually inside the barn, and advancing with much caution along the shaded side of the wall, with his great bludgeon or shilelah, as he called it, under his arm, and ready for murder, I had little doubt. I was just about to rush after him and interfere, when I saw one of the young women give a terrified look towards the place where he was, and say in an agitated voice, –

'Holy Mother of God! if I didn't see Thady Hanlan!' at the same time crossing herself in a great flurry.

The whole group instantly turned their looks upon the intruder, who rushed upon them like a savage, flourishing his bludgeon, and uttering some exclamation in Irish. He aimed a deathblow at the head of the young man; but it was partly stopped by the young woman, who dashed forward and seized his arm at the instant the mortal stroke was descending. The next moment Thady was disarmed and laid prostrate, under the united attack of the whole forces of the barn, male and female.

'Help! master, for the love of Christ!' roared out the vanquished Thady. 'Help! Murder!'

As I really feared they might slaughter the fellow, who had made such a barbarous and cowardly attack upon them, not only without but against my orders, I called out to them to take care what they did, or they might repent it; and at the same time advanced with the labourer towards the entrance, to interfere personally if it should be necessary. I found the door ajar, as Thady had left it; and on reaching the scene of action, the young heroine was pleading hard with the rest to spare Thady's life.

'And for what,' said I, 'would you take the poor fellow's life at all?'

The sound of my voice made them all start up, when the old man, in a trembling voice, replied in the true Irish style –

'Why, bless your Worship's honour, that same boy is no better nor a murderer, and a felon all as one, if you cu'd be after knowing all he done.'

'But, father dear!' said the heroine, 'that's all over and gone now, and Thady wu'dn't been what he is only for the love that was on him, and the drop of whiskey he tuck, bad luck to it!'

'True for you, Nell, my darling!' said Thady, without attempting to raise his head from the ground.

'True!' exclaimed the old man, 'not a ha'p'orth of it! Look there to that innocent chil' in the shroud, rest its soul in glory,' pointing to a corpse over which stood two lighted candles; 'and you, the mother of it, to tell me it is all over and gone. Is not that Thady Hanlan lying there the murderer of it? – of your own chil', Nelly? – and wasn't he after murdering Phil, your own lawful husband, this blessed hour? And you to plead for the false tory robber!'

'It was only the passion was on him that time, and it's over now entirely,' said Nelly.

'Good people,' said I, interfering, 'I do not understand all this; but if you can give any evidence of this man's being a murderer, he had better be secured and taken before a magistrate.'

'It is every evidence in life, we can give,' said the old man, 'bless your Worship's honour! Isn't that chil' there in the shroud,' pointing to the corpse, 'evidence that he was the driving of us all from house and home? And isn't my oul' grey hairs and this roofless barn evidence of that same? – and all through his black ways that driv' us to it?'

The young woman upon this struck in with her version of the story; and the father and the husband talked on also at the same time, while Thady did not utter a word in defence, but lay with his face hid on the floor. After a great deal of this sort of explanation which explained little, I fancied I could gather a few of the real circumstances of the case.

Thady, it would appear, had lived near the barn party in Ireland, had fallen in love with Nelly, and pressed his suit eagerly but unsuccessfully; for she had preferred Phil, her present husband, who was also favoured by her parents, while Thady was discarded and forbidden to repeat his visits. Taking his rejection seriously to heart, he had endeavoured to forget his disappointments by deep drinking, and associating, as a matter of course, with those whom such habits readily brought in his way.

Phil, it would appear, had also been in better circumstances than Thady; for he had taken a farm, and stocked it, before his marriage. This circumstance, as was natural enough, went to Thady's soul, as he considered it one of the temptations which had so cruelly deprived him of his sweetheart; and in his tipsy moments he had frequently uttered dark hints against Phil and his new farm, threatening him with a midnight visit which he did not look for – threats of course exaggerated in repetition.

At length Thady disappeared from the place, and was said to have joined a gang of white-boys,[129] who spread consternation and havoc over the county. Soon after Phil was wakened at midnight by his house being on fire, and it was with great difficulty he escaped with his life; for the ruffians, who had set fire to the house, were ready to receive him when he cleared the flames, and beat and abused him until he was left for dead.

All this the old man maintained was done by Thady himself, who led on the gang with crape over their faces, to conceal his vengeance on his successful and thriving rival.

Phil, however, did not support this charge; and the poor young woman, who seemed eager to protect her rejected lover, denied with vehemence that Thady was at all concerned in the outrage, and maintained that he had gone to England from the first.

Though Phil had suffered a great loss by the burning of his house, he made a struggle to get it rebuilt and put in trim for his marriage; but from that day he never throve. To crown his misfortunes, his barn-yard, or *haggard*, as they called it, was set on fire in the same manner as the house had been; and all his crop, on which he depended to pay his rent and other bills, was destroyed. At last he was compelled to leave the country, and seek his fortune in England; where I now found him holding the wake over his child, which had died probably from the hardships incident to travelling. Such was the story, as far as I was able to make out from the fragments which I could pick up and join together.

The intentions of Thady in first asking the loan of my pistol, and when he could not obtain that, in rushing at Phil with his stick, were easily accounted for (though not to be excused) by the violent feelings of revenge which the sight of the latter had awakened. I did not think myself authorised, taking all the circumstances into consideration, to interfere in the matter; for the evidence of Thady's being concerned in the burning was wholly conjectural. I could readily feel for the poor fellow; and as Nelly was rather a handsome young woman, I perceived that he had some cause for the passions which seemed to madden him. I was, at all events, convinced that Phil was not one of the men whom I sought for; and I would have made an endeavour to reconcile the two enemies, so that their wake for the child might pass over harmoniously without interruption, but I saw it would be in vain; for though they might for a moment profess to agree, it was impossible, from the nature of the case, but that there would always be a smothered resentment, ready, from the slightest cause, to break forth with redoubled fury.

I therefore resolved to leave the poor Irish people in their desolate abode, and take Thady with me to keep him out of harm's way. Nelly was very earnest for her father to give Thady his hand at parting; but the old man was immoveable, and said he would as soon give him his heart's blood. Phil was more manageable, and readily held out his hand; but this Thady would not accept, and the more Nelly tried to soothe him, the more stubborn and dogged did he become.

As this altercation could serve no good purpose, and as I was losing time, I thought proper to put an end to it, and accordingly retired, taking leave of the unhappy party, who in the midst of their misfortunes had deemed it a necessary duty to make merry around the corpse of a favourite child.[130] This I put down as one of the singularities of the Irish character.

Having thus failed in tracing the three church-yard miscreants to the old barn, I thought it hopeless to make any farther attempt this night. If I had been well acquainted with the wood, I should not have left it unexplored; but as I was ignorant of its recesses, and as the labourer was too stupid to render me any assistance, I was obliged to abandon the design. I have little doubt, however, that the desperadoes lurked somewhere thereabouts for the night, and would set out in the morning for their proposed rendezvous with Jones at Lyndhurst, in the New Forest.

Under this view of the case, I thought I should lose nothing by placing myself to watch them at day-break at the outgoings of the wood, in the direction which I supposed they might take. In the mean-time I returned to Duckenhurst to snatch an hour's rest; for I was beginning to feel a good deal exhausted from the exertions of the night, and had planned an immediate excursion to the New Forest in pursuit of Jones, if I could persuade the Rector to consider himself safe from farther disturbance, now that he had secured the mischievous boy, from whom, by proper management, evidence might be extracted, of all the ramifications of the confraternity, and their wicked plots. It was necessary for me, however, to await orders from London, before I could go in pursuit of Jones; and meanwhile I had also to attend to give evidence in the examination of the sexton and his confederate.

As my expedition to the New Forest was partly a speculative one of my own (a considerable reward having been offered for apprehending Jones), and as it was likely to prove hazardous from his being in league with so many ruffians, I was desirous of taking Thady with me, if I could prevail on him to go, and had written to obtain permission for that purpose; a rule which is enforced at Bow Street in all cases where it can be observed.

Thady was in a great measure the sort of person for an expedition of this kind, as he was hardy, strong, and courageous; fearless of danger, and capable of undergoing any privation or fatigue. He was not, I was afraid, quite so cautious as might be wished; but I could scarcely expect to meet with every desirable qualification in one individual.

I may, perhaps, be blamed for having thought of him at all after the accusations which I had heard made against him: but in such an avocation as ours, it would not do to be too scrupulous about such matters; and, in Thady's case, it is to be recollected that there was no evidence besides the vague conjectures of an old man whose mind was irritated, and, it might be, unhinged by misfortunes; for both Nelly and Phil had acquitted him.

I therefore sounded Thady, and found him willing enough to go. I proposed to bear his expenses, and, if we were successful, to give him a portion of the reward offered for apprehending Jones.

The Rector agreed to let me go, on the reasonable condition of returning if he should again require my assistance. By return of post I received the requisite permission from Bow Street, with orders to spare no expense for discovering and securing Jones. For the present, therefore, I bade Cockspur and his sister Miss Dorothy good bye, and prepared for my journey.

CHAPTER XII.

Forest scenes – Castle Malwood and the deer-stealer – Sir Byam Finch and Lord
Blank at Lyndhurst.

It must be confessed that the information upon which I undertook my
present expedition was sufficiently slight; but I had the advantage of personally
knowing Jones, and therefore, if I could light upon him, should not be easily
bammed[131] with an assumed name, if he had recourse to such an artifice. I had
the motive besides (and with me it was a powerful one) of breaking up the whole
gang, which seemed to be extensive in its operations in every species of illegal
traffic and acts of violence.

The three miscreants, when in the church-yard, had not hesitated to lay a plan
for murdering me; and I could not doubt that such deeds were part of their daily
business, when thought to be necessary for their personal security. Whether they
actually engaged in highway robberies and house-breaking, I had no means of
knowing; but men so devoid of all good feeling as to rob the sacred repositories
of the dead, were certainly fit for any other crime.

Their smuggling transactions, though illegal, I looked upon as venial in comparison with this horrible traffic; for though I was now bound by my oath to
regard smugglers as liable to be apprehended and punished, yet, as I had myself
frequently been concerned in little transactions of the kind while sojourning
among the gipsies, I could not bring my mind to think them so *very* criminal.
Our gipsy trade in this way was indeed trifling, and only carried on to supply
with taxed articles ourselves and a few of our friends among the small farmers,
poachers, and others with whom we held occasional intercourse; yet was it in
the eye of the law equally culpable with the traffic of such wholesale dealers in
contraband articles as this Jones, whom I was so anxious to discover.

On the way, I was frequently amused with the rough but ready humour of
my Irish companion, Thady. He was quite illiterate, but having a sharp eye and
a shrewd wit, was never at a loss for a repartee, whatever might be said to him;
and he allowed nobody to pass without some facetious observation, or some
practical joke.

I availed myself of every opportunity, when we halted to take rest or refreshment, to turn the conversation upon brandy, and thence by an easy transition upon smuggling and smugglers, to see whether I could in this way procure any intelligence of Jones and his gang; but I made little of this, for the persons whom I endeavoured to pump happened either to be ignorant of the matter, or unwilling to say any thing lest I might prove to be no 'true man.'

We entered the New Forest by the Romsey road, and came upon the straggling village of Cadenham, so well known from its famous oak, which buds every year at Christmas.[132] We learned at this place that there was to be a forest race, in the course of the week, on the lawn near Lyndhurst, a short distance southward from Cadenham. At this race I thought it likely that some of the gang would make their appearance, and accordingly determined to be present to keep a look-out for them.

On the way, my attention was caught by the ruins of an old castle, which rose upon an eminence to the right; and as such places may always be suspected to form the haunts of those who live by breaking the laws, I thought it might be as well to peep into it on passing, as I might here chance to find the persons whom I sought.

We met a boy mounted on a donkey, of whom I made some inquiries respecting this ruin, and found that it was called Castle Malwood;[133] but he could not tell me whether it was either inhabited or haunted – facts which we had to ascertain for ourselves.

I was particularly charmed with the forest scenery at this place, and wished my old friend Wilton had been with us, to descant on the varied prospect which lay around us as far as the eye could reach. On the north was part of Wiltshire, richly cultivated; while on the south was presented the grand contrast of a lofty plain, garnished with heath and furze, and overlooking the whole sweep of the forest, which spreads before the eye as far as the sea and the Isle of Wight, in one vast expanse. The eye, indeed, travels from wood to wood, and from height to height, over lawns and heaths, through every shade of colouring and perspective, till all distinction is mellowed down and lost in distance; and it becomes doubtful whether the sight is roving over the tufted woods of the forest, or wandering among the knolls of the Isle of Wight, or the hazy streaks of the horizon.

In the nearer distance the heath went down, by a gentle dip, into this vast theatre of trees and lawns; while woody promontories were seen shooting into the vistas, and clumps and single trees of every picturesque form were scattered over the forest lawns between. Herds of deer were also feeding in the openings of the forest, to give life to the scene; and a black-cock, a royal bird which I had not seen since I had been in Westmoreland, rose upon the wing as we passed on.

Castle Malwood I found to be the remains of an old baronial strong-hold; and no doubt it possessed, as usual, subterranean vaults well adapted for the concealment of such merchandise as Jones and his crew trafficked in. On approaching the ruin, I saw a man creeping cautiously out of the next wood, carrying a large fat buck on his shoulders; and with this he was making his entrance at a door-way, when I called out,

'Ho! friend! Can you tell me who lives in this castle?'

The man made no answer, but quickly disappeared with his venison, and shut in our faces an old clumsy door full of large nail-heads. This door, however, did not seem to have been made exactly for the place it now occupied, since there was an open space above which it did not fill; and besides, it stood awry and awkwardly, though close enough to admit of being secured, as I heard the man shoot a bolt; and altogether it was a defence which would not be easily stormed without fire or gun-powder.

This, as a lawyer might say, was a *non pros*[134] to my intention of exploring the recesses of the ruin; and we tried all round for another entrance in vain. It might be considered, indeed, as a sort of impertinent intrusion for me to thrust myself forward into any house or place defended with doors; but as the ruin had a suspicious look, and the man with the fat buck was more than suspicious, I judged that I might, without any legal misdemeanor, try what I could discover. Here, indeed, was evidently a deer-stealer secreting his booty; and whether it might not be provided as a dinner for a party of smugglers or robbers, was very doubtful.

Upon these considerations I summoned the inmates, whoever they might be, to open the door to me; and when no answer was returned, Thady and I prepared to try our united strength in making a forcible entrance.

'By the Holy!' said Thady, 'you might as well think to get out of purgatory without praying, as to get into this devil's den.'

I soon perceived that Thady was right; but I nevertheless felt convinced that the ruin was well worth my search. Had I anticipated the present obstacle, indeed, I could easily have cut off the deer-stealer's retreat before he had effected his entrance; but such is ever the way with the best plans of operation, they always come into one's thoughts when it is too late to do any thing with them, except regret the lost opportunity.

As it was only wasting time to proceed in making vain efforts upon this great ugly door, I thought it best to make a memorandum of the place, whither, if necessary, I might make a secret and unexpected excursion after night-fall, or perhaps at early morn, when the inmates might be caught in their den.

The site, indeed, was conspicuous enough to be easily found; and, as a good land-mark, I afterwards noted that it was close by the celebrated scene of the death of King William Rufus, who was shot here by Tyrrel[135] while hunting in the forest; a most remarkable catastrophe to a prince who had in this very place exercised his power by laying waste and depopulating the whole district for more than thirty miles, turning a fruitful and well cultivated country into a desert, and dilapidating more than fifty villages with their churches, besides houses and cottages innumerable, to make dens for wild beasts of the chace, and gratify his humour of becoming, like Nimrod,[136] a mighty hunter.

The scene of his death is wild, and well fitted for such a deed; a secluded hollow descending from the western heath, screened by a grove of lofty beeches on the east, and all around by scattered clumps of oak and ash, with stripes of greensward running among the avenues – the very place where a hunter, heated with the chace, would like to dismount, as Rufus did, for a moment's repose; at which time, whilst suspecting no danger, the fatal arrow sped him to eternity, and glanced on the oak behind him, which still stands as a monument of the transaction.

Every thing here is picturesque. The town of Lyndhurst, which may be called the capital of the New Forest, from the swain-motes or forest-courts[137] being held there, stands amongst hills, and woods, and pastoral cottages, with heaths stretching away in the distance; whilst the hills of Wilts and Dorset encircle the horizon. The forest race-course, which we passed on our way to the town, is a fine swelling lawn, opening out from the surrounding woods like an inlet of the sea among cluster of islands. It was to this forest-lawn we meant to repair, to keep a look-out for Jones or any of his gang, whom the races might have attracted thither.

I suppose Lyndhurst races are not of sufficient importance to find a place in the Racing Calendar (I have not one by me to refer to); but there is, not-withstanding, some sport as good as can be witnessed at Ascot, Epsom, or Doncaster.[138] There are no fine blood horses, indeed, outstripping the wind in speed, and taking the breath from their riders. All the entered horses are of the genuine forest breed,[139] descended, it is said, from the steeds of Spanish cavaliers shipwrecked at the time of the Armada. They are usually from twelve to thirteen hands in height, somewhat stiff in the jaw, with low croups, flowing tails, rough manes, and streaming forelocks; strong, hardy, sure-footed, and full of life. Most of them, I was told, had been allowed to run wild for several years without provender or shelter other than what they could themselves obtain in the for-est, where they may be seen in troops, feeding among the woods, or gambolling along the glades and openings. They are then either hunted down by horsemen, who relieve one another till the wild horses are exhausted; or they are caught by surprise with a running noose, or run into a bog, and entangled by stratagem.

As we were leaving the race-course on our way to Lyndhurst, I observed two gentlemen at a distance before us, mounted on horses of a very different breed from those of the forest, riding slowly forward in close conversation; and along with them servants with led forest horses, having the usual covering of racers when off duty. A remarkable contrast was presented by their high blood horses, with heads proudly erect, pacing it in company with the little tripping, spirited, foresters; but what surprised me more was, to see gentlemen who could afford to ride fine blood horses in such a place and with such company; for I had understood the Lyndhurst races were chiefly in the hands of yeomen, farmers, and a few scheming fellows who were in fact under-keepers,[140] but set themselves up for jockeys and sportsmen! – that is, swindlers in a small way. The gentlemen before us were evidently none of these; and I conjectured they might be a couple of neighbouring squires, who had come to the races for a mere frolic rather than as a legitimate and fashionable aristocratic sport.

I was never more deceived in a conjecture; for, on coming nearer, I recognised my men at once: they proved to be those two notorious gamblers, Sir Byam Finch and Lord —, both of whom I had for some years lost sight of; nor had I heard any thing respecting either, except that Lord Blank had succeeded unexpectedly (I should rather have said undeservedly) to a large property, and had consequently plunged deeper and deeper into play, and no doubt, as he had begun, into plunder also.

It was no frolic then, it might be sworn to, that had brought this pair of Greeks[141] to such an out-of-the-way place as Lyndhurst races: they must have some better game in view than the purses of the forest yeomen, or the gentlemen-farmers from the borders of Wilts and Dorset – some well-feathered bird which could bear plucking – some raw heir rich in expectancies, and in Jew monies raised thereupon; and at this outlandish spot they would have all the spoil to themselves, without the drawback of shares, hush-money to servants, and other items of reduction to which their town gainings must constantly be liable.

I was not certain whether they might recognise me from the slight intercourse we had had about Wilton's wrestling match on Wimbledon Common; but I thought it would be as well to keep my distance, though I had a strong inclination not to lose sight of their proceedings, as I knew enough of their free principles to infer that they could not mean much good. I therefore instructed Thady, after appointing a rendezvous, to run forward, get as near them as possible, and try if he could pick up any thing from their conversation; while I took a circuit round by the back of the town.

CHAPTER XIII.

Vision of a forest nymph – Female sorrows – Intriguing and counter-working.

I STRUCK into a by-path, therefore, and walked on leisurely, contemplating the fine prospects around me of woods and heaths, and moralizing between whiles on the sequestered life of the forester, who has the spreading oak to canopy his cottage, and the browsing deer for his companions. I had not gone very far, when I overtook a girl who was walking in the same direction, but with a very slow melancholy air.

From her dress I inferred that she was some forest nymph, the flower, probably, of one of the woodland cottages; but from the slightness of her figure, the fineness of her form, and the elegance of her carriage, she seemed to be fitted to grace a much higher station. It is possible, indeed, I might have been influenced by the beauty of the pathway, which threw a charm on all around, to fancy what was not, and deceive myself into a belief of the simple maid being a fairy princess. I am very prone to run into such waking visions; but I like to indulge my imagination in those little deceits, and I could not persuade myself (often as I have been disappointed in similar cases) that this forest girl had not as fair a face as her delicate form led me to anticipate. I even went so far as to quote Shakespeare to myself, and said,

> This is the prettiest low-born lass that ever
> Ran on the greensward; nothing she does, or seems,
> But smacks of something greater than herself;
> Too noble for this place.[142]

But the forest girl did not 'run on the greensward,' for she was evidently in a dejected mood; and as I came nearer, I heard her utter a deep sigh, almost amounting to a smothered moan. It was well I heard this, for I was just about to accost her, in the style of my old friend Bucks, with the words of the song,

> Where are you going, my pretty maid?[143]

when her sigh checked my impertinence.

She must, I fancied, be crossed in love, to be so melancholy when all around was cheerful and gay. I therefore changed the merry song which was at the tip of my tongue to a simple question respecting my way to Lyndhurst; more, however, by way of introduction to the downcast fair one, than to learn what I cared little about; as there was small difficulty of finding the way in such a place.

I was not disappointed in the beauty of her face; though it was not the rural beauty of rosy health, nor the fresh complexion caught from the forest breezes. Her cheeks were pale, with a tint only perceptible of their natural carnation; but her features were exquisitely lovely and lady-like. I perceived that she had been weeping; for the tears still stood in her fine eyes, and it went to my very soul to see so young a creature, apparently formed for joy, the prey of heart-withering sorrow.

'You look sad, my dear,' said I, in a tone of compassion.

'Yes, O yes!' she replied. 'It is my only solace to wander about in these solitudes, and weep.'

I soon discovered, by her accent and her manner, that if she was really a forest girl, as her rural dress indicated, she had some time or other been used to better company than that of the yeomen and keepers. I was grieved and ashamed that I had called her 'my dear:' it was a liberty I should never have presumed to take, had I anticipated the style of her answer. I was loath to intrude farther on her privacy; but my curiosity, or I know not what, got the better of my delicacy, and I said by way of soothing her,

'If you will condescend to take a word of consolation from me, I can tell you that the deepest sorrow will at length pass away. I too have grieved and wept; but the day is gone by now, and I can be as merry as ever; and so will you, pretty maid,' (I thought I might venture upon this expression without offence) 'when time has smoothed away your present crosses.'

'O no! never, never!' she replied, in a tone of despondency. 'Grief and melancholy are now my fixed inheritance in this world.'

'What! with youth to enjoy yourself, and beauty to captivate all around you? It is not natural – it is not just, thus to give yourself up to despair, which cannot, I am certain, whatever be its cause, prove of any avail to you.'

'O! I know it,' answered she; 'I know it too well. That is the very reason why no consolation can ever soothe my sad heart.'

I here made a pause, not, indeed, knowing what to say; or rather my fancy began to be busy in framing a probable history of this pretty girl's distresses. She must, I inferred, be the daughter of a forester, and have fallen a victim to some wealthy seducer, who had been at pains to give her the superior education which her manners showed she had enjoyed. But when I considered her downcast looks, the modesty which I fancied I could perceive in her tearful eye, and withal her simple forest dress, neat, indeed, and very tasteful, but devoid of all tawdry ornament, I indignantly rejected the idea which had previously impressed itself upon my imagination.

She must then, thought I, be the daughter, perhaps the young wife, of some gentleman reduced by losses, and compelled to give up elegance and luxury for a hut in the forest. Yet, if this were the case, she would scarcely have been so forward, (modest as she certainly appeared,) as to tell me, a total stranger, that she solaced herself by weeping, and would never be happy. This, in every point of view, was the most strange and inexplicable circumstance connected with her; and I could not hit upon any solution of the mystery that appeared probable. I was roused from my musing by the girl starting suddenly, and exclaiming, –

'Hark! Did you not hear something?'

I listened in the direction to which she pointed, but could distinguish nothing except the distant tramp of a horse. She seemed, however, to be much agitated, and speaking aside, said, –

'It must be he. What shall I do to be found thus? Will you,' turning to me, 'do me a favour, Sir? I know not how to act.'

'A thousand,' said I, 'if it be in my power.'

'Then – I really am ashamed to ask you, but pray step aside behind this bush for awhile. I hear somebody coming, and I would not be seen with a stranger just now for the world.'

'I see no harm that can come to you,' observed I, hesitating to conceal myself like a culprit, when I was guilty of no indiscretion even in thought. I heard the tramp of a horse in rapid approach, and the girl caught my hand, while, with an entreating look which I could not resist (nobody, I think, could have resisted it), she exclaimed, –

'O for the love of heaven, do conceal yourself till he go. Speed! Haste, I conjure you!'

I, accordingly, though with no very comfortable feelings, yielded to the young woman's pressing intreaty, got behind a thick bush, and in a minute after Sir Byam Finch rode up the path-way alone, and pulled up his steed beside the girl.

'How now, *ma chere*[144] Maria?'[145] said he, addressing her. 'In tears again, I see. Will you never leave off this useless vexation? Why, here you might be as merry as a grig,[146] with so many pretty birds hopping and singing about you the livelong day in the grove.'

'Oh, no! Sir Byam. Mirth is no longer my portion. I was once merry and mad to please you; but those days are gone never to return – no, never!'

'Why, *ma chere*, you are as melancholy as Jacques in the play.[147] I really expect to find you, like him, weeping over the death of a stag one of these days. Come, come! this won't do. You must cheer up; and if you can catch this rich gull Blizzard, you may shine brighter than ever.'

'The very thoughts of him, Sir Byam, would be death to me. I cannot, and I will not, live with another as I have done with you. You were my all! My only thoughts, my only pleasure centred in you; and since I have lost your favour, no man shall again obtain mine. I was young: I was deceived – terribly deceived; but God knows that my thoughts were as true to you as if I had been your wedded wife. No! I will never live with another for all the wealth of the Indies.'

'You must think better of it, Maria. Blizzard is a handsome young man enough; and you may command all his immense wealth – a very pretty thing, let me tell you.'

'I do not want riches, Sir Byam. Your bounty has made me richer than my thoughtless errors deserve. I can live as plainly as a peasant. O that I could be as happy!'

'Come, come, Maria! I shall bring Blizzard to see you; and perhaps you may even get him to marry you – eh? Would not that please you? I was once near the point myself, you know; but it would not do. We are to pass you for the yeoman's daughter, you know; and the eccentricity of the thing will be sure to catch his fancy.'

'I should certainly like to be married, Sir Byam. It would be the only solace to my sorrow on this side the grave; but I will never consent to a deception to procure a husband. I must tell all – all that I have been, though the disclosure should wring my heart. I will not deceive, as I myself have been deceived.'

'Why, girl, this is absolute raving! What he does not know can do him no manner of harm; and I am extremely desirous to turn the thing to your advantage – upon my soul, I am. Though you and I can no longer be what we have been, I still feel an interest in you; but if you reject all the plans I have made in your favour, why, there is an end of it, and I have my trouble for my pains.'

'O, Sir Byam, you distress me greatly, indeed you do. I am very grateful for your thinking at all of a poor lost creature like me; but you ask me to do what I cannot bring my mind to. If any body would have me for a wife after I had told them all, I feel a spirit within me by virtue of which every nerve would be strained to do my duty, even if my husband were the meanest peasant; but this, alas! is a vision that will never be realized by me.'

'Aye, Maria, talking of peasants, I fancied I saw a young fellow with you as I rode up; but when I looked again he was gone. Some of the forest youths fallen in love with your pretty face – eh?'

'Ah! Sir Byam, you are still the same man I perceive,' ejaculated the poor girl; 'still jealous of me, though I am discarded. Yet, God knows I never gave you cause, but was as faithful to you as a wedded wife, in spite of all the multiplied temptations which assailed me. You call my face pretty – once, indeed, I thought so myself; but that is all over now. Sorrow has blasted the young bloom of my cheek, and dimmed the lustre of the eyes you used to admire. Alas! alas! those days are gone never to return!'

'Hang the wench! she is growing poetical. Come, come, Maria! I'm not to be caught again. It would be *mauvaise ton*,[148] you know, to take you back; so make up your mind to try Blizzard. I'll bring him to see you as the yeoman's daughter, mind me; and if that don't do, why then you may set your cap at the young peasant, if you please. I'm sure I saw him, say what you will. So farewell, cheer up, and be a good girl.'

It may be easily supposed that I listened with keen interest to this conversation, not a syllable of which I would have lost for the world. The settled melancholy of the young creature had, from the first, melted me into compassion; and now, when I learned that she had been the confiding victim of such a man as Sir Byam Finch, I pitied her the more. I was somewhat surprised, indeed, that he treated her with so much lenity and so little gross ruffianism, seeing that he had cast her off; but who could have been rude to such a woman?

If I had been in Sir Byam's place – if I had heard from the lips of beauty such a declaration of affection and constancy, I know what I should have done, even had my rank been far above his – I would have set the world's opinion at defiance, and married her. What though she was looked upon as fallen and lost? Was it not her confiding love to him that was the cause? and ought he not, therefore, to have braved the scorn and spite of society that he might cure the wounds he had inflicted? But no: he appeared a coward, striving to continue his deceptions by inveigling a youth, probably under the pretence of friendship; while Maria, delicate and sorrowing as she was, stood up with the firmness of a heroine for principles of virtue which, alas! nobody would now give her any credit for possessing.

I confess I was originally caught by Maria's elegant figure – I was yet farther charmed with her fine features; but the conversation between her and her seducer made me admire still more her delicate feelings of propriety. I was already half in love (Heaven help me!) with the cast-off mistress of a fashionable profligate!

The idea made me start. I dared not contemplate the picture which my imagination now drew, though I could not forbear looking at the unconscious object of it standing woe-begone and thoughtful, with her eyes fixed on the ground, and seeming more sad than ever. I hesitated, and was altogether at a loss what to do. I was strongly impelled to go up and renew our conversation; but I had also an ominous presentiment of the consequences of trusting myself again within the spell of her fascinating melancholy, which to me was more irresistible than 'quips, and cranks, and wreathed smiles.'[149]

It was needless, however, I felt, to attempt resisting the impulse, for I was already ensnared and could not escape; though to quiet any unpleasant whispering of conscience, I tried to make myself believe that it was only pity for misfortune, and the wish to aid a fellow-creature in distress, which influenced me to approach her again instead of passing onwards, as perhaps my readers may think I ought to have done. She was so much cast down that she did not observe me, and started at the sound of my voice when I asked if I could do any thing to assist her.

'No, thank you, Sir!' she answered. 'I fear you can do nothing for me. I am ashamed that you should have been already troubled; but you have heard all, and now know that I am a poor degraded outcast, rejected by the man in whom I thoughtlessly confided, and, what is still more distressing – O, Sir! you cannot think how my poor heart burns with indignation at the very thought – insulted by the most odious proposals!'

'I pity you, madam, from the bottom of my soul,' said I, passionately.

'O, if your pity then could save me from this! Pity is so new to me, the very sound of the word revives my sinking spirits and my buried hopes. I am used to contempt, and scorn, and taunting insult; but nobody has pitied me;' and the poor damsel's tears again flowed.

'What then can I do? Tell me how I can save you; and, if it is within the compass of possibility, command me to the last drop of my blood.'

'Alas! alas!' replied she, 'I know not. I asked what cannot be done. No; I must meet my sad fate. I must endure the odious language of profligacy – I must undergo the booby stare of this new friend of Sir Byam's, and perhaps be spurned for my endurance – I must suffer the ignominy in silence, till death – sweet death – shall come to end my misery.'

'Say not so, madam!' cried I, very earnestly. 'You are young, and may outlive all the distress which now weighs upon you. Why can you not escape to some retired spot, where you might not be exposed to the intrusion of insult?'

'Eagerly – gladly would I do so – O! most gladly. But where can I go out of the reach of misery? If I go where I am known, I *cannot* escape it. If I go where I am not known, that very circumstance, unprotected as I am, would only make my case the worse. No; I am hopelessly wretched, and wretched I must remain.'

'Madam,' said I; 'it is but little that is in my power; yet that little, I repeat, you may command, if I can serve you. I pity you – I am strongly interested for you; and if there is any way in which my protection can avail you, I am most ready to give it.'

'O! Sir, I know not how to be sufficiently grateful for your kindness. I cannot tell you all my sad story; you have, indeed, already heard what saves me the pain and the shame of a confession. For the ostensible purpose of recruiting my health, which grief is rapidly undermining, Sir Byam pressed me to come down hither; and though I had grown indifferent where I went, a lingering fondness for him, though he deserves it not, made me comply with his request. I now find that he had other designs than any regard for my health. These you know also: you heard the abandoned profligate make me the base proposal. Does such a wretch deserve to be loved? Alas! I have loved him – doted on him – adored him! But that folly has passed – to-day has quenched it utterly. I'll banish his name from my heart, and all memorial of him from my sight; nor will I outlive another such insult as that you have unfortunately witnessed.'

Upon saying this, she snatched a locket from her breast, and tore a ring from her finger, threw them upon the ground, and trampled upon them with her feet.

I could well sympathise with this just indignation. It was a burst of virtuous passion, which did honour to the girl's feelings; and, I may say that it tended to rivet the fetters in which I found myself hopelessly bound. Some may suppose that, on her part, it was all acting, all a premeditated design to try what she could make of me; nay, that the whole affair, from its commencement, was a deep-laid plot to ensnare me.

Yet this could not be: I could not be so far deceived. There was no affectation in those natural bursts of feeling – no meretricious pouting or pretence – no arts meant to allure. Her pale cheek told that her story was too true; and the scene with her profligate seducer stamped her as a woman of high and honourable purpose, whatever might have been her errors in unsuspecting youth and confiding inexperience. I should as soon have distrusted my own senses, as the genuine language of the heart which I could read in her beautiful eyes. I looked up to her with respect: I could not persuade myself that her character was stained.

The die was cast. My resolution was taken: I thought not of consequences, but was hurried on by my fate. I must either abandon her, or provide for her safety; and quashing every rising suggestion of prudence, determined for the latter.

'My dear Madam,' said I, after this brief struggle, 'I will protect you from insult at the risk of my life, if that should be necessary. If you can trust to me, as yet a stranger, leave your present abode, and I will try to procure you another until you have time to consider what steps to take.'

'You are a stranger, Sir, it is true,' rejoined Maria; 'but I feel that I cannot distrust you. How it was, I know not; but I thought I saw, from the first, that in you which made me bold to speak as I have done; and what is more – indeed every thing, – after knowing all you still treat me with respect, to which I have been long unused even from the lowest menials. I *will* trust you, Sir; and O! may Heaven reward you for your kindness to a poor, lost, friendless girl!'

'I shall be richly rewarded, my dear Madam, if I can accomplish your deliverance from future insult, and find any way to promote your happiness.'

When I said this, I perceived a faint smile flutter over her cheek, like a ray of broken sunshine on a drooping lily; and I felt as if a new tide of blood was rushing through my own heart, when I saw this eloquent token of rekindled hope. I could have kissed her pale cheek, but sorrow had rendered it sacred. I may be called a timid, bashful, simpleton, to be thus awed into distant respect in such a case. I care not. I would not wantonly wound the feelings of the veriest midnight wretch; and *such* a woman, sinking under sorrow – her young bosom chilled and sickened by heartless neglect – her virtuous resolutions treated with mockery and insult – No, no! I hope I have a heart to feel, and a conscience to consult; and I care neither for the smiles nor the taunts of a selfish and sensual world.

We agreed that she should go to the cottage where she lodged, get together such necessaries as she could, and steal out again to me. She could not trust the people of the cottage with her designs, not knowing what influence Sir Byam might possess over them; otherwise I should have proposed her continuance there for a time.

When she was gone, I picked up the trinkets which she had so indignantly trampled upon, and, so far as I could judge, they were of considerable value, both being set with what appeared to be fine brilliants. My purse was not particularly well stocked, and I did not know what money she might possess, if any; yet money was indispensable to all our plans, and I looked upon the trinkets as a means of supply which had most opportunely fallen in my way. She would have left them, I have no doubt, to be picked up by the first forester who passed.

We took a range as wide as our time would permit from her former lodging, and were fortunate in finding a neat comfortable cottage, into which my fair protegée was admitted for what I considered a small, but what the cottagers looked upon as a handsome gratuity.

The poor girl seemed to be quite transported with gratitude for being again treated with respect and kindness; and I think she must have perceived that I had still more tender feelings towards her than I had yet dared to express to her, or even perhaps confess plainly to myself. Love is an adept at making stolen marches, and often quietly seizes a vantage-ground before you are aware. A glance or a smile will lurk in your memory, and haunt your dreams till you are bewitched by the spell, and surrender your heart at discretion. Or, in other cases, a word or a tone of the voice will linger in your ear like distant music, and

> Softly sweet, in Lydian measure,
> Oft will wrap the soul in pleasure:
>   Soft the measure;
>   Rich the treasure;
>   Sweet the pleasure;
>   Blent with pain![150]

I have felt all this, and can speak to it: I take not my notions from whining poetasters and sentimental novelists.

But I was plunging headlong into love fancies, when I should have been looking after business, and attending to my duty. I therefore left Maria, promising a speedy return, of which she saw from my looks there was no fear.

CHAPTER XIV.

Greek speculations upon a gentleman eccentric – Jones at Lyndhurst.

I FOUND that it was little less difficult to procure beds at Lyndhurst during the race week, contemptible as I had imagined the sport would be, than at Doncaster or Epsom at a similar period. The landlord of the inn at which I put up, however, had, to increase the number of his rooms, hit upon a contrivance which I have sometimes seen practised in country inns to meet extraordinary demands for accommodation. This was, to divide such rooms as were large enough to be divisible by means of a temporary wooden partition, which slid in grooves, and could be removed when no longer wanted.

Into one of these half or quarter apartments (I am not certain which it was) I obtained admission by paying about thrice the ordinary price of the best room which mine host had; and I was not displeased to find that he had put the titled gamblers into the divisions next mine. These were larger and better furnished; but I suppose they cared not, in the mean-time, for accommodation, so that they could succeed in their designs.

Thady returned rather late, with the excuse that he had been having a drop, to make him comfortable at the same time that he got thereby gracious with a brother tippler who was undergroom to Sir Byam, and had found means to pry into more of their schemes than they had any notion of. Many servants, indeed, make this the occasion of extorting considerable sums of money from their profligate masters, when they are knowing enough to give hints which cannot be misunderstood. Some will even go so far as to provoke their masters to quarrel with them and threaten to dismiss them, in order to get a good opportunity for introducing their private knowledge with the more effect and advantage; and when by such conduct they have once got their masters into their power, they take care to put them in frequent remembrance of it, at the expense of their purses.

Whether Jack Dobson, Sir Byam's under-groom, was playing a game of this sort I cannot tell; but over his glass, Thady found means to get out of him all he knew of the history of his master's expedition to the Lyndhurst races. From

Dobson's account, it would appear that the gamblers had picked up a fool of the first water, descended by the father's side from a family of West India planters, and by the mother's from an African princess, whom the chances of negro warfare had consigned to slavery in the British colonies.

This young creole, as I suppose I may call him, was immensely rich, and passionately fond of showing it by spending his money in making himself ridiculous, under the notion that he was an eccentric, and that eccentricity was the best passport to fashion.

Upon one point the gamblers found him not so well adapted for their modes of plunder: – he had imbibed the idea that gambling was a stupid commonplace amusement, which every booby took to; and that, therefore, no gentleman eccentric[151] would think of touching a card, a cue, or a dice-box. Betting, indeed, he might occasionally be brought into, as it saved him the trouble of thinking and arguing; but he was not inclined to bet upon ordinary matters. It must be something out of the common line to strike his fancy; such, for instance, as, – which of two live frogs would leap highest and farthest? or, whether a hedge-hog or a guinea-pig would swim best in a horse-pond? Upon such matters as these, which he looked upon as the essence of high eccentricity and ton,[152] he would as freely sport his thousands as a chimney-sweeper would bet his sixpence upon a game of chuck-farthing.[153]

Such, it appeared, was Mr. Ellice Blizzard, who had been persuaded by the gamblers that all the *crack*[154] races, as they are termed, were becoming quite a bore, and only fit for the everyday vulgar; that blood-horses were now stale, and as plenty as blackberries; and that in a few years nobody, who had any pretensions to ton, would patronise the Derby, the Oaks, or the St. Leger.[155] But at Lyndhurst, in the New Forest, they continued, there were races really worth patronizing, if any gentleman of influence would be *eccentric* enough to countenance them, and lead the ton where there was so fine an opening.

It was meant, of course, that if Mr. Blizzard, who was a gentleman of influence, at least in his own estimation, would go down to Lyndhurst and patronize the forest races, they must soon eclipse all the *crack* blood-horse races in the kingdom, whilst his name would be immortalized as the leader of the fashionable world.

Blizzard, notwithstanding all the tempting baits in this well-laid snare, was not, however, caught till he was told that the race-horses at Lyndhurst were not only real denizens of the forest, but actually wild horses caught on purpose; many of which would fly open-mouthed at the grooms who were mounting them. The notion of a wild horse-race was precisely the thing to tickle Blizzard's fancy, and he decided to go; while Sir Byam, Lord Blank, and their friends, had equally decided to rook[156] Blizzard, before his return, of as many thousands as they could prevail upon him to venture upon what they were pleased to call wild horses.

This, however, was only the first part of their design, the mere opening or prologue of the play which they intended to enact. It was necessary not only to buy forest horses – that they could easily do for twelve, fifteen, or twenty pounds[157] a horse – but to ascertain their comparative mettle and powers of running; otherwise their bets would be mere lottery and dabbling in the dark; and Blizzard, fool though he was, might by chance succeed at such a game as well as any of them.

It was upon such a trial of skill respecting their newly purchased forest racers, that they had been on the race lawn when I first descried them. As soon as this had been ascertained, they would play their cards accordingly, with some certainty of winning.

There was, besides this, the underplot of turning Maria over to Blizzard, in order, if possible, that Sir Byam might thus get rid of an annuity which he had incautiously granted her when at Cambridge. Maria, indeed, was the Miss Cherry mentioned in a former page as Sir Byam's mistress. Her annuity he found it very inconvenient to pay, and was, therefore, extremely anxious to find some means of getting rid of it, and of being quit of her altogether. The Lyndhurst expedition was caught at as being quite the thing for throwing her in the way of Blizzard, and if he could pass her upon him for a forest girl, he considered his success as certain. Sir Byam had not calculated upon her opposition to this scheme, which was thereby, I hoped, entirely defeated.

But the most important information which Thady had picked up was, that one Jones had been written to by Sir Byam to procure the horses; and I had hopes that it might turn out to be the delinquent of many crimes whom I was so anxious to secure; for one scoundrel (I beg Sir Byam's pardon) usually finds out another, when there is any scheme of fraud or villainy to execute by proxy; and Jones seemed to have so great an itch for traffic of all kinds, that I verily believe he would not have hesitated to sell his own father provided that the terms offered should satisfy his avarice. The enormity of the crime would be no obstacle to such a wretch.

If it was really this Jones who had been dealing in the forest horses, I have no doubt that he procured them for a mere trifle, such as a few pounds of tea or tobacco, or a skin of brandy, and that he did not part with them again for less than twenty or thirty pounds each on the nail.

Be that as it might, I resolved to make strict inquiry after this forest horse-jockey, in order to prove or disprove my suspicions; while, in the mean-time, I should also give a side-look at the proceedings of Sir Byam and his friends. Besides what I had thus learned, I overheard, through the thin boarded partition which divided my apartment from theirs, the following conversation between Sir Byam and Lord Blank.

'I think,' said Sir Byam, 'we have the raff[158] now as tight as a glove. Mum is the word, you know.'

'But has he brought any stuff with him, do you know? Has he "put money in his purse?"'[159]

'*N' importe*;[160] his note of hand will do as well; or I think we may take his word itself when witnesses are by.'

'I sha'n't, for one. For mark ye, Finch, he manages all his concerns, I find, through a rascally pettyfogging attorney; and if he smoke out a debt of honour to the tune of a few thousands, he may tip us something unpleasant, don't you see?'

''Gad! you are quite out there. Blizz is too much afraid of losing caste. He would not, I am convinced, shirk his word to save him from beggary.'

'O! you don't know the lawyers. They are deeper than we, a devilish deal; and a raff like Blizz is so easily bammed. A shrewd attorney might readily persuade him to anything, even to the making over all his property to said attorney, and turning hermit.'

'Aye, I grant you he might be gulled into such a whim, but it would be to gain the laurel of eccentricity; a very different affair from cutting the *haut ton*[161] by shirking a debt of honour, and taking advantage of the gambling laws.'

'Well, if we can't make it better, we must rest content, though I prefer the bankers. But what is to be done about the odds on the grey, and saddling him with that stiff-jawed colt?'

'O! Jones will manage that. He undertakes to persuade him that the colt is the better horse – quite *wild* – only caught yesterday – and fit to run down the fleetest buck that ever started; while we carry the grey against the field at any odds we can persuade him to.'

'This Jones seems to be the very devil, I think. You have him in every thing – jockeying for you, pimping for you, and now manager in chief for pigeoning[162] a raff. A deuced[163] excellent factotum, to be sure!'

'Ay, and he can do more than all that. He can chip you off[164] any inconvenient rascal who may know more of your concerns than he ought; and when he has done the job, can make a good bargain with the surgeons for the body, so that it may tell no tales. There is a deep one for you! Would *you* venture upon such a *comédie larmoyante?*'[165]

'Zounds![166] venture? I think you at least need not put that question after what you know of me. But when you have such a useful friend as this Jones, why don't you get him to put this Miss Cherry of yours into one of his spare sacks?'

'O Lord! no, poor thing! I'm not quite so heartless yet as that comes to. This annuity of her's,[167] indeed, is a dead weight round my neck; but I must try the scheme for her with Blizz. A sack and the surgeons? Good God! do you take me for a Turk?[168] No, no; that would be too bad, indeed. Why, the poor thing has a sort of liking for me, I believe, after all, in her own way, and would give me every farthing she has now, were I to ask her. You don't know Maria so well as I do.'

'Try her, try her! and if she give you a single *tonic*[169] to save you from hanging, I'll take her annuity on myself.'

'Done! done! You are in for it to a certainty. Dead and done for.'

'In that case I suppose your friend Jones would willingly become the undertaker, if he were ordered to find a sack instead of a coffin. Zounds! I wonder how the fellow escapes being nabbed.'

'Luck – all luck. He has been pulled up once or twice, but he always finds some loop-hole to creep out at, and gets off till the storm blow over. And yet he has not much brains, you would say, for anything, – rather a common-place sort of a fellow, but contrives to get through very ticklish affairs where cleverer men would stick fast in the mud. The only cunning he can boast of has been beat into him by running his head so often against the gallows' post.'

'There he'll stick at last, if the devil is the boy I take him for.'

'I don't know that: he has too many friends in court to have much to fear. There is scarcely a magistrate, for instance, in this county and the next who would back a warrant for his apprehension; or if they did, he would contrive to avoid being committed by some flaw in the evidence, or by means of a keg of brandy, or a snug supply of prime claret to the committing magistrate, or a present of imperial "*gunpowder*,"[170] purporting to come direct from the particular tea-store of the Emperor of China, to the magistrate's lady. Stupid as he is, Jones has pluck enough for all that.'

From this confidential confab[171] of the two titled swindlers (I might have used a stronger term with no injustice), I perceived that I should have more difficulties to encounter than I had foreseen, with regard to the chief object of my journey. I had now no doubt whatever about the identity of this Hampshire Jones with him of Battersea, though I wondered why the fellow had not thought of changing his name into some *alias*,[172] which might have served so far to protect him. The only explanation I could give of this was, that Jones was so very common a name as not to be liable to excite suspicion; and it might be of much advantage to come into court (the fear of which must be ever before his eyes) without the suspicious circumstance of an *alias* in the warrant or indictment.

If I did find the miscreant, I was at a loss what to do with him, seeing he had so many means of eluding justice. But it would be no fault of mine if I got him once clear off my hands. I was not, luckily, responsible for the conduct of magistrates, particularly those who would take bribes of smuggled merchandise to manœuvre a delinquent out of a trial for his crimes – so, at least, said Sir Byam Finch: I hoped for the honour of the Hampshire Commission of the Peace, that it was not so; but such things, I know, are certainly done in other parts besides Hampshire.

All that I had to do, however, was, if possible, to secure the desperado: after that they might either hang him, or make a justice of him for aught I cared: I confess I should not have felt much compunction in the event of his receiving the full reward of his numerous delinquencies.

With regard to the plot formed against Blizzard, I at first thought of introducing myself, and opening his eyes to the character of his *friends;* but upon farther consideration I perceived that this would serve very little purpose; for if he did not lose his money to them by betting on forest horses, he would be certain to lose it to the first Jew who could find him out, for some childish bauble pretended to be unique: – a rifle fowling-piece (not made for firing), which would unscrew and go into the waistcoat pocket; or a dish of strawberries, said to have been produced on the summit of Mont Blanc, would beguile him of hundreds.

It was a pity, however, to see good money passing into the purses of such fellows as the gamblers, one of whom had been ruffian enough to propose the murder of the beautiful girl who had fallen a victim to the other titled scoundrel. If any circumstance, therefore, occurred by which I could prevent their designs of plunder, I should take care not to lose the opportunity.

CHAPTER XV.

Wild horse-race on Lyndhurst lawn – The pigeon and the rooks – Irish method of doctoring a lame horse.

Next morning I did not forget to pay a visit to my fair protegée, and told her as much of what I had learned as I thought might do no harm. I took care, indeed, not to mention the expressions of interest respecting her that Sir Byam had dropt, as I foresaw it would require but little to revive her affection for her seducer, and this for my own sake I wished to avoid.

It was partly, perhaps, my apprehensions that this affection was not extinguished which proved an excitement to the interest I had begun to feel; for I have often remarked that the instant all doubt is at an end, there comes over the heart a dull deadening flatness, a stagnation of the living energy which had before been so restless. It is, in fact, the termination of hope, and the beginning of still life and sluggish indifference.

I had no right, indeed, to question the affections of Maria, as I had myself preferred no claim; but that did not prevent me from desiring a place in her thoughts – that is, the chief place; and the uncertainty of obtaining my wish had made me spend a sleepless night, and prompted me to pay her an early visit.

She received me with the most lively expressions of gratitude; and though it was apparent that her thoughts were confused and wandering in uncertainty, (how could it be otherwise?) she had become less depressed and more cheerful. Still she did not feel that she was altogether secure from her enemies, and looked forward with uncertainty to the future. She had formed no plan; and I dared not trust my fancy with building castles in the stability of which she might be concerned, as I had, in spite of the contempt which I wished to bestow on the world's opinion, a strong presentiment of the difficulties that might arise from my interesting myself on her behalf.

This was the least of my embarrassments. I had not yet dared to hint that I entertained for her any feeling more tender than sympathy with her sorrows. I conceived that, under the present circumstances, any warmer sentiment might indicate a want of sufficient delicacy and respect, and awaken the painful notion that I wished to take improper advantage of her unprotected condition, and was no better than those profligates from whose power I had aided her to escape. Any suspicion of this kind I was very careful to prevent. I was convinced that her own feelings were delicate, and in her present painful circumstances would be more easily wounded than if she were moving in a different sphere. On this account I always spoke to her and treated her as if she were a sister in distress.

For the present I could make no farther arrangement towards her accommodation; and I could not counsel her removal elsewhere without affording her my protection, which my public duty would, for some time perhaps, prevent me from rendering. Besides, it did not appear where she could be better settled, till some permanent plan might be devised for the future.

I was afraid, indeed, that the profligates might find out her retreat; but if they did, she knew where to send to me for assistance, and I had little doubt but she would in that case avail herself of my protection; for although, as I have said, I did not express in words all that I felt for her, I could not disguise my looks, which she would not fail to read: every woman is well skilled in the interpretation of this silent language of the heart. From the respect also with which I treated her, she must have perceived that I entertained no sinister designs; to which, however, I have remarked, that women are for the most part unaccountably blind, till they often find it too late to recede.

From her mind being somewhat lightened of depressing thoughts, Maria appeared to be much more handsome than I had even imagined; and I regretted that I could not with safety escort her to the race-ground, the amusements of which might have tended perhaps still more to make her cheerful. I went so far as to picture her in the costume of a female equestrian, displaying her fine figure on horseback, and attracting every eye by the elegance of her movements. But it might not be; and I had reluctantly to leave her to the solitude of the cottage, while I attended to my official duties.

When the day of the races arrived, I repaired to the lawn to take my station. The first object which attracted my notice was a carriage of a most singularly grotesque construction – an odd mixture of the antique and the modern – drawn by no less than ten horses, with five postilions in *outré*[173] liveries.

It is superfluous to say that the whole assemblage of people were set agaze at this strange equipage. The rustics stared, and the gentlemen-farmers swore their biggest oaths at the extravaganza. The forest girls, who had come decked out in their best holiday apparel, were universally of opinion that it was some of the royal princes, if not the King himself, who had come to honour Lyndhurst races in the state coach. The state coach itself of course they had never seen, with all its gilded and gaudy trappings, otherwise they could not have committed such a mistake.

The person who sat in this odd vehicle was no less fantastic in his dress. He wore a high black fur cap, shaped somewhat like a bishop's mitre, and similar to those which I have seen worn by Armenian merchants on the Exchange; but with this difference, that there was a plume of feathers stuck in the front, and supported by a knot of gaudy ribbands of many colours, like the cockade of a recruiting serjeant. The remaining part of his attire I cannot so easily describe, but it appeared to be equally grotesque.

He was withal a young man, and not unhandsome, though his complexion was dark – too dark for that of an Englishman. In a word, it was no less a personage than Mr. Ellice Blizzard, the would-be 'gentleman eccentric,' who had considered it indispensable to his success in stamping the Lyndhurst races as a place of fashionable resort, to open his campaign in this mountebank style of tasteless extravagance. He had set his heart upon having a Lapland sledge drawn by reindeer; but this was an equipage which all his wealth could not command. The sledge, indeed, or something called so, he might have procured in the metropolis; but the reindeer were not to be had, and they could not be manufactured, even by London ingenuity, out of any other species of animal that would draw in a carriage. I have since understood, indeed, that one of Mr. Blizzard's Hebrew friends did make the attempt to transform a set of galloways[174] into reindeer by decorating their heads with antlers, and other contrivances; but the horses could not be made into passable stags, and the attempt was abandoned, to the great grief of the Jew speculator, and the sad disappointment of Blizzard, who had to content himself with ordinary steeds for his extraordinary carriage.

It was this disappointment about the reindeer, perhaps, which was preying on his mind; for he did not seem to be in spirits on the present occasion, but looked cross and sullen. Independent of the reindeer, indeed, he might well feel dissatisfied if he had expected to see in the forest, so far from the metropolis, a phalanx of splendid carriages lining the race-course, and filled with the chief beauty and fashion of England. He had no doubt exerted his influence and his eloquence in the circle wherein he moved to bring down to the forest as many *crack* people as he could; but though some might promise to make up parties to honour the new place, not one probably ever thought more of the subject, or if they did, it would only be to laugh at the folly of the proposer.

The original projectors of the expedition, Sir Byam and Lord Blank, had the best reasons imaginable for keeping it private, because they could conduct their machinations much more effectually when out of the range of their fashionable connections, who might otherwise wish to participate in the plunder they had marked out. Their only importations from the capital were one or two desperate broken-down gamblers, who were to assume the dress and character of foresters, (to be ready to catch Blizzard upon all points,) and to share largely in their winnings with the projectors.

From the disappointed looks of Blizzard, however, it seemed a question whether he might not, after all their trouble, give them the slip, and order his postilions to drive for town. To prevent this consummation, they found it necessary to pique his pride by representing that his credit was staked to go through with what he had undertaken, and that if he could make any display at all this year, they might hope for better sport the next.

The horses, *wild* and tame, were at length ready to start, and I could single out the two which I had formerly heard mentioned as the colt and the grey; the latter belonging to Sir Byam, and the former to Blizzard, who had been persuaded to give a hundred and fifty guineas[175] for it, though it was not worth more than ten: Jones might probably have charged them twenty or thirty. This bargain, indeed, was the commencement of their present nefarious system. The colt, though stiff-necked and badly formed, was palmed upon Blizzard as quite wild, newly caught, and able to outstrip the best blood-horse in speed. As this false character of the animal was not given by the profligates themselves, who pretended to know nothing of it though they had made a careful but secret comparative trial, no blame could attach to them from the anticipated defeat.

Blizzard had swallowed all he had been told respecting this extraordinary colt, whose very defects had been made the subject of panegyric, and exhibited as excellencies. The stiff neck was said to be evidence of its uncontaminated breed, all the finest forest horses, and particularly all which had been winners at Lyndhurst, having had that point in perfection.

The praises which had been so lavishly bestowed upon the colt made Blizzard as vain of possessing it as he was of his fantastic carriage, or his Armenian fur cap; and he was quite in the vein for offering any odds in its favour. This opportunity was not to be lost, for Blizzard was too fickle to be depended upon for an hour at any time. Several thousands, accordingly, were soon staked upon the event of the race. I know not the precise amount, as I judged it prudent to keep aloof for fear of being recognised. The sum, however, I understood to be considerable; and though the riders, who were knowing fellows, and partly in the secret, jockeyed the horses admirably to keep up the deception, yet nobody could doubt, from the relative appearance of the animals, which was certain to be the winner.

To the terrible chagrin of Blizzard, who was almost ready to stake his life upon the colt, the grey shot a-head, and won the race easily, and with it a round sum of the West Indian's cash.

Blizzard cared little about his money, as he had a great deal more of it than he knew how to spend; but he was palpably annoyed at his *wild* colt having run so scurvily. Both wise men and fools, however, have a mortal dislike to confess themselves mistaken; and the loss of the race, so far from putting Blizzard out of conceit with the colt, made him more determined than ever to look upon it as an extraordinary animal, and he was convinced that the race had been lost wholly in consequence of bad riding. Had he himself been on the colt, he could have won the race, he said, even in the teeth of Eclipse, Highflyer,[176] or any other horse of celebrity.

These particulars I afterwards learned; for, as I have said, I took care not to mingle too closely with those who might have recognised me. Blizzard's casual boast of his own skill in riding was eagerly caught at by the gamblers to tempt him to another trial of the *wild* colt, and they failed not to urge him to undertake the exploit. Here, however, they found an insuperable obstacle in Blizzard's personal fears; for though he scrupled not to talk of his feats and his fortitude, he was a very dastard when there was any serious apprehension of danger; and to mount a *wild* forest colt, he prudently concluded, might bring his neck into peril if it should take a fancy to run off with him to its native woods. He found means, therefore, to decline this adventure; but he was eager to enter the colt for another trial, under the management of a different rider.

My Irish friend Thady had taken as keen an interest in the sport as any of the London party; and when he discovered this new arrangement, he set himself to defeat the scheme. His plan, which he disclosed to me, was truly Irish, though I have since understood that it has sometimes been practised in England. He had seen, he said, a horse that was lame in one foot cured of halting by rendering him lame in another! for which purpose, driving a nail through the hoof into the quick was the expedient which would run least hazard of immediate detection.

Upon this barbarous principle Thady proposed to render the grey horse, on which the conspirators depended, lame in both the fore feet, so that it might not appear in his walking, but would be certain to prevent his winning the race, even though the colt were less fleet than it was. Thady would find ways and means, he said, to get into the stable; and the devil was in it if Blizzard did not gain back all he had lost, with something handsome to boot.

I approved of Thady's desire to defeat the gamblers, but did not like the cruelty of the measure which he meant to practise on the poor horse, though it certainly appeared to offer the most effectual means of success.

It may be supposed, perhaps, from all this racing detail, that I had lost sight of Jones; but though I had been a good deal interested in the movements of the gamblers, I was not meanwhile forgetful of my duty. I searched, however, for the culprit to no purpose, as he did not make his appearance on the race-ground; and I began to fear he might have received intimation of my arrival from some of his numerous confederates. Yet this was scarcely possible; for nobody at Lyndhurst, except Thady, knew the business I had come upon; and though Sir Byam or Lord Blank might perhaps recollect my features, they could not know my avocation. Possibly he might be afraid to venture himself in so public a place as the race-ground, well knowing that there might be some who would point him out for what he was.

Thady, however, whom I began to find very useful in procuring information, had learned that he was certainly in the neighbourhood; and Jack Dobson, the under-groom, had even had an offer from him to engage as a smuggling rider on the liberal terms of thirty shillings a week, and a guinea a day for expenses, with as much brandy gratis[177] as he chose to drink, provided that he did not thereby unfit himself for business.

Dobson liked the terms well enough; but he did not like scampering about for life or death amidst showers of excisemen's pistol-bullets, or fighting his way with cold iron through squads belonging to the preventive service.[178] He preferred a quiet bed and a sound sleep in the attic of Sir Byam's stables, with money enough for a rasher of bacon through the week, a roast rib of beef for Sunday, and a comfortable cheerer of gin with a pipe, in an evening, at the nearest tap. But though Dobson declined commencing smuggler, he was of opinion that it might suit Thady if his genius lay among brandy and broken heads, and offered his influence to procure him the situation.

By this means, then, if Thady managed well and remained true to his trust, we might to a certainty discover Jones's haunts, and surprise him when he supposed himself to be most secure. I was not very fond of placing much reliance on the Irishman, for I confess I was prejudiced by the common opinion entertained of his national character; not, indeed, that I had myself any experience of Irish duplicity. Yet, from all I had hitherto seen of Thady, he appeared to be faithful; and the prospect of sharing the reward would of course operate strongly in preserving his fidelity.

I could not discover whether he had any inclination to join the smuggling party; but that was of little consequence, for he had national cunning enough to be able to betray Jones, and afterwards make terms for himself as if nothing particular had happened.

I accordingly gave Thady proper instructions to discover, if he could, some of the haunts of Jones, or to fix a place of meeting with him, in order to make sure of our prize. Even were it at midnight, in the subterranean vaults of Castle Malwood ruins, I should not shrink from making an attempt to secure him. All this Thady faithfully promised to do; and I was compelled to trust to his fidelity, or rather to his interested hopes of sharing the reward – always a much more trusty bond than friendship, honour, or even a deed legally engrossed.

I took care not to confide to Thady the secret of Maria's escape and retreat; for here I had no proper hold over his tongue, if he were inclined to gossip. It was not probable, during the bustle of their gambling transactions, that the profligates were yet aware of her escape; though it was likely enough that, the race being ended, the concerted story of the yeoman's pretty daughter would, over their wine, be thrown out to Blizzard by way of lure. The bet was also to be decided between Lord Blank and Sir Byam, whether or not she would from affection consent to resign her only means of present support; a point of no small interest to both parties, considering their eagerness for money. This would be likely to occasion an early visit to the cottage which she had left, when her flight would be disclosed.

CHAPTER XVI.

All for love, and a fig for the world.

As the races for this day were over at an early hour, I had a little leisure to look around me, and accordingly sauntered into the woods without any definite design, though I hoped I might come by chance upon some of Jones's smuggling parties; and as one quarter was as likely as another, I took the direction of the cottage where I had placed Maria.

I tried to persuade myself that this was quite accidental, and that I was indifferent whither I went; but this attempted self-deception was too flimsy to bear scrutiny, and I was forced to confess to my conscience that there was more than accident in my selecting that particular path. The notion of meeting with the smugglers, indeed, soon vanished before the more interesting thoughts of the fair Maria and her hapless fate.

I had no intention of paying her another visit that day, though I was already not very far from the cottage; and I would most willingly have gone if I could have discovered any passable pretence, but fancy refused to aid me in devising one; and all the gratification I could afford to my feelings was to obtain a view of the cottage by climbing up to the higher branches of an oak that stood near the path. This may be considered a piece of puerile folly, as I could only see the roof of the cottage and its curling smoke; but, whatever may be thought of it, I have recorded the circumstance as it happened: it will at least be an indication (if it *should* be esteemed foolish) of the state of my feelings towards Maria, when I could dwell with delight upon a distant and imperfect view of the cottage wherein she lived.

I might as well, indeed, have gone forward at the first, for I could not eventually restrain myself from stepping in for a minute to acquaint her with the events of the race. I now recollected also that she might be alone, as the cottagers would probably have gone to see the sport. This was an inducement which was not to be withstood, as we could the better talk over our plans without fear of interruption.

As I drew near the cottage, I eagerly looked through every opening of the trees, with the hope of seeing Maria while I remained unseen – not, indeed, with a design of acting the impertinent spy, but to indulge those sentiments which were rapidly growing in my bosom. I did see her. She was sitting by the cottage door at work with her needle, the very picture of beauty and innocence; and though other thoughts painfully intruded upon me, I tried to banish them, with a sigh, and, though the resemblance was forced, fondly repeated to myself the pretty pastoral verses of Cunningham:

> The Cottager Peace is well known as her sire,
> And the shepherds have named her Content.[179]

Maria, however, was far from being 'content:' it was impossible she could be so in her present state of uncertainty; but the quiet of the cottage door threw an air of peace around her which she could not but feel, although she was beset with difficulties, and troubled in thought.

I know not how long I might have indulged in musing on the lights and shadows of the picture before me; for the longer I gazed, the more reluctant, or rather bashful, I became to intrude myself upon her notice. In spite of the painful circumstances in which she was placed, and of her throwing herself upon my protection, I could not help considering her as a superior being to whom I should look up, and possessed of refined feelings which I was at a loss how to treat.

The presumed absence of the cottagers, which I had at first considered an advantage, I now began to look upon as a difficulty that would only increase my embarrassment in speaking to Maria. When we had to whisper, and to watch that nobody was listening to what we said, it brought us more upon a footing of equality, on the natural principle that 'all are fellows in their need;'[180] but in a conversation solitary and unwitnessed, the circumstances, I felt, were very different.

As I was debating the point with myself, whether to venture forward or return contented with having seen Maria, I was roused from my deliberations by the sound of a horse approaching along the bridle-road that led to the cottage. There was nothing extraordinary in this, as it might be some of the foresters returning from the races; but in my present mood I should as lief have dispensed with it. I had no suspicions that it could be Sir Byam, about to repeat his odious proposals, for he did not, I hoped, know where Maria was; and I was certainly not prepared for the apparition of Blizzard in his fantastic costume, bestriding a bay Arabian, and ambling it through the forest alone, having detached himself from his innumerable suit of lacqueys and postilions to enjoy a solitary eccentric ride before dinner.

As his road lay past the cottage door, he could not fail to see Maria; and I naturally enough felt uneasy for the consequences. He must be struck with her beauty; nobody, I was certain, could look upon her with indifference; and if he fell in love with her, as I had done, at first sight, I could not foresee what might result from the influence of his wealth. I recollected, indeed, that she had called him a booby; but she had never seen him, and at that time she was violently prepossessed against him by the proposal of Sir Byam. She would, as I foresaw, look upon him in a very different light when he came in her way by accident. She might, perhaps, dislike his mulatto complexion and his fantastic dress – these afforded me some hope; but I was altogether very much afraid I might lose, before I had gained, her; for though I might consider myself as her temporary protector, I had yet preferred no farther claim.

On passing the cottage, Blizzard was evidently struck with the appearance of Maria, for he reined up his steed, and stuck his eye-glass[181] over his eye in the Bond Street[182] style, a movement which I could not but think presented a curious contrast to his Oriental costume. His admiration of Maria, however, appeared, to my great relief, to terminate in this eye-glass view; at least he did not speak to her, but spurred forward with the utmost nonchalance.

As yet, then, she was safe; and I resolved, on the instant, that I would endeavour to prevent any future chance of losing her. In short, however mad or foolish I might be reckoned, I determined forthwith to make her proposals of marriage.

I clearly saw all the objections to such a step: the sneers of the world, the taunts of acquaintances, the remonstrance or the pity of friends, and perhaps even the occasional pains of self-condemnation – all these I could anticipate; and, if I knew any thing of myself, I felt prepared to brave them. There was a time, indeed, when I looked forward to a very different sort of life from what I was now leading, and when the mere mention of such a marriage would have gone nigh to drive me mad.

Upon considering it coolly (I fancied I could still do so), it did appear to carry with it a stain which I should have most gladly dispensed with, and which would surely be regarded as vile by the world. The very mention of the circumstances would be bad beyond all question; that is, if the case were to be considered as an ordinary one. The grand difference, to me at least, lay in my confirmed reliance on Maria's good principles and steady fidelity, the knowledge of which would, of course, be confined chiefly to ourselves; yet, if we were agreed in this, what need should we have to concern ourselves about the opinions of others?

Had my situation in life been different, I should have found many more obstacles, and, probably, some that were insurmountable, unless I chose to renounce all intercourse with society.[183] But, as it was, I had already in part renounced the circle of respectable middle life in which I might have moved, and was now a sort of outcast, except among my brother officers or persons of similar rank, who would not probably take much notice of my marriage.

There was a possibility, too, of keeping Maria's painful story a secret, for she had been but little in London, and was quite unknown there; and while she had been at Cambridge, she had lived very retired. Besides, she had lived in a style of splendour which would have no resemblance to the plain manner which my circumstances required. If secrecy, then, could be effected, it would give me all I wished for on this side Heaven.

Independent, altogether, of the love I had for Maria, it was not to be supposed that I could aspire to the hand of any female who had received a good education, and been used to respectable society; and any other I could not associate with in the close domestic intimacy of marriage. Maria and I seemed, in this respect, to be well matched. I had not, indeed, forfeited my respectability by any thing besides adopting, first, a wandering life, and afterwards enrolling myself at Bow Street; but still I was not what I had or might have been, if I had followed a different course.

Maria, on the other hand, could hardly expect any offer of wedlock, even from the lowest and most ignorant, if they were informed of her condition; she would not, at least, readily meet with a young man like myself, who knew something of education and polished life, though not of the same high degree to which she had been accustomed: and what was more, I was willing to forget all, or at least to consider her in the light of a young and virtuous widow; as, indeed, she well deserved, I thought, to be esteemed, from the attachment she had preserved towards her deceiver, until he had forfeited all claims to her love by his unmanly and degrading proposal of palming her upon another.

Such were a few of the reflections which passed rapidly through my mind as I advanced to the cottage; and I took courage to mention the subject to Maria, though with as much delicacy as possible, lest I might unintentionally hurt her feelings. I told her that I had mentioned my wishes, at this early stage of our acquaintance, to prevent her from having any suspicions of my conduct towards her, and to give her something to look forward to in her present destitution of hope.

My proposal came upon her so unexpectedly that she seemed struck with astonishment, and looked extremely doubtful whether to think me serious or only jesting. Marriage, in any way, was so entirely out of the range of her hopes, though uppermost in her wishes, that she could scarcely be persuaded it was not a dream.

With respect to me, the proposer, she could not of course form much opinion, as she knew so very little of me, except that I had assisted her to escape from Sir Byam, and had treated her with the most delicate respect. I flattered myself, however, that I could perceive she was pleased with the offer of my hand, though she did not (and I could not expect it) give me any decided answer. She was, indeed, boundless in her expressions of gratitude for my good opinion of her, and led me to entertain hopes of succeeding in my fondest wishes, if she were allowed a little time to calm her mind after the agitation which she had so recently suffered.

I ventured to take her hand; and, though I could not exactly say she gave it, yet I was overjoyed that she did not withdraw it, but kept her eyes fixed on the ground, while a slight blush flitted over her pale cheek. This was a token of genuine modesty which I could not mistake, and which I shall never forget. From that moment her image was indelibly stamped on my heart.

It may well be conceived that, in this state of mind, I was but ill fitted for official duties; yet was it indispensable that I should attend to these, now that I had discovered a probable method, through means of Thady, of succeeding in my expedition. With many a struggling wish, therefore, to prolong my visit, I at length mustered resolution to take leave of my beautiful Maria (the application of the word 'my' was still, indeed, doubtful), and returned to Lyndhurst.

CHAPTER XVII.

Puzzled, not pleased.

I WAS very anxious to know what Blizzard had thought of Maria, though I could not devise any means of discovering his opinion. I might have been satisfied, perhaps, with his riding on without speaking to her; but it did not follow that he thought no more about her, or that he did not return by the cottage. If I had thought of this sooner, I should certainly have protracted my stay there; but I was at Lyndhurst before the idea struck me. I had not mentioned the fantastic gentleman to Maria at all: my mind was too full of what was to me a more interesting subject; and after her thoughts had been turned into a similar channel, it was not likely that she would trouble herself about him and his impertinent quizzing-glass.

I confess, however, that I particularly disliked the notion of his seeing her again on his return; and had Thady been in our secret, I would have despatched him on purpose to watch. As I could not do this, I perplexed myself in hoping at one time that he would return in a different direction, and fancying at another that he had actually thrown himself at Maria's feet.

Thady put an end to these idle dreams by informing me he had received certain intelligence that Jones had left the vicinity of Lyndhurst, and was gone to superintend a grand smuggling party at Norley, between Lymington and Beaulieu,[184] where Thady had instructions to meet him, if he wished to enlist in his honourable corps of ruffians.

This news was not to be neglected; and as it became necessary for me to follow up the game with all activity, I conceived it requisite for that purpose to set off next day for Norley.

I must needs of course leave Maria behind me; and this I could not bring my mind to acquiesce in, when I considered her vicinity to Lyndhurst, and the probability of her being discovered by some of Sir Byam's crew of retainers. Whether he would give himself any farther trouble about her, indeed, was uncertain; for he seemed to take no interest in her except what was connected with her annuity, and this I had no doubt he would have been glad to get again into his own power.

I was prepared to pass the night in turning over in my mind every plan I could imagine to insure Maria's safety, and at the same time accomplish the object of my expedition. It was useless to think of sleeping, or, indeed, of going to bed; and accordingly having ordered something to keep my brains stirring, I sat down to ruminate on the various circumstances in which I found myself involved.

I anticipated a desperate affray with Jones, unless I could detach him by stratagem from his gang, or, as Norley was near the coast, obtain the assistance of a preventive corps to secure the whole party. I could not, however, determine upon any measures of this kind till I should be on the spot. If, indeed, I should by any means succeed in detaching Jones and securing him myself, it would be preferable to sharing the adventure and the reward with others; but I must needs bend to circumstances.

In the adjoining room all was still and quiet till a late or rather an early hour, when my two profligate neighbours returned from some of their night experiments upon the purse of Blizzard. I soon distinguished by their tone that they had not succeeded according to their wishes, and had met with something to chagrin them, notwithstanding their large winnings on the race-ground.

'A cursed unlucky bore, this!' I heard Sir Byam say, as they entered. 'Cursed unlucky! to lose sight of him, and let him gallop about the forest alone.'

'Zounds!' replied Lord Blank, 'and just at the time too when the raff might have been caught. I had schemed it all snug – after dinner to yawn over our wine – curse the dullness of country inns – order cards, and you and I to have a rubber to keep us awake; take no notice of him, but leave him to beat the devil's tatoo,[185] while we pretended to enjoy ourselves: at last hook him in for mere company – offer to let him win back his race-ground losings; and then, hurra! for plucking the raff out-and-out, just to make him feel as if he were alive.'

'A capital scheme! but it is gone to the dogs, hang it! How cursed unlucky!'

'But do you think that this forest girl he is raving about can be your Maria?'

'I know not what to think. If he gives his route correctly, it can't be; yet his description agrees in all other points. If it be so, there will be one good hit to balance our ill luck, I mean on your account; for you would be certain to lose your bet, and be saddled with her annuity.'

'That we shall see to-morrow, if it please fortune.'

'No, no: not so soon by my advice. I know Maria; if it is she, as I hope, leave Blizz to take his own way with her. He is mad enough to propose an elopement with her to Gretna Green,[186] in that queer ten-horse concern of his. We might have quizzed him into any sort of humbug. 'Gad,[187] I believe he would have gone to give the girl a midnight serenade, if he had been well prompted.'

'Zounds! but if it is not Maria after all, Sir Byam?'

'Why then, Blizz has got the start of us in finding a forest beauty, that's all. I saw none at the races worth having; but if it is not Maria, we must have a plot to cut him out. Maria is good enough for such a raff. It would be treason to let him poach on the pure forest preserve.'

'Cut him out, the goose! Why, zounds, he confessed that he did not say one word to this paragon of beauty and innocence, though he passed her twice. He expected her, I suppose, to begin the game, and drop into his mouth like manna,[188] by making love to his fantastic fur cap and his mulatto phiz;[189] and when she said nothing, he did not know what to do, but passed on, hoping, doubtless, that she would incontinently follow him.'

'Yes, but he meant to make amends for this *niaiserie*[190] to-morrow, and show himself a very Lothario[191] in making love.'

'Zounds, then! if it is not your Maria, we must lend him a hand, were it on no other account than for his bamming us to-night, and wenching it upon us so pertinaciously when we had baited our card-trap so well. He ought in all good manners to have submitted to be plucked *en regle*.'[192]

'As for lending him a hand with the girl, leave that to me, if you please. I shall make a trip in the morning towards the quarter he talked of, to see this forest beauty; and if it be Maria, you know the affair is mine. If it prove to be a new face, and worth the trouble, why then we can cut the cards for the chance of having her – all fair, you know.'

'No, no, Sir Byam, it is not all fair. I know you of old. You have tricked me on that score more than once; and I shall take care not to leave it all to your management this time. Blizz goes early to-morrow, he says, to try his luck with her. Permit me to go earlier; I know what to do in such cases.'

'Well, hang it! take your own way. We have the colt concern right before the wind, at all events – an out-and-out pluck; better, I take it, than all the pretty girls in the forest.'

In reckoning, however, upon 'the colt concern,' Sir Byam of course had no suspicions of the Irish trick which Thady, as he told me, had found means to carry into effect according to the scheme before explained; and which, as I afterwards learned, proved successful in baffling all their wicked ingenuity for plundering the young fool.

This conversation, it may be supposed, supplied me with abundant materials for musing upon; for Maria, now the chief object of my concern, was in danger, it appeared, of being carried off to Gretna Green in Blizzard's fantastic carriage. The notion, indeed, was absurd enough, as he was not likely to be pursued if she had been a forester's daughter, as he probably supposed; but it was not more absurd than many of his other movements. On the other hand, Sir Byam was certain to discover her retreat; and it was hard to say what might be the consequences of an interview. Notwithstanding the arrangement which the two profligates had agreed in, I was almost certain that each of them would try to steal a march upon the other, and endeavour to get first to the cottage, which they supposed to contain this forest beauty, of whom Blizzard had become so enamoured.

To anticipate them, and secure Maria from intrusion, it would be indispensable for me to remove her from the vicinity of Lyndhurst as early as possible on the ensuing morning; and as I was obliged to proceed to the coast at the same time, to make sure of Jones, she might accompany me to Lymington or Beaulieu. As soon as the sun was up, therefore, I lost no time in going to the cottage to concert such measures with her as it might, under the circumstances, be most advisable to adopt.

CHAPTER XVIII.

Irish hopes and cottage pictures – The Hampshire magistrates and Mr. M—d
– Smuggling arrangements.

THADY had eagerly set his heart upon his promised share of the reward, and
had begun, in his own way, to build as fine castles in the air as ever entered into
the prolific fancy of a pennyless Irishman. He had already planned an immediate
return to his native isle, the entire purchase of a cabin 'ilegantly' white-washed,
with a pig in one corner and a cow in the other, besides a paddock for the cow to
graze in, and a nice bit of ground where he could grow potatoes for a daily supply of eatables, and flax to give winter's work at the spinning-wheel to his wife
and daughters, both of which he meant to have as indispensable parts of his live
stock.

Since his unfortunate refusal from Nelly, however, he had not met with any
young woman whom he should deem worthy of honouring with the title of Mrs.
Hanlan, and the reversion of the cabin which he intended to purchase. But this
would be a matter more easily settled when he became proprietor of the said
snug cabin, than whilst he was only poor Thady Hanlan, without a *tenpenny* in
the world to bless himself upon.

'Hurra! never fear!' he shouted, skipping about in the full tide of such great
anticipations. 'Thady's the right boy for the girls, long life to every mother's son
of them! Agh! master, and you may believe me for that entirely. There's na'er a
colleen in Connaught[193] wu'dn't lip up out of her petticoat to raech such a bit of
a cabin as that, wid the pig, and the pratees, and the cow, and the butter-milk:
and it's a christening we'll have of that same, and it's Barney we'll be after calling
it.'

'The cabin, Thady? Will you call your cabin Barney?' said I.

'Is it the cabin, master? Jasus be wid you! Agh! and it isn't now at all at all. It's
the pig I was spaking about; for once't we had a slip of a pig com'd home from
Ballyclogher, and there was the whisky galore, and Dan Flannigan and his fiddle,
and dancing and fighting your bellyfull for pure love; and sure as Shrove-tide[194]
we christened the leprighaun[195] wid a noggin of the cratur,[196] and the pig's name

was Barney. Agh! it's myself wud have the right fun that night when I go to oul' Ireland agin. Hurra! I pray God, Amen!'

'Why, Thady, you will become stark staring mad if you get on at this rate.'

'Is it myself you mane? Agh! let me alone for that! once't I get snug in the cabin sure that blessed day, and all the boys drinking and fighting about the hearth rightly, 'case of my coming home amongst them agin; and the colleens will be smirking and smiling, and "How d'ye do, Thady Hanlan?" they'll all be saying to me. That wud be great; and it's myself will be the biggest boy of them all entirely that night, Jasus be praised for the good luck you put upon me. Long life to you, master dear, and a thousand blessings for that same.'

'But you cut before the point, Thady. We have not the reward yet, nor the rascal for whose apprehension we are to get it.'

'True for you, master dear! But he's all as one as caught entirely, when once't I get houl' of the tory.'

'Yes, indeed, when once you get hold of him; but you should keep your rejoicings till then. You may meet, perhaps, with a disappointment.'

'Devil an inch of it! It's myself that wud bear all the disappointment in life, were I once't in oul' Ireland agin; hurra!'

Thady's notion of returning to Ireland was rather a singular trait of character; for very few of the numerous Irish emigrants show any desire of being 'gathered unto their fathers.'[197] I confess that I liked the poor fellow's unexpected nationality. It gained him more of my confidence than he had yet shared, because, perhaps, his fancied cabin brought to mind my own Derbyshire cottage, which I so frequently dream about and look forward to; and at this time I was more than ever enamoured of my visionary picture of happiness in retirement.

Without such glances, indeed, at future comforts, life would seldom be worth having; at least, the unsettled random life which I had so long led. My cottage pictures had now the additional charm of being enlivened by the vision of Maria, whose image mingled with all my fancies, though I was still kept in harassing doubt whether I should ever obtain her.

But I must here make a pause in my story, so far as Maria is concerned, to attend to adventures of a very different caste from pastoral philandering in a forest. It will be requisite, indeed, that I should now make an effort to redeem my character for vigilance and activity in duty, which some honest-hearted readers may say I have been sadly neglecting for idle and foolish flirtation. My only apology is, that I could not help it; –

> Since my Creator formed me
>   With passions wild and strong;
> And list'ning to their witching voice
>   Has often led me wrong.[198]

The occurrences at Lyndhurst, it may be said, present an instance of my errors from this cause; yet, were I placed again in similar circumstances, I think I could not avoid acting in the same manner, by giving myself up to the feelings of the moment without much regard to consequences.

It was important that we should get to Norley in time to circumvent the enterprise of Jones, and entrap the delinquent himself, lest he might again elude us by some counter-movement. If Thady's information could be depended upon, we were yet in good time; and we accordingly hastened to reach Lymington, where we might establish our head-quarters and place of rendezvous, till we had formed definite plans of operation.

Thady, by my advice, obtained a night interview with the wholesale dealer in illegal traffic under the pretence of learning more particularly what would be required of him, and also the probable items of what he might be called on to expend; a subject of the first interest in the proposed undertaking, and an inquiry most likely to blind Jones to any suspicion of treachery. Thady was likewise to discover, if he could, the disposable forces of the party, and their several stations.

This latter, indeed, it was not very likely he would be wholly intrusted with, for fear of accidents; but he would learn, at all events, the nature of his own service, and probably the number of the particular gang with whom he would have to co-operate. All that he might be told of these circumstances, indeed, was not to be entirely relied upon, as Jones would take care to render the business sufficiently mysterious; but if he managed well (and Thady had enough of the Irishman in him for that), we might learn what would be sufficient for our purpose.

It may be supposed that, in this arrangement, I was putting off time with half measures, when I could have at once settled the business by pouncing upon Jones at his interview with Thady. But it is not fair to pronounce hastily upon any plan, without taking all the circumstances into account. Probably, had I ventured upon this, as, in truth, I had first intended, I might have fallen into an ambush of cut-throats, and lost my life without obtaining my object; for it was not likely that Jones would meet an untried and unknown Irishman upon such a business without some sturdy attendants within call, in case of need. He could not have forgotten, indeed, in what manner I myself had served him on an occasion in some degree similar; and he would have been a fool to put himself in such hazard again, with the recollection of the former upon him. It appeared, therefore, that any premature attempt on my part would only be rushing upon mortal danger to no purpose.

A still more dispiriting view of the matter was suggested by the alleged feelings of the Hampshire magistracy towards the delinquent. I had no proof of this, it is true, farther than the general assertion of Sir Byam Finch, who could not be supposed to have other sources of information than mere casual reports, or, perhaps, only his own suppositions respecting a county where he was but a chance visitor. Jones himself would take care not to boast of such immunities from justice if he really possessed them; but if he did not, he might get such a report put into circulation to intimidate the local constables, and keep them occasionally at bay. I judged it prudent, however, to act as if Jones were really under magisterial protection, because I was well aware such things are but too common; and, though I might be mistaken in the present case, it was well to be prepared against such an accident, which might render all my previous trouble and expense unavailing.

Thady acted his part very shrewdly; persuaded Jones that he was the only person whom he had ever employed that was worthy of entire confidence; got himself introduced to two or three of the inferiors of the gang; and, finally, obtained intelligence of their numerical strength, and their intended movements and operations; all which he hastened to communicate to me, under the prompting influence of his fancied white-washed cabin, with its Irish accompaniments.

It appeared from Thady's account, that the smuggling corps was more formidable in numbers than I had anticipated, and consisted of fifteen *riders*, as they are termed, with about half a score of *cads*[199] to act as assistants, spies, watermen, or whatever might be necessary for the good of the business.

These riders were furnished with good horses, upon which the various contraband merchandise was carried in the pack-saddle fashion, for the most part during the night; but in places thinly inhabited, or when there was little chance of a surprisal, they rode in open day. A party, indeed, of ten or fifteen daring resolute fellows, well armed with fire-arms and cutlasses, could march through most parts of the country, avoiding the more considerable towns, in defiance of the laws; particularly as the mass of the people think it no crime to rob the revenue, and would more willingly assist in the escape than in the apprehension of a smuggler.

It was seldom requisite, however, as Thady understood, to muster the whole force of the corps, and was more usual to proceed by detachments of four, five, or six riders, according to the importance of the risk, and the probable danger which they might have to encounter.

In the expedition which was now about to be undertaken, it had been resolved to employ the whole body, but in two separate divisions, which were to take their turns at intervals. The goods to be removed consisted of tea, brandy, and tobacco, which were already landed and concealed; part in Norley Wood, and part under a cliff on the sea-shore opposite the Isle of Wight.

The intended route of the cavalcade was through Ringwood towards Salisbury, where a wholesale receiver, who dealt largely with Jones, was to warehouse the goods for farther disposal. Such, at least, was the information which Thady had been able to procure. Concerning their ultimate destination, however, I cared nothing, provided I could make sure of their place of assembling or any pass on the road where they might be most easily intercepted; and particularly, if I could ascertain where Jones would station himself as commander-in-chief.

The latter point Thady could not discover, with all his Irish cunning; but he learned that, though Jones seldom accompanied the riders on their journeys, he generally directed them in person, upon their setting out, as to the disposal of the packages and their subsequent destination. The chief difficulty would be to find out whether he would go to the wood or the cliff, as both were points from which the riders were to start.

This was an important consideration in the plot which I had been contriving to secure him. My intention was, if possible, to have all the credit of apprehending Jones to myself; and, for this purpose, to endeavour to detach him from his followers, or waylay him when he was going to or leaving them; while I should have an armed party of marines or preventives,[200] if I could procure them, to deal with the rabble-rout of riders and cads, the capture of whom was with me a very secondary concern.

My first object now, therefore, was to obtain such a party for the purpose of cutting off all assistance from the chief delinquent, while I and Thady should take care that he did not escape. Upon inquiry, I learned that several of his Majesty's revenue-cutters were stationed in the Solent off the mouth of Lymington River, and the opposite harbour of Yarmouth, besides a disposable force of the preventive service on land; so that I should easily obtain such a party as I might want. It was necessary, nevertheless, that I should manage all this part of the business personally; and I, therefore, proceeded to the coast, and took a boat to row out to the nearest revenue-cutter on the station.

I took this step first, to provide a safer prison for Jones, if I should be fortunate enough to apprehend him, than I might be able to obtain on shore; as I was impressed with the notion, that the commander of one of his Majesty's vessels would not be so easily tampered with as a mercenary jailer, or even as a claret-loving magistrate.

The naval officer must support his honour through all temptations: it is as indispensable as his own life's blood to the situation which he holds. But the jailer would only consider in what manner he could make the most of his prisoner; and the magistrate, having no interest in keeping a culprit secure, might find a thousand shifts to screen himself from exposure, if he thought it of advantage to refuse backing the warrant, or to twist or mar the evidence in case of an application for committal. The naval officer, besides, would have the additional stimulus of making a seizure of merchandise, of more value than any bribe which might probably be offered to seduce him from his duty.

Lieutenant Frampton, the commander of the vessel which I hailed, was a surly, cross-grained-looking man; and, if I might judge from a large scar over his left eye, had seen some active service in his day; though I was uncharitable enough to suppose that the scar might have been as readily got in a brothel-row at Wapping or Gravesend, as in serving his Majesty on the high seas. Perhaps I should not have made such a supposition, however, if I had not at first sight disliked Frampton's looks, and, in consequence thereof, augured badly of my cause if I should have to depend much upon him.

I was never more agreeably disappointed in a conjecture; for the Lieutenant at once entered eagerly upon the business, and, as he knew more of the smugglers and their haunts than I could possibly do, said he would soon find a method of *doing up*[201] the whole gang, upon the information which I had procured.

Frampton proposed to moor his vessel off shore, send a strong party in a boat to the cliff, and procure a land-party for Norley Wood; according to which arrangement, I should be at liberty to make whatever movements I might think proper. Frampton, in pursuance of this plan, immediately despatched a message to Captain Ormesdale of the preventive service, requesting to have a party in readiness; and I returned, at the same time, to get my Bow Street warrant backed by a Hampshire magistrate.

Frampton recommended me to apply to W—m M—d, Esq., as a gentleman who was not likely to be influenced by Jones's claret or cognac; though, he added, he would not answer for it but that the worthy magistrate might be strongly tempted with curious outlandish books, which nobody besides himself, in these parts, could read or understand. This, however, was a commodity entirely out of the smuggling line. I hastened, therefore, to this gentleman's mansion, which was in the vicinity, was ushered into his library, and obtained his signature to my warrant without demur.

I had left Thady to make all the farther inquiries he could among the riders and cads with whom he had so soon formed acquaintance. The only point of any moment which he learned was, that they would cross Boldre Bridge; where, as I conceived, a party of preventives might be certain to intercept them, if they should escape our previous ambuscades.

I began now to entertain the most sanguine hopes of effecting, by these arrangements, a grand capture of the whole crew; and Thady was even more than sanguine – he was quite certain, he imagined, of his cabin and its comfortable adjuncts, – that is, of the money which was to procure them.

In this state of his notions I placed the utmost reliance upon the Irishman; and it was so far fortunate, since it would be indispensable that one of us, at the time appointed, should go to the cliff and the other to the wood, lest after all our prize should escape. Thady, indeed, had no authority to act himself; but, as the distance was not great, and as he was to be furnished with a horse in his pretended capacity of rider, he could, in the course of an hour or two, apprize me if my assistance should be necessary. He was to take the wood station, while I should proceed to the cliff, to co-operate with Lieutenant Frampton.

When the night arrived, Thady posted away to Norley Wood with his head much fuller of his Irish cabin than of deadly skirmishing with smugglers; that, indeed, was a matter of which he made little account. He seemed to have no fear of wounding and maiming, and cared as little about a broken head as a broken tobacco-pipe; though he was shrewd enough (as will presently be seen) to get himself out of danger when it actually came in his way. In fact, an Irishman seldom looks forward to consequences at all, be they what they may; though it may perhaps be objected that Thady's cabin anticipations were somewhat of an exception to this general rule.

END OF VOL. II.

RICHMOND;

OR,

SCENES

IN THE

LIFE OF A BOW STREET OFFICER,

DRAWN UP FROM HIS PRIVATE MEMORANDA.

Some be'th of war, and some of woe,
And some of fun and fudge also,
Some of escapes, and guile, and death;
Also of love forsooth there be'th.

LE FRÊNE.

IN THREE VOLUMES.

VOL. III.

LONDON: HENRY COLBURN.
1827.

CONTENTS
OF
THE THIRD VOLUME.

CHAP. XI.

Way to get up a breach of promise in marriage

CHAP. XII.

Pocket-picking at Astley's

CHAP. XIII.

A blindfold adventure on the Thames

CHAP. XIV.

Billiards – Whist – Tête-a-tête with Mrs. —

CHAP. XV.

Gambling and intriguing

CHAP. XVI.

Easy methods of getting rid of a fortune

CHAP. XVII.

Doings of a night party from Bow Street

RICHMOND.

CHAPTER I.

Dead for a ducat[1] – Ould Bill Hughes – Price of a good opinion.

IT was night-fall when I reached the shore, in the vicinity of the cliff where the smugglers were to rendezvous. I was quite alone, and wished to be so, that I might obtain as much personal reputation as possible, and have no other claimants besides Thady upon the reward, supposing I should be successful in the adventure. This was a consideration of some interest; for if Frampton and his party were to become sharers, it would leave but a sorry item for each, and poor Thady would stand a bad chance, after all, for the cabin upon which he had set his heart.

Just as I got to the beach, I heard the bumping of oars towards the right, which I imagined to be Lieutenant Frampton and his party; but by looking carefully over the surface of the water, I descried a small boat with only a solitary rower plying a pair of oars. At another time I should not have thought there was any thing singular in this; but as my mind was strongly excited, and my fancy awake, I imagined that the boatman might be connected with the smuggling expedition, and actually on the look-out lest there should be any surprise from seaward. If this were the case, Frampton would not be able to land without a signal of alarm being given. I watched the boat, therefore, with some anxiety, to see if I could discover by its manœuvres whether my suspicions were just. It did seem to ply off and on, without steering any certain course, although it made nearer the shore than when I had first descried it.

Whilst I was thus eagerly on the watch, I was startled by a strange sound which I could not account for, though it resembled the rustling of a forest in a storm; but this it could not be, as there was scarcely a breath of wind, and no trees sufficiently near. I taxed my imagination to discover the cause, but could think of nothing except the bustling departure of Jones's riders, though it was yet much earlier than I had expected them. It required some stretch of fancy, indeed, to make this a probable conjecture; for the noise certainly did not much resemble the trampling of horses, unless it might be that the sands produced a very considerable deadening effect upon it. The clearest description which I can give of it is, that it was a rustling, rushing, sound, and appeared to come from an opening between the cliffs, where there was a small inlet of the sea at flood-tide, the channel of which was dry, or at least passable, at low water. My road lay over the sands here, as it was now ebb tide; and I could calculate on three hours or thereabouts before the sands would be covered.

The sound which had so perplexingly attracted my attention at length gradually died away, and I could hear nothing but the oars of the boat, which I perceived made for the inlet; and as that was not far from the smugglers' cliff, this movement served to confirm my suspicions. The twilight, however, was rapidly departing; and it was with the utmost difficulty and at the hazard of being discovered, that I crept nearer the water's edge, and crouched, to prevent the boatman's perceiving me between him and the sky. Just as I got close to the break of the waves, I saw the man run his boat in upon the sand, and throwing out an anchor, leave her there, carrying with him what appeared to be the oars, though it was too dark for me to distinguish with certainty.

As the man took the direction of the cliff, I became convinced that he was one of the smugglers, probably Jones himself, who might have landed from some of the free traders in the offing, and, after giving his directions, might perhaps intend to return thither in the boat which he had so carefully moored. If it really were Jones, I considered myself in excellent luck; and at all events I was determined to accost the man, as I was well armed and prepared for mortal resistance, should such be offered. I may remark, also, that I could not detect the least symptom of fear in my own heart.

The man appeared to be afraid of being discovered; for, as I advanced, I could see him crouching and running along the sands, in a similar manner to what I had myself been just doing to avoid his observing me. It did not appear, however, that he had observed me, otherwise he would not perhaps have landed at all, or at least he would have shown some tokens of his discovery; but he did not once turn his head, and still pressed onwards in the direction of the cliff. Although he kept up a sort of running movement, I soon gained upon him, and was just on the point of stepping up to him to ascertain whether he was the man I wanted, when he stopped short, and the moment after discharged a musket.

I dropped down quite senseless. If I had been shot through the heart, I could not have been more suddenly levelled with the earth. His firing was so instantaneous and unexpected, that though I had my pistol ready cocked in my hand, I could not fire in return. I must confess, how much soever I may be censured, that though I did expect deadly resistance, I was quite taken by surprise, not having the most remote notion that I was discovered.

I must have lain for some little time upon the sands in this sort of stupor; and as I regained my senses by degrees, I fancied (very naturally) that I was mortally wounded; though in what place I was unable to conceive, for I could not say that I felt any pain. I thought this not a little strange, till I began to recollect I had heard soldiers who had been in the wars assert that a ball-wound gives at first no pain whatever, not even if it should be mortal, but, at the same time, stuns the person struck, just as I had been stunned.

This was a very unlucky recollection, for it made me forebode a dreadful death on the sands, where I was certain to be overflowed by the returning tide, if I were not able to get up and escape. I made an effort, therefore, to raise myself, determining, if it were unsuccessful, to cry for help, in which case possibly some of Frampton's party might hear me and come to my assistance. The miscreant himself, who had fired the piece, would of course leave me to my fate; though, when I had time to reflect, I thought it somewhat strange that he had not made surer work of it, and lent me, before his departure, a knock on the head to aid the effect of the bullet.

I found to my great joy that I could scramble up; and as I felt no pain, began to examine where I was wounded. I searched every part of my body, but in vain: I could find no trace of blood; and it appeared that I should be forced to come to the mortifying conclusion, that I was not wounded at all!

I may as well confess the whole at once, at the risk of whatever bad opinion may be formed of my spirit and courage. My falling had been wholly the effect of surprise. I would fain believe that from the suddenness of the thing it could not be fear; for the effect was instantaneous–I had *not time* to become afraid. My surprise was greatly increased by the darkness, the quiet, and above all by the excited state of my mind; for I have often remarked, in such cases, that every species of feeling and passion is more easily roused and more intense than in an ordinary state of tranquillity. Joy in this way will kindle hope; love will stimulate ambition; and, as in my present case, anxiety will render surprise more intense.

In other circumstances, I should have been irresistibly disposed to laugh at my own folly; but as I could not arrive at any satisfactory explanation of what had occurred, and as I had still to make my way to the chief scene of action, other thoughts than those of mirth employed me.

I again pressed forward towards the cliff, but had not gone many yards when my progress was interrupted by one of those irregular ponds of water and sludge which the tide so frequently leaves on a sandy shore. As it was now quite dark, I did not know what might be the extent of this obstacle; but as I found it impossible to cross it, I was compelled to grope my way along the edge.

It appeared, however, that it might be passed by those who knew the ground; for I immediately descried the boatman in the midst of it, wading and splashing about as if he had lost his way, and stooping, at times, like a gleaner in a harvest-field. He soon perceived me, and called out in a hoarse voice, –

'Who comes?'

'A friend,' said I, in an assumed tone, for I did not know but I might be recognised.

'A friend? Aw! I knows as much. A friend to the free trade as well, I know; but I don't meddle in them things. It sha'n't never be said that ould Bill Hughes 'peached a free trader; only I likes a bit of 'bacca now and again, and my ould woman like tea and brandy, you understand. Bill Hughes won't never 'peach; only it be as well to drap him some of them there good things as be a going, just for his favourable opinion now and again.'

'And who may Bill Hughes be,' said I, 'that offers his good opinion on such reasonable terms?'

'Aw! you are young in the business, I see, not to know ould Bill. Why, I be's known on this here coast all alongst for forty years – a fisherman when fish be plenty, and a fowler when I can scratch up anything that way for a bit and sup; but I may muddle and puddle in the dark among this here sludge long enough afore I can pick up a morsel of living.'

'So you have been firing on a roost of sea-mews in the dark, have you?'

'Aw! thof ne'er a one on 'em I can find, but a beggarly half-dozen.'

'Pretty good sport, I think, for one shot.'

'One shot! why, Lord bless you! I fired four on'em,–two double-barrelled rifles double-charged. I should ha' had two dozen birds with me for that, out o' the main great flock, what I heard alighting on the sludge; you might ha' heard the whiz on 'em a good mile off.'

'But why should you fire in the dark? Could you not take better aim in daylight?'

'Aw! so be you could get at the birds; but they're too sly a deal for that game. Lord, Sir! they will smell your powder a good mile off: d— their noses, I say, for bringing me out amongst this here cold sludge in the dark!'

'Well, honest Bill, if that is your name – '

'*Ould* Bill if you please. It is Bill Chadwick as they calls *honest* Bill.'

'Well, *Ould* Bill, since it must be so, I wish to get across this same sludge, if you can point out the way.'

'Right across, – you can't miss it, so be you've got mud-shoes.'

'Well, but as I am not so provided, what am I to do?'

'There's no help for you, but go round by the cockle-bed, and keep to the right of the porpoise.'

As I knew neither the extent of the sludge, the situation of the cockle-bed, nor what he meant by the porpoise, I was as much at a loss a loss as from the want of mud-shoes. My only chance, therefore, was to give Old Bill a trifle to extricate me from the labyrinth. It was no easy matter, however, to satisfy him with a trifle; for he made so many excuses about leaving his birds (if there were any more) to be swept away by the tide, and of losing his boat itself if he were not back in time, that I was forced to give three times what I had intended before he would budge a foot.

At length he waddled out with his great mud-shoes, soled with a long piece of board, to prevent sinking in the sludge. He had his fowls in a wallet which hung at his side; his rifles, I suppose he had, after firing, carried back to the boat. He soon disencumbered himself of his mud-shoes, and we proceeded towards the aforesaid cockle-bed, and a piece of low rock which he called the porpoise, and which marked the boundary of the sludge on the land side.

As we were going along, it struck me that I might obtain some important information from my guide, if I could get properly round him. It would be necessary, however, for this purpose, that I should assume the character of a free trader, as he was pleased to denominate the smugglers; – in short, pretend to be one of Jones's men, out upon a night expedition.

'So, Old Bill,' said I, in a sort of questioning tone, 'you know something of my friends, the free traders?'

'Aw! know them! to be sure I does. These forty odd years I be on and off a-knowing some'at on 'em.'

'And Jones, our master, I suppose you know?'

'Aw! I knows 'im for a rare 'un! He might ha' been worth a power o' money but for the wenches, what he won't leave alone. He spends all on his girls, and neglects business as well: he's always a-running arter 'em; the more fool he, I say. Why, I have know'd him belay and dangle about that there cottage in the bend of the cliff inshore, till the bull-dogs were at his heels; and all for a bit of a wench as came there, ne'er a soul know'd when, why, nor wherefore.'

'Then,' said I, 'it is to be hoped he won't do so to-night, when so much depends on his coming to time.'

'He'll stay at the cottage to the very last minute, I'll be bound,' said Bill.

'By Jove! then,' said I, 'it will be necessary, if you are sure of that, to put him in mind of his duty. I will go to the cottage myself and jog his memory a bit.'

'Aw! *you* may, but *I* wouldn't, if I didn't wish to put myself in the way o' being murdered. He don't like being smoked[2] with his wenches, Jones don't; no more didn't I when I was a young 'un. He wouldn't mind losing a good cargo as soon, I know.'

'O! for that matter I don't much mind murdering,' said I. 'So, Bill, if you show me this cottage, I'll beat up his quarters, and put him in mind of what's to be done before morning.'

'Aw! young 'uns be always too forwardsome. Belay a bit till you be as ould as I be, and you won't be so fond o' being murdered, I know. Howsomever, if you ben't afeard of a bullet in your belly, or a cutlass to your throat, there is the cottage at the light there under the cliff, and go to't in the devil's name! but you won't say I sent you, thof.'

'No, no, Ould Bill, I won't 'peach you to master, I give you my word.'

'Aw! but I must back to my boat afore the tide be getting hould o' her; so God speed you, young 'un.'

'Success to your night fowling, and good bye, Old Bill.'

I now made all haste towards the cottage-light which Bill had pointed out, and I was so eager to get thither lest Jones, if he were there, should escape me, that I had no leisure to reflect on my good fortune in meeting with the night-fowler, even though I had been so unaccountably thunderstruck with his rifle-firing: there were four successive discharges, however, it will be recollected, almost at my ear; in the dark too, and quite unexpected.

CHAPTER II.

Peep into a smuggler's haunt – Attack upon Mother Carey – Courage and cunning of Thady Hanlan.

I SOON reached the cottage; but as it was not my intention to make a forcible entry, and spring upon Jones in his castle, if he really were there, I judged it advisable to wait till he might come forth to go to the cliff, when I could more certainly master him in the open field. But the first point was to ascertain if he were in the house; if not, I should have to proceed to the general rendezvous.

I therefore crept with the greatest caution up to the window from which the light came, and on looking in at the side, so as to conceal my face if I should chance to be observed, I saw enough to convince me that old Bill was quite correct in his information; though, if he had guessed who I was, he might not have been so communicative.

Jones was sitting, as I perceived, by the cottage chimney-corner, with a bouncing, blooming Dolly on his knee, and a little round table beside him, on which stood a bottle and glasses. There was also an old woman bustling about the apartment, who seemed to take no notice of what was going on in the chimney-corner, where

> Each smack still
> Did crack still,
> Just like a cadger's whip.[3]

The wench was precisely such a beauty as I should suppose an unpolished varlet like Jones to fancy. She might be, I imagine, some six or eight-and-twenty, stout, plump, mutton-fisted, and ready to laugh and show her great white teeth on every occasion. Her vocabulary seemed to be rather meagerly furnished, being all comprised in a few nonsensical exclamations, such as, 'My grief!' 'Mr. Jones, is it possible!' but these, and a few other phrases of equal 'pith and moment,'[4] she did not fail to repeat often enough to keep her tongue wagging.

From the colour of the liquor which they were drinking, I concluded it to be claret or port; and as Jones did not spare it, I anticipated that he would be in very good trim for my purpose, if, from the same cause, he did not forget to make his exit at all.

I was resolved not to lose sight of the miscreant now on any account, even if I should watch during the whole night and the following day. I considered him as sure game, if I could avoid coming into contact with his gang at the cliff, and get him once under the charge of Lieutenant Frampton. If, on the other hand, I should fall in with the smugglers, I might make up my mind to be despatched without ceremony.

I waited a considerable time, and with great impatience; but Jones, meanwhile, was making himself too happy with wine and wassail to think of venturing forth upon the dangers which awaited him. While I remained near the cottage, moreover, several horsemen passed me, whom I inferred to be his riders repairing to the muster. This gave me the unpleasant foreboding that I might be interrupted in the performance of my duty by some of those fellows chancing to pass at the nick of time, and effecting a rescue.

At length I had the pleasure of seeing Jones prepare to leave his lady-bird and the snug chimney-corner; and I hoped it would be long enough before he was at liberty to return thither. He seemed, indeed, very reluctant to depart, and was palpably afraid of some catastrophe. I could not make out whether his fear arose from any hint which he might have received to keep on his guard, or whether it was merely a general presentiment, such as he must frequently experience.

Be this as it may, he was so much under the influence of fear, that he got his womenkind to furnish him with female apparel, as a blind, of course, to those who might be seeking him for harm. Under a large cloak, I saw him bestow a dangerous-looking cutlass, and in his bosom he stuck two formidable pistols. The old crone appeared to be very assiduous to serve him, and to take a deep interest in setting all his things right. When she had finished the adjustment to her mind, she said to him in a fawning tone,

'Now, for God's sake take care of yourself, Mr. Jones, and keep out o' harm's way: I wouldn't for the whole world any thing should come over ye. Oh, what would become of us but for your kindness!'

The wench, meanwhile, did not fail to laugh heartily at his grotesque habiliments, by way of keeping up his spirits, or rather, perhaps, of playing off her own; but *his* fit of humour was past, and he seemed more inclined to treat her with a box on the ear than to join in the fun. The more testy he appeared, however, the louder did she laugh, till he could no longer bear to be made the butt of her jest; and, clenching his fist, he struck her such a blow on the face as knocked her down upon the floor, exclaiming,

'Lay you there, ye — — ! till I come back! I'll teach you better manners nor make your game o' me!' And, on saying this, he sallied forth to take his chance in the adventures of the night.

Notwithstanding the affray he had just had with his mistress, I was unwilling to cause any alarm by seizing him, till he was at some distance from the cottage. Jones himself, however, defeated my design in this, in consequence of the state of his brain from the fumes of the wine, jumbled up with alternate fear and courage, in all the hubbub of confusion.

By the side of the road, and not far from the cottage, stood a piece of rock, or a large stone, which might have passed with a little fancy for an effigy of Lot's wife.[5] This was an apparition which Jones did not seem to like encountering, and he made a dead pause to consider what to do. As I was only a few paces from him, I was astonished to hear the click of his pistol, as if he were preparing to fire, which, indeed, he immediately did without saying a word; and not contented with one discharge, he followed it up with another; but when he perceived that his imaginary enemy made no movement, he discovered his mistake, and muttered out, 'D— it, if it an't nothing but Mother Carey hatching her chickens,[6] as the sailors say, after all.'

I was afraid that this premature explosion might mar my plans; for the firing in this direction might attract some of his own troopers, if they knew where he was as well as old Bill Hughes had done. At all events, the women at the cottage could not fail to hear it, and might alarm the gang by some concerted signal. I was soon relieved from the latter fear by hearing a bustle at the cottage door, and I could distinguish the old crone saying,

'I tell ye nay, wench! It an't no place for you for to be a-going amongst murderers and cut-throats.'

'Let me pass! let me pass! I can fight as well as the best on 'em,' said the girl.

'Nay, I tell ye! What's the use? Let him take it; he'll come to't in the long run for certain. Would ye risk your life for a cut-throat villain, what would kiss you one minute, and knock you down the next? I would ha' more spirit in me nor that comes to. God rid us of the rubbishing scoundrel! we can do without sich as him.'

As I heard no more of this edifying conversation, I suppose the old crone's eloquence must have been successful; and if Jones overheard it, as he might, he took no notice, but passed on. I allowed him, however, to advance some distance farther before attacking him, as I wanted to get as near as possible to the station where I hoped Frampton was already posted with his marines.

I had now, indeed, nothing to fear except Jones's personal strength, since he had been so foolish as to discharge his pistols at Mother Carey; and as I had marked where his cutlass was buckled, I could secure that at the first onset. I knew, besides, that he had a good deal of the coward in him, notwithstanding the hazardous life which he had chosen to lead.

Accordingly, when I had got him into a part of the road suitable for my purpose, I suddenly rushed upon him, seized his cutlass with one band, and with the other held a pistol to his head, telling him I would blow out his brains if he offered any resistance, or attempted to give any alarm.

'My name is Richmond,' I continued, 'and I want you at Bow Street again for the old business.'

The dastardly miscreant was taken quite aback; he made no attempt either to escape or resist. He tried, indeed, to gain me, as he had done before at Battersea, by the offer of money; but I told him it was in vain to tempt me, and would be just as well to submit quietly to save farther trouble, as Lieutenant Frampton and his party were almost within call.

'And my fellows all betrayed, I suppose,' said the prisoner in a despairing tone.

'All safe in custody by this time, Mr. Jones, I have no doubt; and now I must try my derbies[7] on yourself.'

My prisoner shuddered at the touch of the cold iron; and well he might, for he was aware of his numerous crimes, and that if he were once brought to trial, he could not again escape as he had hitherto done. When I had taken the requisite means for securing him, we proceeded in the direction of the cliff, with all caution and some delay on my part, for I was necessarily in doubt respecting Frampton's party, and if he had not arrived, or had been unsuccessful, then all my success would be worse than useless, as I must submit without a struggle to the smuggling gang.

Passing onwards, we heard the report of firearms in the direction of the cliff; and as there were repeated discharges, it was of the most intense interest, though of opposite kinds, to us both. The contest was clearly not decided, but going on with deadly struggle. I had, consequently, to keep strict hold of my prisoner, who might otherwise escape to his friends. I thought it proper, moreover, to pause, for it would serve no good purpose to involve myself in that strife which was the more peculiar province of Frampton and his men, while I might lose my prisoner, whose apprehension had cost me so much trouble and anxiety.

Whilst deliberating what to do, I was considerably alarmed by the trampling of a horse, which seemed to approach from the direction of the cottage, and probably bore one of the riders, late, to the rendezvous. I held my pistol ready, and told Jones if he dared to call for help, or utter a single word, I would shoot him without ceremony or apprisal.

The trooper accordingly passed us undisturbed, and was followed at some distance by another, who seemed to be in a merry mood, singing as if he had been trotting to a fair on May-day. As he came nearer, I could distinguish the words of his song to be a gibberish which at first I took to be Welsh, and thence concluded the singer to be a countryman of his master's; but on his nearer approach, I recognised the voice of Thady Hanlan, who was chaunting a stave of an Irish coronach[8] (or, I know not what they call it,) to keep his courage awake, and brighten up his fancy.

'That's the d— Irishman as I have just took on,' muttered Jones to himself.

'Ho, friend! whither so fast?' said I, being now well assured that I could speak without hazard.

'By Dad! then, if that isn't Master Richmond was spaking,' said Thady to himself, in a sort of hesitation whether he should answer till he was more certain of his ground.

'Come, come, Thady!' said I, 'no muttering, but tell us what news.'

'Why, long life to you, master, not a ha'p'orth;[9] only I had the devil's own run for it that time, in respect of a bit of a slip I put upon the shavers[10] at the wood unknown'st to every boy of them.'

'The d— traitor!' muttered Jones, with rage and vexation.

'Agh! by the Holy, and what boy is that wid you there at all, master dear, for good or bad?'

'You shall know all that in good time, Thady; but in the meanwhile you must ride forward, and see how Frampton succeeds in his skirmish at the cliff; and I shall go down to the water's edge and wait your return.'

'I see, I see. Then sure, master, I can be doing that same; but if one of them bullets take a fancy to come acrass myself, and pop me off to purgatory, God rest me! you may wait and wait long enough for Thady's returning.'

'Come, come, Thady! no flinching; but keep up your courage like a true Irishman.'

'Is it me, you mane? Lord purtect ye! I'm the very boy wud never flinch a ha'p'orth for the biggest regiment of peelers and tories[11] that ever was; only there was one of them boys after me out of the wood like the very devil when they foun' out I was off for no good; but let me alone for that, by Dad,[12] I jinked[13] him any how; for when I heard him galloping and blowing all alongst behind me, I trated him wid a bit of a thrick by just walking my baste into the fields to graze, at the next turning; and so away rid the boy after nothing at all, and then myself after him, laughing like Larrey Callaghan over a noggin of potheen;[14] and here I am all right and tight for a bit of fun.'

'Well, Thady, that was clever "any how," as you say; but in the mean time ride on and see what is doing forwards.'

'I see, I see; but if I wud meet in wid the boy I thricked, master?'

'Why then, Thady, you can "thrick" him again, that's all; though I see you are a little afraid of him.'

'Is it myself that's afeard? Jasus keep me from all sin, if I wudn't skiver[15] the spalpeen like a skinned eel; but Frampton's boys may be after mistaking me for a throoper, and the boy may have toul' the throopers how I giv'd them the slip, and all of the tories may fire upon poor Thady at once't, and wid your leave, master, that's too much for any Christian sowl to stand, let alone a poor Irishman.'

'Then, Thady, as you appear to be in the unfortunate situation of the frog and the harrow,[16] it may be as well to dismount, and if you have no objection to make a woman of yourself, here are a hood and a cloak to cover you up, when you will be the better able to get among the skirmishers without danger.'

'Agh! long life to you, master, but that's the very thrick I wud like to be after putting upon the tories.'

Accordingly I took the liberty to disencumber Jones, (who stood muttering and grumbling the while,) of his outer and upper habiliments and transferred them to the person of Thady. I took care, however, not to tell the Irishman that it was Jones I had in custody, lest by any mischance or thoughtless blunder he might defeat my plans.

I instructed him to go cautiously forward to the field of battle, in which direction there was still occasional firing, and bring me intelligence of the state of affairs, that I might take my measures accordingly. To prevent accidents, I therefore marched my prisoner out of the road towards the beach, to wait for Thady's return.

We had not gone many yards, however, when I heard a bustle upon the road as of flight and pursuit; and a skirmish and clashing of weapons ensued, but no firing, probably for want of ammunition or want of leisure to load. Thady must have met this party, and if he chose to lend his aid to Frampton's men, it would no doubt tend to bring this affair at least to a close; for there did not seem to be more than four or five altogether, including both friends and enemies. Thady, I soon found, was in the midst of the fray, for I heard him shouting,

'Hurra! hurra! down wid the spalpeens[17] entirely! Hurra! for ever and amen!'

At the same time I distinguished the hoarse seaman's voice of Lieutenant Frampton, exclaiming,

'Steady, my lads, steady! Cut 'em up, if they won't strike their colours.'[18]

The combat, if I might judge in the dark from the clashing of weapons, waxed hotter and bloodier; but this at length gradually declined, and it was apparent that victory had declared for one side or the other. All the while I took care to keep fast hold of Jones, and to have my arms ready; for otherwise he might have found means to escape to his friends. When I understood, however, from the cessation of hostilities and the boisterous exclamations of Thady, that Frampton was master of the field, I deemed it time to make my appearance, and add my prisoner to the number which it was probable he had secured.

I found that Frampton had two fellows severely wounded in custody, and that a third had got away; but at the cliff they had gained a complete victory, having taken them all prisoners except two, who were killed in the skirmish, or at least left for dead.

He had sent them all on board his cutter, and proposed, for greater security, that I should, as had been previously agreed on, accompany my prisoner on board also. But upon second thoughts, I deemed it more advisable to have Jones conveyed to the nearest jail, for there might be a possibility of his escaping from the cutter, or on the way thither, as well as from the jail, and the proclamation for the reward expressly stated, that whoever lodged the said Jones in any of his Majesty's jails would be entitled to receive the same.

I suggested that, as the cottage was so near, we should adjourn thither, for the sake of obtaining some refreshment after our labours of the night; and this being agreed to, we prepared to beat up[19] the quarters of Jones's womenkind for the purpose of tasting some of the good things which I knew they had in store.

When we got to the cottage, I tapped at the door; but, though there was a light blazing, no answer was returned. I therefore peeped in at the window, when I saw the old crone busy bathing the wench's eye, to which the blow she had received from Jones had given a touch of Day and Martin,[20] I tapped again, but not being more successful than at first, was obliged to request Jones himself to make a signal which might be understood and answered; and this he was perhaps the more willing to do, from a notion that he might be called on to partake, for the last time probably, of the stores of his own providing.

At his well-known signal, the door was instantly opened by the old crone, who warmly welcomed him notwithstanding the epithets of 'villain, scoundrel, and cut-throat,' which she had not spared a short time before: the girl also said something about 'My dear Mr. Jones!' but when they got a glimpse of his unwelcome companions, they both drew back in great terror, real or assumed. The old crone, however, soon perceiving how matters stood, and that Jones was pinned past redemption, threw off the mask which she considered it useless to wear any longer, and began to greet her quondam[21] master with the most abusive virulence.

'O you gallows vagabond!' she went on, 'I was always a-telling you as how it was on the cards you would be topped[22] one day, and it is no more nor such a rotten, rubbishing, shab[23] as you desarves; no more it an't, you sneaking scamping, rascal you! The gallows is too good for sich as you!'

The wench, in the mean-while, was taking a survey of the company for the purpose, perhaps, of pitching upon one of us to replace her friend in trouble; and as a good opening for such a design, she thought proper to chime in with the crone in abusing the prisoner.

'A pretty piece of rubbish he is, indeed!' she said, addressing me. 'My grief! if I would'nt dance under the gallows when he's a being topped, the rotten-hearted villain, for to purtend to come arter I with his buttered[24] blarney! I would spit upon the very name of Jones, for spite at sich a sneaking wretch!'

'Jones! Jones! Hurra!' shouted Thady, capering about as if escaped from a mad-house. 'Is that same fellow Jones, master, long life to you? Hurra and amen! I pray God for ever!'

The poor fellow seemed quite crazed with joy at the discovery of my successful capture, which I had hitherto concealed from him; and he could not himself know Jones, for it may be recollected that his former interview with him had been under the colour of night, when he could not see his features.

'Now, Thady, for "ould Ireland," and the nice bit of a cabin,' said I.

'Agh! and long life to every inch of you, master, I pray God! And snug sure the cabin is, every ha'p'orth, expicting myself home and happy to dig the murphies[25] anyhow, by Dad!'

'So you have fixed on one to purchase, have you?'

'Is it the cabin ye mane? Throth[26] and sure it's itself that's just waiting till I come over agin; and it's Tony Sullivan and Mick Flaherty are the boys to raer it for me tight and right, wid such proper fresh turf you never seen alive the day you were born, master!'

Thady having got upon his cabin hobby,[27] there was not much chance of getting him off from it, if we chose to listen to his interminable fancies thereupon. But we were more anxious to see some of the old crone's wine and other good things, which I had not even the trouble of asking for; since, as soon as she had given vent to the overflowings of her wrath against Jones, she bustled off in all haste to her larder, or pantry, or whatever she called it; threw a cloth, which by the bye was none of the cleanest, over the aforesaid round table, and covered it with all sorts of scraps and fragments, such as legs and breasts of chickens, cold fried flounders, &c.; and, by way of having something hot, she proceeded to cut some clumsy rashers of bacon from a flitch which hung by the chimney-corner, and flung them on the gridiron.

Her wine, however, (or rather Jones's wine) we found to make up amply for her supper *set-out*,[28] as it proved to be excellent claret. But Frampton and his men voted it too cold and washy without a drop of brandy to qualify it; and on tasting their mixture, I had no difficulty in agreeing with them, particularly as I was so much exhausted and worn out with the fatigues of the night, which was now considerably advanced.

The women were as eager to please their new guests as they were to abuse Jones, who being now 'fallen from his high estate,'[29] was, in the natural course of things, ungratefully deserted by his quondam *friends*. The wench, as we have seen, chorused her companion's ditty with much seeming good will, and exerted all her powers of attraction by exclaiming, 'My grief!' as a tail-piece to every remark; following up 'her grief' with a mechanical laugh, and epiloguing the laugh with a toss of her head, to get rid of a huge bunch of uncombed curls which hung dangling over her eyes. I remarked, however, that she took all care not to disturb those curls so far as to unveil the eye which Jones had hostilely visited, though they did not quite answer the purpose intended; for Thady, who was the only beau she seemed to have any chance of entangling, fixed upon the unfortunate eye at the very outset of his courtship.

'Why, botheration to it, my darling!' said he, (an Irishman in such cases has always 'darling' and 'jewel' tripping from his tongue) 'if you haven't got one of them purtty eyes of your own in mourning for its sins, I've a notion.'

'My grief! is it possible?' said the girl, pretending astonishment. 'But I knows what it all was; the great, big, ugly handle of the pump bounced right in my face, as I was a-going in the dark for a pitcher o' water.'

Jones, upon this, seemed to be contemplating a piece of revenge, and was just commencing an explanation, to put the girl out of countenance, when he suddenly checked himself, and relapsed into the sullen silence which he had hitherto preserved. Perhaps he foresaw, in good time, that he would gain no honour by his genuine edition of the eye-story; and might draw upon himself the immediate personal vengeance of Thady, who, as I perceived, was so eager to procure a wife to grace his cabin, that he did not seem to be very nice in his choice. I have little doubt, indeed, that the wench might have caught the poor fellow had she been allowed time to practise upon him; but I took effectual care to prevent such a consummation.

CHAPTER III.

Elopement from the cottage – The seaman not a milk-sop – Potheen *versus* blue ruin.

HAVING changed my mind respecting the immediate disposal of my prisoner, I resolved to have him brought before Mr. M—d, who had backed my warrant, in order to get him fully committed. I was the more anxious for this as I did not like to undertake the responsibility of escorting him to Guildford, where it would be requisite he should be tried for the kidnapping affair. He had done enough, I was convinced, in Hampshire, to afford ample grounds for his committal in this county, ensure me the proclaimed reward, and, what was no less important, secure to poor Thady that share of it with which he meant to achieve so many wonders in the way of Irish comforts. I had other reasons, besides, which may appear as I proceed in the narrative.

After partaking of the crone's refreshment, I suggested the propriety, as it was now wearing very late, of taking up my own and Thady's abode at the cottage for the night; while Frampton returned to his vessel with his prisoners securely pinioned, but leaving one of his men to assist Thady and myself in guarding Jones till we could remove him in the morning. I was not much afraid of any rescue being attempted, for Frampton had completely settled the cliff party, all but one, who had made his escape, and was not likely to return.

I did not yet know, indeed, the fate of the gang which Thady had left at Norley Wood; but I had no fears of any attack from that quarter, as they had little chance of being informed that Jones was in trouble, and it was more than probable that the preventives would prove as successful with them as Frampton had been at the cliff; for they knew the numbers of the smugglers, and the fault would be their own if they did not take a sufficient force for the attack.

As for any chance stragglers of the crew coming upon us, there was little fear; since, according to "Old Bill Hughes," it was not very safe for any of them to intrude upon Jones in his cottage retreats; he wishing, no doubt, to keep his preserves as clear as possible from poachers.

When Frampton had bid me good night, my first care was to order off the old crone and the girl to their separate apartment, as I had not only become tired and disgusted with their nonsense, but wished to keep Thady and the seaman out of harm's way; for I did not know what plot the wench might have devised to effect the liberation of Jones, though she had openly abused him, if she could once get either of them into a quiet corner for the purpose of practising her stratagems. For my own part, I resolved to forego sleep altogether for the night. I had too great a stake at issue to trust even Thady with the custody of the prisoner, as a bribe would, I doubt not, have proved a temptation too powerful for his resistance. Jones, I remarked, went to sleep on a bench by the fire as soundly as if he had been in his own bed, and nothing the matter; so much, I suppose, had habit reconciled him to impending dangers, that a circumstance like the present appeared to be a matter of course.

At an early hour in the morning I roused the old woman to get us some breakfast, as I anticipated excellent tea, free of all duty and debentures. In this I was not disappointed; but Thady looked a little mulish because the young one, whose qualifications as a cabin companion he had been weighing all night in the balance of his fancy, did not think fit to make her appearance. She probably thought that, as she had failed over night to make the impression she expected, she had much less chance in the morning, when her unfortunate accident would be certain to tell to her disadvantage, daylight being always an unwelcome intruder on the deeds of darkness. She might, perhaps, think also, that Thady was not a fish worth angling for; and that it would be more profitable to reserve herself for a more likely suitor; or, what she understood best, a wealthy profligate *friend*, such as the prisoner Jones.

The rascal still remained silent and sulky, casting many a wistful look towards the door, as if he had some hopes of either a rescue or an escape. I had carefully tried to prevent all private communication between the women and him, but I more than once observed him making signs to them; and it came into my mind that their abuse might be partly feigned in order to lull our suspicions.

As his anxiety palpably increased during breakfast, I began to form unpleasant conjectures respecting the absence of the girl, who might have other reasons than those I had at first fancied for her non-appearance. It was possible, indeed, that she might have got out by the window of her apartment, which I had unaccountably neglected to secure, and given the alarm to some of Jones's friends, of which, perhaps, in spite of my vigilance, he had procured intelligence.

I therefore ordered the old woman, in the most peremptory way, to summon the wench instantly from her chamber. She pretended to do so, but in a manner go suspicious, that I was convinced all was not right. The dark-eyed lady-bird, indeed, was flown; but whether she was off on her own business, or to effect the rescue of my prisoner, it was important that I should not remain another moment in the cottage. I therefore made all haste to conduct my prisoner before Mr. M—d, with a view to his committal.

We luckily arrived at Mr. M—d's without accident; but not, I am persuaded, without the girl having done her utmost to get us intercepted, as a proper punishment for the neglect with which I had treated her proffered advances. Indeed, I perceived her at some distance hurrying across the fields homewards, but with a dash of disappointment in her gait; at least I was inclined to fancy so, though I did not stop to parley with her, and I question whether she even perceived us.

'There goes the stray craft,' said the seaman, 'all sails set, and scudding it away round the headland; howsomedever, she may now hoist her signals in lubber-land, so we've got the prize safe under weigh.'

'True for you,' said Thady, casting 'a longing, lingering, look'[30] after the wench; 'but sure and sure she's a swate jewel any how, and cru'l purtty she is. I cud just like the moral[31] of her, barring she is an English colleen, and wudn't take kindly to murphies and butter-milk, I've a notion; bad luck to her for that same.'

'No more wouldn't I be a sniv'ling milksop,' said the seaman.

'And sure,' retorted Thady, smartly, 'I wasn't the boy wud be axing you at all at all; only if I was once't in oul' Ireland agin, I cud trate you wid a drop of the cratur you never saw in England the day you were alive; barring it was gin, and that's no better nor ditch-water by the side of the ilegant potheen, all as bright as a jewel, and as strong as that great Sampson[32] in the oul' ancient times.'

My two attendants went on in the same strain till we arrived at our destination, discussing the advantages and disadvantages of the sister kingdoms, in respect of their favourite articles of diet and drink; in which discussion the seaman railed pertinaciously at butter-milk, and dwelt a good deal on his sea-notions of a *milk-sop;* while Thady launched out eloquently on the peculiar demerits of cheese, hard dumplings, and other viands of English preparation, which were no more to his taste than gin; and this, in comparison with 'the whiskey,' he held in most sovereign contempt.

CHAPTER IV.

Adventures at Norley Wood and Boldre Bridge – Qualms of conscience, official and domestic.

AT Mr. M—d's, we met with Captain Ormesdale, (the officer of the preventives who had been at Norley Wood,) who was there on a similar errand to mine, having some prisoners with him for examination. He had made a resolute attack upon the gang in the wood, and it had been a very sharp affair, for some of his men were severely if not mortally wounded, while the desperadoes whom he had taken prisoners had suffered equally. I took considerable interest in his narrative, not only from having been engaged in concerting the plot for surprising both the parties, but also because I had little doubt that, if the Norley gang had not been cut up, the cottage-wench might have found means to bring them upon us for the rescue of her paramour Jones.

Whilst we were waiting Mr. M—d's leisure, the Captain told me he had arrived about dusk near the spot indicated in the information, concealing his men among the underwood till he had examined the ground in person, for the purpose of deciding upon his future proceedings.

There was a considerable rivulet hard by, which Ormesdale thought would be worth surveying, as he knew the smugglers to be very partial to the concealment of their merchandise under water; and he was unwilling to have all the fatigue and the danger of attacking them without getting hold, if he could, of some of their booty. He was well acquainted, he said, with this stream, from having frequented it for the purpose of angling; and be knew of a pool somewhat farther down than his ambuscade, which, on account of its depth and seclusion, was a likely place for an aquatic depot of tea, tobacco, or brandy – all, of course, well defended against wet, according to custom, by wrappers of water-tight oil-skin.

This pool was partly concealed by trees and thickets, which grew to the very water's edge, and consequently the Captain had to get quite close to it before he could ascertain whether any illegal proceedings were going on there. When he had got through the underwood, however, to the edge of a brow overlooking the pool, he distinctly heard a muttering of voices, and between whiles a splashing of the water, which, together with an occasional glimmering of light, probably from dark lanterns, left him no doubt as to the operations in progress.

It was too dark for him to distinguish any of the party, even if the thick bushes had not intervened; but he ventured near enough to mark the spot, to which he might return at his leisure, if he should survive the skirmish that was certain to ensue. In the meanwhile, he resolved upon attacking the water-party, by bringing up his men under cover of the wood.

He soon found, however, that the smugglers were not to be so easily surprised as he had sanguinely fancied; for, as he was returning, he was challenged by one of them who had been stationed, by way of piquet, at the approach to the pool. Thady's desertion, indeed, had probably been known by this time, and might have put them on the alert.

Ormesdale was not prepared to meet a sentinel in this spot, but he had presence of mind enough to answer the challenge by instantly discharging his blunderbuss at the fellow. Had he delayed a moment, he would, to a certainty, have been shot himself; but though the ruffian was not killed, he was disabled from returning the fire.

The discharge of the Captain's piece operated to excite general alarm in both parties. His men came up to the spot, as he expressed it, 'in double-quick time;' and the smugglers, who had no knowledge of the force brought against them, determining not to fly their colours nor abandon their goods without a struggle, advanced at the same moment. It afterwards appeared, however, that part of them stayed behind, to re-consign the bales which they had been dragging from the pool to their former place, of concealment, while the rest undertook to repel the hostile intruders.

Ormesdale's party were more than double the number of the smugglers; but unless they had used the utmost caution, there was great danger, in consequence of the darkness, of their losing one another in the wood, and of fighting against their comrades in the confusion which would soon be unavoidable. In order to prevent this as much as possible, the Captain left the disabled sentinel, ran forward to meet his men, formed them in line as well as the nature of the ground would admit, and, as soon as he heard the smugglers advancing, ordered them to fire at random among the bushes, as any attempt to take aim was out of the question.

He then issued strict orders that none of them were to fire nor even to load again, but betake themselves to the cutlass and the bayonet; which, however, they were not in any case to employ, except against such as did not return the pass-words of the night, three different ones having been given out, lest the desperadoes should get hold of a single one and defeat its use.

Ormesdale's men fired a platoon[33] as they were directed, but with what effect, if with any, it was impossible to ascertain. Their firing, however, checked the advance of the smugglers, who immediately fell back upon their reserve at the pool, closely pursued by the preventives.

As the thickness of the wood prevented the entire party from advancing by the route which the Captain had taken to reconnoitre the pool, they were forced to proceed by a more open, though rather circuitous path. Here they fortunately came upon the horses of the smugglers, some of which were tied to the trees, while others were loose, with their riders mounted and ready to escape. One or two of these did set off, and were put down by Ormesdale's men as cowards; the rest were pounced upon and secured, at the expense of as many wounds as they could succeed in bestowing on their assailants.

When the horsemen were mastered, Ormesdale pushed forward to the pool, where he had to maintain a more obstinate struggle, as there was at once a greater number to be grappled with, and, in consequence of the trees and brushwood, it was extremely difficult to discover the marauders, who took care to let their presence be known only by making passes with their cutlasses at some of his men: in this, as well as all other methods of bush-fighting in the dark, they were, indeed, well skilled.

Torches might, it is true, have served to detect the fellows in their lurking places, from which they made incessant springs and sallies, instantly retreating again; but any sort of light carried by the preventives would only have served to bring upon them the well-aimed bullets of the smugglers. They were, therefore, forced to stab at random among the bushes, and turn sharply and closely upon those who took them at unawares.

By means of their greater numbers, however, and by attending strictly to their watch-words, Ormesdale's party were ultimately successful in securing the greater number of the gang; though it was probable that several of the latter found it prudent to escape when they perceived the hopeless state of the contest.

Ormesdale himself had some difficulty in mastering one of the party, who made a violent push at him with a bayonet fixed to the muzzle of a blunderbuss. He was fortunate, however, in being able to parry the thrust, to twist the weapon out of the scoundrel's hand, and to become assailant in his turn. The fellow now gave way, and retreated towards the pool; but the Captain followed him closely, and supposing, from his exclamations, that that he was wounded, called upon him to surrender, which, however, he was not disposed to do; on the contrary, he still drew back, whereupon the Captain made a grasp at his collar to seize him. The ruffian instantly emulated his opponent, grasped Ormesdale's stock,[34] and, being close upon the edge of the pool, leaped into it, dragging the Captain after him. He was resolved, it should seem, being a very muscular fellow, to make up for the loss of his weapon by stratagem and bodily strength; and had not the Captain been also a powerful man, his life would, in all probability, have paid the forfeit of his rashness in following up the desperado. Even with all his resources, Ormesdale was in considerable danger; for the fellow, having taken him so completely by surprise, was careful to make the most of his advantage, and got him at first fairly under the water, which was at that place of some depth. In attempting, however, to push him still farther into the pool, the smuggler made a false step and stumbled, upon which Ormesdale seized the moment to get his head above water, and succeeded both in recovering his ground, and in giving the alarm of his danger to his friends.

The Captain had lost his weapon also in the scuffle, and was consequently upon equal terms with his opponent; and their relative strength was likewise so much upon a par, that victory was in the highest degree doubtful. Ormesdale, therefore, thought he was authorised, without any impeachment of his courage, to call for assistance, on the arrival of which the fellow was secured.

This man was amongst the prisoners brought to Mr. M—d's; and as Ormesdale's story directed my attention to him, I soon recognised in him one of the three ruffians who had personated the ghosts in the church-yard at Duckenhurst; he was, indeed, the very miscreant by whom my murder had been so unceremoniously proposed, and I was not, it may be inferred, sorry to see the rascal in custody.

Those members of the band who had escaped from the wood, if they pursued their intended route towards Ringwood, were certain to be intercepted at Boldre Bridge, which is a short distance up the river above Lymington; for here Ormesdale had taken care to post a few chosen men, who would try their mettle if they offered any resistance. In truth, as the affair had turned out both at the cliff and at Norley Wood, there was little left for the men stationed at the bridge to do. They had a few pickings, however, among those who effected their escape on Ormesdale's first attack, as well as in one who had probably been seized with alarm, and had galloped off, when Thady's desertion was discovered; for he had preceded the others by an hour or more. If it was really cowardice which had induced this man to take precedence of his companions in galloping to the bridge, he may be quoted as a striking instance of the effect which danger will produce in eliciting courage even from a dastard – courage, however, of a particular kind, and differing considerably from that which stirs up a man to rush forward upon a formidable enemy in a scene of strife, or boldly to face a mad dog or an unchained bear. The ruffian rider did not seem calculated for feats of this description; but when he saw that it would be impossible to force his way through his opponents on the bridge, and, on turning back, found his retreat intercepted likewise, he determined, having no mind either to fight or surrender, upon the only other alternative in his choice, and accordingly forced his horse to leap over the parapet of the bridge into the river. The horse was killed upon the spot, but the desperado could not be found; and it was not ascertained whether he was drowned, or had contrived to save himself by swimming ashore and slinking off; a design to which the time of the evening (for it was now dusk) would be favourable, if he had not been much disabled by the adventurous leap.

The business of the committals being all satisfactorily settled by Mr. M—d, I had nothing farther to do than transfer my prisoner to the local authorities, to be dealt with according to the laws he had offended. At the ensuing assizes a verdict of guilty was recorded against him upon a single charge, no other being brought forward; and he was sentenced to be transported, though, as the old crone had justly said, 'the gallows was too good for him.' I never heard, nor wished to hear, more of the miscreant: that he was *not* sentenced to execution, however, eased my mind of a very disagreeable feeling connected with the emoluments arising from the capital conviction of criminals. I would much rather never touch a guinea, than have the reflection of its being the price of life, even though the convict had committed crimes of the deepest dye. Forty pounds[35] would prove but a poor recompense to me for the consciousness of having been the chief instrument in bringing a miserable wretch to the gallows.

This feeling, I foresee, may subject me to the accusation of inconsistency, since my principal duty as an officer must be to apprehend criminals who have to take their chance of capital conviction. Well, it may be inconsistent; I cannot help it. All I can say is, that I have a very different feeling about a capital punishment and a sentence of transportation.

After all, it seems to be an inconsistency which I share with those exquisitely tender-hearted people (the poet Thomson[36] for instance) who whine over the slaughter of 'honest, harmless, oxen' and 'peaceful flocks',[37] but have no scruples about using tanned hides, feather beds, and fleecy hosiery; or (so they are not actual witnesses of the slaughter), will regale, with as much delight as Justice Greedy[38] in the play, on 'a loin of veal'[39] or a smoking sirloin.

I was now at liberty, in so far as official business was concerned, to return to town, and claim the reward; but I had still the private duty of attending to Maria, who had removed by my advice to Lymington, till we could come to an ultimate understanding about what was farther to be done. Her very consent to leave Lyndhurst under my escort showed plainly enough how she wished the affair to end; and, in short, (as no reader will thank me for prosing any longer upon such a subject,) we were finally married, my naval friend Lieutenant Frampton kindly attending to give away the bride.

During the bustle which these nuptials created, I had no time (nor had I any desire) to reflect on the important step I was so rashly taking. I was quite carried away by the whirl of passion, and looked forward only to an uninterrupted stream of happiness, – a long sunny summer-day, to the close of life. But the moment I was alone, and all around me moving in the ordinary routine, clouds began to gather and to darken the bright vision which had floated into my mind. I grew melancholy, and fancied many, many things which were not.

Maria had cheerfully let herself down from the splendour of a profligate establishment to live in a forest cottage; but this was a very different scene from the confined habitation she would henceforth have to occupy in the metropolis. This change, I anticipated with a bitter sigh, would soon make her repent of the match, though it did so much for her reputation, saved her from being farther degraded, and in some degree introduced her anew into society.

These, with other reflections of a similar cast, tended for awhile to embitter my mind; but experience soon proved that they were entirely groundless. Maria was cheerfully contented with the small establishment to which my limited income confined us, and seemed not to regret the very different style of her former life, which, indeed, she never even hinted at, whilst I had too much regard for her feelings ever to remind her that it lived in my remembrance.

CHAPTER V.

The joys and sorrows of an Irishman in London.

The reader will recollect that I had a claimant upon a share of the reward, in the person of my assistant Thady, whose Irish anticipations, it may be supposed, would not be much cooled by his seeing me so happily settled for life. As the poor fellow had been of such essential service, I deemed it just to give him considerably more than I had at first intended. The reward, indeed, was itself handsome, and there was besides no small addition, arising from my share in the seizure of the run-goods at the cliff and at Norley Wood; so that I could well afford to be liberal to the Irishman, by whose aid the adventure had been achieved.

I was not, however, well assured that Thady would turn his money to so useful an account as he had been sanguinely planning; for you can never calculate on the movements of an Irishman. His mind is such a complete *tabula rasa*,[40] as Figgens was wont to say, and his head so light and empty, that they are certain to be seized upon and filled by the first folly or gewgaw that comes in his way; and of such, sharpers and swindlers have always an abundant stock, whenever they can get scent of a well-filled purse to pay for them.

Knowing this, I gave Thady, along with the money, a few hints to take care of it. All I could get from him in reply was a profusion of exclamatory thanks, and a chorus of 'never fear! I'm not the boy for to be chated, anyhow!' and no doubt he thought so 'entirely;' but it often happens, I have remarked, that those who deem themselves the most knowing and the most secure against roguery, are peculiarly liable to be ensnared; and Thady, I am sorry to say, proved an exemplification of, rather than an exception to, the general rule.

When he had got the money fairly into his own hand, it is impossible to describe the singular gesticulations and capers which he exhibited. It seemed to me as if a current of quicksilver had got into his veins instead of their natural blood; for there was not an inch of his body which he did not twist and twine about in every form of joyous though ludicrous extortion. And withal, he made such faces! – looking, by turns, sly, simple, and roguish, and wondering, with open mouth and staring eyes, as if he were not very well assured of his own identity.

'Well, Thady,' said I, 'and what will you do first with all this *lot* of money?'

'Is it what I'll do wid it?' said he, casting by turns a devouring look on the cash, and a glance at his patched coat. 'Why, sure, I'll first — but I won't be telling you now, 'case you'd be after laughing at that same.'

In consequence of this notion having taken possession of Thady, I could not prevail upon him to tell me what grand movement he contemplated; but it afterwards turned out that he found his way to the Jewish repositories of old wearables in Holywell Street, and proceeded to get himself equipped in the cast hat of a Bond Street exquisite, one-half too small for his bullety head, with a top-coat which might have served to envelope half-a-dozen such fellows as he. In order, also, to make his inside garments correspond to his national notions of fine dress, he replaced his old shirt, which (he had long lamented) was of all colours but white, with a ready-made article of 'rael ilegant Coulraine.'[41] Thus equipped, at an expense which (in spite of his genuine Irish propensity of haggling for several hours over every bargain,) the Jews had found means to make triple what it ought to have been, Thady sallied forth in quest of adventure.

One of the national foibles inherent in most Irishmen with whom I have been acquainted, is a love of bravado, and of exalting themselves, so far at least as words can be made a manageable instrument of magnification. Thady strongly indicated his Milesian[42] descent, in this way, by boasting to Jack Dobson, whom he accidentally met in Piccadilly, that a rich relation of his in Ireland had taken a fancy to die and leave him a 'great legacy,' which *fact* he proved by showing Jack a handful of money, at the same time reckoning every shilling he possessed as guineas.

Dobson would probably have regarded Thady's *talking* as mere Irish blarney, but he could not distrust the evidence of his eye-sight, and stared in wonder when he heard the genuine chink of the good hard cash. It may well be supposed that Dobson had not spent his time in the service of Sir Byam Finch without picking up some of his master's methods of 'raising the wind'[43] upon occasion, by *pigeoning a flat;*[44] and that he was quite prepared to exhibit a specimen of 'high life below stairs,'[45] in the art of gambling. Thady's windfall presented a golden opportunity; and Jack was of course immediately and fully resolved to spare no pains in profiting by it, and transferring the gold to his own empty pockets.

Nobody can be long in the company of an Irishman of Thady's class, without hearing the praises of whiskey said and sung with endless variety; and the poor fellow did not fail to treat Dobson, over their cups, with a specimen of his eloquence upon this inspiriting theme. It now became Jack's cue to take up the ditty, knowing that it was the most likely way of getting Thady within his grasp, to invite him to drink a glass of genuine Inishowen,[46] which he opportunely knew was to be found in Sir Byam's cellar, and could readily be come at by letting the butler go snacks[47] in the plunder of the unsuspecting 'boy.'

Jack would doubtless have dispensed with sharing Thady's gold with a second party, had any other plausible scheme suggested itself; but as he would probably require an assistant at any rate, in *doing* or rather *undoing* poor Thady, it was as well to have the butler, who could furnish the main instrument – the whiskey. He might afterwards have an opportunity perhaps, (as gamblers of all ranks prey without mercy on their associates and accomplices) of pigeoning the butler himself, not only of his share in this spoil, but of other winnings no less considerable, of which he knew him to be possessed.

Thady was accordingly decoyed without the least difficulty into the snare thus baited; and it was an easy matter to foresee the increasing of his potations from what he called 'the laste taste in life of the cratur,' to the swallowing of dram after dram, till he would be ripe for suffering any scheme of villainy which they might choose to practise upon him.

Thus far I could make out an intelligible story from what Thady recollected of first meeting Dobson in Piccadilly, till they adjourned to his trap-stair apartment[48] over the stables; but farther, except some confused remembrances about a dice-box, he could recollect nothing till he found himself next morning in the watch-house,[49] terribly bruised and bespattered, and without a single 'thirteen'[50] in his purse out of all the money I had given him the day before. The whole had vanished, and with it his vision of the cabin, which, however, had begun to wax rather dim in his fancy the instant he perceived that he could procure immediate enjoyments for his money, instead of trusting to the uncertain future.

Finding himself in trouble, and not knowing how to get out of it, Thady was advised to send for me to speak to his character; and, upon learning how matters stood, I was at no loss to conjecture that Dobson and his friend the butler, as soon as they had got hold of their spoil, had conducted him to the street. In order, likewise, to get rid of him altogether, they had probably contrived to involve him in a row, a matter of no great difficulty in the case of an Irishman well primed with whiskey.

I pitied the poor fellow heartily, but I could do little more for him, as he could not swear to Dobson or the butler having either robbed or cheated him out of his money; and though I had no doubt of the fact, Thady himself had so little distrust in such 'good fellows,' that he would not have scrupled to go again with them for 'the laste taste in life of the whiskey,' with all the money in the world in his pocket. His notion of his loss was, that he had been robbed by the watchman who had taken him into custody for riotous behaviour, making a row, and disturbing him on his beat. Under other circumstances, indeed, this might have been the true state of the case; but it was not likely that Dobson would leave any gleanings for the watchman. The others who had been engaged in the fray took care to make Thady their scape-goat, while they made off from the scene of danger.

My pity, therefore, was all the consolation I could bestow on the luckless Hibernian; though perhaps, after all, it was as well for him that his money was gone, since he would have taken to nothing while it lasted but getting himself into the way of bad company; whereas, being pennyless, he was not very likely to be ensnared, and would meanwhile be forced to take to some employment to earn a living, which would contribute to keep him out of mischief. Dobson, indeed, deserved most richly to suffer, since it was very probable that he and his accomplice the butler had not even taken the trouble of gambling for the money, when once they found Thady fairly 'malted;'[51] for it would be as easy for them to rifle his pockets as to mystify his tipsy wits. But, in consequence of the deficiency of evidence, nothing could be done; and Thady was, of course, obliged to begin afresh his meditations upon empty pockets, and the means of replenishing them – a study in which he had, like many others, been all his life unsuccessfully engaged. I remarked that he did not now hint a word about the return to Ireland which had so lately animated his hopes. The scheme, indeed, was, in all probability, quashed for ever; and Thady would have to rest contented with watery gin and hard dumplings for the remainder of his life in 'merry England.'[52]

CHAPTER VI.

Scene at Bow Street – New readings of Shakespeare.

SOMETIME after the above events, I was in attendance at the office, when, just as the routine business of the day had been got over, an elderly personage in a great pucker,[53] accompanied by a pert-looking minx, desired to see the chief magistrate.

In most cases, it is possible to give a shrewd guess at the rank and character of a stranger from the cut of his coat, or the colour of his complexion; and, upon this principle, I proceeded to infer that the personage in question was probably a city merchant, or wealthy tradesman, retired from business to enjoy his 'wine and walnuts' in some suburban villa, or cottage ornée,[54] as the auctioneers' bills have it. His face at least, ample and ruddy withal, betokened that he was no water-drinker; and the quakerish style of his garments, though his coat was not altogether capeless, gave him a commercial look, which did not comport at all with the flurry he was when he made his appearance at Bow Street; for men of business, at least in London, cannot afford leisure to get into passions; besides which, it is indispensable to their success to preserve equanimity and method.

In this respect, then, the old gentleman was not quite in keeping with the character I had fancied, and I had consequently to try him by other standards; but I am not certain that I should ever have discovered him to be a village proprietor of shops, cottages, ale-houses, and other tenements, which yielded him a good rental, and placed him above the necessity of any other employment than that of attending regularly upon his stomach, a duty which he had never been known to neglect.

I was almost confident as to the minx, however, at the first glance; for there was no mistaking her gaudy gaiety, her flaunting and ill-matched finery, somewhat extravagant on the score of expense, and, above all, her impudent and irrepressible forwardness. She could be no other than a thriving domestic, who had either got into a place where she could 'rule the roast,'[55] or had discovered other methods of obtaining money besides her regular wages, and acquired therewith what she would no doubt call a *high spirit*, but which appeared to every body else to be saucy impertinence. Except for this repulsive quality, indeed, she might have passed for a rather good-looking maiden, turned of five-and-twenty, and well-fed.

Upon the old gentleman being asked the nature of his business, the hussey, being used to take such liberties perhaps, determined to have the honour to herself of speaking first in the affair, and stepped forward to commence her story; but the magistrate was ungallant enough not to lend his countenance to this palpable encroachment upon the legitimate order of precedence, and would assign her maidship nothing more than the second place in point of sequence. To this she submitted with a very ill grace, and gave divers audible tokens of her desire to show that she had a *spirit* within her not much accustomed to the curb and the rein.

Order being at length restored, and the previous question repeated, the old gentleman, having the idea of his grievance strong upon his mind, answered as if the magistrate had known his whole story.

'Why, your Worship, I want to have the law of the rascal, so be we can get hold on 'im.'

'Who do you mean, Sir?' said the magistrate, perceiving that the complainant was not over clear in his conceptions.

'Why, your Worship, who should I mean but Joe Banbury, Esquire? Woe betide the day when my Becky took up with such as he, for all his lands and his money! when she had the choice of Squire Foxleigh and Mr. Eldforte as well.'

'But you knows, Mr. Crickles, both on 'em was old enough to ha' been Miss Rebecca's grandfathers for matter o' that,' interrupted the Abigail.[56]

'Peace, Nancy! I tell ye, and mind what his worship said; only I wish Becky had took up with any body but this Joe Banbury.'

'And pray,' said the magistrate, 'what has Mr. Banbury done? Has he seduced the young lady, or what?'

'Bless your Worship!' rejoined the agitated Crickles, 'worse than that! much worse than that. Woe's me that I should live to see the day!'

'I cannot,' said the magistrate, 'imagine any thing much worse to befal a young lady, unless he have murdered her.'

'O! worse than that too,' exclaimed the old gentleman; 'a great deal worse, I assure you.'

'Then come to the point at once, Sir; and we shall see what can be done.'

'Why, then, your Worship, the amount of the misfortune is – he has *married* her; and I think that a great deal worse than murder, as matters have turned out.'

'It must certainly,' observed the magistrate, 'be some terrible matter that makes marrying a young lady worse than seducing or murdering her.'

'Terrible enough,' answered the complainant, 'I assure you. Why, he's mad! as mad as a March hare![57] and he is driving Becky mad; and that will drive me mad. I feel it here already, I do;' pointing fearfully to his head. 'And I leave your Worship to judge whether all that is not worse than murder.'

'Indeed, if the case be as you represent it,' said the magistrate, 'it is bad enough; but why don't you have him locked up, to prevent mischief?'

'O! for that matter, he's as good as locked up already,' sighed Crickles: 'he takes care o' that; but the misfortune is that Becky is locked up wi' 'un in the old house, what he calls Banbury Castle; but no more like a castle it is, than chalk is like cheese – an old rickety rubbish of a place! as I tell him, the very materials an't worth carting off of the premises.'

'I have nothing to do, Sir, with the value of this Banbury Castle,' interposed the magistrate; 'but why don't you take means to undo his locks, if he is as mad as you say?'

'The reason is, your Worship, that nobody dares go near 'im.'

'We shall find those who both dare and will, I promise you,' said the magistrate.

'That, your Worship, is the very thing I want! Once catch hold of the mad-cap, – get Becky out o' his clutches, and clap him snug into Bedlam!⁵⁸ – the only place fit for such as he; but the officers you send had need be bullet-proof, or I wouldn't answer for the life of ere a one on 'em.'

'You may safely leave that to themselves,' was the rejoinder. 'There is little fear but they will find a scheme to get at him, if they should take him when he is asleep.'

'Lord bless your Worship!' cried the applicant, 'it matters not whether he be asleep or awake; for he has the place all stuck over with spring-guns,⁵⁹ so that nobody can get within a mile of it without being shot dead!'

'Then there's mischief, if not method in his madness, I perceive. A danger-ous sort of subject he appears to be,' said the magistrate, who seemed a good deal puzzled what to think about the case. Indeed, old Crickles talked so very strangely of this Mr. Banbury, that it was not over clear but he might himself be a little touched in the wits.

'Method and mischief enough for the county, or the kingdom either,' answered he, 'and cunning as a fox, – the very strongest sign, as I hear say, of a true madman. Nay, for that matter, I know some'at on't myself, and had my Christmas dinner spoiled by it.'

'Ah! *that was* a misfortune!' said the magistrate, archly.

'It was indeed; for there was Jerry Holt, the born *natural*,⁶⁰ got into my kitchen, went right up to the fire, and before the cook could say Jack Robinson, stirred the soot down all over the joint on the spit: "now," says Jerry, "you can't eat that there beef, but I can." There was a piece of mad cunning, your Worship! and that is nothing to Joe Banbury.'

Every body within hearing, including the worthy magistrate himself, laughed heartily at the *natural* catastrophe of the old gentleman's Christmas beef, or rather at the rueful recollections which the recital called up in his mind, and spread over his countenance. It seemed, however, to afford no matter of mirth to him, any more than Joe Banbury's spring-guns, of which he could not speak without terror.

'Well then,' said the magistrate, 'you wish to have this Mr. Banbury apprehended?'

'O! by all means, your Worship. It cannot be done too soon, if the thing is possible.'

'I'll answer for its possibility; but you have made no specific charge against him, except his setting spring-guns about his premises, and that he has a right by law to do.'

'Nay, but has he a right to drive my daughter mad? I should like to know that.'

'It will depend very much on the means he employs. If he puts her in bodily fear of her life, or commits any personal assault, (farther than beating her with a rod, wand, or cane, not exceeding a finger's thickness,[61]) I can grant you a warrant to have him apprehended.'

'For that matter, I'll be sworn she is not sure of her life an hour while she bides in the house; and out of it she can't get without his permission – can she, Nancy?'

'No, indeed, that she can't,' said the minx, glad at last to get her tongue at liberty; 'no more could'nt I get out, till I cut and run from 'un. He allows of nobody going outside the great gate ever since he took to drilling[62] Missis so.'

'What do you mean by drilling?' said the magistrate.

'O! saving your Worship's reverence,' replied the girl, 'just doing a mort[63] of all manner o' queerish things. Master's a rum chap for that.'

'Well, but what queerish things; are they he actually does to your mistress? Does he set her up as a mark for his spring-guns, or what?'

'No, bless your Worship's reverence,' cried Nancy, 'he's too fond on her by half for that. Shoot her with a spring-gun! bless you, I've heard him with my own ears say he would'nt allow of "the winds of heaven itself to pay a visit to her rough face."[64] Them are his own very words.'

''Fore George![65] and did Joe really say so? the rascal!' exclaimed old Crickles. 'There can be no question but he's mad – quite horn mad;[66] for a smoother face than Becky's is not to be found in seven counties – she had always a soft silky skin, from a baby. O! the mad rascal, to call her face rough!'

'Then, if he is so fond of her as the girl says,' continued the magistrate, 'her life does not seem to be in much danger, unless he kill her with kindness, as some husbands have been said to do by their wives.'

'Pox take such kindness!' said Nancy, who was determined to retain her liberty of speech, 'I have no patience with his goings on. Why, it an't many days agone when he wouldn't allow Missis to touch a morsel of dinner, all out o' his whims, 'cause he said the "mutton was burnt, and so was all the meat," and wasn't fit for nothing but "to 'gender anger," though you never see any thing so nicely underdone.'

'He's mad to a certainty!' interrupted Crickles.

'But that was nothing!' continued the girl. 'He put all the house in a mort of fright, – catched up the dishes from the table, and chucked them all about the floor, and called us all such queerish names, you never heard the like. Missis, good soul, made a try to quiet him all she could; but it wasn't no use, for the more she tried, he turned the more rumbustical.[67] You have no notion of his queer goings on.'

From Nancy's tragical history of the dinner, I began to perceive that Mr. Joe Banbury was probably setting himself up to enact the character of Petruchio,[68] in either mad or sober earnest. Indeed, the minx's cross-reading about the 'winds of heaven,' and Mrs. Banbury's 'rough face,' was a palpable hint that his studies were of a theatrical cast; and if he were crazy at all, it appeared that he must be *stage-struck*.

The whole of the girl's stories, in fact, tended to confirm this conclusion; for such expressions as she recollected him to have used, though most of them had undergone a strange metamorphosis in their passage through her memory, were evidently of dramatic origin. The magistrate seemed to draw the same inference; and as he had nothing particularly pressing upon his time, he had let the complainant and his pert attendant run on at greater length than would otherwise have been permitted. He now once more addressed Crickles, and said, 'Pray, may I ask if this Mr. Banbury is a player?'

'Not that I know on, these some years,' answered Crickles, 'except a turn at backgammon of an evening or so; but I've seen him mad after cricket, and fives, and that sort of thing.'

'It would appear, then, that this is not the first of his madness; but I don't mean such games as those you have named: I alluded to the theatre; did he ever act?'

''Fore George! if you mean a play-actor, he shouldn't have married my daughter if he had been, I know.'

'He appears, however,' said the magistrate, 'to have some little knowledge that way, by his attempting to perform in his own house Shakespeare's facetious comedy of The Taming of the Shrew; perhaps he judged it might be useful to employ a little kind instruction of this sort upon his wife, on setting out in his matrimonial career, to prevent any shrewishness afterwards.'

''Fore George, Sir,' returned the angry Crickles, 'if the madcap rascal says my Becky's a shrew, he deserves to have his nose pulled, that's all; for a milder, sweeter, gentler creature is not to be found. It is worse a deal than calling her face rough, and God knows that was a scandalous libel enough on the poor thing.'

'But cannot she make her escape from him by some means or other, when he treats her in this manner?'

'La! your Worship,' said Nancy, 'that wouldn't be no easy matter, I assure you; for he sermons her so about the "virtue in a lock and key;"[69] and when she offers to go out, he cries, "softly! you stir not hence except to breathe with me"[70] – his very words – I remember them because I thought them so comical. But la! your Worship, he beat that all to nothing one day, and swore the sun was the moon,[71] and wanted Missis to say so, right or wrong; but she wouldn't humour him in it for no consideration, and she was all of a tremble with fear to see Master so out o' his mind.'

'The case is plain then,' said the magistrate. 'You swear that Mr. Banbury, whom you presume to be *non compos mentis*,[72] has put Mrs. Banbury, your daughter, in bodily fear of her life, and under these circumstances has committed divers assaults upon her person.'

'No, your Worship,' said Crickles, 'I won't swear to the latter, for I don't know as he ever beat Becky; it is bad enough to drive her mad without the scandal of beating her.'

'Then you swear to his putting her in bodily fear of her life?'

'Yes, truly, as you have heard Nancy say, he absolutely starves her; for no sooner is there a good dinner on the table than he falls into one of his fits, and won't let her taste a morsel, pretending that beef is "choleric," and mutton breeds "anger," and what not;[73] and with that falls to scolding the servants, and telling Becky to "pluck up her spirits," to be "merry" and "patient," and what not.[74] And he an't content with starving on her – he won't let her have a bit of sleep neither, as Nancy can testify.'

'That I can, your Worship,' shouted the girl; 'for he chucks all the bed-things about just as he does the dishes at dinner, and says his "sweeting," his "honey-love"[75] sha'n't never lay in such a "whoreson" bed. Missis has not been a-bed for two or three nights, with his goings on; and when he sees her nod on her chair, he bawls in her ear, as how there's "no rest for the wicked,"[76] and the likes o' that.'

'Well,' exclaimed old Crickles, 'I'll have the law of the mad-cap rascal! to call my daughter "wicked," and "rough i' the face," and a "shrew," and what not. I won't stand it, indeed I won't, no longer.'

The magistrate soon grew tired of this stuff, as I fear the reader has been long ago; and a warrant having been made out against Mr. Joseph Banbury, its execution was intrusted to me; but as this would-be-Petruchio was reported to deal in fire-arms, it was deemed adviseable that I should have an assistant, in case of accidents or resistance, and I chose Jem Bucks for the purpose, as it was an adventure which would square well with his humour.

CHAPTER VII.

Banbury Castle, with its approach – More doings of the Squire in the comedy
line.

FROM the whole story, it appeared to me that this Joe Banbury must either
be actually crazed, or a goose of the first water, to dream of turning a wild and
improbable farce (I think I may call it so without offence) like the Taming of the
Shrew, into a serious domestic performance. He had, therefore, met with all the
success he deserved; and instead of *taming* poor Mrs. Banbury, was in the fair
way, it appeared, of *untaming* her, by either making her mad in good earnest, or
exciting her to effect her escape from his mad discipline.

It seemed, likewise, that he had carried the joke to a great length, in beset-
ting his premises with spring-guns to prevent all intrusion upon his 'school for
wives.'[77] At least such was the representation of the complainant, whose account,
however, was not altogether to be trusted, as he had evidently warped many
facts, and magnified others so as to suit his own notions; in which he had been
largely aided by Nancy, who seemed, if I might judge from the sly smirks and
simpering whispers that she played off while they were in the office, to have her
own designs upon him. Her lures, I could also perceive, were not thrown away.
The bait took; and I was not therefore surprised to see them afterwards going
into a haberdasher's in the Strand, the pert hussey hanging upon the old fellow's
arm, and smiling upon him most lovingly. I doubt not but she found means to
cajole him out of a good addition of tasteless finery to her already overstocked
band-boxes: it is no more than proper, indeed, that old fools like him, – ay, and
young ones too, – should pay smartly for their folly.

The business which Crickles was thus forgetting for the bought smiles of the
minx, it was my duty to attend to; and accordingly Bucks and I held a council
of war, to determine how we should proceed with this odd gentleman, Joe Banbury. One point we were agreed upon; indeed we make it a general rule in such
cases, – namely, to conceal our object, and even our office, till we find a fitting
time and place to appear in our true colours.

In the present case, Jem proposed that we might have a bit of fun to make ourselves merry withal, and perform our duty at the same time. The hint was undoubtedly good, and accorded well with Jem's favourite song,

> Laugh while you live,
> For life is a jest,
> And who laughs most
> Is sure to live best.[78]

But I did not like his device of our appearing at Banbury Castle in the character of players, with offers of our assistance or instruction in the process of wife-training. Were we to do so, we should get no fun except by prompting Banbury to add to the acts complained of, and that would not only be a dereliction of duty, but would subject poor Mrs. Banbury to a continuance of what was probably already more than human patience could endure, which would be both cruel and ungallant. She had, by all accounts, suffered quite enough, even if she *were* a bit of a shrew, of which there was not one tittle of evidence. On the contrary, her father averred that she was mild, sweet, gentle, and, what was more, smooth-faced, – a sort of countenance which no shrew ever owned from the days of the notorious Xantippe[79] downwards.

It might be necessary, indeed, to take into account the opposite assertion of Banbury himself, as reported by Nancy, and bearing that his wife's face was 'rough'; but this we were old-enough stagers to detect as a small slip in the minx's memory, if it were not rather a twisting of the evidence from malice *prepense*,[80] in order to aim a sly hit at a face prettier than her own: I have known such things done in my time. But be Mrs. Banbury what she might, rough or smooth, shrewish or gentle, she had plainly had her share of mad pranks, and it was but just that her husband, Squire Joe, should have his quota likewise, if it were practicable to come round such a spring-gun Hotspur[81] as he was represented to be.

My plan, therefore, was to gain admittance to him under whatever pretence should seem most likely to succeed when we arrived, and then to announce ourselves to be *mad doctors*[82] (as they are called) commissioned to try his sanity in consequence of his recent proceedings. Such an announcement would most probably make him mad enough in all conscience, even were his mind ever so sound, and then we might pursue the joke by dextrously clapping him in a strait waistcoat,[83] if we could beg, borrow, or steal one for the purpose, before setting out.

This was, it is true, altogether a more ticklish game than that proposed by Bucks; but if Banbury were really crack-witted, as I had some guess he was, the strait-waistcoat would be the safest way to secure him, and our warrant would bear us out in such a case for the violence we might have to employ. Jem was liberal enough to concede that my plan was the best; and we therefore set about procuring the strait-waistcoat; changing our dress a little, the better to play our parts, and making other necessary preparations for our journey.

Mr. Banbury's residence being at no immeasurable distance from the metropolis, we determined to get thither next day in time to interrupt a repetition of the dinner scene, if Joe still stuck by the fancy of 'chucking' the dishes off the table to prevent Mrs. Banbury from following the dictates of nature by eating thereof.

One thing was sufficiently clear, namely, that if he adhered rigidly to this 'order of the day,'[84] he could not long preserve her alive, and must of necessity have relaxed something of his discipline, to keep up the farce so long as had been hinted at in the evidence of the complainant. Mrs. Banbury, indeed, might probably yield to his absurd humours so far as to procure herself a bit of dinner; on the same principle as Nancy might, against the grain, humour old Crickles, in order to coax him out of a new gown; but the feigned acquiescence, with the accompanying fair face, would of course be thrown off when no longer wanted; and the mistress and the maid would return to their former courses as if nothing had happened.

It was an odd whim enough to call the place a castle, for we found it to be nothing more than an ordinary house of the farm fashion; somewhat large, indeed, old, weather-stained, and like the proprietor, rather crazy[85] in the upper works, – the chimneys being partly dilapidated, and what remained of them ready to topple down on the attack of the next storm. The great gate, formerly alluded to in Nancy's evidence, was in similar progress towards ruin, – the two white marble globes that had formerly stood in proud display over its square brick columns, now reposing neglected in the adjacent ditch, all chipped, splintered, and begreened with moss; while their former 'high estate'[86] was occupied by clumps of house-leek and other wall-weeds. The only thing which bore any mark of recent erection was a large board, giving notice of the aforesaid spring-guns to all trespassers and intruders.

As we stood awhile, to take a view of these desolate premises, we perceived a number of people approaching from the *castle*, loaded with bandboxes[87] and other trumpery, which made us conjecture that Squire Joe, finding Mrs. Banbury *untameable*, had allowed her to remove with all her goods and chattels; and that this was the very procession in the act of taking final leave. This idea was strengthened by the appearance of a well-dressed female, whom we concluded to be Mrs. Banbury herself.

Our conjectures on this point, however, as it turned out, were quite astray; for instead of Mrs. Banbury, the female (we afterwards learned) was no other than a fashionable milliner, who looked any thing but the picture of 'patience on a monument,'[88] since she seemed resolved to appear in a pet or a passion, or to show off contemptuous high spirits; and her affected endeavours to act the fine lady affronted produced the most laughable caricature of vanquished vanity, trying to outbrave disgrace, which I ever witnessed. She bridled up, and bounced, and tossed back her head, as if she disdained to breathe the very air of such a place as Banbury Castle. To suppose that this piece of absurd affectation could be poor Mrs. Banbury was a worse libel upon her than any which we had heard reported as applied by Joe himself.

I was not long in perceiving that the whole party, about to make their exit through the gate, were divers purveyors of female finery, who had, I supposed, been sent for to perform an indispensable scene in Joe's revival of the shrew-taming farce. All of them had much the air of people whom I have seen trying either to escape observation or to defy it, in the instance of those absurd hoaxes sometimes played off by sending a number of tradesmen with their goods to a house where they are not wanted.

The present company, however, had probably been forced to bear both the disappointment and a volley of farcical abuse to boot, even if Banbury had 'spoken no more than was set down for him'[89] in the play. We were not held long in suspense respecting the events which had just occurred at the *castle;* for one of the party, seeing us about to enter the gate in defiance of Banbury's spring-guns, and having, which is rather unusual in such cases, more compassion than malicious mischief in him, honestly warned us of the reception we might expect to meet with.

"Od[90] rot 'im, Sir!' said this man, addressing me, 'if he an't, for certain, out o' his seven senses! You haven't no notion of how he is a going on – tumbling every thing about, and swearing and stamping: he's mad for certain!'

'Mad or not,' the little milliner struck in, 'it was a shame to you, Mr. Blount, and a shame to the whole lot on ye – vasn't it? – for to see a lady insulted in such a manner: there an't one on ye a gentleman, no more there an't. My gracious! I vould spit upon such low, mean, dirty, warmint as the best on ye, I vould!'

'So ho! Mrs. Whistle-chops![91] what's that all about, can ye tell me?' said another of the party. '*You* don't mean to call yourself a lady, do ye?'

'Don't speak to me, Mr. Tickel![92] Don't missis me; you know I an't no missis!' replied the *lady*, tossing up her head in a high pet.

'But who insulted you, Ma'am?' said I, with the hopes of leading her back to Mr. Banbury and his farce.

'Vhy, Sir, I'll tell you all 'ow it vas. Mr. Banbury sends for to horder a dress-cap o' me in the wery nooest fashion for Mrs. Banbury; so the Banburys being hold customers and good pay, I cuts hout van: it vas a very 'andsome van indeed, trimmed vith sooper-sooper-Brussels lace, and the wery moral[93] o' that in the Lady's Magazine,[94] vhat I has from the libraly: and it is such a booty, as every body said!'

'I for one didn't say so,' cried Tickel, with a sneer intended, I suppose, to convey a doubt respecting the quality of the super-super-Brussels lace.

'And who vould ax *you*, I should like to know?' retorted the *lady*, again turning to me. 'So, Sir, as I vas a-saying, I brings this bootiful cap punckshal to the minuet; and Mrs. Banbury, good soul, vas wery much pleased vith it; but, my gracious! 'ow Banbury took on about it! He aboosed the fashion on't, called it a "baby's cockle-shell," "a valnut-pie-crust," a "coffin for a custard," and said it vas "mouldy like a porringer:" you've no hidear vhat rum[95] things he say?'

'Then, Ma'am, I suppose you took all this as an insult upon your skill!'

'My gracious! No, Sir, if he held vith that, it vould been nothing; but he falls on me as vell, vith such tremenjuous horrid names, it puts me into a faint to think being called such things, if it vasn't he vas mad, Sir.'

'Ay, my life to a pin he is mad!' said Blount, who turned out to be the tailor on the occasion; 'for he served us all the same as Miss tells you. Why, there was a habit I made by his own order, which Mrs. Banbury admired of all things, and d'ye know, Sir, he said it was like "a barber's shop," and that the "sleeve was an apple-tart:" upon which, rot 'im! he called me a "winter-cricket," and bid me "hop about over the kennels"[96] – I'll take my Bible oath of it he's mad!'

'Don't you believe a word on't, Sir!' said Tickel to me. 'Don't you see, Sir, all this is to gammon[97] you away, and keep Banbury's loaves and fishes among themselves? Don't you, if you're wise, lose a good customer for their chaffing! Why, Mr. Banbury is as grave as a judge, if you'll believe me.'

'Believe you?' said I archly, 'rest assured I shall not lose a good customer when I have such an *honest* adviser as you at my elbow.'

Tickel was one of those who delight in seeing others get into the same scrape with themselves; but in this instance he made a slight mistake respecting our avocation, which defeated the joke he expected to enjoy at our expense.

It is worth remarking here that there is nobody from whom, by taking proper means, one may not pick up some little useful hint or other; and, accordingly, I discovered from Tickel one important point, namely, that the spring-guns (rather a dangerous out-work to encounter) were muzzled for the nonce, to give safe ingress and egress to the several tradespeople who had been sent to mock poor Mrs. Banbury with finery which it was never intended she should have.

I would not have altogether trusted Tickel upon this point, after his attempt to deceive me; but 'in the multitude of counsellors there is safety'[98] and they all agreed about the guns. Indeed, it was not likely that the little milliner, even with the hope of good money before her eyes, would have ventured her dear person within an atmosphere of gunpowder, had she not been insured of her absolute safety. Our task, of course, would probably be easy; for in the midst of all this bustle of his crazy comedy, he would have little suspicion of a surprisal. As I had now a good opportunity, however, I wished to know somewhat more of my man than I had yet heard, before I proceeded to business. From such inquiries, therefore, as I made of Blount and the others, I learned that Banbury had always been rather a whimsical sort of person, as is not unusual among those who can afford to be idle, and are rich enough to

> Quarrel with minced pies, and disparage
> Their best and dearest friend, plum-porridge.[99]

One marked point of his character seemed to be, to *perform* his whims as well as *contrive* them, and to persevere in acting any absurdity which he undertook, till it was displaced by another. He cared not about expense in such cases, not knowing what it was to want money; but it was fortunate that he had never hit upon any folly except one, which was of a very costly description.

The whim alluded to accounted for the desolate and ruined appearance of his premises. Somebody had persuaded him (for it did not appear he was enough given to reading to catch the mania from books) that nothing made a place look more respectable and imposing than visible marks of the footsteps of time. Proceeding literally upon this notion, he laboured for a whole summer in demolishing bits of walls, pulling down the corners of chimneys, displacing the marble globes at the gate, and at last went so far as to break one of the sail-frames of a windmill, in order to give it a respectable veteran appearance. It was even reported, according to Blount, that having christened his house a castle, and completed his out-of-door plans, or grown tired of them, he had actually begun to make the household furniture match with his battered walls and broken windmill, and had been hard at work (for he liked to do things himself) hammering and defacing chairs, tables, and sofas, and committing other pieces of similar folly; when, all at once, it should appear that 'a change came o'er the spirit of his dream;'[100] and he betook himself to some other piece of business equally absurd.

CHAPTER VIII.

Honest servants – Feats of Mrs. Banbury – Might and right.

Of the details of Banbury's marriage I could learn little in addition to what I previously knew, except that his wooing had been something of the oddest; and, though Miss Crickles had at first treated his proposals more as matter of jest than earnest, he had, by dint of unwearied perseverance and importunity, at last succeeded. After this event, (which had happened several months before it was my duty to take part in these whimsical scenes,) Banbury had no doubt been pursuing other eccentricities: – the only fact, however, necessary to my history is, that during a visit to London, he had been induced to go with an acquaintance, for the first time, to one of the theatres, when 'The Taming of the Shrew' had been performed; which had so caught his fancy, that he immediately set himself to try the experiment suggested thereby, and, in order to acquire perfection, actually commenced a requisite course of theatrical study.

It was not the least absurd part of the whim, that Mrs. Banbury had less of the shrew than most women, and had been justly enough described by her father as kind and gentle. She had, indeed, tried all the lawful means which a wife may employ to wean her husband from his pranks, and when both coaxing and mild expostulation failed, had not scrupled to vary her method of attack by throwing out a joke once and again. These jokes, however, Banbury had no patience with, and instead of yielding to the force of ridicule, he only became the more stubborn in following up what he had begun. It had, I have no doubt, been some of those jokes (a little more tart probably than usual) which had set his fancy agog, and produced strange trains of association whilst he was at the theatre, and stranger proceedings when he returned home.

Mrs. Banbury, it would appear, had not been altogether so quiescent under this new regimen as might have been expected from her gentle nature. The thing, indeed, was too much for human endurance, – at least, beyond the bounds of a Turkish harem, and even there it would scarcely be submitted to but from dread of the sack or bowstring,[101] which are always at hand, and not sparingly employed. She now became convinced of what she had long suspected, namely, that her husband was really out of his mind, and had therefore assisted Nancy to escape, in order that her father might be apprized of what was going forward.

It would have been better, perhaps, had she escaped herself; but this was found to be impracticable, as Banbury was cunning enough to suppose that she might have a wish to that effect, and had accordingly taken every measure which he judged necessary to prevent it. Indeed he never lost sight of her even for a moment, keeping by his text-book to the very letter.

When we arrived before the *castle* to summon it to a surrender, we heard a great racket proceeding from one of the upper rooms – battering of doors, voices in loud altercation, and other tokens of actual warfare, which astonished us the more that they were unexpected, since we could scarcely conceive the mild and gentle Mrs. Banbury to have commenced forcible retaliation for the insults and injuries with which her mad-cap husband was hourly treating her. Yet it was by no means impossible; for the most pacific disposition may be goaded beyond endurance, and forced, in self-defence, to repulse wanton insult.

Thus, indeed, it turned out. The scene with the little milliner and the rest was too much for her. She had borne hunger and want of sleep, and had suffered the plain evidence of her eye-sight to be questioned; but to be mocked with handsome caps, gowns, and other matters of *dress*, was such an overflowing measure of injustice as no woman could be expected to tolerate for one moment.

All the servants, with the exception of Nancy, had hitherto been on their master's side; indeed they had become so accustomed to his oddities, that, so far from interfering therewith, they gladly assisted him in making himself a fool, while they enjoyed the sport. In his present prank, however, he had found it requisite to bribe them to bear with his humours, it being necessary to the perfection of his performance that he should treat them with great seeming severity and violence.

When menials once touch any thing in the shape of a bribe, they begin to think there should be no end of it. Their avarice is insatiable; and when it meets with refusal, recourse will be had to every means, right or wrong, to satisfy its cravings. It is probable that this same spirit of avarice had been taken advantage of by Mrs. Banbury to gain over those who had exhausted the liberality of her husband, to aid her in repelling his insults.

Be this as it may, they had all turned against Banbury, it appeared, after the departure of the tradespeople, and were in the very act of shutting him up in one of the apartments at the time we approached. He was now fairly caught in his own trap, and was no less impatient under the yoke than he had before been eager to impose it, though nobody was likely to pity his distress or assist him in his troubles.

'Rascals! ruffians!' we heard him bawling out, 'release me instantly, or I'll send you all to the pillory by the lump.'[102]

Upon this the noise of thumping at the door grew louder, as if he had been employing a battering-ram, of the days of old, wherewith to effect his escape; though the more likely weapon was some of the fire-irons, or whatever other implement he could find in the room.

'No use, Master,' we heard somebody reply. 'No use to worrit so, for we won't let you out, that's all.'

'Dear Banbury!' a female voice rejoined in a soothing tone, 'you know I don't wish to confine you or have you ill-used; though really, my dear, if you consider, you have carried things too far to-day. But if you promise to leave me at peace, and not play off your tricks upon me, I shall give orders to unlock the door immediately.'

Banbury replied to this conciliatory proposal in scrap lines from the play; part of which we could not distinguish, though it sounded like

> 'I love thee well in that thou lik'st it not.
> And now my sweeting and my honey-love,
> Will we return unto thy father's house?'[103]

'No, no!' replied Mrs. Banbury, 'you must promise to give up this nonsense, or out you sha'n't get. You've done nothing but repeat this "sweeting" and "honey-love," since you began your pranks upon me, and you must give your word to lay aside that with the rest of the folly; on which condition *only* will I accompany you to my father's.'

> 'Then, come on, o' God's name! once more to our father's.
> Good Lord, how bright and goodly shines the moon!'[104]

'Now, my dear Banbury, do give up this nonsense, or I shall be forced to think you are really mad. What folly is it to be thus repeating, day after day, that the sun is the moon. If you talk so incoherently, it will be absolutely necessary to keep you in strict confinement.'

This sensible speech was followed by another volley of blows upon the door, from which it appeared that Banbury was resolved to stand his ground to the last. It was now, I thought, my turn to interfere by knocking at the house-door, and inquiring for Mr. Banbury. A servant told me that he was ill, and could not be seen; but I *insisted* on seeing him, and made good my entrance, with Bucks at my side, in spite of the menial's remonstrances to the contrary. On proceeding to the scene of discord, we found the lady standing at the door whence the noise proceeded, in a state of some agitation, though calmer than might from the circumstances have been supposed.

'Madam!' said I, 'your father has sent us to give you what assistance you may want.'

Upon this announcement, I perceived that the servants appeared to look somewhat blank and disappointed, perceiving, no doubt, that the reign of folly was likely to be at an end, and with it their harvest of bonuses and bribes. I communicated to Mrs. Banbury in a few words that we intended to examine the late proceedings of her husband, who still kept up his racketing at the door, and seemed to be in the fair way of adding its shattered remains to the rest of his manufactured antiques.

Mrs. Banbury appeared at first to be delighted with our arrival; but I could perceive, from her countenance, that a reluctance and dislike to have her private circumstances exposed to strangers began to arise in her mind. It was this, I have no doubt, which made her endeavour to soften and explain away the strange conduct of her husband; which explanation, however, accorded ill with his furious attacks upon the door.

Had it not been for this circumstance, indeed, I am persuaded that, from her goodness of heart and wish to prevent farther unpleasant consequences, she would have tried to get rid of us, and add another instance to thousands more, that we are least contented when we obtain our most anxious wishes. But Banbury's continued thumping and battering made her at last give a reluctant consent to retire and allow us to unkennel him.

We accordingly opened the prison-door, when Banbury sprang out like a house-dog loosed from his chain, so overflowing with the feelings of freedom, that he did not know what to do first, though he had palpably a wish to be avenged on the servants who had deserted him in his need. It was doubtless this which prompted him to leap open-mouthed on Jem Bucks, without perceiving, in his hurry, that he was a stranger.

It was pretty evident, however, that Banbury's spirit of revenge was far from being deadly; for it evaporated in giving Bucks two or three shakes which Jem took good-humouredly, without uttering a word, or attempting to resist. Banbury was plainly afraid to go the length of a blow, but had no lack of abusive words conned from the comedy, and did not spare calling Bucks 'a whoreson, malt-horse drudge,' 'a beetle-headed flap-eared knave,'[105] with other goodly additions of like quality. He had not proceeded far, when he perceived that he had mistaken his man, which made him 'grin horrible a ghastly smile' at his error; but it did nothing to cure him of his folly, for perceiving Mrs. Banbury peeping from a corner to see what was going forward, he addressed her with

> — 'We're beset with thieves;
> But fear not, sweet wench, they shall not touch thee.
> I'll buckler thee against a million!'[106]

Upon this, giving Bucks the wink to be on the alert, I stepped up behind him, pinioned his arms, and proceeded to fit on the strait-waistcoat. Banbury was so taken by surprise at the rapidity of my movements, that he was secured before he had time to think of resistance; but when he found himself in helpless durance, he raged and stormed in a much more natural and earnest guise than in his dramatic rehearsals.

'Villains! robbers!' he cried, 'I won't be confined! I am an Englishman, and will have my freedom! Out of my premises, I say, you thieving house-breakers! or I'll have my action against ye for assault and battery.'

'Yes!' replied I, 'when you are sound enough in the wits to sustain an action; but not till then, I promise you, Mr. Banbury.'

'I say again, be off out of my premises! I won't be talked to in my own house by robbers and villains!'

'It will be better for you,' said I, 'once for all to be quiet. We are neither robbers nor villains; and if you will promise faithfully, on the word of a gentleman, to lay aside your whims, and not distress Mrs. Banbury with them, I will instantly release you.'

'And d— you, Sir! who are you, to tell me how I am to behave to my wife? I am a free-born Englishman, and I won't let any man speak so to me.'

'When once you *are* free, Mr. Banbury, you may talk thus; but you perceive that in the mean time you must rest contented till you give the promise I mentioned.'

'O dear me!' cried Mrs. Banbury, advancing from her concealment, 'what shall I do? what shall I do? You must not be so hard upon him, indeed you must not. Let him go, and I'll promise for him any-thing you please.'

As this all arose out of tenderness for her husband, without any consideration of consequences, I did not think it my duty to comply with her request, particularly as Banbury himself naturally grew more obstreperous on account of her supporting his cause. Bucks proposed to cool his hot-headed folly by sousing him with a few buckets of water; but I was more anxious to get his promise, which I had some confidence he would keep, notwithstanding his odd fancies, could it be extorted from him.

Seeing, however, that I could make nothing of him by persuasion, I bethought me of paying him back in his own coin, that is, allowing him neither food nor sleep till he showed tokens of recovery from his stage-struck fit; and I told Mrs. Banbury I would compromise the matter with her upon that understanding. To this she agreed, though not with the best grace; but when he saw the table covered with the good things of this life, his heart could not withstand the temptation. The mutton might 'be burnt,' and the beef 'engender choler,' but Banbury was determined not to see them vanish without having his accustomed share, if that could be procured by apologies and promises, of which he became as lavish as he had before been niggardly. As the lady appeared quite satisfied with these, and as I deemed the promise of a gentleman (though he might be a little cracked in the wits,) a sacred pledge, I did not hesitate to set him at liberty and make my bow, without letting any of them know in what capacity I and Bucks had acted.

On our approach to London we met old Crickles and the maid Nancy returning together as lovingly as if they were about to be married, which was very probably the game she was pursuing, being, of course, in love with his purse and his houses, for which he might, perhaps, consider that her laughing countenance and pert looks would prove a good equivalent.

CHAPTER IX.

Shopping extraordinary of a lady of fashion.

SOME months after my expedition to Banbury Castle, I was one day walking along Bond Street, at the fashionable shopping hour, when my attention was attracted by a very fine carriage, remarkable, among the rest of the equipages which crowded the street, for the richness of its ornaments, and the splendid liveries of the servants. Curiosity respecting rank and riches is always on the alert and easily excited, and it was this feeling which induced me to inquire, though without success, to whom this fine carriage belonged. I little thought how soon I should learn personally more than I could have dreamed of, and more, in some respects, than I would ever have wished to know respecting it.

I cannot tell how it was, but I was irresistibly inclined to keep my eye upon this carriage. As it stopped before a jeweller's shop, I drew nearer to examine the arms on the pannel, but, being ignorant of heraldry, this only served to tantalize me; for nothing rouses curiosity more readily than an obstacle. If our path is smooth and unimpeded, we linger along with listless indifference; but the instant a difficulty starts up, all our dormant powers are summoned to overcome it. Thus, it is very likely, if I had, on my first inquiry, been told that the equipage belonged to the Marquis of A—, or the Countess of S—, I might have thought no more about it; but the answers of 'don't know' and 'can't say,' which were repeated to me more than once, induced me not to lose sight of my object.

It halted, as I have said, at a jeweller's, into whose shop a lady stepped from it, in a costume rich, elegant, and tasteful; and, as I thought, with that dignified and noble air which can only be inherited within the pale of rank. If I was before curious to learn to whom the carriage belonged, I was now far more desirous of knowing who this lady was. Female elegance and splendor of dress have ever had a charm for me, independently of the beauty of the wearer. It may be that they serve to whet the fancy; and, indeed, I have often remarked that this is the case. In the present instance, although the lady I speak of displayed an air and figure of the finest character, I was not fortunate enough to obtain a sight of her features. I was so impertinent, however, as to make a stand at the shop-door, to indulge in conjecture till I should have the opportunity of realising it. It was suggested to me that the lady could be no other than — —, of whose fascinations in the highest circles I had heard so much; but why she should be alone did not appear. It is by no means unusual, I know, for some ladies to go shopping by themselves; but I was not aware that this was customary in the higher ranks, and I was inclined to look upon it as contrary to etiquette.

Be this as it may, the lady *was* alone; though, from what soon happened, it turned out that she would not have been the worse for a protector. She had not been long in the shop, when I perceived the jeweller looking very suspiciously at a bank-note, holding it up between his eye and the light, and giving his head an ominous shake, in confirmation of his doubts. I heard him repeat the word 'forged,' and at the same instant the lady made a snatch at the note across the counter. I thought this passing strange. Had she requested to have it returned, I saw no reason why the jeweller should refuse her, since it was highly improbable that a lady of her apparent rank and consequence would attempt to palm upon him a note which she knew to be forged. She did not succeed in snatching it from him, and appeared to be much agitated. I could not distinguish what she said; but, from her gestures, imagined that she was employing all the eloquence of female intreaty to obtain the note. She offered him another in lieu of it, which, after much hesitation, he at last took, and gave her some change in return.

I looked upon the whole occurrence as so very singular, that I was resolved to keep a watchful eye upon this lady's subsequent shoppings; if, indeed, what had taken place at the jeweller's should not have damped for that day her pursuit after finery and fashions. She immediately, however, drove off to a silk mercer's lower down the street, whither I followed her, to see if she would again try her suspicious bank-note. I was extremely anxious for the event, hoping there could be no real ground to suspect a lady of her appearance; yet I knew well that such things had been and might be; that few are proof against strong temptation when it is thrown in their way, how virtuous soever they may fancy themselves, or may be reckoned by the world. Supposing, in another view of the case, that the lady had become honestly possessed of the note, and was short of pin-money, she might naturally wish not to lose it, if the sum were considerable, and might quiet her conscience with the salvo[107] that she might fairly pass it, as it had been passed to her. Besides, the jeweller might possibly be mistaken, and after all, the note prove genuine. Such were the thoughts which passed through my mind on considering this occurrence; but I had soon an opportunity of rectifying them by new facts.

I remarked that she was not long in selecting what she wanted at the silk mercer's, to whom she also gave a bank-note in payment, and received what appeared to be a considerable balance in cash. There would have been nothing singular in this, if I had not seen the previous transaction at the jeweller's. Even as it was, the note passed to the mercer might not be the one objected to as forged; yet, altogether, I could not help suspecting that it was the same, and that this was a scheme to get rid of it.

Having settled with the mercer, this gay dame of fashion, and (for aught I knew) of title, drove off to a lace-shop, whither I still followed to watch her proceedings. Should she, in the present instance, again offer a note in payment, it would strongly increase my suspicion that all was not right; while, on the other hand, if she gave the money which she had received in change, it would serve to acquit her at least of systematic fraud. I had already taken so much interest in the affair, that I was not a little anxious it might turn out to be in the lady's favour, though it might, in some respects, be more advantageous to myself if I could detect her in the act of breaking the laws. At the lace-shop she again offered a bank-note; though the shopman, like the jeweller, looked very narrowly at it, he at last put it up, and, as in former instances, handed her the balance.

I was now painfully convinced that the lady regularly trafficked in passing notes of large amount; and that these were forged, was, by consequence, self-evident. With such impressions, I felt it my duty to the public to sift the matter thoroughly. This, indeed, would also be justice to the lady, who might possibly be far above the commission of such a crime; though, (with all due deference to the virtuous,) as a general principle, suspicions of evil in this wicked world have more chance to be correct than erroneous.

I learned, at length, that the lady who had thus excited my curiosity, was Mrs. —, sufficiently notorious in the great world as a dashing beauty now somewhat on the wane, and altogether careless of attending to those strict rules of female propriety, so indispensable in every rank. Probably she herself mistook this carelessness for high spirit; but it had frequently obtained for her the honour of having her name coupled in gossiping circles with mysterious nods and broad inuendoes; though it did not appear that any thing had as yet transpired, flagrant enough to exile her from what is called good society, which, indeed, tolerates every vice, so that it be kept within the strict limits of *concealment*. I understood that, combined with all this, Mrs. — was at the head of a splendid establishment, where routs and other fashionable parties were given with unusual frequency and unrivalled magnificence.

All this information, coupled with the stories I had so often heard among my brother-officers, of the illegal resources of dashing fashionables at the West End, induced me to mark out her *ladyship* for farther observation. My first care was to discover her address, which was easily effected by means of the Red Book;[108] and next day I stationed myself in the neighbourhood to watch her movements. Though I had taken the precaution to go early lest she might escape me, I was very near losing sight of her for the day, as she was ready to go out several hours before the fashionable time. I did not like to go too near the door, lest I might excite suspicion, since I had the day before been hanging so much about the carriage. I therefore employed a lad to get amongst the servants, and learn, if he could, where the carriage was to drive. He soon returned, informing me that he had heard orders given, to drive to Ludgate Hill;[109] and I accordingly took a hackney-coach and proceeded to the same place, being now pretty certain that I should find Mrs. — playing the same part in the City as I had before seen her do in Bond Street.

The first shop which the lady entered on Ludgate Hill was a haberdasher's; and it immediately struck me that I might get a nearer view of her proceedings by entering the shop myself, and purchasing some trifle for Maria, calculating that the shopmen would not attend me with much alacrity, whilst they had a better customer to serve. It happened as I had anticipated. I was allowed to stand as if I had been a pauper asking alms, every individual of the establishment bustling to serve Mrs. —. She was not long in making her selection of articles, as she cared less about these than the money which she was to receive in exchange. She produced, as before, a bank-note, purporting to be for twenty pounds,[110] to settle a bill of about as many shillings. This, it appeared to me, was making the most of illegal traffic, and (leaving the risk of life and reputation[111] out of the question,) was turning a profit of enormous amount, supposing as I did, that the note was forged.

The haberdasher of Ludgate Hill, it would appear, was of a similar opinion with the Bond Street jeweller, and looked with equal doubt at the paper. The lady did not seem to feel easy during the scrutiny; but when he handed her back the note, and told her not to trouble herself about the trifling bill, which she could settle at any future time, she seemed to be both relieved from anxiety, and mortified at her failure. He did not say that he could not give her the balance, but told her plainly enough that he 'did not like the look of the note, though for all that it might be genuine; yet there were so many forged bank-notes in circulation, that he was compelled to be cautious, and the note in question had some of the suspicious marks,' he said, 'which had been notified from the Bank.'[112]

I imagined that, after this plain intimation of the state of the case, Mrs. — would have ventured no farther in the business; but in this I was mistaken, for she pursued her course with the same effrontery, and with similar success to what had attended her on the preceding day.

Had I not been swayed by other feelings than those of duty, I should now have found no difficulty in determining what to do. There could be no doubt that the lady was deeply engaged in criminal transactions, and the proofs would probably have been more easily obtained than she imagined; for it would only have been necessary to apprehend her and search her person when she was engaged on a shopping expedition, or to bring forward any of the tradesmen to whom she had passed her bank-notes.

She no doubt considered that her rank and consequence would secure her from suspicion, and protect her from arrest; but the guilty often think themselves most secure when they are upon the very brink of detection and ruin, and it would have been so in the present case had I not been influenced by pity, or rather, perhaps, fascinated by the splendour and beauty of the delinquent, whom I could not bring my resolution to expose to disgrace. This was the predominant idea occupying my mind; though I confess I had also fears that I might have misinterpreted her proceedings, or that at least I should not be able to establish proof sufficient to bring home the crime of passing bank-notes, knowing them to be forged. If matters should turn out so, I might incur serious trouble by involving myself in the vengeance wherewith her powerful friends might pursue me.

The passing of so great a number of large bank-notes, however, for payment of sums comparatively small, soon set me at ease on this point, for I saw her enter more than a dozen shops in the City, and though I was afraid to venture near enough to see every transaction, I saw sufficient to assure me that they were all of the same description. Yet it was probable she might have some method of concealing them, if she should be apprehended; or I might choose a time when she had none in her custody; and in either case nothing satisfactory could be proved against her.

Upon considering the subject farther, I thought it would be a pity to sacrifice so fine a woman, how criminal soever she might prove, and allow others to escape; for it was not to be supposed that she was both the forger and the utterer.[113] There must be others employed in a crime of this kind; probably a whole gang of delinquents, who by such means might support a style of the most splendid extravagance. If this were so, and even if the lady were to save herself by becoming approver[114] and informing against her accomplices, I felt a sort of shuddering repugnance at the thought of subjecting her to the lowest degradation into which a criminal can fall.

Looking upon it in this point of view, only two plans of proceeding suggested themselves. In the first place, humanity whispered I should give the lady a hint that she was in danger, which might perhaps put a stop to her continuing the illegal traffic, and thus prove as useful to her as a trial and punishment. It did not strike me then so forcibly as it would now, that there is but very little chance of any delinquent reforming after having triumphed for a time in security, and that this generally applies most strongly to females; yet, even if I had considered the case clogged with all the adverse facts resulting from an enlarged experience, my disposition would have led me to save the lady, if it were possible.

My second plan, however, appeared to be more eligible; namely, to allow the lady to pursue her course for a short time unmolested, while I should endeavour to trace her accomplices by every means in my power. If I could discover them, I might at once check the crime and save the lady, who might, it was possible, be forced to act illegally, contrary to her inclination, by the influence of her husband, if he were now living. Such cases have occurred, and, on the lady's account, I hoped this might be one of them; for though the disgrace of her husband might involve her in ruin, yet, if she were not also involved in the crime, no reduction of circumstances would be so bad as a conviction for felony.

I thought at first of gaining over one or more of the servants, to see whether I could learn any thing through their means; but upon farther consideration it appeared to me that some, or all of them, might be deep in the transaction, a circumstance by no means unfrequent in the history of such affairs. The slightest advances, therefore, on my part, might spread alarm through the whole establishment, and defeat my purpose. Yet, deprived of this resource, which in some cases might have been made available, what was I to do? I could devise no mode of gaining a nearer view of what was going on in the recesses of the house; and merely watching the sort of persons who went in and out might, for a long while, lead to no result.

I determined, however, to do nothing rashly in a case which appeared to be of so much moment; and after having seen the lady finish her shopping perambulations, and returned to the office to see what was stirring, I spent the early part of the evening at home with Maria. As I was here enjoying all the comforts of domestic happiness, the thought naturally rose in my mind that I had, by a strong[115] effort, saved one deserving woman from impending ruin; and it would be a noble subject of self-gratulation if I could succeed in saving another from a fate no less disgraceful, Maria's gratitude to me knew no bounds, and I was desirous of equally meriting, though in a very different way, the thanks of Mrs. —.

When it was wearing late, I sallied forth to see whether I could discover any thing going on at —'s house, though I had little expectation of eliciting much more; and yet, thought I, perhaps my trouble may not be in vain.

CHAPTER X.

Night scene in Hyde Park.

It was already past midnight, dark, gusty, and threatening rain, though none had yet fallen, when I observed a person issue abruptly out of the house I was watching, and hurry along, as if something serious were the matter. As I was on the opposite side of the street, I could not, with the scanty light afforded by the lamps, tell whether it was a gentleman or a servant. If the latter, I concluded that he must be despatched on very urgent business; and if it were a gentleman, that he must be actuated by some powerful feeling. On no other supposition could I account for the violence and rapidity of his movements.

At first, I thought I might as well remain where I was, to see whether he would return; but in that case I might lose sight of him; whilst, if I followed him, I might fall upon some trace of the illegal connections of the establishment. It was no easy matter, however, to keep up with the person in question, who dashed on with the utmost speed, as if life itself were at stake. His movements had all the appearance of flight prompted by fear, though it was possible enough for me to mistake in such a case.

Supposing that he was urged by fear, and in the very act of making an escape from pursuit, could it be, that while I was eagerly watching, a discovery and surprisal had already been effected? This would be sufficiently mortifying; but if it were so, I was determined that the runaway should not get off so easily; and I therefore pursued him with all the keenness which the supposition awakened in my mind.

He had not run far before he suddenly stopped, as if he had forgotten something, took two or three hasty strides back, and then as suddenly checked himself again, and proceeded with the same violent rapidity in his first course. This was scarcely compatible, I imagined, with the notion of flight, though it served to confirm my conclusion, that he was under the influence of some strong emotion.

In a short time after, he stopped a second time; and while he leaned against a lamp-post, I could perceive, being now pretty near him, that he was greatly agitated, and seemed to grasp it to avoid falling. I went close up to him as if I were passing accidentally along the street, when I heard him ejaculate in a low, desponding tone, 'O God! has it come to this!'

The light of the lamp, dim as it was, showed me that he was without question a gentleman, well dressed and apparently young withal. I was now more than ever at a loss to conjecture the cause of his violent feelings and seeming despondency. I did not wish, and indeed had no right, to obtrude myself upon him, though I should have liked much to ascertain whether he was connected in any way with the bank-notes passed by Mrs. —, and presumed to be forged. As the case at present stood, I could not well do any thing more than watch the young gentleman's farther proceedings.

There was evidently a tempest of emotion at work in his breast, for he groaned by starts as if his heart would have burst, and then he would strike his forehead, and clench his fists with frightful violence. Could it be remorse for lending himself to crime which was thus maddening him? or could it be vexation at having been detected? Fear it could not be; for the agitations of fear manifest themselves in a very different manner.

He repeatedly ejaculated, 'It is all over!' and sometimes, 'I must do it!' in a tone indicating that he meditated some deed of desperation. At length he seemed to have resolved what to do, remained for a time in a calmer mood, as if absorbed in thought, and then walked away at a hurried pace, but with none of his former rapid violence.

I followed him till he entered Hyde Park;[116] but he had not gone far when he again paused, apparently hesitating whether to proceed in his intended route, whatever that might be. I still kept aloof, lest he might observe me, though there was less chance of this, considering the strong excitement which he was suffering. When he got amongst the trees, also, I could easily screen myself, and at the same time keep sufficiently near him. The moon was up, indeed, but her light was much dimmed by the driving clouds.

He at last took one of the paths which lead to the Serpentine River,[117] hurrying on with considerable discomposure. It now struck me, from all the circumstances, that he probably contemplated suicide, as I could not on any other supposition account for his strange conduct. If this were his intention, I deemed it so far fortunate that I had watched and followed him; for I might be the means of preventing a serious and irrevocable crime, – a duty no less meritorious than the detection which I was aiming at of illegal acts.

My conjecture proved to be right. The young gentleman approached the edge of the river, and again his agitation became terrific. He cast a fearful look into the water, shuddered convulsively, and starting back as if horror-stricken, paced distractedly up and down the bank for a short distance, threw himself on his knees in a praying posture, but instantly rose again as if he dared not pray; tore open his clothes, and as quickly buttoned them up again, in momentary repentance perhaps, or probably unconscious of what he was doing.

I concluded that it would not be safe to permit his longer continuance in this state of, at least, temporary insanity, without interfering to prevent his doing anything rashly. He had no weapons that I could perceive, but there could be little doubt that he meditated self-destruction by leaping into the water; and even if he did not, his state of agitation was such, I thought, as authorized me to accost him, and try whether I could be of any use in soothing his distress; for it gave me great pain to see such palpable tokens of mental torture. I had myself suffered much, and could strongly sympathise even with a stranger; though there is something so horrible in the idea of suicide, that it partly represses sympathy. It is, in fact, a deed so revolting, that, except under the delusions of insanity, we cannot look upon it as having its origin in human nature.

Pondering in this manner, I resolved on the instant to prevent his intention; but I was too late, for just as I stepped up to accost him, he sprang from the bank, plunged into the water, and disappeared. Had I been a moment sooner, I could have saved him; and now I feared it was beyond my ability, though I was determined to spare no effort. I marked the spot where he had disappeared, and fixed my eye upon the water with intense anxiety, to see whether he would rise to its surface; for it would have been madness to dive, in the dark, with the design of rescuing him: it would only have been courting inevitable destruction for myself. I had the idea strongly impressed upon my mind (for its correctness I cannot answer) that he could not remain many seconds without thus rising; and I also recollected an instance of a person who had thrown himself into a pond, but was soon as anxious to get out as he had been to get in, and I hoped this might be the case in the present instance.

It could not be more than a minute, or at most two, when I thought I perceived, by the obscure light of the clouded moon, a dark object on the surface of the water, which, though at some distance from the spot I had marked out for observation, might, I hoped, be the body of the unfortunate gentleman. A smothered groan immediately convinced me it was so, and I hesitated not a moment to leap into the water, depending on my powers as a swimmer to effect his rescue.

He was palpably struggling to keep himself from sinking; at least, he appeared to be making such efforts as a person ignorant of swimming would do, upon falling by accident into deep water. I reached him just at the time when he seemed to be exhausted, and about finally to sink. I laid hold of him so as to keep up his head with one hand, while I used the other with all the strength I could put forth to buoy us till we reached the bank, which was happily near, or otherwise we might both have gone down; for now that the drowning man understood what I was about, he clung to me with a despairing grasp, more calculated to destroy than to assist my endeavours. I was fortunate in getting him safe to the bank, though he was so much exhausted as to be unable to speak. The joy of having succeeded in my somewhat hazardous attempt banished my own feelings of weariness, and I was all anxiety for the poor fellow who had thus narrowly escaped a premature death.

The lateness of the hour, and the distance of the place from any house, were difficulties which, in our circumstances, were not easily overcome. If I could have procured him dry clothes and something hot to drink, I imagined that he would have been speedily restored; as it was, I had no alternative but endeavouring to get him on his legs, and keep him, if possible, in a state of motion; for, little as I knew of such things, I concluded that if he were allowed to be motionless with his cold wet clothes about him, he must inevitably perish. I succeeded at last in getting him to stand, and, after some trials and much urging, to walk a few steps. Still he could not speak, and so far as I could see his face in the glimmering light, it was rather vacant than wild, showing as much exhaustion of thought as his bodily frame did of life.

With considerable difficulty I at length, by dint of urging and dragging him along (his arm within mine), got him to Hyde Park Corner. He now also began to mutter, and at times incoherent exclamations escaped from him; but his mind did not seem sufficiently clear or calm to understand what I said to him. I therefore continued to help him along till we might reach some place where I could see him taken proper care of.

When I considered the unseasonable hour, however, and our wretched plight, I perceived it was hopeless to think of getting into any house of entertainment, and the watch-house was certainly a very unsuitable resource under such circumstances. I could think of no place, indeed, in the least adapted to the purpose except my own house, which was still at some distance; but as he could now walk tolerably, it appeared to be the only unexceptionable plan which I could adopt, to take him home. If he were once freed from his dripping clothes, and placed in a warm bed, there was little doubt of his complete restoration so far as the body was concerned; his mental affliction would, in all probability, prove more stubborn, unless the violent measures which he had attempted might have a favourable effect – an event which, I have been told, sometimes happens in such cases.

It did not escape me that, if he recovered, I might be able to obtain from him such information respecting the illegal connections of Mrs. —, as would lead me to trace the mysterious transactions which I was certain were in progress. How far he himself might be mixed up with these I did not know, though it seemed highly probable that something of this kind had prompted him to the rash act he had just committed. Of course I could not expect him to accuse or criminate himself; nor was it likely that a person of his gentlemanly appearance would betray even his enemies, if he had become acquainted with their secrets, much less turn informer against his accomplices in illegality, if such he had. Yet, independent of all this, I might get at some facts of importance, upon which I could act in following up the cue which I had already discovered.

I was seldom from home, even officially, at so unseasonable an hour as this; but as Maria knew upon what expedition I had gone, she had sat up to wait for my return, with her usual unwearied and unweariable attention to my comfort. She was not a little alarmed when she saw me in such a plight, and still more so at the sight of my companion with his dripping garments and his pale, ghastly, vacant countenance; while, from the cold and feverish state in which he necessarily was, he shivered as if suffering under an ague fit. It was fortunate that he was calm and manageable; indeed, he permitted us to do anything we pleased with him, and appeared to be as helpless and passive as an infant. I found no difficulty, therefore, either in making him swallow some hot tea (I was afraid of giving him any thing stronger), or in putting him to bed, where he soon sank into a deep sleep, forgetful, as I hoped, of all his mishaps, whatever they might be.

I did not well know what to do about informing his friends, who would naturally be alarmed if he were missing. I was still unacquainted with his name; and though I had seen him come from the suspected house, I knew not in what relation he stood to its inmates. It was not likely that he would be capable of being removed, much less of being intrusted to his own management. I could, indeed, give notice of the circumstance at the office, but I wished, if possible, to avoid that; for if I did so, he would probably be removed from my charge, and I had no wish to part with him till I had endeavoured to procure such information as he could give respecting Mrs. — and her establishment. Besides, if he were connected, as his dress and appearance betokened him to be, with any family of rank or fashion, they might not like to have the attempted suicide blazoned through the public prints,[118] and would rather thank me for concealing it.

Taking all these things into consideration, I concluded that it would be my best plan to send a note in the morning to Mrs. —, acquainting her that the gentleman who had left her house some time after midnight, in an agitated state of mind, was for the present safe, and would return in a day or two. I was aware that this was not the precise course which strict duty pointed out; but it is not easy to be always strict, and little harm could ensue from it, while it might eventually lead to the best results for the purposes of justice.

I sat up to watch by the gentleman's bedside during the remainder of the morning, though this, as it turned out, was quite superfluous; for, except a sudden start or two, he slept as calmly as if nothing had happened to him till about noon, when he awoke like a person who had been terrified by some awful dream, and was not quite assured whether it were real.

The finding himself in a strange bed would, no doubt, add strongly to his perplexity; yet, notwithstanding his strange looks and some exclamations which escaped him, I was glad to perceive (or at least I fancied I perceived) that his mind was not much, if at all, deranged. He began, indeed, to talk quite rationally, and to ask such questions about the things around him, which he had no distinct recollection of having seen before, as would naturally occur to any person in the same situation.

I evaded, as much as I could, saying any thing which might lead his attention to the painful events that had taken place at the Serpentine, though it would probably be impossible, in the end, to conceal them from him. I was desirous, however, of keeping his mind away from the subject as long as possible, lest his recovery might be retarded.

The calm which he enjoyed after awakening, and at which I was so delighted, was but of short duration; for little more than an hour had elapsed, when he sank into a reverie, continued a considerable time without speaking, and then burst out into wild and passionate exclamations, while his whole frame was dreadfully disturbed. Maria became greatly alarmed at this, and feared that it would end in confirmed derangement; but I, who had seen and experienced more of the violent workings of the passions, entertained little apprehension on this account, since his present agitation must soon exhaust him, and he might then sleep again, and awaken calm as before.

The event proved that I was right in these anticipations. He continued, indeed, alternately agitated and calm during the whole day and the following night. Still, however, there was nothing like confirmed aberration of mind, and I had, in consequence, strong hopes of his recovery. Our chief difficulty was, that from not knowing the cause of his distress, we could not give him any consolation.

On talking over the melancholy subject with Maria, we came to the conclusion that it might tend greatly to relieve his mind, if he could be induced to unburden it of the load which weighed so heavily upon him. The best way, indeed of mastering a painful passion is, not to shrink from a contemplation of its causes, but to confront them boldly; to turn over the distressing ideas and associations in every point of view, and to court their recurrence till they become familiar and tame, like a serpent deprived of its sting. It is in this very way, indeed, together with the effect of the sympathies usually manifested by friendship, that the detailing of our griefs and grievances to others always lessens their poignancy. Even privately writing such details, I am convinced, would have a similar effect; and I should thence conclude that, of all other men, a poet is the least likely to go mad, or die of a broken heart.[119]

I therefore decided to sound the poor fellow on the causes of his distressing feelings. At first I could get him to say nothing, but that he was ruined, and that it was all over with him; though, when I pressed him warmly to say whether there was any thing I could do to relieve him, and told him I was willing and ready to undertake whatever might be for his advantage, he became a little more communicative. He said I had a *right* to know something of his history; an expression which gave me to understand that he had a pretty distinct notion of what I had done for him, though he did not expressly say so; and I had too much delicacy to press him for an explanation. I had hopes, indeed, that the painful recollection of his attempted suicide had been the chief cause of his recent relapses into severe mental affliction; and if so, he might get the better in time of the horror which could not but arise from such a circumstance.

CHAPTER XI.

Way to get up a breach of promise of marriage.

THE young gentleman's story, so far as I became acquainted with it, was in its outlines by no means uncommon, though many of the particular circumstances were rare – at least, for the honour of humanity I hope so. The details which I obtained from him at different times, both then and afterwards, threw so much light on the transactions I wished to investigate, that it may not be unimportant to give a sketch of them from the facts that came to my knowledge.

The young gentleman's name was Percy,[120] and I understood him to have no remote chance of becoming heir to a splendid title with its accompanying estates; but, independently of this, he had already inherited a large property which devolved on him from an uncle, who had depended more on his own exertions in commerce than on the reversionary store of his ancestors.

Mr. Percy, it appeared, had only come to this property a few months before the event above related, though he had long been in expectation of it, and had (not very prudently) acted as if it were already his own; that is, he had spared no expense, however great, in the gratification of his wishes; and of course, like all young men who can command money, had allowed his passions to run riot, and plunged into all the follies which are current among the fashionable and dissipated. It was true, he had not yet the actual command of his uncle's money; but it was not long before he discovered, or rather was himself discovered by, those who were willing to advance him whatever sums he wanted, on the faith of his coming into possession at no distant day, with the usual proviso of an exorbitant premium to cover the risk.

Being by these means furnished with a well-stocked purse, young Percy, raw and inexperienced in the duplicities and frauds of the world, had in the usual way fallen into the snares which are always laid for such as he by people who live by their wits upon those that have none. He was accordingly beset wherever he went by horse-jockeys, dog-fanciers, and projectors[121] of all descriptions; while the neighbouring squires, and sometimes their sons, took the liberty of borrowing from him (as if by accident,) such sums as they thought he might be able to spare, without troubling their memories about it in future. By these various out-lets, he soon found that his money escaped from his possession with marvellous rapidity; so much so, indeed, that he more than once, he said, ran himself short of a guinea, while he imagined he had still a large sum left.

In this state of things, a partial stop was put to his profligate expenditure by a person who had contrived, as it appeared, a deeper scheme to entrap him than the crafty knaves who were plundering him of his ready money. This schemer was a speculating farmer, Grinstead by name, with whom Percy had accidentally come into contact in some business respecting horses. Grinstead, like most other men, seems to have had a keen eye to his own interest in every transaction; and upon considering the prospects of Percy, and calculating on his youth and inex-perience, he thought that more unlikely things had come about than his falling in love with Miss Grinstead, who was allowed by all the parish to be quite a none-so-pretty.[122]

The farmer accordingly exerted himself to lure Percy to his house by seeming to be much taken with him, flattering him upon his appearance, and exhibiting a deep knowledge of horses, about which he talked in a way most likely to gain the young gentleman's ear. As Percy was easily led, he soon found himself seated in Grinstead's parlour, and the young *lady* doing her best to look pleasing and pretty.

Marriage was an idea which had never entered Percy's thoughts. He was not, indeed, insensible to female attractions, as will afterwards appear more at length; but all the companions with whom he was in the habit of associating laughed at wedlock as a thing so utterly absurd for a young gentleman just beginning life, that he would almost as soon have thought of hanging himself as of marrying. He would flirt, or dance, or talk nonsense, whenever opportunity offered; but this was the sum and substance of his gallantries, when Miss Grinstead, under the instructions, it would appear, of her father, laid close siege to his heart, or rather to his expected fortunes.

Grinstead seems to have been no less knowing in the management of his scheme than in the points of a good horse. In fact, he was a very crafty old fellow, and proved himself so in this instance by instructing the girl to ply the young man as warmly as decency would permit, till she could once gain his notice, or, in his own pithy phrase, 'hook in him,' after which it would not be so difficult to play him to their purpose.

Percy said he was very much struck with the manner in which the girl behaved to him, and could not at first understand what she meant; but when they were accidentally (it would be more correct perhaps to say on purpose) left together by themselves, he could no longer doubt that she intended mischief, in endeav-ouring to carry his affections by a *coup de main*.[123]

As it was somewhat new for him to be placed in such circumstances, the novelty (like all other novelties at his age,) pleased him; and after he had got rid of a little of his awkward bashfulness, he did not hesitate to return her advances. Young people in such cases, indeed, soon understand one another, and require no prompter besides nature to lead them from the first look of kindness on to the most extravagant vows of eternal fidelity. Percy, it is true, had not yet proceeded so far as this; but enough had been said and looked between him and the farmer's daughter, to induce him to think of it after he was gone, and to make him contrive a pretext about horses, to repeat his visit next day.

Grinstead no doubt saw that his plan was beginning to work, and therefore took care to whet Percy's anxiety by avoiding all mention of Miss Grinstead, who did not make her appearance. Percy had neglected, on his first salutation, to ask for her, expecting that he should see her as a matter of course; and when he was disappointed and lingered about on the fret in consequence, he did not exactly like to say any thing to the old fellow about his daughter. At length he took his leave, but contrived, as he no doubt imagined, another pretext for returning on the following day, when the stratagems of war seem to have been altogether changed: – the father had been *called unexpectedly* from home, and Miss Grinstead was dressed out in her best gown and her sweetest smiles to do the honours of the house. She acted no longer, however, her former part of a coquette to ensnare him. She now appeared coy, modest, and not to be won at a word; and instead of making any of her former advances, seemed more inclined to retract what she had before accorded. Percy was upon this somewhat non-plussed,[124] and did not well know what to make of her; but he had already gone rather too far to retreat with a good grace, and in such cases advancing or retreating are the only alternatives; there can be no stand-still medium in affairs of love, as this I suppose must be denominated.

Percy, therefore, determined to declare his admiration of her attractions, and request permission to repeat his visit, to render her all the homage due from a lover. The matter, accordingly, was soon settled, and Percy received in proper form as the acknowledged suitor of the farmer's daughter.

Still he had never dreamed of what was uppermost in her mind, and never even hinted at *marriage*. The correspondence, however, it was evident, could not go on long without some explanation on this point; and several cunning devices appear to have been had recourse to by old Grinstead, to bring about the wished-for eclaircissement.[125] Percy was not shrewd enough to see through these, any more than he had penetrated the cunning manner in which he had been led on in the first instance; but from the account which he himself gave, I found no difficulty in interpreting the facts, and tracing them to their true source: a person, indeed, like Percy, who is duped or hood-winked, is always the last to discover it.

The young man was, of course, allowed to pay his addresses according to his fondest wishes, and was for a length of time very assiduous, haunting the farm, as he said, like a ghost, and never happy but when he was there. Still he thought nothing of marriage, and gave no hints of any intention farther than mere coquetting. This, however, was not at all to old Grinstead's taste, though he had gladly countenanced it as a beginning to more important and permanent measures. Accordingly, after some weeks, or months it may have been (for Percy, I found, was by no means accurate in dates), spent in this dangling kind of idle and dangerous courtship, Grinstead, it seems, showed that he at least was in sober earnest in the matter, and began to sound Percy as to his ultimate intentions. As it was a question which he had never asked his own conscience (not contemplating aught beyond mere pastime), he was not of course prepared to respond satisfactorily to the farmer's interrogatories. These could not fail, however, to show him more than he liked to see of the consequences of his flirtation; and when he began to consider how Miss Grinstead would appear, in the character of his future lady, among his high fashionable relatives, all his love for her (if it might be called by that name,) could not blind him to her obvious deficiencies, nor banish his anticipations of the ridicule which such a step would draw upon him.

These reflections had the effect of preventing his return to Grinstead's for a whole day; but he passed it miserably, because he had of late given up all his former amusements in favour of coquetting and romping[126] at the farm, and had now nothing to fly to in order to escape from his own fancies. He tried every thing he could think of, but remained restless and dissatisfied with each. His fowling-piece was out of order; his fishing-tackle was still worse; he could not get his favourite dog to obey him without beating, which he had never before required; and his horse seemed to be more in the humour of going backwards than forwards. The night was no better than the day, as he could not sleep for fretting; at one time blaming himself for ever having gone near the farmer's, and at another wishing that he *were* there, as a romp with Miss Grinstead would cure him of the painful vacuity of thought which he had endured and was enduring.

It was not difficult to prophesy how all this would end. The morrow found him, after several turnings and returnings, on the way to the farm, with the hopes – faint, indeed, but not extinct – of renewing his flirtation, or whatever it might be called, without committing himself farther upon the subject of matrimony – a point on which he was fully determined not to give in, though Miss Grinstead had been more indispensable to his happiness than she really was. Old Grinstead, on his part, was no doubt equally determined not to concede the point of flirtation. Indeed, it soon appeared that they had already begun to act upon the defensive; for, when Percy arrived, he could not see the coquette, who was expressly denied to him, though he was certain, he thought, that she was at home. This was a disappointment which he had not anticipated, and, of course, he felt it to be the more galling. He soon departed, therefore, and determined to give himself no farther trouble about the affair.

It was much easier, as the reader must well know, to come to such a determination than to keep it. Upon leaving the house, chagrined at the unexpected denial of Miss Grinstead, and indignant at the way in which her father had talked to him, he felt a spirit of resentment rising in his bosom, and it is not unlikely that his thoughts were too big for utterance. He resolved and re-resolved that his departure from the house should be final, and in order to keep firm to his resolution, intended to set out that very day to visit a friend at a considerable distance, and hastened home to put his design in execution, by getting ready his horse and other things.

It so happened, however, that he thought he might as well call and bid Miss Grinstead a final farewell before setting out, and then he would be done with her, as he said, 'forthwith and for ever.' This, indeed, was breaking through his resolution almost as soon as he had taken it; but he convinced himself very easily that that it was only the first step in following it up. Accordingly, he assumed what he called an air of consequence, cool and indifferent (though it is more probable that it looked like pique or offended pride), and went boldly to announce that he came to take his final leave.

This was a consummation which had been as little anticipated by Miss Grinstead and her father as her denial in the morning had been by Percy. She soon, therefore, made her appearance, in a dejected and forlorn state, as became a forsaken maiden; and when he hinted (for he had not courage to speak out) that he intended to be absent for a considerable time, the girl burst into tears. These may have been affected, though I will not affirm as much, since it is by no means improbable that she felt a genuine affection for him, he being a good-looking young man, though it might have been perceived that he was too bashful, and not sufficiently knowing, to be a very successful gallant.

It will easily be perceived that this scene was well calculated to interrupt his purposed journey, and put all his resolutions to flight. He was, for that day at least, effectually prevented from going away; for he could not think of leaving the hitherto laughing, romping, flirting, coquetting girl, to cry her little heart out in his absence. Their mutual differences were, therefore, soon buried in silence, and the day was spent, as many others had been, amidst the fooleries current in such cases, pleasant enough to the parties themselves, but mawkish and impertinent to all besides.

For some time after this the subject of marriage, which had caused all the difference, was not hinted at on either side, and the intercourse of idle flirtation was continued as before. Grinstead, no doubt, was well aware of the sort of person he had to deal with, otherwise he would not have permitted so dangerous a game to be kept up; but though it is probable he had no great fear for sinister consequences, he must nevertheless have been anxious to secure Percy, if possible, and as soon too as might be, for fear he should be led off in some other direction.

In this state of things, Miss Grinstead was taken ill; I will not be so uncharitable as to suggest that she only pretended to be so, but it was evidently made the most of to 'hook in' Percy farther than he dreamed of. It was only he, they informed him, who could give her consolation, and support her sinking spirits; and Grinstead told him that he believed it was love alone which was her disorder.

By such representations and artifices as these, Percy was at length cajoled into an implied promise of marriage, or at least what was construed by Grinstead as such, though he himself had not given the matter a thought. As Percy could not see Miss Grinstead during her illness, he became tired of dancing attendance upon her father, and listening to his doleful news from the sick room; and, as a natural consequence, his visits began to be 'few and far between.'[127] In short, he gradually returned to his former amusements, and the idea of Miss Grinstead waxed correspondingly faint in his fancy, giving place to a miscellany of dogs, horses, and fowling-pieces, which occupied the better portion of his thoughts by night and by day.

All this was sufficiently natural; and Percy, at length, thought and felt as if no such person as Miss Grinstead existed, or had existed – at least to him. His intercourse with her family in the same way declined so rapidly, that when the farmer and he met by accident, they barely exchanged the commonest civilities. Miss Grinstead's illness had not been deadly: she soon recovered, and Percy had met her more than once, but without the slightest feeling of pleasure, and not a strong one even of recognition. He said that she appeared to him to be a good deal like some stranger whom he had before seen, and had forgotten even by name. I well understood what he meant by this, as I had more than once observed the same thing in similar circumstances.

From this 'unvarnished tale,'[128] I was at no loss to anticipate the deep game which the farmer was playing upon this inexperienced young man, who was roused from his state of forgetfulness towards Miss Grinstead by a formal visit from her father, to put him in mind of the promise of marriage. Percy, if he had ever given the subject any consideration, had of course supposed the Grinsteads (from their late conduct) to be no less indifferent than he was; and, had there been no money in prospect, and no estates and title to hope for, they might probably have allowed the thing to drop; but these were attractions of too paramount importance to be resigned without a struggle.

Percy was naturally, as may have already appeared, a timid, soft, bashful, young man; but such are not always the most manageable or easily led when they are irritated or threatened with compulsory measures. Percy, therefore, so far from being intimidated by the serious tone of old Grinstead, stoutly denied his having ever given an explicit promise, which was indeed the truth; and told him that whatever he had said was more by way of jest than anything meant in earnest.

Grinstead, however, was not to be put off with explanations. Money was his object, and money he was determined to have before he had done with Percy. Accordingly, when he perceived that he could not gain him over to acknowledge the promise by fair play, he changed his tone, and threatened him with an action at law. This was the best hit which the farmer, with all his scheming, had yet made; for Percy, like most young men of his timid caste of mind, when unbronzed[129] by bad company, had a horror of having his name dragged into the publicity of a court of law. He had felt very uneasy at some passing jokes which he had formerly encountered on account of his acquaintance with Miss Grinstead; but those were trifles compared with the scrutiny into his private history, which would be the consequence of an action. Yet how was he to avoid this? He neither could nor would marry the girl, for whom all his fondness had vanished; and nothing less, it appeared, would satisfy her father; so that an action seemed to be inevitable.

Percy, in this dilemma, thought it requisite to consult his attorney, and, of course, the man of law *honestly* advised him to defend the action by all means, if it should go so far. This advice, however, was not to his taste, since he was resolved to put in no defence; for let the business go as it might, he should at least in this way prevent discussions, siftings, and scrutinies, which he abhorred.

As the attorney had failed to give him any other consolation than that he might gain the action if it were properly defended, he thought he would again try Grinstead himself, and endeavour to bring him to reason; for he could not persist, Percy thought, in a thing so absurd as to force him into a marriage against his will, particularly as it must have appeared evident, from the whole tenour of his conduct, that he never had any serious intentions of wedding the girl. Percy was simple enough to think that an explanation of this sort, made in the spirit of candour, could not but satisfy all concerned. He did not see Grinstead's drift of turning it into pecuniary advantage; but the *honest* farmer did not leave him long in doubt as to his views, and asked him, in so many words, what he would be disposed to give to be quit of the whole affair.

'Why,' said Percy, musing for a space upon a proposal so unexpected, 'why, what would you think of a matter of twenty pounds? My attorney tells me it will take at least fifty to bring it into court, and you may think yourself well off to get twenty pounds for nothing at all, as I may say.'

'Twenty pounds! twenty pounds!' shouted Grinstead, as if he had been offered as many farthings. 'Twenty pounds! Mark ye, Mr. P. I'm too old to be fooled by you; and hark ye, Sir! I intend to have the damages laid at ten thousand pounds,[130] hark ye! Twenty pounds indeed! What an old ass you must take me for!'

Percy was thunderstruck: ten thousand pounds, notwithstanding his uncle's large property, was a sum which he quailed to think of. He had indeed looked forward to the possession of a great deal of money, but had never had the absolute command himself of one thousand, much less of ten. He thought, at first, that Grinstead was mad; yet when he saw that he persisted most obstinately and seriously in the business, without consenting to abate a jot of his demand, Percy became really alarmed, and began to weigh the several measures proposed to him more narrowly than he had hitherto done. He even half thought of marrying the girl rather than lose so large a sum of money; but as his fondness for her had fled beyond recal, he could not bring his mind to that in any form wherein it could be viewed. If the action, again, were to go forward, there would not only be the chance of his losing the money, but the public exposure, which Percy dreaded worse than death. It would be better at once to pay down the money than run the chance of this; but there was a bar even to such an arrangement, for he had not the money to pay, however well disposed he might have been to be gulled.

Grinstead, there can be no doubt, would soon perceive that Percy was in the trim[131] to do any thing which he might desire, save and except the grand point of marrying Miss Grinstead; and being eager not to lose so fair an opportunity of enriching himself at little hazard, proposed that he should forthwith execute a bond in his favour for five thousand pounds, his conscience probably smiting him for avariciously grasping at double that sum. Percy, in the hurry of the moment, consented to this, and the bond was accordingly signed; but even here, in this important measure, his simplicity was undiminished, for he forgot to obtain a release, and Grinstead was cunning enough not to insert any condition in the bond, so that poor Percy was now as much in his power as before.

This was the first considerable sum which he had been swindled out of, and it gave him more bitter vexation than he had ever experienced. Grinstead, indeed, added a double sting to his rapacity, by refusing, with a sarcastic sneer, to sign a release from the promise of marriage, when he called next day in time, as he simply imagined, to redeem his error of not getting it when he signed the bond.

The thoughts of this iniquitous transaction, and vexation at his own simplicity in being so begulled, drove him almost mad. He could not, for very shame, look any of his acquaintance in the face, for fear that they knew the circumstances. Indeed, he fancied that every body was talking of it, and laughing at his folly. This was beyond endurance; and he therefore took a sudden resolution of quitting the country, which had thus become so disagreeable, and of plunging for relief into the bustle of the metropolis.

We shall see, as we proceed, that he was no less unfortunate in London, and that the dashing Mrs. — was a still more successful schemer in money matters than old Grinstead.

CHAPTER XII.

Pocket-picking at Astley's.

Percy had only been once in London, and then but for a few days, previous to his expedition to dissipate his vexation, or at least conceal it from those who might be aware of its cause. He had few personal acquaintance, and such as he had he wished to avoid, choosing rather to mix unknown with the crowds at the theatres and other places of public resort, which he assiduously frequented.

He soon felt the want of associates, however; for all the bustle of public amusement becomes tiresome, when there is nobody to share our interest, or take a part in the passing remark. Strangers, indeed, will occasionally enter upon a transient conversation; but that is not sufficient to supply the natural cravings of the social principle. Percy was constitutionally social, and seldom easy unless he had some friend or acquaintance with whom he could pass part of his time – a very dangerous quality for one so inexperienced as he was in the metropolis, where swarms of knaves and swindlers of imposing and plausible manners are always prowling about to ensnare the unwary. Percy was an excellent subject for harpies of this class; and as he was not difficult to start, he could not long escape being discovered and hunted into the toils.[132]

Amongst the public places where he spent his evenings, Astley's[133] was his greatest favourite as he fancied he had some little knowledge of horses, and delighted to see the extraordinary feats performed there more than in the best acting exhibited upon the stage. It is probable that he had here given some tokens of his rawness and rusticity, of easy interpretation by those who were on the watch for prey. The very look of eager curiosity and unrestrained delight, which is so common in a stranger to such sights, would be quite enough to mark him out for plunder; and if he were at any time (a thing not unlikely) betrayed into a rustic burst of applause, it would be an unequivocal signal to all the pick-pockets within hearing to pounce upon him.

Something of this sort had probably occurred at Astley's to point out young Percy; for one night, when leaving the house, he was jostled in the crowd, and immediately afterwards missed both his watch and pocket-book. On looking round in hopes of discovering the thief, his eye caught a man whose looks he did not like, seeming, as he thought, to endeavour to escape with his booty. The movements of this ill-looking fellow confirmed Percy's suspicions, and he therefore pressed through the crowd till he came up with him, when he did not hesitate to collar him and charge him with having picked his pocket. The fellow looked so conscience-stricken, Percy said, that he had no doubt he had pitched upon the right man; but he denied the crime with the greatest effrontery, affirmed that he was an honest tradesman, and offered to be searched on the spot, or to go before a magistrate and submit to any examination which might be deemed proper. All this had so much the appearance of innocence, that Percy was staggered in his belief: instead of pressing the charge, he pitied the man, and would have given him money, had it not been for very shame of his mistake.

The altercation, in so public a place, could not fail to attract a crowd, and Percy soon found himself surrounded with a motley group, eager to learn what was going forward. When he liberated the man, however, and expressed himself satisfied of his innocence, the crowd gradually dispersed, and Percy was left to make the best of his way home to ruminate on his losses.

As he was crossing Westminster Bridge, a gentleman came up to him and asked if he were the person who had just been robbed at Astley's of his watch and pocket-book. Upon Percy replying in the affirmative, the stranger said, he thought he knew the robber to be a notorious character who prowled about in that neighbourhood; and, if his suspicions were just, he might be able, perhaps, to retrieve the property. Percy told him it would be an obligation to him which he could not easily repay, as there were some valuable papers in the pocket-book useless to any body but himself; and the watch having been his father's, he would not have parted with it for any money, though it was not of much real value.

The stranger, upon this, hinted that it would be a bad plan to inform the police, as he said he had at first thought would be best; for as the property was so important, if the robber dreamed of pursuit, he would take care to destroy or conceal what might lead to convict him. There were other means, he said, of getting at stolen property which were sometimes more successfully had recourse to; but, so far as he had heard, these were both expensive and somewhat hazardous; yet many gentlemen (he knew) of honour and probity had not scrupled to treat with the confederates of thieves, for the recovery of what could not otherwise be replaced for money. It was a course which, in the present instance, it would be far best to follow; for pickpockets always destroyed private papers which were not so recovered, because this was the only way in which they could make anything by them; whereas, if they were found, evidence might thence be drawn to bring home the crime.

Percy was rejoiced to hear of any means of recovering things of so much adventitious value, and he looked upon the stranger as a good angel sent to console him in his misfortune. He thanked him warmly for the interest he had taken respecting his loss, but feared at the same time that nothing could be done, as he was so little acquainted with the town, and less with the means to be pursued in such a case.

The stranger said that he was himself altogether unacquainted with the class of persons with whom it would be necessary to treat – nobody could be desirous of having such acquaintance; but a friend of his had recently been engaged in a case precisely similar, which had also happened at Astley's; and as he had been successful in retrieving his property by treating with some of the confederates of the pickpockets, perhaps through this friend, who knew by painful experience how to correspond with the gang, Percy might be put upon the way of managing the business to his satisfaction.

The more Percy considered the representations of the stranger, the more plausible they appeared; and he would have immediately set about taking the necessary steps, had he not felt reluctant in giving so much trouble to a person he did not know. The stranger himself was more anxious, it appeared, to ascertain whether Percy would be disposed to go to any expense in the affair, than concerned about the personal trouble which he might incur. The expense was a consideration which gave Percy no concern: he was willing to spend any reasonable sum to recover what he had lost, if he could only be certain of success by this or any other means. The stranger said it would be too much to *assure* him of success – he could not venture to do that; but the instance of his friend, he thought, afforded a strong probability in favour of it.

The stranger then went on to tell Percy that it was now too late to introduce him to this friend; but added, that he would himself use the privilege of intimacy by calling and making the necessary inquiries, which he would communicate without fail, at as early an hour next day as Percy might choose to appoint. With a great many apologies for the trouble which he was giving him, Percy named ten o'clock, and handed his card, while the stranger at the same time frankly gave him his in return.

If Percy had known any thing at all of the town, the conduct of this person, though he appeared to be a gentleman, would have excited strong suspicions of his motives in being so officious; but Percy, unsophisticated in the ways of crime, saw nothing in it except disinterested kindness and generosity. It would, indeed, have been almost impossible to impress him with the notion that this very *gentleman* was not improbably the man who had picked his pocket, and was now endeavouring to make the most of the plunder by trafficking with him on exorbitant terms for his own property; or, if he were not the actual depredator, that he was at least one of the gang, who calculated largely on Percy's ignorance.

Such were nevertheless the opinions which I formed to the disadvantage of the stranger, whose card bore the name of Dawkins, with the fashionable address of Grosvenor Street.[134] Percy allowed, however, it did seem a little curious that a gentleman to whom he was entirely unknown should, all at once, take so deep an interest in his loss; but still he thought it no more than he would have been apt to do himself, if it had lain in his power. It is in this manner that the innocent become an easy prey to the guilty: they compare the hypocrisies of fraud with their own upright intentions, and conclude upon their complete accordance.

Percy could not sleep for thinking of his loss, and of the singular interest which Dawkins had manifested in the business; and he looked forward, therefore, with great impatience to the hour when he was to hear from him. He had thought little over-night of the money which might be required; but he now recollected that Dawkins had spoken very particularly on this point, and he accordingly put a sum in his purse, such as he supposed the pickpocket might be glad to have for his things, if he were lucky enough to discover how these could be treated for.

The hour at last came, but Dawkins was not punctual to his appointment, and Percy was consequently kept in that state of anxiety which is almost certain to accompany suspense. Hour after hour passed away, and still he neither appeared himself, nor did any message come from him. Percy's anxiety would not let him remain at home longer than noon, when he resolved to lay aside his bashfulness and timidity, and call on Dawkins in Grosvenor Street. He did so, but was told he was not at home, and he therefore remained now as far from recovering his things as at the moment he lost them. He wandered about in great uneasiness all the day, and went home so dissatisfied, that he had no heart to go to any of his usual resorts for the evening.

CHAPTER XIII.

A blindfold adventure on the Thames.

PERCY had already begun to alter his opinion of Dawkins, but he could not think what motive that person had for pretending to take so much interest in his loss, leading him on to form almost certain expectations, and then deserting him as if he were not worth the trouble of thinking about. He was ruminating, he said, in this manner just before candles were brought in, when Dawkins himself was announced to apologize for not keeping his appointment in the morning.

He had not been able, he said, readily to meet with his friend who understood the secrets of recovering stolen property, and he had also been so hurried with important business, that he could not find a moment to send a note to Mr. Percy; but he would now make amends for his apparent neglect by taking him direct to his friend, who had told him he was quite certain of recovering the things, if the demands of the thieves could be satisfied with regard to money. Dawkins professed to know nothing of what would be asked, but talked in no measured terms of their rapacity, and of the danger of entering upon the thing at all without yielding to this.

Percy of course did not much like the money part of the business so soon after the loss of the five thousand pounds to Grinstead; but since there was no other way practicable, he was compelled to submit. Dawkins took him to a tavern near Westminster Bridge, where he was to meet his friend, whose name I think was stated to be Hodges. This Hodges had not the gentlemanly look of Dawkins, though he was fashionably dressed, and received Percy with great politeness, telling him that he would do any thing to serve Dawkins, particularly in an affair so similar to one in which he himself had suffered seriously, and had bought his experience dearly, as every body must, he remarked, who falls into the hands of rogues and pickpockets.

Hodges farther represented the business as peculiarly dangerous in a personal point of view; for as it involved the original depredator and also his confederates (who would be in the act of trafficking with his property) in a capital crime, they would feel it necessary to use very strong precautions for their own safety, the least infringement whereof might be visited with fatal consequences. Hodges said it was necessary to tell Percy all this before he entered upon the adventure, otherwise he might be led into a worse scrape still than the losses which he had suffered, and might possibly conclude, without just grounds, that he had been betrayed. This latter, indeed, was the light which Percy ought to have viewed the business in, from his first meeting with Dawkins; but by talking in this manner, Hodges lulled all suspicion of deceit on their part, and Percy did not hesitate to take directions how to proceed.

Hodges, upon this, told him that he would have to engage a waterman,[135] (whom he would point out,) at Westminster Bridge, who would take him in his boat to the person he would have to treat with; but it was a necessary preliminary that he should submit to be blindfolded before landing, otherwise there would be an end of the matter. It was what he (Hodges) had submitted to, and without this precaution the waterman dared not, on peril of his life, land him at the wished-for spot. To this condition Percy inwardly demurred, but his anxiety to regain possession of his watch and papers overcame his scruples, and he consented.

The preliminaries being thus settled, Dawkins took leave, but said he would call next day to learn how Percy had succeeded; and the latter, accompanied by Hodges, went towards the bridge to find the *knowing* waterman. Hodges continued to impress him strongly with the idea of the danger he would run, if he did not comply with all that was required of him, particularly on the score of money. As they approached the bridge, however, Hodges ceased speaking, began humming an air, and from humming went on to whistle the same air, as if he had been sauntering alone. Percy thought this a very bad specimen of London manners; but it is probable Hodges had more meaning in his whistling than mere pastime, and it could scarcely be a piece of gratuitous rudeness towards his companion.

The waterman, as it happened, was not on the station when they came thither, and Hodges manifested great impatience, but continued humming and whistling his air by turns, while he looked anxiously over the parapet, as if waiting for the appearance of his man. At length, Percy heard a boat rowing in to the landing-place, and soon after a tall fellow ran up the steps, and pried about as if looking for some one he expected to meet.

'That is the man,' said Hodges, in a whisper. 'You must make your own bargain with him, and tell him what you want. I must not be seen in the business, and you must on no account tell that I directed you to him.'

He then squeezed Percy's hand and slunk away lest, as he said, the waterman might see him. It was now quite dark, and Percy was left to advance or recede in the adventure which he had undertaken. He was naturally timid, as I have already mentioned, but it does not appear that he was a dastard, since he could muster resolution to intrust himself in the dark, on the water, with a man in confederacy with robbers, and who was farther to have the liberty of blindfolding him and carrying him wherever he chose. He did pause however, he said, before he could venture to accost the tall fellow, who looked by the light of the lamps to be very ruffian-like, and too powerful to cope with, if there should chance to arise any difference between them.

The fellow himself put an end to Percy's hesitation by asking him the waterman's usual question if he wanted a boat. Percy, assuming courage, told him he did, if he could land him where he might purchase a lost watch and pocket-book. The fellow upon this came close up to him, looked narrowly into his face, and cross-questioned him at some length as to the time, place, and circumstances, of the loss he had suffered, probably with a view of ascertaining that he was not imposed upon. When he was satisfied on these points, he told Percy that his regular fare for such a voyage was a guinea; but if he chose to be liberal for superior treatment, he might make it as much more as he had a mind.

Poor Percy was now, as it may be seen, in the hands of the Philistines,[136] and had to submit to this as well as to other demands equally exorbitant. He accordingly gave a guinea and a-half to the fellow, who muttered a discontented grumble that he had not made it even money; and Percy was under the necessity of adding another half-guinea to insure the good treatment which was promised as the reward of extra liberality.

As they rowed out into the stream of the river, Percy said he shuddered to look at the dark scowling face of his companion, and think what sort of business they were engaged in. His fears were not lessened, it may well be imagined, when the waterman told him, in a tone not at all mellowed by the additional guinea, that he must now submit to be blindfolded during the remainder of their expedition, to prevent him, he said, from seeing what he ought not to see. Percy was not over-certain that he might not afterwards rifle his pockets and throw him into the river, for he was now no less suspicious of his tall companion than he had been unsuspicious of Dawkins and Hodges. They rowed on, however, in silence for about half an hour or more, as Percy calculated; though, in his state of agitation, it is not likely that he could keep a very correct reckoning of time.

At length they landed, and he was first led up what appeared to be a wharf-stair, and then through several turnings of what he took for lanes and courts. He was enjoined absolute silence, and though the tall fellow did not threaten him with any consequences in case of disobedience, yet he did not forget the cautions of Hodges, that his life might be in jeopardy if he did not comply with what was required of him.

He was very anxious to get a peep from under his bandage at the sort of place he was in; but the fellow had taken too much care, in its adjustment, to admit of this, and he had therefore to content himself with mere conjectures. He did not even know on what side of the river he had been landed, nor whether he was above or below the bridge, where he had gone into the boat. This, however, was a matter of little consequence with regard to the main object of his adventure.

After turning several times from right to left and from left to right, he was desired to enter at a door which was so low that he was obliged to stoop. He was thence led through a winding passage, and down a short flight of steps, at the bottom of which the waterman told him he must leave him. While he was standing here in great uncertainty as to what was next to happen, he was accosted by a person in a strange, squeaking, cracked voice, (probably assumed,) and asked what he wanted. Upon answering that he wished to purchase a watch and pocketbook, he was desired to describe them, and particularly to mention the contents of the latter. The questioner then told him it was probable they could be procured, if he were ready to come down with any thing handsome.[137] The word 'handsome,' however, in such cases, has so wide a signification, that Percy did not well know what to say to this. He had before imagined that five or at most ten shillings would be a very handsome fare for the waterman, though the fellow had been barely contented with two guineas. If 'handsome' was to be taken with equal latitude of meaning in the proposed purchase, he did not know what sum to offer, nor indeed that he had cash enough to satisfy the avarice of the miscreants. At length, after some consideration he thought it best to sound his way by inquiring what price was expected, professing at the same time his readiness to give any thing reasonable.

'O! we never make prices,' squeaked the trafficker in stolen goods; 'but if you come down with any thing *handsome*, we'll see what can be done.'

'And what would you call handsome?' rejoined Percy, afraid to commit himself, and recollecting, no doubt, how far he had been mistaken in estimating the rapacity of Farmer Grinstead, in a case not altogether dissimilar. He could get no answer to his question, however, but a repetition of the words 'handsome' and 'liberal,' and he was forced at last to name a sum which, though *he* thought handsome, (and amounting to within a trifle of all he had in his purse,) was treated with as great contempt as Farmer Grinstead had before displayed at his mention of twenty pounds.

After much altercation, however, and every possible attempt made to overreach him, (as he might well have expected,) a bargain was concluded, and upon paying the money (which amounted to a larger sum than he was willing to acknowledge), he had his property restored to him.

He was then conducted, as he thought, (for he was still blindfolded,) by a different way to that by which he had entered; and when he got out of the house, the tall fellow was in waiting to receive him, and lead him back to the boat. When they got to the wharf-stairs, it struck Percy that he might again be robbed of his property by the ruffian waterman, over whom he had no check; and if he had heard any body at hand, he would have tried to have him secured by giving the alarm for assistance; but as all was silent, and he knew well he could do nothing with such a powerful man alone, he was compelled, though much against his will, to re-imbark in the boat.

The fellow said nothing till they were about to land, when he had the impudence to ask him for another guinea to drink his health. Percy, however, had not a guinea left to give him; his crack-voiced friend had taken care of that, and the tall ruffian was therefore obliged to rest satisfied with a single shilling and some odd pence, the entire remainder of Percy's well-stored purse. It was not probable, indeed, that such a gang would leave the young man a halfpenny, when they found him so pliable and easily imposed on. The wonder to me was, that they had returned him the watch and the pocket-book, since they could as easily have retained them as the money which he gave for them. His having got these safe again, though he had paid smartly for them, made me suspect (from his own story) that they had not done with him, and had found out that he was too good a flat[138] to let escape, so long as he had any thing worth plundering.

As Percy was by no means a fool in many things, it was rather inexplicable to me that he should not have suspected Dawkins, when he found him connected with Hodges, who had a manifest understanding with the tall waterman. The truth is, that young people hear the wickedness and deceit of the world so much talked about, that the words call up no ideas in their minds any more than the rhymes of a hymn, or the sing-song of the catechism, does in a school-boy. Percy had, in this way, heard of the frauds of London;[139] but he thought of them only as things at a distance, and not likely to cross his own path. There is no method of acquiring a true knowledge of London frauds except by being their victim; and then, perhaps, the knowledge may come too late. Percy was, indeed, doomed to be the victim of deceit; and had it not been for my accidental interference, experience might in his case have been too late.

CHAPTER XIV.

Billiards – Whist – Tête-a-tête with Mrs. —.

ACCORDING as I had anticipated from Percy's narrative, his *friend* Dawkins paid him a visit early next morning, ostensibly to learn what success he had met with in retrieving his things, though really, as I had no doubt, to keep up and extend his acquaintance with a young man whom he understood, from his apparent disregard of money, and other hints which he might pick up from his conversation, to have good prospects.

From this time forth, indeed, Dawkins and Percy advanced, from being visiting acquaintance, to becoming sworn and inseparable friends. Dawkins had a thorough knowledge of the town, and took Percy to every place where he thought he would be most amused, making himself, of course, as agreeable as possible, by studying the tastes and humours of his young friend.

It was not long before he offered to introduce him to certain private parties, where he could spend his evenings more pleasantly than at Astley's or other theatres. Percy was delighted with this proposal, for his friend's acquaintance were not likely to know any thing of his country connection with the Grinsteads, the very idea of which he could not endure. He would thus, also, get some notion of London society, and make up for the painful solitude which he had suffered since his coming to town. He had some fears, indeed, of being rather unfit for mixing with fine people; but the idea he entertained of his prospects, and the certainty of getting his uncle's property, at least in a short time, impressed on him his own importance, and tended not a little to support his courage.

Such were his thoughts, Percy said, in anticipation of the introduction which Dawkins had promised him; but he found these, like many other anticipations, deceitful. He was first introduced to a set who spent their evenings at billiards; but, in this circle, so far from being able to assume the consequence which he had resolved to do, he was a mere cypher, and could not even understand their language; nor was it likely he should, for among such a set it would of course be high *flash*,[140] altogether above the comprehension of a young man like Percy, fresh from the country. He was not, moreover, much of a billiard player, though he had taken a cue upon occasion before coming to town. He was at all events, he soon perceived, no match for the London proficients; and could not be persuaded to attempt playing, out of fear that he might be laughed at.

Dawkins, therefore, failed in his first attempt to involve Percy in the vortex of gambling, as was no doubt his intention, founded probably on his telling him that he could play a little. It does not appear that he even challenged him to bet upon the players, a circumstance which may be accounted for on the supposition that he was contriving a deeper plot than merely gaining a few unimportant bets, and did not, therefore, wish to give a premature alarm as to his designs, lest they might be frustrated before he could bring them to bear.

The next plan of Dawkins, since he had been unsuccessful in interesting Percy with the billiard party, was to try the influence of female attraction, a thing which rarely fails, in the case of young men, to lead them wherever it may be wished by the crafty and the designing. It must have been with this view that he first took Percy to a private party at Mrs. —'s, where, however, such parties were not, as I understood, the order of the day,[141] except to serve some particular design, such as the plundering an unsuspecting youth like Percy, or, at least, preparing him to submit with a good grace to lose his all.

On the night, accordingly, when Percy was introduced, there were only a few select friends to sip coffee, talk scandal, and play a rubber at whist,[142] which Percy, indeed, was rather partial to, and probably had told Dawkins as much. He was at first, he said, dazzled beyond expression by Mrs. —, whose dress, manners, and appearance, were very far above all that he had conceived of female charms. She would, no doubt, appear to be a being of a different species from the farmer's daughter; but it did not follow that it was more safe to come within the sphere of her attractions. When women are bent upon evil, they are much more dangerous than men, as they are more artful in acquiring power, and more crafty in turning it to their own purposes.

Though Percy was at first overawed by Mrs. — more than by any of the other ladies present, she spoke to him with so much good-humoured affability and freedom, that in a short time he found courage to take part in the conversation. He was quite fascinated, he said, and felt as if he were in a new world. Whist appeared to him, for the first time, to be a *bore,* as he could never tire of listening to the conversation of Mrs. — It is highly probable, indeed, that she not only played off her own attractions to the best advantage, but flattered Percy upon the points where she found him most easily accessible.

The lady, to his great delight, did not join in the rubber, and attached herself to him, inquiring in the kindest manner about his prospects and connections. Fascinated as he professed to be, it is not probable that he would talk of himself or his prospects in a manner likely to diminish his consequence; and of course nothing could be a stronger inducement for a lady of her stamp to make the most of him. She never asked him to take a hand at whist, and pretended that she cared little about cards, though she found it indispensible, she said, to comply more than she wished with the fashion of the times.

This sort of half confidential *tête-a-tête*[143] was interrupted by a dispute which arose at the whist table, and which was proceeding to high words, between Dawkins and another gentleman, who seemed to insinuate that there had been something unfair, a circumstance I think very probable, though Dawkins repelled the charge with great indignation. Mrs. —, of course, must have had a strong wish to conceal this scene from Percy, and accordingly she told him she could not endure wrangling and disputes. She made this a pretence for instantly leaving them to settle their differences as they best might, inviting him to follow her, unless, she added in a jocular tone, he took pleasure in card quarrels, and had a genius for peace-making.

He could not resist following her, and the disputants were becoming too hot to take any notice of his quitting the room. She ushered him into a splendid apartment, fitted up in the most luxurious and expensive style, and continued to talk to him in the same strain of lively familiarity, though he did not, he said, feel so much at his ease as he had done in the whist room. There he had the rest of the company to keep him in countenance, though they were at a little distance and deep in their game; but here he had to encounter the lady's fascinations without any resource to fly to in aid of his timidity and false shame. She perceived this, and began to rally him upon his rustic bashfulness, proffering her services to cure him by showing him a little of the gaieties of the West End.[144] For this purpose, as a commencement, she gave him a general invitation to make free in calling when his evenings were not otherwise engaged. In short, he was to have the *entrée*, make what use of it he afterwards might.

Percy, it may well be conceived, returned home with his head full of the scene to which he had been introduced. Dawkins, who accompanied him, was very anxious to impress him with the notion that the fracas at the whist table had all originated in a mistake; that the gentleman had, on explanation, made a handsome apology, otherwise he would have called him out for the insinuations he had rashly ventured on, and in such a case he would have taken the liberty of requesting Mr. Percy's assistance in quality of second. As it had turned out, there was no necessity for having this honour thrust upon him. The story, however, would have the effect of impressing Percy with a high notion of his friend's honour and courage; though it was not difficult, if the matter had been sifted to the bottom, to foresee that a very different conclusion would have resulted.

It gave Percy but little concern how the matter was settled, for his thoughts were all running on the lady, of whom he could not tell what to think. His conjectures were the more vague concerning her, that Dawkins had not told him whether she was married or a widow. If she were married, it was singular, he thought, that he had not seen her husband, or that she should not have mentioned him in the course of the night, at the very least when giving him so particular an invitation, – not to speak of her taking him apart from the rest of the company, and talking to him in the free manner she had done. He had no notion of a married lady doing such things; and, on reflection, it appeared no less singular in a widow, if such she were, though he remarked that, at least, she did not wear weeds.[145]

He spent the greater part of the night in cogitations of this kind, but could not satisfy himself upon any point. One thing, however, is sufficiently plain; namely, that Mrs. — would make a powerful impression upon a young man so little experienced in the gay world, particularly when it is presumed that she had exerted unusual efforts to allure him, a circumstance which might have upset one more guarded than Percy as to female artifice, when an end is to be gained.

From what I had myself seen of Mrs. — in her carriage-costume, commonly the least attractive form of female drapery, I could well conceive the effect of her appearance in the superior elegance of an evening dress, and surrounded with all the splendour and luxury of wealth. When I thought also of her shopping devices to get rid of so many bank-notes, I had not a doubt that, from the first, she had had designs upon Percy of a very different kind from those which he had flattered himself by supposing.

It is not to be wondered at, indeed, that on turning over in his mind all she had said to him (and he did so a hundred times before he slept), he should form, or wish to form, the notion so flattering to his vanity, that she had been taken with his person. This, I say, is not to be wondered at, since it is probable that she had directed all her efforts to make such an impression; which, by the way, is never in similar cases a matter of much difficulty. Percy, of course, had his head completely turned, and rushed into the toils which were spread for him with all the alacrity that could be wished.

His first concern accordingly, next morning, was to run to Dawkins, to inquire whether Mrs. — were a widow or not, – the point he was chiefly interested in ascertaining. He was angry with himself that he had not asked him this important question whilst they were returning home, as it might have saved him a great deal of anxiety and painful conjecture; but the truth was, that Dawkins had been too full of his whist dispute to have leisure or inclination to talk of any thing else.

At this stage of the story I could not foresee exactly the part which Dawkins meant to act. That it was disinterested, however, I had no conception; but why he should lead Percy to Mrs. —'s, when he might have found other means of managing him to his wishes, I could not fathom. If it was intended, as the gamblers say, to *pigeon*[146] him, as was highly probable, Mrs. — would, of course, come in for a share of the plunder; whereas, if Dawkins had been dextrous enough, he might have had all in his own pocket. I could only explain his conduct, therefore, on the supposition of some very close connection of interests between Mrs. — and him, or of some insurmountable obstacle which had been conjured up or discovered to lie in his way.

How eager soever Percy may have been to ascertain if Mrs. — was a widow or a wife, and though he went to call on Dawkins for the express purpose of asking, his false shame overcame his anxiety, and he dared not venture to put the question for fear of disclosing his thoughts, and thereby exposing himself to raillery, a thing which he dreaded more than all other evils. Instead of getting his doubts resolved, he had again to endure the history of the whist dispute, which Dawkins inflicted upon him in all its minutest circumstances; and so warm was he upon the subject, that he never inquired what Percy thought of the party, and did not propose to return to Mrs. —'s at any future time. On the contrary, he asked Percy to go with him that evening to another party, where he was to meet the disputant, and settle all differences over another rubber.

With his head full of Mrs. —, and his teasing uncertainties about her condition, this was the most unwelcome proposal which could have been made; yet he did not well know how to avoid compliance. He would much more gladly have taken early advantage of the general invitation which he had received from Mrs. —, and returned to the scene which had so bewitched him. Dawkins had not calculated on his hesitation, far less on his refusal; and, upon perceiving him to be musing and absent when he should have answered his question, he began to rally him as being haunted with the blue devils;[147] and though he did not hint at the subject uppermost in Percy's thoughts, the latter had so much fear of this that he gave his consent to make one at the whist party, though at the same time wishing all whist and whist players at the bottom of the Red Sea. Upon this understanding, however, they separated for the time, Percy being left in the same dilemma with respect to Mrs. —.

Having nothing besides to occupy his mind, he sauntered about the streets restless and aimless, sometimes hesitating whether he might not devise an excuse to get off from Dawkins in the evening and steal away to Mrs. —, or whether it would not be better to pick up a little courage, and pay her a morning visit then. He was afraid that this might be a breach of etiquette, but he was still more apprehensive that she might scan too narrowly the thoughts which he wished to conceal, and of which he was himself so ashamed that he more than once blushed, though alone.

As the evening drew on, after a long, long day spent in self-tormenting, he had nearly made up his mind to give Dawkins the slip, and dispose of his time in a way more to his liking. But when he considered that it would be almost impossible, by any scheme, to conceal his movements from his friend, whose ridicule he sorely dreaded, he could not make up his mind to the attempt.

He bethought him, at this critical juncture, of sending a note to Mrs. —, stating that he had intended to call, but was prevented by his engagement with Dawkins. This device pleased him much, for he could venture to introduce a compliment in a note which he would have blushed to utter in person. He accordingly addressed himself to the task, and after writing and rejecting more than one, he at last hit upon a form of expression which pleased him. He instantly despatched the note, and went to join Dawkins with a lighter heart than he had anticipated; for he had now got over the painful preliminary of making his first advance to an acquaintance with the most fascinating woman he had ever seen. How the affair might end, he as yet knew not; but he cherished the hope that he should soon know in what light he was to regard Mrs. —.

CHAPTER XV.

Gambling and intriguing.

THE whist party turned out very different from the expectations formed respecting it, for the disputant did not think fit to make his appearance; a circumstance which seemed to give Dawkins great annoyance, and incited him to commence anew his demonstrations to Percy, that he had played honourably on the previous evening, a thing about which the youth had never taken any interest. To one more experienced in reading mankind than Percy, the anxiety of his friend on this point would have proved a strong ground of suspicion; for the guilty are always feverishly desirous to assert their innocence, even when it is not questioned. The disputant, if he were not one of the set, had probably made some discoveries respecting his antagonist, which had prevented him from joining the party; or, what was not unlikely, it may have been altogether a scheme on the part of Dawkins to get Percy himself to take the vacant hand, and thus break the ice towards the prosecution of deeper designs.

Whether this had been previously planned or not, the proposal was made; but Percy was still in his absent mood, and unfit either for play or company. Dawkins got quite exasperated at this, and was on the point of quarrelling with Percy, had not one of the party interfered, and proposed an adjournment to the theatre, postponing their rubber till another opportunity. Dawkins, after some demur, agreed, perceiving, doubtless, that his impatience might betray him, and prematurely expose his plans (whatever these might be) before they were ripe for operation. Percy, however, was in no humour for theatricals, and pleaded indisposition to get off from the set, and indulge his anxieties alone.

He had no sooner got rid of his companions than he hurried away to Mrs. —'s, not with the intention of calling (he could not presume, he thought, to do this after sending his note), but with the hope of seeing what company might be entering or departing, or – in fact he could not well analyse his motive. While pacing along the foot-way in melancholy mood, it struck him that she might possibly answer his note next morning, though he had not requested such a favour. This notion, slight as the foundation for it was, put him in high hopes, and after a good deal of extravagant castle-building,[148] he went home to dream over the prospects in which he had foolishly indulged.

Next morning he watched for the knock of the postman with as much intensity as if his doom had depended on it. He got up at least two hours earlier than usual, as people will do in such cases, under the false notion that this may speed 'the lazy foot of time;'[149] but it only served to put him in a passion with his watch, which he applied again and again to his ear to ascertain if it had not actually stopped. He threw up the window-sash, and scrutinized every passenger whom be supposed to be in the least like a postman; and in his haste, as he confessed, positively stopped a postman who was on his way to another district, to inquire for the expected letter.

At length, to his inexpressible joy, a note did come to him – the address in a pretty female hand too. He tore open the seal with breathless anxiety, and ran his eye like lightning over the contents; but though it really was from Mrs. —, and very kindly inviting him to one of her *soirées*,[150] I think he called it, there was nothing in it to satisfy the doubts which harassed him respecting her. He thought it would be very strange indeed, if, after all this, she could be married. At all events, if it were so, she must certainly have had her husband's consent to the invitation, though she did not mention him in her note. He was more pleased, however, with the idea of her being a widow; and having concluded upon this as the true state of the case, he waited with great impatience for the appointed hour, which (according to his country notions, and in his state of mind,) appeared to be unconscionably late.

Percy did not choose to describe to me so minutely his reception on this evening as he had done with regard to the former one. His recollections, indeed, of all that had happened to him from this time forth were so painful, that he was unwilling to dwell upon them; yet from what he did say, I was enabled to make out the main facts of his story up to the time when I so luckily rescued him from the water.

Before he discovered that Mrs. — was *not*, as he had sanguinely hoped, a widow, she had entangled him so deeply that he could no longer muster courage to escape from her fascinations. He became spell-bound, and rushed upon destruction, which he plainly saw, but could not avoid. When the appalling fact flashed on him that he was paying his court, and surrendering his best affections, to a married lady, he was shocked beyond expression. He was not yet bronzed by the shameless effrontery, (so lamentably common in this profligate age) of exulting in criminal intrigues.[151] He had too much good old-fashioned country morality for this. But the best principles may be upset by the storms of passion, and Percy soon found, to his cost, that a smile from Mrs. — was too powerful to be combated by abstract principles of morality: thus, like Adam, falling into the snare that was laid for him:

Against his better knowledge not *deceived*.
But fondly *overcome* by female charms.[152]

The chief excuses for his conduct were furnished him by the lady herself, whose husband, it appeared, usually spent his nights in Curzon Street[153] with a mistress for whom he kept up an expensive establishment, leaving her quite at liberty to do as she pleased. This was a sort of excuse, though a very weak and wicked one, for the lady; but it was none for Percy, who, however, by dint of sophistication, considered it as rendering the crime comparatively pardonable, and calculated to quiet in part those twinges of conscience which recurred the more frequently the more he endeavoured to repress them.

Other excuses, still less tenable, were artfully suggested to Percy, drawn from the common example of the fashionable world, where *liaisons*[154] of this kind were almost as common as marriage itself. They had been customary indeed, it was urged, among distinguished people in all ages of the world, from King David and the Trojan Prince[155] to the present times; and why, therefore, might not they be allowed to follow the illustrious examples of the great in defiance of crabbed morality and gossiping scandal? This wicked sophistry had considerable effect in removing Percy's scruples and unhinging his best resolves; and all his deliberations and determinations were too frail to save him from plunging deeper and deeper into error and crime.

But what motive could Mrs. — have for thus misleading a young and unsophisticated gentleman from the path of rectitude? At the very first glance, it did not appear to me that a lady of her caste could be so readily swayed by personal considerations as Percy's story seemed to imply. She must have some deeper aim than amorous gratification, otherwise she would not have been so eager to pounce upon him, as she had done, the moment he had been introduced. From all that I had heard of Dawkins also, who had taken him to Mrs. —, I augured that there had been mischief intended; but whether Dawkins had merely introduced him to help off any suspicions he might conceive about play, and lead him on by degrees to gamble till he was ruined, or, whether he had acted as a purveyor of *pigeons* for Mrs. —'s select parties, does not clearly appear; though the latter supposition is the more probable, and derives confirmation from the circumstance of Dawkins, after the evening of the whist-party, discontinuing his pressing attentions to Percy (being then, perhaps, engaged in the pursuit of other game,) whom he, no doubt, considered as fairly hunted into the toils. There can be little scruple, however, in believing, if this were the case, that Dawkins had, at first setting out, other views in the affair, which circumstances, best known to himself, might probably have conspired to baffle.

The views of Mrs. — upon Percy were, I was convinced, of a pecuniary kind; and her object, in attracting him, to smooth the way more effectually for successful plunder. Nevertheless, I could not well understand why both Dawkins and she had taken so much trouble, when they must have perceived at once how manageable Percy was. The only explanation of this which I could fancy was, that they were well aware he had not yet the actual command of money, and were afraid of losing him by premature measures; at the same time, they might, perhaps, contemplate the double game of *lending* him money (forged bank-notes would answer their purpose) upon bonds, or other recognizances; and thus, one way or other, plundering him of his last guinea.

This proved, in fact, to be the very snare which had been laid for the poor young man, though I have a notion that the catastrophe[156] was kept for some months from bursting over him by some consideration (probably personal) on the part of the lady, so far as such a woman, amidst the whirl of dissipation, could feel any thing like affection. It was impossible, of course, this should last longer than any novelty which engrosses for a time, then palls, and is finally forgotten to give place to some other object destined to the same career. But be that as it may, Percy was slowly dragged on to his destruction by silken cords. He was not even allowed time to pause and reflect on the consequences of his folly; for no sooner was one scene of dissipation ended than another was contrived, and he made no effort to get out of the current which was sweeping him along to inevitable perdition.

A considerable time had elapsed before Percy was initiated into the mysteries of losing his money; but when, by a series of manœuvres, he at length found himself seated at Mrs. —'s gambling-tables, (which were regularly kept up, though with all possible privacy,) and when he saw guinea after guinea escaping from his purse never to return, he felt even more compunction of conscience than he had done on first finding himself the gallant of a profligate lady of fashion. But here also he was involved beyond the power of retracting; for he was both under the spell of female influence to urge him on, and also plunged in the vortex of gambling, from which nobody ever escapes except by miracle.

In the mean time he was forced to borrow largely (on his expected property) at exorbitant premiums, and was cajoled the while by Mrs. — with hopes that, by some fortunate run of luck, he would not only clear all his premiums, but double or triple his fortune, how large soever it might be. Percy, of course, was ready to believe whatever she chose to assert; and though he was at first extremely reluctant to raise money in the way alluded to, yet this reluctance gradually wore off, or was mastered by the stronger desire of retrieving his losses, or rather of gaining an immense overplus, the notion always uppermost in the mind of a really honourable gambler, unacquainted, as Percy certainly was, with the gross frauds and tricks of sharpers by profession.

Still, the farther he ventured in his stakes and bets, the farther he seemed to be from the attainment of his object, although he had frequently such extraordinary runs of luck, that he imagined himself just upon the point of realizing all the golden hopes with which Mrs. — had filled his fancy. On one occasion in particular, he had in the course of the night gained, in money and bonds (fabricated perhaps for the purpose), upwards of seven thousand pounds. This was unquestionably an irresistible inducement to *proceed* in so lucrative a speculation; but fortune soon changed her smiles into frowns, and instead of seven thousand pounds *gained*, he was glad to escape with a *loss* of two or three thousand, which he had recently borrowed of one of Mrs. —'s friends, who was always ready to supply his wants on the usual terms.

Meanwhile, the affairs of his late uncle having been brought to a settlement, the executors, in conformity to the will, transferred to Percy money and property to a very large amount. The precise sum he did not mention; but it could not have been less (as I estimated from different items which he casually recounted) than a plum,[157] and probably a great deal more – a sum far too large to be entrusted to the management of one so inexperienced. Considering the terms on which he now was with Mrs. —, it cannot be wondered at that she would be among the first to learn these good news, if good they might be called. To Percy himself they proved to be the *worst* news which he had ever received, as they hastened on that destruction which had for so long a time been hanging over him. Following up the plot which had been laid, now was the moment for the conspirators to secure their prey, to prevent it from falling into other hands.

Percy of course would not disclose to Mrs. — his transactions with farmer Grinstead, the consequences of which he would now have to feel by payment of the bond, it having been made due when he should come to his uncle's property. The farmer had received information of the proceedings of the executors almost as early as Percy himself; and it is not to be imagined that he would be slow in securing the money while it was yet attainable. Accordingly, on the very next day the bond was presented for payment; at which time, before taking it up, Percy ought to have insisted on an acknowledgment cancelling all future claims upon him on the same subject. This he had not foresight enough to think of; but he was not long in being made aware of the consequences of his neglect. Grinstead had scarcely got the money safe in his grasp, when he gave Percy to understand that he would forthwith commence an action against him for breach of promise of marriage in spite of the compromise, for which the latter could produce no voucher.

This was a piece of deliberate swindling, of which Percy had no conception. He had already, indeed, discovered Grinstead to be a knave, but thought he might have been well contented with the payment of the bond, without loading his conscience with a second villainous plot to gratify his avarice; so little did poor Percy yet know of the extent of human depravity. The very dawn of his good fortune was thus overclouded with too certain forebodings of the gathering storm, which was soon to overtake him. He could not help telling Grinstead, in plain terms, that he looked upon him as a scoundrel; but the farmer only replied by a sarcastic laugh, and told him to guard his words better, if he did not wish to have another action against him for slander, to accompany that already determined on for breach of promise. Percy could endure this no longer; and was proceeding to make forcible ejectment of the body of the aforesaid Grinstead into the street or the gutter, as it might be; but the farmer, who appeared to have a competent knowledge of the laws relating to the rights of the subject, bawled out 'assault and battery!' and Percy was again counter-checked in his proceedings.

With all the smooth cunning which villainy knows so well how to assume, Grinstead quashed his wrath at this unceremonious treatment, and advanced to Percy with a simper, as if they had been the best friends in the world. Percy was even more astonished at this than at his previous conduct, and could not imagine what the farmer could now mean, unless his conscience had all of a sudden smitten him to make an apology, and return part of the money. These, however, were the very last things which Grinstead would have dreamed of: he knew too well the sort of man he had to deal with, to forego his fraudulent claims merely for the purpose of humouring his own conscience. His object, as it had been all along, was *money, money;* and in its pursuit he was not ashamed to ask Percy to compromise the *three* actions, for breach of promise, slander, and assault, by the forfeiture of a few more thousands, which he could now so well spare!

Percy, however, did not choose to comply on the instant with this impudent proposal, but said he would take time to consider of it. This was precisely what Grinstead wished to avoid; and, rather than consent to it, he was willing to reduce the terms of the 'compromise,' so as to make them quite accord with Mr. Percy's convenience. Accordingly, after exhausting all the plans which he could devise, he at last proposed to grant a release in full for the three actions threatened in lieu of a single thousand pounds, which Percy was fool enough to add to the five thousand of the bond. This time, however, he took care to have a release properly executed before he parted with his cash.

Grinstead was scarcely gone, when a host of other bills and bonds for money advanced came pouring in upon him from the country; and of course he had to draw largely on his funds to meet these records of his past expenditure. A mere trifle, however, sufficed for them all, in comparison with what would be required to settle with Mrs. —'s friend, who had so *kindly* lent him several large sums already lost at the gaming-table. His country bonds brought the latter strongly to his memory, and he accordingly set aside a sum for their speedy payment.

How anxious soever Mrs. — must have been to prevent any of this good money from passing beyond her grasp, she was not aware of what was going on; and being altogether ignorant of his country bonds, could have no idea of interfering to prevent his taking them up; but she had the idea of getting as much as possible, if she could not get all, and as soon too as the execution of her plots would admit.

CHAPTER XVI.

Easy methods of getting rid of a fortune.

THE actual possession of what Percy had looked forward to so long, drove all thoughts of gambling from his mind; for why should he now trouble himself with large winnings at play, when he had already more than he knew what to do with? The store appeared to him inexhaustible; for after having paid off the demands which had given him uneasiness, and which he had been in the habit of considering enormous, there was still (according to his arithmetic) a residue sufficient to last him for life.

This frame of mind was not at all to the taste of Mrs. —, who, like all her class, was feverishly eager to grasp at money, and had anticipated, the first night he subsequently passed at her house, an extraordinary harvest of golden plunder. What wine might do it was impossible to tell; but in his sober moments Percy was fully resolved to abandon play for ever. He had not, indeed, calculated on the influence which Mrs. — had over him, and which was sufficient to put to flight much stronger resolutions than he could form. A sally of wit or of playful ridicule would be enough to unhinge any preconcerted line of conduct which he might have taken the trouble to lay down for himself.

The first thing, indeed, which she said to him was, that he could now afford to sport a few thousands to keep up the respectability of her set; and though he should get the name of a *roué*,[158] that would be the best passport to the highest circles of fashion. He attempted to parry this by the argument which had weighed most with himself, namely, that he did not now *require* to play for gain, and thought he might spend his spare thousands to better purpose than losing them at cards. She readily replied to this, that if he were averse to playing at the table for the credit of her establishment, she would challenge him herself to a few throws at dice, a proposition which she was sure he could not withstand. In short, she teased and bantered him till he consented to give her the chance of winning a few hundreds by way of passing the time. This was a bad beginning, and a palpable renouncement of his resolution, which of course would in the end lead to all the lady desired.

The process of plunder, however, seemed to go on much more tardily than had perhaps been anticipated; for Percy kept so far to his resolution, that he would not join the gamblers at the table as heretofore; and though he lost a hundred or so every night to Mrs. —, he steadily refused to go into what is called deep play, on the very reasonable ground that he did not wish either to win or lose large sums. Had he always been as prudent, he might have saved himself from a great many of the troubles in which his folly involved him; but Mrs. — was altogether too crafty to be baffled even by his steadiest resolutions; for when one device failed, she had a thousand others ready to put in requisition. She would not of course be long in discovering that her purpose could not be effectually accomplished by means of the dice-box, how dextrously soever she might manage; and afraid, it may justly be imagined, that if much time were lost, somebody else might have the *honour* of plucking the young man, she fell upon a more speedy method of gaining her ends.

Accordingly, instead of challenging him to try the chance of a few throws as usual, the next evening, as soon as he arrived, she put on an air of profound grief, as if some serious misfortune had befallen her; took him apart with greater appearance of secrecy than she had ever done, and employed all the blandishments in her possession to excite his interest and compassion. She refused a considerable time to disclose the cause of her grief, for the purpose, no doubt, of making her dupe more eager and curious in his inquiries. At last he wrung from her a confession, that she was in great difficulty from being short of money to support the credit of her gaming-table. She had been compelled to withdraw a large sum to meet the immediate expenses of the establishment, and there had been an unprecedented run of ill-luck against the pool, which she did not know how to get over. It was, however, quite a temporary embarrassment, she said; and if she could get a little assistance for a week or so, all would be right again. It was most unfortunate, too, for her, that her friend, who used to advance such sums as Percy had formerly required, was out of town, otherwise he could have raised her any money she might please to want at a few hours' notice.

After such a tale, heightened as it would be by tears and all the moving eloquence of beauty in distress, Percy, supposing it quite genuine, was liberal enough to offer his assistance to any extent which the lady might require; but this seemed to give her still more uneasiness. She could not think of troubling him in such a case, though he was the dearest friend she had in the world, and there was nobody else to whom she could unburden her mind. Besides, as her embarrassments did not proceed from real poverty, but were occasioned wholly by a temporary want of ready cash, – it was a storm which would blow over in a few days.

These representations (as was obviously intended) only made Percy the more anxious to relieve her; and reiterating his offers of service, such pressing kindness made her soon retract her refusal, at the same time pretending that she had no idea what sum might be requisite. Percy said this was of no consequence, he having a large amount lodged at his banker's, previous to its investiture in the funds,[159] according to advice given him; that any part of it was quite at her disposal; and indeed, for that matter, he would sign a blank cheque to be filled up at her pleasure!

This was a piece of simplicity and infatuation which Mrs. — could scarcely have calculated upon his committing, fool as she must have known him to be; but since he had made an offer of the kind, she was not slow in improving on it, and hinted that, as he was so very liberal, he might as well give her *two or three* of those same blanks, – not that she would probably want more than a hundred pounds or so, yet it would be as well to be provided against unexpected demands. She backed this impudent and insidious request with her most winning smiles and caresses, so that Percy hesitated not, in the warmth of his liberality, to sign for her about half-a-dozen blank cheques, the only acknowledgement which he received consisting in hollow protestations of gratitude, as profuse as they were deceitful. Considered as a piece of gallantry, it would have been sacrilege to require the lady to give him any document guaranteeing payment. This was the very thing, of course, which she wished to elude, as Percy too soon found to his cost.

No sooner had this artful woman obtained her long-anticipated prize, and in a form too which she could not have hoped for, than she excused herself from remaining any longer with him that evening, upon the plea of having to attend to important concerns which could not stand over. Percy had not foreseen this movement, or perhaps he would not have been so ready with his cheques. In fact, he looked forward to a few hours of small talk, flirting, and gallantry, as the least premium he could expect for his generosity. Mrs. — it appeared, had a very different notion of the affair, and wanted to pursue the speediest measures for converting the cheques into cash, and take counsel of some of her advisers how she might contrive to fill them up with very large sums without exciting suspicion at the banker's, and causing a reference to Percy himself, which might not be expedient when *thousands* were to be drawn for instead of *hundreds*.

So far all was going on as well as villainy could desire against the honest unsuspecting Percy, who would at no distant period be, at this rate, plundered of his last guinea before his eyes were opened to the system. The effrontery, indeed, with which the whole design was conducted might have alarmed him, had he not been of so really good a natural disposition, that he could scarcely conceive such depravity in others as was now directed against himself. The scene, however, was drawing to a close, and the splendor which had dazzled him was about to exhibit a very different-tinted glare.

He called the following evening on Mrs. — rather earlier than usual, to make up, as he fondly fancied, for the time which had been curtailed at his last interview. To his utter astonishment, he was told that she had gone out of town, but was expected back next day at farthest. She had told him nothing of this, nor had she even left him a line in explanation of her sudden departure, though Percy imagined this was the least she ought to have done when under such peculiar obligations to him. He thought that perhaps her absence regarded some important business connected with her embarrassments, and this led him to think of his blank cheques, at first with a sort of regret, and finally with some little suspicion that all was not right; yet, on the other hand, he conceived it next to impossible that she should deceive him, and appear all the while so extremely complaisant and loving. Little was he aware of the duplicity which so frequently lurks in female smiles, or of the smooth serpent tongue concealing the poisonous sting, ready to strike when opportunity offers. Had the banking-house been open, however, he would have gone directly thither to ascertain what sums had been drawn for with his cheques; but at this hour he could obtain no access there, and was forced to spend the night in sleepless conjectures.

On the morrow he was at his banker's the moment the doors were opened, and was informed that all the cheques had been presented by a Mr. Johnson, who represented himself to be a stock-broker, and said he had been commissioned to buy stock for Mr. Percy to the amount of all which was in the banker's hands except a mere trifle; and that the money had accordingly been paid to him, as the cheques were considered to be genuine, and the signatures correct. This, indeed, comprised all the ready cash which Percy now possessed, after paying his various borrowings and debts of honour. He was so taken by surprise at the intelligence, that he could scarcely believe it. He could not imagine it possible for Mrs. — to deceive him so far. She had only pretended to want a few hundreds, and here was the greater part of his fortune swept away at once, without giving him the slightest hint; and what was more, the man Johnson, who had presented the cheques, had made a false representation, which unequivocally showed the intention of fraud.

He hurried from the banker's in great perturbation, to see whether Mrs. — had returned, but was told she had sent word not to be expected for a week or two. The servant pretended he did not know her address; but if Mr. Percy wished to leave any message, it would be despatched by a messenger who knew where to go, and who proposed setting out in the afternoon.

Percy was thus non-plussed in every quarter, and ignorant how to act. Shame would not allow him to confess to his banker the real state of the case, nor to consult with his solicitor, who might have been able to take some steps to recover the whole or part of the money. He resolved rather to bear his loss than acknowledge he had been befooled by an intriguing woman. This resolution, however, it was easier to form than to abide by; for he would soon be so short of ready money, that it would be no easy matter to conceal his embarrassments. He had still, it is true, considerable property left, which might be converted into cash; but this could not be readily effected without an awkward exposure of his necessities among his friends.

Notwithstanding the plain facts which thus proved to him that Mrs. — had taken iniquitous advantage of his liberality, he was very loth to admit the conviction, and devised all imaginable excuses for her, even going so far as to fancy the cheques might have been stolen by Johnson or some of his confederates. He had evidently, indeed, become so much attached to this female harpy, that he could not force his mind to believe her guilty of fraud; and of course never for a moment admitted the notion that her encouragement (or rather courting) of his own gallantries was more wicked and criminal by far, than the affair of the cheques. Conscience had not yet begun to punish him for this part of his conduct, though he had been, not unjustly as I thought, punished in his purse.

He waited with great impatience for several days, expecting that Mrs. — would come to town and give him some explanation of her extraordinary behaviour; but a full week passed without producing any farther intelligence than he had obtained when he first called; and he had consequently to abandon, one by one, all the excuses which he had ingeniously set up, because, even if she had lost the cheques, or they had been stolen from her, she ought to have given him immediate information (at least by letter) of so important an occurrence.

When this painful conclusion was at length forced upon him, he had to set about devising in what manner he was to raise a few pounds for his daily expenses, – to such a state had his folly in a few weeks reduced him. He tried to borrow some money from those who had before accommodated him, but soon found, by bitter experience, that he was no longer looked on as his uncle's heir, nor could he in this way procure a single guinea! It is highly probable, indeed, that those to whom he applied, as being Mrs. —'s own friends, were sufficiently apprised of the state of his finances to be on their guard. He perceived, therefore, that he had no other resource than the disposal of his remaining property for ready money, how much soever such a step might expose him to unpleasant remark.

It was very soon after this time that I began to notice the singular proceedings of Mrs. — in the way of shopping; and when I heard Percy's story, I inferred that she must have very quickly lost or disposed of all the money she had procured for his cheques, enormous as the sum was, otherwise she would not so soon have had recourse to the dangerous practice of passing forged bank-notes. It is highly probable, indeed, that Johnson, whom she had employed to cash the cheques, had taken care to help himself to a large share of the booty, or that her husband (who perhaps possessed more influence over her movements than she pretended to Percy,) had laid his hands upon the whole, and had, it might be, squandered it in gambling. Ill-gotten wealth, indeed, seldom prospers; and it is very likely some such fate as I have just conjectured followed the money so ungratefully filched from Percy.

How long Mrs. — had been in town before her victim was apprised of it he did not know; for she was always denied, as at first, whenever he called. My own opinion is, that she had never gone out of town at all, though it did not appear that she was very particular in concealing herself, as Percy one day observed her carriage in Piccadilly, and was quite certain she was in it; but it drove on, and he lost sight of it, while he was procuring a hackney-coach to give it chace. He did not neglect to call both that same evening and the next morning, but with no better success than before.

This could scarcely fail to irritate the most placid man who ever existed. It drove Percy almost mad. Such treatment was even worse, he thought, than cajoling him out of his blank cheques, for it deprived him at 'one fell swoop'[160] of both his money and his mistress. He was determined, however, now that he was convinced she was in town, to get access to her by some means or other, were it for no other purpose than to vent his indignation. He therefore prepared to watch her movements; and his knowledge of her habits, and the hours which she was accustomed to keep, enabled him on the following day to trace her to St. James's Street, and just as she was alighting from her carriage, he stepped up to accost her with as much forbearance as he could assume in the public street.

He was thunder-struck (though it was what he might well have expected,) when she pretended, with the utmost *nonchalance*, that she did not know him, and declared she could have nothing to say to one who was not of her acquaintance.

Poor Percy, it may easily be imagined, would feel himself, from this fresh instance of ingratitude, deep 'in the gall of bitterness.'[161] He turned away from the Jezabel[162] without uttering a word, for his heart was near bursting to think that such a thing could really have happened to him. It exhibited a view of human nature, and of female knavery, which he could never have dreamed of, and could scarcely bring himself to believe, though he was not able to get rid of the evidence of his senses. After enduring this galling insult from a woman whom he had fondly fancied to be every thing that was generous and high-spirited, he felt himself ready to undergo any other species of degradation.

Under this impression, he resolved to part with such portions of his remaining property as were most likely to bring him an immediate supply; and for this purpose he could devise no better way than applying to the *same* money-lenders who had so recently refused his offer of personal security, but who might possibly change their tone if something more tangible was placed in their possession. By resorting to them, also, he would escape the disgrace of letting his other friends know any thing of his embarrassed circumstances. He concluded, therefore, upon immediately taking this step, and proceeded with all the coolness which he could muster to prepare the necessary documents.

His proceedings, however, were interrupted by the very unexpected arrival of a note from Mrs. —, purporting to be an apology for her conduct towards him, but at the same time reserving an explanation till she saw himself, if he would take the trouble of calling upon her as usual in the evening. He did not know what to think of this strange epistle; it appeared more like a dream than any of the things which had recently befallen him. He did suspect, indeed, that it might be intended to entrap him farther; but the high opinion which he had previously formed of Mrs. — still lingered in his mind, and made him imagine that she had only been playing off a joke upon him in the case of the cheques, and that the money would still be all safe.

This, in truth, was his final hope, and he clung to it as pertinaciously as if it had been founded on the most absolute certainty. He forgot, of course, that it was not very like a joke to use a false pretext, in order to lull any suspicions which might have arisen in the mind of the banker when the cheques were presented. He was, at all hazards, resolved to keep the appointment, whatever might be the event.

There could not be a doubt that Mrs. — had some new design upon the poor fellow, whom she had found to be so easily gulled; though one might have thought she had got enough, for once, to satisfy her avarice. It struck me that she might have obtained intelligence of the nature and value of his remaining property, and thence formed some plan for swindling him out of the whole. If this were so, she must have calculated very largely indeed upon his simplicity; for after the affair of the cheques he was not very likely to part with any thing more without better security than her loving word of honour.

On going at the time appointed, Mrs. — received him in the most caressing manner imaginable, with a profusion of apologies as fulsome and flattering as they were unmeaning; but she said not a word withal about the cheques. She persuaded him, however, that her pretending not to know him in St. James's Street was a piece of cunning to give the lie to a report which she said had been gossiped over the town respecting their intimacy, and which she did not wish exactly to reach the ears of Mr. —, lest it might involve Percy in trouble; for though her husband left her time pretty much at her own disposal, he would be forced to take notice of any very flagrant gallantry or flirtation which might be maliciously reported to him; and she was by no means certain, from hints which he had let fall, that this was not the case now.

Percy was sufficiently willing to take all this in good part; but still the cheques stuck in his throat, as did also the long disappearance of Mrs. — from town; though he was so subdued by her flattering manner, that he could not find courage to mention that which preyed so deeply on his mind. It was absolutely necessary, however, to come to an understanding upon this important point, before there could be any of the former harmony between them; and in spite of all her caressing attentions and merry gaiety, he could not help being moody and absent, the unfailing consequence of a guinea-less purse.

The crafty dame must soon have perceived this, and could be at no loss to know the cause, though it did not suit her views to begin the explanation. After a good deal of manœuvring, she at length brought him to hint at the money which had been obtained by means of his cheques. At this she affected the utmost astonishment, and was quite indignant that he should suppose such a thing done by her connivance. She had only drawn for a few hundreds, which she would repay, she said, in a week or two, and professed to be altogether ignorant of the very large sum which had actually been obtained by Johnson. She farther pretended to have no knowledge at all of this Johnson, and said she had passed the cheques to different people in the ordinary course of payments.

Poor Percy knew not what to make of this confident denial, though he was glad to learn that she would so soon return the few hundreds which she confessed to having received. His suspicions of her, though not altogether removed, were now much fainter, and he was half convinced that she herself had been imposed on by Johnson, or some of his confederates. Be it as it might, however, the money was gone, to all appearance irretrievably; and though he might hope to recover what Mrs. — confessed to have drawn, I was pretty certain that he would in the end be deceived even in that.

As the lady was suggesting a thousand imaginary ways by which the cheques might have been altered after they went out of her possession, a thundering knock was heard at the door which threw her into great terror and agitation, as she knew it, she said, to be her husband's, who had lately taken a fit of watching her very closely, on account, as she supposed, of some malicious reports respecting her evening visiters. She knew not, she added, what to do with Percy, as he might take a fancy to search every corner and concealment in the house, which he had more than once done of late.

Percy, of coarse, was not a little frightened at this announcement, particularly as they were at the moment in Mrs. —'s boudoir, the first place to which the furious husband was likely to come. He ran to the window, threw up the sash, and would have made a grand leap, at the hazard of his limbs, had she not caught hold of him, and, with a suppressed scream, intreated him not to endanger himself rashly, saying she would endeavour to conceal him. She accordingly, under this pretext, hurried him into the adjoining bed-chamber, and made him get into bed, while she covered him snugly up, and was in the very act of drawing the curtains, when Mr. — gave a loud knock at the door of the boudoir, and she left poor Percy in all the agony of fear lest his hiding-place might be discovered.

This bed, indeed, was the very place, of all others, where in prudence he ought not to have been, under such circumstances; and if he had given the subject a minute's consideration, he would, I think, have refused to go into it. But he was destined to be infatuated and played upon by those who knew how to take advantage of him. There can be extremely little doubt, indeed, that the whole was a preconcerted scheme between the lady and her husband, to entrap Percy for the nefarious purpose of obtaining more money. Whether they were aware of his present embarrassment does not appear; but even if they were, they must have had some guess of his remaining property, or they would have taken no farther trouble about him.

The lady bustled off to let in her obstreperous husband, who began to rate her in no gentle terms, as Percy inferred from the loud tone of his voice, though he could not at first distinguish what was said, except that he fancied hearing his own name, or something like it, a circumstance which did not tend to make him feel more comfortable on his bed of thorns.

After a good deal of altercation, and, as Percy thought, some whispering in the intervals, Mr. – at length insisted upon getting admission into the bed-chamber, which the lady appeared strongly to resist, both by persuasion, and by personally defending the door. Percy, it may well be conceived, saw nothing before him but detection, and cursed the hour that he had ever entered the house. He started up, and again intended to try the window, or to get under the bed, or into some corner, when Mr. – overpowered the personal opposition of his wife, and burst into the room, breathing death and fury towards whomsoever he might find there.

Percy was not, as I think I have before remarked, of a cowardly disposition, though soft and easily imposed upon. In the present instance, his courage was greatly damped by the consciousness of his being in rather a criminal and critical predicament; yet when he foresaw that he would be compelled to brave the vengeance of Mr. – , he resolved to make a stand at least for his life.

Mr. – went directly to the bed, as if he were proceeding on particular information; found Percy hidden under the bed-clothes, and swore the most horrid oaths that he would cut him to pieces. Percy got upon his legs in a moment, and darted past his assailant into the boudoir, with the intention of effecting his escape; but they were prepared, it seems, for this movement, for the door of the boudoir was fast locked, and poor Percy fairly caught in the snare which had evidently been baited for him.

When he perceived that his retreat was thus cut off, and escape hopeless, he turned about to face his foe in the deadly combat which he fully expected would ensue. He did not anticipate, however, that he would have to contend against fire-arms, which would render any personal effort of no avail; but so it was, for Mr. – was prepared to receive him with a brace of pistols, one of which he instantly presented, and threatened to shoot him through the head. Mrs. —, in conformity to female etiquette, screamed out, and placed herself before Percy to protect him; but she soon shifted her ground when she was herself threatened with danger. Percy, therefore, had no resource left but to submit to be fired at, if Mr. — chose to do so, or to beg for his life, which the first law of nature prompted him to do. There seemed, however, to be no mercy in the breast of the enraged husband, who appeared to thirst greedily for Percy's blood. Mrs. —, after being driven from her defensive position, began to entreat, with great seeming earnestness, for the life of the victim she had beguiled into her toils; but her husband, so far from relenting, grew more furious, and again threatened to make her the first object of his vengeance, if she did not desist from her solicitations. Percy in turn begged for her life, and, to enforce his petition, said he would be most willing to agree to any terms which Mr. — might choose to dictate.

As this was, in all probability, the very point on account of which the whole plot had been devised, it is not to be wondered at that it tended in some degree to mollify the wrath of Mr. —; but it was with great difficulty, and after much pressing, that he could be brought to listen to any accommodation. At length, he condescended to ask what terms Percy would propose, to save himself from being shot through the head upon the spot, which was the doom threatened. This question was one which he was exceedingly puzzled to answer; but Mr. — came to the grand point at once, by saying that he must have a round sum of money in lieu[163] of his forbearance.

A more unfortunate time could not have occurred to Percy for such a demand, as he had no money for his own immediate wants, much less for a purpose like this; and the Grinstead business came not very seasonably to his memory, bringing the suggestion that it would take some thousands to purchase his release from this ill-fated boudoir. He accordingly hesitated, and stammered out he knew not what; for this money matter had terrified him much more than any personal danger in which he might be. Mr. —, however, left him no time to hesitate, but with the cocked pistol in his hand pressed him to name what sum he was disposed to pay down.

When he found there was no avoiding it, Percy candidly told him that he had no money at his command, and it would be necessary to delay till he could retrieve himself from some recent embarrassments. His tormentor, however, had no notion of being put off with any such excuse. With him, as he said, it was money or vengeance, and if he chose to bring an action against him, he would lay the damages at not less than fifteen or twenty thousand pounds. This was a thunder-stroke to Percy, for the whole of his property, even were it made the most of, would not amount to so much, since his loss of the very large sum by means of those accursed cheques. He candidly told Mr. —, therefore, that he was not worth so much in the world, even if he were willing to give it; but this confession, though it really was the truth, was not believed, and payment on the spot, of one or other of these sums, was peremptorily insisted on.

Percy was driven to absolute distraction by this accumulation of misfortunes. On the one hand, there was this infuriate husband ready to shoot him, as he believed, though it was, in my opinion, very far from his intention; on the other, there were his embarrassed finances, and the new demand upon him, which would sweep away all he had left. Even were an action at law to be the result, his property, and, what to Percy was no less, his character, would irretrievably suffer. But Mr. — left him no alternative. He was a much more formidable person to deal with than old Grinstead, bad as *he* was; for, independent of his personal powers, which were by no means contemptible, his connections in the great world had an imposing influence on the idea which Percy had conceived of him, even before he had so unexpectedly and unfortunately encountered him.

At length, to end the altercation, Mr. — proposed three things for him to choose between. First, and principally, to stand fire and have a brace of bullets lodged in his head or heart, as the case might be; secondly, to sign a bond, with judgment, for fifteen or twenty thousand pounds; or, thirdly, to pay him down a thousand pounds, or a bond for the same, on the spot, as the purchase-money of a respite for twenty-four hours from fulfilling either of the other two conditions – at the same time giving in writing his word as a gentleman not to stir out of the boudoir. Percy did not long hesitate in making choice of the last of these hard conditions, as he had then some space left to hope for a favourable change in the storm which threatened him.

Upon his signing the documents prepared by Mr. —, he was left to ruminate on his misfortunes in solitude, the lady, of course, being ordered to a distant part of the house. His first thought was to attempt an escape; for though he had given his word as a gentleman, and in writing too, that he would not, yet he had the salvo[164] of his having been *forced* to do this, and no forced promise is binding.

He was by no means certain, however, that Mr. — trusted altogether to his word, otherwise, from his knowledge of the house, he thought he might have effected his purpose. If there was a watch set upon him, it would be a different matter; but he thought he would at all hazards try the window. To his great joy, they had forgotten to fasten it, though the height which he would have to leap was rather startling. The worst of it was, it did not look into the street, but into the back premises of the mansion. The stone walls, however, which enclosed the circumscribed spot designated a garden, were by no means high, and he thought he had performed a greater feat than scaling them. The window was higher than would be safe for him to leap from, particularly as he would have to make the pavement his landing-place; but it was possible to let himself down, if he could procure any thing strong enough to use for a rope.

In this exigency, accordingly, he thought it would be no harm to make free with the window-curtains, or the furniture of the ottomans;[165] though, upon consideration, he determined that it would be better to delay his operations till the night was farther advanced, to avoid interruption.

Meanwhile he turned over in his mind the consequences of his escape, among which the most appalling to him was the threatened action at law. He saw no means of avoiding this disgrace, but flying the country; and he would rather suffer death, he thought, than this. It was probably at this time, when the notion of committing suicide first entered his breast; though he said nothing of that to me, and I felt too much for his state of mind to draw him into any confession upon so distressing a subject. Whether his recent pecuniary difficulties, under circumstances which must have produced so much self-condemnation, had led him to think of terminating his existence, I have no way of knowing, though this is by no means improbable. I am more inclined to think that it might be rather an impulse of the moment, from the state of distraction into which he had been thrown by so many untoward circumstances.

When he deemed the night, or rather the morning, sufficiently advanced for his purpose, he commenced operations by tying and twisting together whatever he could find about the room wherewith to make his rope. He succeeded better than he had expected, and after some little delay, got the one end securely fastened so as to bear his weight, while he swung the other out at the window, by which to let himself down.

He descended without accident, and, to his great joy, found himself once more, as he thought, in comparative freedom. He hastened, therefore, to examine the walls, which it would also be necessary to scale, in order to reach the open street.

Here he was met by an obstacle which he had not anticipated, in the shape of a great tall fellow walking about like a soldier on guard. It was fortunate that he saw this man before he had advanced to reconnoitre the walls, and it was probable he had not himself been observed, for the window whence he had descended was not within sight of his *beat*, being screened by a projecting angle of the building. Having thus obtained an opportune hint to take care how he proceeded, he concealed himself with all the caution which fear on such occasions naturally suggests, endeavouring at the same time to watch the movements of the tall fellow, whose figure strongly reminded him of the waterman at Westminster Bridge; though, in the dark, the identity of the man must, of course, have been a mere conjecture. Percy could not understand why he was pacing about here at such an hour, if it were not for the purpose of preventing his escape; and yet, if this were the design, why had he not taken his stand immediately under the window?

After remaining for some time in his concealment, and perceiving the man pacing the same unvaried round, he thought he might venture to steal along by the side of the wall, to ascertain whether he could not elude the vigilance of the sentinel, if sentinel he were, and find some place over which he could effect his escape unperceived.

There were no lights in view, and the wall, from being high, rendered the shaded space dark enough to conceal him. He was on the opposite side of the court, or garden, to the man; and though he was near enough to hear his step, and to remark his making occasional visits to a snuff-box, he hoped that he might himself avoid detection. He was much alarmed, however, by the sudden opening of a door in a low building near to the left-hand wall, whence a faint light issued, as if from a lamp or candle at some distance within; and a lady, whom he recognised to be Mrs. — herself, made her appearance with a bag in her hand, such as he had seen her have for the gold to supply the pool at the gambling-table. If it were so (for he could not be quite certain in the dark), he thought this was a very singular place to deposit money.

When she was gone, the door was again shut; but the tall fellow accompanied her towards the house, while Percy could hear mutual whisperings going forward. This appeared to him very mysterious, and, while the fellow was absent, he stole over to the low building to see if he could make out what was doing there; for the light, he could perceive, was left burning after Mrs. —'s departure, and it was probable somebody was left with it, in charge, perhaps, of the cash, if she kept her strong-box there. Percy, of course, had too much of the feelings and high principles of a gentleman, to think of making any secret attack upon this same strong-box, even if he did discover it, and though it was most probably filled with the plunder of his own purse. Had it been my own case, it would, perhaps, have been the first thing which I should have devised, under such circumstances.

He got close to the door of the low building, but it was fast shut, and there was not the smallest chink through which he might observe any thing that was going on within. He could distinguish, indeed, certain sounds, as of some mechanical operation, such as the creaking of a mangle[166] at work; but he could not understand what it could be if it were not a mangle, though it was a singular time, he thought, for such work to be going forward.

He went all round the building to see whether he could not make something of this mangle-house, or depôt of money, for it seemed, according to his conjectures, to serve both purposes. All his prying, however, led to no farther discovery, and it had well nigh led to his own detection; for he heard the tall fellow returning at a quick pace, and had to make all imaginable haste to the farther end of the garden, to avoid encountering him.

Although Percy could not penetrate the mystery of the mangle-house, I perceived at once the value of his discovery; for I had extremely little doubt, taking all circumstances under consideration, that this was the bank-note manufactory, or something of the same illegal description. For if it had been any common operation, why carry it on at such an hour, and under the surveillance too of a sentinel? It was very unlikely, also, that a lady of Mrs. —'s habits would be looking after any of her domestic concerns at all, much less at such an hour as this. From all these considerations, I deemed Percy's account of this mangle-house, (if I may call it so) the most important which I had yet received from him, connected with the investigation that had led to our acquaintance. I did not, however, let him know what I thought upon the subject, lest he might take alarm at being brought in as an informer, but I resolved to proceed with all expedition upon the hint.

Percy could find no exit from the garden: the wall was too high to scale without the aid of a ladder, or something as a substitute; for, as he could not reach the top with his hand, there was no means of climbing over. He was consequently much worse off than before, exposed as he was to the night air; and if he should remain there till morning, he was sure to be detected, and did not know what construction Mr. — might put upon the circumstance in order to make farther demands on his purse. There was no help for him, however; he must brave the storm, rage as it might, for all his efforts to scale the wall were wholly fruitless.

It would have struck me at the first, in a dilemma like this, to have tried to bribe the sentinel; but the low state of Percy's purse probably made him think this hopeless, and he continued his efforts to scale the wall, till at length he alarmed the tall fellow, who came running to the spot, and demanded with a great oath what he wanted. Percy was speechless; for when he recognised the voice of the tall waterman, he had no hope of any lenient treatment, and reluctantly resigned himself to his fate. The tall fellow did not seem, indeed, to make much ceremony about the matter, and was preparing to make Percy's 'quietus,'[167] and put an end to his earthly troubles.

His conscience, however, seems to have checked him just as he was about to perpetrate the deed, and he repeated his interrogation in a still more rough and peremptory manner. Percy muttered out some unmeaning answer, upon which the fellow quickly recognised his *blindfolded* companion in the boat expedition, and this, as might have been expected, led to a temporary truce. Money of course, come how or whence it might, was the main pursuit with the sentinel, as well as with his superiors, and Percy was accordingly assailed with a fresh demand upon his now meagre purse. If all he then had could have tempted the fellow to connive at his escape, he would have given it cheerfully, though he knew not well when or where he was to procure another shilling; but he had no sum at command enough to satisfy the rapacity of the man, and no credit is ever allowed in such cases: it is an established rule of villainy which is never violated. What then was to be done? Percy would have promised him largely, though he did not well know how he might be able to fulfil any pecuniary engagement. The fellow, however, would listen to nothing except the chink of the ready cash, and told Percy that he must needs secure him as an intruder into a place where he had no right to be.

Finding himself thus disappointed, Percy, in the simplicity of his heart, then tried to excite the fellow's compassion, by candidly telling him part of his story; but his hearer was made of 'sterner stuff'[168] than to be moved by a tale of misfortune. He foresaw, perhaps, that securing Percy might be for his advantage as proving his vigilance; upon which notion I have no doubt it was, that he laid hold of the unfortunate young man, and dragged him back into the house.

Mr. — was not in the way, and though the lady certainly was, she took care not to make her appearance, so that the tall ruffian had to take the trouble upon himself of finding a strong room wherein to lodge his prisoner. He was not, it may be supposed, very nice in considering the subject of accommodation, and made no ceremony of thrusting Percy down into a cellar which was used for the stowage of every species of lumber; but what had probably most attracted him, in making the selection, was a massive door with a huge padlock, offering a strong token of its capability of being secured. Percy might well regret leaving the elegance of the boudoir for this wretched place, where, to add to his misery, he was left without a light.

He bethought him now, when it was too late, of crying out for help, with the faint hope of drawing the attention of some compassionate menial, or even of any chance passenger in the street, or of some of the inmates of the neighbouring houses. He had little faith, it is true, in any of the servants, for in the heyday of his visits he had not been liberal enough with regard to the article of *vails;*[169] that is, the domestics of such an establishment are never satisfied, since they necessarily see so much requiring hush-money, to bribe them to silence, that ordinary vails are looked upon with contempt. The chance, on the other hand, of making himself heard beyond the limits of the premises, shut up as he now was, appeared to be very small. He therefore abandoned this hopeless scheme, and again resigned himself to his fate. At this time, also, I imagine his thoughts may have been turned upon self-destruction; for he had the whole of the following day to ruminate upon his situation, with the exception of the incident of a visit of condolence from Mrs. — herself.

Notwithstanding the very strong causes of suspicion which he had against the lady, he could not help being rejoiced to see her, the more particularly too, as she had the kindness to bring him some breakfast, of which, in consequence of the agitation he had suffered, he stood very much in need. The crafty dame pretended that she did all this by stealth, and at the utmost peril to herself; but that she would hazard even her life for him, to save him from danger. In the present difficulty, however, she was extremely sorry she could lend him no assistance, for Mr. — had been so very strict in having all her motions watched, that it was only by means of a large bribe to a surly domestic, that she had been able to come to him at all. He pressed her very hard to contrive some means of escape for him, but she represented the thing as altogether impracticable without a larger sum of money (for the purpose of purchasing silence of those whom it would be necessary to trust) than she could then command; and she well knew that Percy had now no immediate pecuniary resource. At the same time, she would leave no scheme untried to effect his liberation.

The lady's chief aim, however, in this visit seems to have been to learn whether he were disposed to grant the bond, which of course was the grand object of their machinations. She affected to advise him to resist compliance with this condition so long as he could by any shift avoid it, an advice which he did not require a prompter to follow; though he was simple enough to confess to her that he saw no way to escape the evil except by granting the bond, and this to him would be absolute ruin, as the sum demanded was more than he was now worth in the world.

As a small consolation to this gloomy view of the matter, she took an opportunity of reminding Percy of the few hundreds which she owed him, and would pay very soon, and this perhaps might serve him till fortune changed her frowns into smiles. Percy, however, knew too well that these few hundreds would be every shilling required to liquidate the debts which his recent embarrassments had compelled him to contract. After a good deal of this sort of manœuvring conversation, the lady got him wound up to abandon himself to his fate, and sign the bond.

Altogether, it struck me as a thing at the first glance almost impossible, that Percy should have allowed himself to be so much imposed on, and in a manner so outrageously illegal, without taking some decided step to obtain his release and punish Mr. —. If he had thought for a moment on the same principle which made him attempt his escape after giving his written word of honour to the contrary, he would have at once signed the bond, and applied to a magistrate to apprehend Mr. —. I can account for his infatuation, indeed, on no other grounds than that his mind was so agitated and unsettled by the general state of his affairs, that he was incapable of calm reflection. I have no doubt, also, that his notions of the character of a gentleman had a considerable influence on his mind; for he would have deemed it disreputable to take any legal steps against Mr. —, when he felt himself in the wrong. His only notion of punishing him was that of bringing him to the test of the laws of honor in a duel, as if this could have done away with the insults and shameless plunder which he had suffered:

such are the conventional deceptions of education and prejudice. I can imagine no other plausible causes than the above, of Percy's infatuation.

The period of his respite having expired (and in this instance good faith was kept with him), he was brought from his place of confinement to meet the inexorable Mr. —, and settle as to the conditions proposed for his selection and acceptance. At this interview there was a renewal of the scene of the previous night, with this variation, that, instead of his pistols, Mr. — held out the threat of having a couple of bailiffs in readiness to secure him, if he were determined upon refusal or resistance. This, however, could be nothing more than a mere bugbear,[170] got up on the faith of Percy's inexperience and ignorance.

Be this as it may, it was effectual in bringing him into a compliance with their avaricious measures. Scarcely knowing what he did, he signed the document required, which would deprive him of all his remaining property, and for this valuable consideration he obtained liberty of egress from the house of his ensnarers.

As he was hastening out into the street, he accidentally encountered Mrs. —, who favoured him with a farewell smile of triumph, while she hesitated not to tell him, in a tone of the most heartless cruelty, that he was a ninny, and she hoped, she said, that he would never show her his fool's face more. It was then that he first got a glimpse of the real nature of the arts which had been practised upon him, and he rushed madly out of the house. The reader has already been told what followed. He had been goaded by a series of misfortunes and insults till his mind was unhinged, and he was, in an evil hour, tempted to the horrid act from which I rescued him.

CHAPTER XVII.

Doings of a night party from Bow Street.

It was now my duty to follow up the information derived from Percy; but I was at the same time anxious not to let him know any thing of my movements, for fear of alarming his *honourable* prejudices. I had a strong wish to recover the poor fellow's money for him; but I was much afraid that, from such a gang of miscreants, nothing could ever be obtained, even with justice and the law on our side. In the case of the cheques it would be impossible to do any thing, as they had been given under such peculiar circumstances, and as no process whatever could be raised without his own instructions, which I was almost certain he would not consent to give. I had no patience with this sort of punctilio,[171] and could have wished all the absurdities of the code of honour pitched to purgatory. It was necessary for me, however, to do what my duty required in bringing the delinquents to justice, whether or not it was to be of any benefit to Percy.

I was happy, in the meantime, to see the poor fellow restored in a great measure to strength again, through the attentions which we paid to him; and even if he should lose all, it would be a lesson which he would not soon forget, were he ever to attain to the title and its accompanying property which he had in prospect, though somewhat doubtfully. There was still the chance left for him of saving the sum in the bond, if I could get hold of Mr. — in sufficient time to prevent him from enforcing payment, unless, as I dreaded, he had already put it into the hands of some of his confederates in villainy. If this could be accomplished, it would be of the utmost importance to the poor young man, who had perhaps been sufficiently punished for his errors and imprudence, independently of this.

I was at a loss in what manner to proceed in order to a complete detection and capture of the whole gang, none of whom, I conceived, not even the lady with all her fascinations, deserved to escape condign punishment; for it was clear to me that Percy was only one of many victims who had fallen under their merciless clutches in one way or other, though his case was probably a rare one, in so far as they obtained so much money with so little trouble.

It struck me that if I could get myself introduced to their gambling-table as one who was not unwilling to sport a little cash, I might attain my object better than by an open attack upon the premises; yet, even in this there was danger, for I was beginning to be a little known about town in my official capacity, at least I had the vanity to suppose so; and I knew well that nobody keeps a more keen eye upon our honourable fraternity than the sort of people with whom I was now concerned; and if I were prematurely discovered in a prank of this sort, I had no doubt that I should have to pay the forfeit with my life. If Percy, out of a spirit of revenge, could have been persuaded to assist in the affair, we could have succeeded to a certainty; but after sounding him as narrowly as I dared upon general principles, I had to give up this notion as altogether hopeless.

As I was not less anxious to know something more of the mysteries of the low building (above designated the mangle-house,) than to secure Mr. — and his confederates, I had a strong desire to get hold of the tall waterman, or watchman, or whatever he might be, who was evidently a factotum-agent of the gang, though in an inferior capacity. Such a fellow as this would more readily consent to become approver[172] than Dawkins, or any of those who moved in a higher sphere of villainy. The difficulty, however, would be to get hold of this tall ruffian; for though he might be in the back premises as a watch for one night, it was very probable that on the following he might be acting as a night-waterman on the Thames for some illegal purpose. Had I been certain of his standing sentinel at the door of the mangle-house on any particular night, I would have proposed that Jem Bucks and I should, by some contrivance, get cautiously over the walls, take him by surprise, and gag him, to prevent his giving any alarm, while we would promise him his life on condition that he afforded us a clue to the various ramifications of iniquity with which he was connected. If we could accomplish thus much without noise, we should have it in our power to capture the chief delinquents at our leisure, and to put an end to the operations carried on in the mangle-house, which I strongly suspected to be nothing less than a wholesale manufactory of forged bank-notes.

Whatever might come of it, I was resolved to attempt this latter stratagem; and in order to make sure of something at least when we were about it, I thought it advisable to have a strong party stationed on all the outlets of the premises. Our enterprise, indeed, required the utmost secrecy and promptitude, for those miscreants are well known to be always fully prepared for flight or concealment, by means of trap-doors, secret closets, and other ingenious devices suggested by their fears. If the premises, however, were wholly beset with those whose business it is to circumvent such contrivances, there would be little chance, at least, for them all to escape our vigilance.

Proceeding upon this scheme, I immediately took the necessary steps for secretly obtaining the sanction and warrant of the magistrates to organize a select party, to act under my directions, according to the information which I had procured. I had some difficulty in determining upon the hour of commencing operations. This was a very material point to hit, for if we were too early, we might be disappointed in finding our game at their rendezvous; and it would be imprudent, on the other hand, to delay too long. After cross-questioning the unsuspecting Percy, and consulting with Bucks, I determined upon commencing about midnight.

The chief doubt which I had of our success was founded upon the alarm likely to have arisen through the whole establishment, from the note which I had sent respecting Percy. It was not, indeed, very explicit as to what had happened to him; but it was expressed so that Mrs. — must have inferred something very particular, and knowing, as she did, the injuries and insults which he had suffered, it was by no means improbable that she might form conjectures respecting him not far from the truth. If she had any idea of his disclosing the shameful transactions at her house, it was probable that measures had already been taken to secure a retreat from justice with what they could contrive to save of their ill-gotten wealth.

The only safeguard, in fact, which they could cling to was Percy's character, and they would naturally distrust even that after all they had done to destroy it, by showing him the villainy of his dearest associates naked and undisguised. His attempted escape, after pledging his word of honour in writing, was a circumstance which they could not fail to remember and dread, if he should think of following it up with disclosures of the restraints put upon him for the purpose of obtaining money. Except, indeed, for his imprudent, if not criminal, gallantries with Mrs. —, he had been as palpably robbed, as if he had been waylaid by a highwayman. Withal, however, even if they had taken partial alarm, it was not likely that the whole establishment would be broken up, though the principals might be *non est inventus*,[173] as the lawyers say, and this would be a grievous disappointment to our hopes both of gain and reputation.

The time approached, however, when all my doubts and conjectures would have to give place to effort and energy in conducting the enterprise which I had undertaken. In the first place, I stationed a strong party in front of the house, though not too near to create suspicion, should they chance to be observed. I next appointed others in the most probable places for escape behind the premises; and when all was 'well ordered and sure,'[174] Bucks and I made an attempt to get over the garden wall by means of rope-ladders, which we had taken care to provide for the purpose. We got over safely, but found nothing stirring, and all dark, so far at least as we could make out by a cursory glance; but we were too cautious to hurry into the scene of action, and endanger our lives without obtaining our object. After creeping with great caution along the wall, I at length distinguished the sound of footsteps, which I conjectured to be those of the guardian of the mangle-house.

'Hist!' said Bucks, in a low whisper, 'there he goes. I think I can make out something of his shape, dark as it is.'

'Is it the tall one, do you think?' replied I, 'for I confess I can't make out any thing but the sound of his footsteps.'

'O! for that matter,' answered Jem, 'I can't say to an inch as to his tallness; but he's no dwarf, I can see, however.'

'Then, Jem,' said I, 'we'll have need of all our strength to manage him as we wish; we must come upon him warily, or all will be lost.'

'Take him on the stern quarter, as we say at sea,' rejoined Bucks; 'you hook the gag over his head, while I pinion his *fams*.'[175]

A cat was never more wary in lying in wait for her prey, than Jem and I for this understrapper[176] of crime. We were fortunate in obtaining a station at the west corner of the mangle-house, just upon the turn of his *beat*, where we remained for a minute or two ready to pounce upon him as he turned upon his heel to measure back his round.

We dared not now even whisper – we scarcely ventured to breathe; for if we had given him any cause to suspect intruders so near him, he would probably have greeted us with a discharge of fire-arms, which he doubtless carried. We were standing on the alert, and ready to spring upon him, when I heard him patting what I took to be the lid of his snuff-box, and I held Jem's arm for a minute to give him time to take his snuff, thinking it a pity to balk him of this brief pleasure, which was soon to be exchanged (in case of our success) for the pain of the handcuffs.

He had treated himself, I suppose, to an extra pinch from his box, for it made him sneeze violently, and we did not fail to take this as a signal of attack. A fortunate omen, too, it proved; for we mastered our man with less noise than we could have expected, though not without vigorous struggles on his part to disengage himself. I succeeded, however, effectually in gagging him at the first onset, and instantly after presented a pistol to his head, threatening to shoot him on the spot if he made the slightest noise, while Bucks was expeditious in the use of his implements of trade.

When we had finally secured the tall ruffian, as it turned out to be, we led him off to the top of the garden where our ladder was ready placed to secure our retreat, had that been necessary. By means of what I sometimes call *pistol eloquence*, we persuaded him, against his will, to mount, and soon transferred him safely to one of our number who was in waiting to assist us. When we had got him thus fairly out of reach of alarming his employers and confederates, I ungagged him and promised to use every means for saving him, if he would give us any information that might enable us to secure the rest.

The fellow hesitated a good deal at first; but when he saw little prospect of escape in any other way, he reluctantly told us how to get access to the mangle-house; namely, by giving three gentle taps at the door, together with the watch-word of the night, which he communicated. There was only one man, he said, at work; but he left it to ourselves to discover what he was about. It struck me, indeed, that he might not himself know much of the secrets within, farther than that something was going forward contrary to the laws. That he knew it to be a manufactory of spurious bank-notes I much doubted, though he certainly was acquainted with many things connected with the crimes of the gang.

When we had obtained from this ruffian as much information as he could be induced to contribute, we removed our ladders, to return to the mangle-house, for the purpose of exploring its recesses. When we got to the door, we could hear the sound which Percy had compared to that of a mangle, but which appeared to me to be more like that of a copper-plate press. In this, however, my fancy was doubtless aided by the conjectures which I had previously formed. I tapped at the door, according to the tall fellow's instructions, and this signal was answered, after some little delay, by a sort of half whisper demanding the watch-word of the night, which I gave in a similar tone. I was much afraid, at the same time, that notwithstanding my speaking in this tone, (in which a voice is not so easily distinguished,) the person within might suspect all was not right; and if he should prove to be inquisitive, I could not escape detection. Fortunately he was satisfied with my answer, when Bucks and I rushed in and seized him; a feat which we were successful in accomplishing with less noise than, from the violence of the measure, we could well have foreseen. The man, in truth, scarcely made a shadow of resistance; a circumstance very common among criminals when apprehended, and which may be partly explained from their always looking forward to such a fate, and partly from their being benumbed with mingled surprise and fear. When he saw that resistance was useless, he contented himself with saying,

'Then it's all dickey[177] with me at last, however.'

'Ay, dickey enough, I'll be *bound*,' said Bucks.

'And will you just allow me to *bind* you, then, with them d—d derbies?'[178] replied the man in a jeering, waggish, tone, which proved him at once to be hardened in crime and reckless of consequences.

'O, no!' Bucks replied; 'I'll teach you a trick worth two o' that, if you show us all over this devil's den of yours.'

'Catch me there if you can,' said the prisoner. 'I'm not the chap to tell tales, however. Too old a cock to be caught with chaff,[179] by jingo.'

We could make nothing farther out of him; and accordingly, when we had secured him, we had to commence our search without his assistance. We were balked, however, at the very outset, in getting at his machine, whatever it might be; for our progress was stopped by a door that had no visible lock nor latch, but was nevertheless securely fastened, a thing which he had taken care not to neglect even when summoned by a genuine signal; and, indeed, we could distinguish the creaking of a door within immediately after we had tapped. I tried in every direction, with the notion of finding a spring, but could not discover the secret with all my endeavours, while I had to endure the chuckling sneers of the prisoner, of which he was not sparing.

Bucks tried to bandy wit with him, but was foiled at every point, till at last he got into a passion, and threatened to give him more weighty matters to exercise his thoughts upon; for which, however, he seemed neither to care nor fear. I was more interested in discovering the trick of the door; and at length I did hit the secret, and gained access into the concealed work-shop, where we found, as I had anticipated, a new copper-plate press, apparently of first-rate workmanship, and several spurious notes recently thrown off, and ready to be signed and numbered. The prisoner, though somewhat crest-fallen to see the secrets of his den thus laid open, did not lose his spirits so far as to forego his jest; he had even the impudence to tell me that the notes would not make a rope strong enough to hang a heavy fellow like him.

'Ay,' said Bucks; 'but they will serve to *purchase* ropes to hang every mother's son of ye that we can find in them premises-master and man, mistress and maid, of ye, if law gets its proper swing.'

'O! ye may hang 'em all,' said the fellow, 'when you once *nab* them; but I learned at school never to count my chickens till they were hatched, and mayhap, friend, you may be off your eggs this bout.'

This was a hint broad enough to spur us on to the completion of the enterprise which we had so prosperously begun; and we accordingly seized such notes as were worked off, and a quantity of paper ready for farther operations, and led away the prisoner to join his companion in custody, while I cast many a prying look into the great house, where I hoped the chief delinquents were still safe and unapprized of the danger hanging over them. If they were really in the house, my party being stationed as it was, there was no possibility of their escape, for the officers had strict and positive orders to seize every body who issued from the premises, under any pretence whatever.

I was almost certain that we had managed to capture our two prisoners so quickly, that no suspicion could have been excited within doors by any noise thus occasioned. My chief cause of fear was, that some of them might pay a visit to the back premises before we were quite ready with our arrangements; and, in that case, the absence of their tall sentinel would immediately advertise them of something being wrong. This notion suggested the device of sending Bucks off with the prisoner to our party outside the garden wall, while I assumed the part of the tall sentinel, and began to pace up and down the *beat* where we had captured him, with the consequential air of official importance. I wanted some inches, indeed, of the stature of my predecessor; but that, in the darkness, would probably not be remarked.

It was well that I had thought of this scheme, for Bucks was not a minute gone when I heard the creak of a back-door in the great house, and soon after a man came directly forward to my station, and without saying a word to me, went to the outer door of the work-shop of forgery, and gave the three signal-taps. I knew he would not be answered, and therefore took the opportunity of passing pretty near him, to see if I could discover whether he were a gentleman or one of the inferiors, but it was too dark for me to satisfy myself in this. On his part, he did not like my coming too near him, and, in a growling tone, ordered me to keep my distance. This, although intended to check the impertinence of the tall sentinel, served to nettle me; and, though I knew not what odds against me he might call from out the house, whilst, in the temporary absence of Bucks, I was single-handed, yet I could not restrain myself from rushing upon the fellow, and ordering him to surrender under pain of immediate death.

'By whose authority?' said he, quite coolly.

'By authority,' said I, 'of a warrant from Bow Street, where you are wanted for the crimes committed in this establishment.'

'I know of no crimes,' he continued in the same cool tone. 'There must surely be some mistake in this: you must have come to the wrong house.'

'We shall see that,' said I, 'when the examinations are taken, and the new bank-notes are scrutinized; in the meantime you are my prisoner, if you please.'

'I'll be d— first!' he cried in a resolute tone, and made a pass at me with some sort of weapon, which struck my left arm, though I did not feel that I was very severely wounded. I immediately discharged a pistol at the man, but without being able to take aim, and, indeed, I did not wish so much to kill as to terrify him for a moment, and give the alarm to the party in front, who were instructed to break into the house whenever they should hear the report of fire-arms behind. At the same moment Bucks returned to assist me, and we soon secured my opponent, who proved to be no other than Dawkins, the fellow who had first decoyed Percy into this den of plunder and crime.

We had now three of the miscreants in custody, and I hoped that our party in front would be successful in securing the rest. It may be thought that I should have laid a plan for discovering and demolishing the gambling table, when I knew there was such a thing in the house, and that I should also have endeavoured to surprise the gamblers in the act of playing, in order to prove the case. All this, of course, I should have taken care to do, had gambling been the only crime chargeable on the establishment; but I deemed it of more importance to discover the bank-note manufactory, and procure sufficient evidence to bring the crime of forgery home to the proprietors. If this could be successfully accomplished, the proof of the gambling was an inferior consideration; though I might, indeed, have managed to execute both designs, but not without greater numbers and much more trouble.

I was glad to hear, in a short time, that our men had proved successful in gaining an entrance at the front, and being joined in the garden by some of those who were stationed behind, I endeavoured to obtain access at the back doors, which was a matter of less difficulty, inasmuch as several of the servants, understanding that they might be in danger, were endeavouring to make their escape in this direction.

I did not choose to encumber myself by securing these, as I was anxious to get hold of their master or mistress. I was too late, however, I was much afraid, for being 'in at the death,'[180] as a huntsman would say, since the front party had got the start of me, and were ranging all over the house. I was, I confess, rather vexed at this, for I should have liked to have had the honour of capturing Mrs. —, as I took the credit of first tracing her illegal proceedings. I made anxious inquiry, accordingly, of every one I met, whether they had seen any thing of the lady; but I got the same negative answer from all, from the servants of the house as well as from our own people, who had been making search into all suspected places.

I myself conjectured that, if Mrs. — were not shut up in her boudoir, where it was probable she was when our attack commenced, she had succeeded in getting into some secret closet, or down by some trap-door, into a place of security, for it was fair to conclude, from the analogy of the secret door in the work-shop, that there were conveniences of this kind for the purposes of retreat in different parts of the house. I hastened, therefore, to the boudoir, with the intention of making a thorough search there for the lady who was missing, but who was certainly in the house, as I accidentally heard one of the servants whispering to another,

'Where the deuce can Missis have hid herself in all the *row?*'

'Aw! she knows a thing or two!' replied the other. 'She is as snug by this as a mouse in a mill, I know.'

From the experience which I had just acquired in discovering the spring of a concealed door, I was in great hopes of unearthing the lady from her lurking place, if she really had taken refuge in any secret closet, as I strongly suspected. I found the boudoir and the adjoining bed-chamber empty, as I had anticipated, but was resolved not to leave an inch of the walls or partitions unexplored. I first applied my ear to the places which I suspected most, and listened with intense anxiety, that I might, if possible, distinguish her breathing, which would naturally be hurried and louder than usual, from agitation and fear. I was disappointed in receiving any indication from this token; but at length I perceived a small chink in one of the partitions of the boudoir, which had much the appearance of the secret door of the work-shop, and as the same person had probably been employed in the construction, I felt pretty confident of finding some concealment, whether the lady might be there or not. The spring did turn out to be similar to the former, and I experienced no difficulty in opening the door, which disclosed a very small apartment, with room only for a sofa. Here lay Mrs. —, panting and terrified for the fate which awaited her, and which she had long dreaded and prepared for. When she saw me enter, she exclaimed in a voice almost stifled by agitation,

'Ah me! my time is come at last; but I have still one friend left, thank God!'

Upon this she drew something from her bosom, and turning her head away, I did not exactly perceive what she was doing, till she dashed an empty phial on the floor, and looking me wildly in the face, cried,

'Now it is done! – all is over! Take me where you please!'

From the smell which was diffused from the phial, I was convinced she had swallowed a quantity of laudanum,[181] for the dreadful purpose doubtless of destroying herself; and I was so agitated at the idea, that I had scarcely any power left either of speaking or acting. I was horror-stricken to see so fine a woman, formed to be the ornament of society and an honour to her sex, driven by a headlong career of vice and crime to the commission of such a deed. Here was beauty levelled with the most degraded felon, and rushing into the presence of her Maker flushed with all her crimes, unrepented of and never regretted, save when obstacles interrupted their pursuit. The sight was painfully humiliating; but there was a necessity for acting, and promptly too, rather than losing precious time in moralizing. I therefore despatched a message express for the nearest apothecary or surgeon who could be found, to come immediately and try what could be done to avert the effects of the poison, if she had really taken the laudanum with the intent of destroying herself; though it might be, that she was in the habit of dosing herself with the drug, to drown care and thought in temporary oblivion – a practice which I am given to understand is lamentably common in the upper ranks, and particularly among ladies, who are denied by the usages of decorous society to indulge in wine. Her wild expressions, however, proved but too plainly that she had meant it to be the termination of all her earthly troubles. This effect, it appeared, was quickly about to be accomplished, for after a few incoherent exclamations of delirious rapture, she sank into a state of death-like sleep, and before medical aid could be procured at this unseasonable hour, fell into dreadful convulsions, and expired in the greatest agony. It was one of the most appalling scenes which I ever witnessed, and harrowed up my feelings the more, that I considered myself as the immediate cause of the catastrophe, though it must eventually have come independent of my surprisal of the house on that particular evening.

We could not find Mr. — himself; but it was reported next morning that he had fallen in a duel by the hand of Percy, who had fled instantly to the continent, to avoid the consequences of a trial.

It will not be of any interest, I conceive, to the readers of my narrative, to follow it up with a detail of what occurred before the coroner on the inquest held upon the body of the unfortunate Mrs. —, or at the Old Bailey, in the trials of the several criminals whom we took on the night in question. My purpose will be answered if what I have recorded in these volumes shall serve to beguile an idle hour, or show to those, who are inexperienced, the innumerable snares which beset the path of life, particularly in this overgrown and bustling metropolis.

THE END.

EXPLANATORY NOTES

Volume I

1. *LE FRÊNE*: apparently invented by Gaspey.
2. *HENRY COLBURN*: Colburn (1784/5–1855) was one of the most enterprising publishers of the early nineteenth century. Rumoured to be the illegitimate son of Lord Lansdowne, he began his career in the book trade as proprietor of a commercial circulating (lending) library and then turned publisher, specializing in English and French books of the day and fashionable novels in particular. He went on to publish the *New Monthly Magazine* (1814–84), and was also part owner of another prominent literary periodical, the *Athenaeum*. As a businessman, Colburn was known for deviousness.
3. *assafœtida*: an ill-smelling resin.
4. *salamander*: salamanders were believed to be able to survive amidst fire.
5. bring ... in: reduce to submission.
6. Figends: 'fig' could mean 'something worthless'.
7. *take off*: mimic.
8. *Crusty*: 'crusty' could mean 'short-tempered'.
9. *plashed*: (or 'pleached') intertwined.
10. *firkin*: small cask of one quarter barrel measure (about forty-one litres).
11. *strolling*: itinerant.
12. *Walker's Dictionary, and Enfield's Speaker*: famous guides to 'good' spoken and written English – John Walker's pronouncing dictionary (1775) and William Enfield's anthology, *The Speaker* (1774).
13. *Austin's Chironomia*: Gilbert Austin, *Chironomia; or, A Treatise on Rhetorical Delivery* (1806).
14. *Inkle and Yarico*: title of a very popular comic opera (1787) by George Colman the younger.
15. *Drury Lane*: one of the long-established licensed theatres of London, as distinct from the increasing number of theatres only permitted to put on musical dramas and entertainments.
16. *Bucks*: 'buck' could mean 'dashing fellow'.
17. *Mrs. Radcliffe's wild stories*: Ann Radcliffe (1764–1823), pioneering author of Gothic novels, such as *The Mysteries of Udolpho* (1794), in which a virtuous heroine is persecuted by villains amid picturesque French or Italian scenery.
18. *living and loving*: phrase used by a number of writers.
19. *romping*: love-play.

20. *counting-house*: accounts office.
21. *Liverpool*: a major port in the north-west of England, on the Irish Sea.
22. *spouting club*: club where young men got together to declaim speeches from plays.
23. *Ormskirk*: a market town in west Lancashire, in the north-west of England.
24. *Preston*: a town in Lancashire.
25. *Lancaster*: a town in Lancashire.
26. *assizes*: trials held at periodic intervals in a particular place, at that time the occasion for social gatherings and entertainments of various kinds.
27. *blood*: pedigree or thoroughbred.
28. derbies: handcuffs (slang).
29. *Lancaster Castle*: housing the town jail.
30. *flats*: dullards; dupes.
31. *Garstang*: a small town between Lancaster and Preston.
32. *Penrith and Kendal*: market towns in Cumberland and Westmorland respectively, in north-west England, near the Lake District.
33. *Douglas*: title of very popular play (1756) by John Home; Norval was a role to be performed by any actor with pretensions to talent.
34. *Shap*: a wild area in the Lake District of north-west England.
35. *romantic*: at this time mainly signifying 'characteristic of romance', that is, appealing to imagination, picturesque.
36. *Lowther Castle*: a castle-like country mansion owned by the Lowther family, principal proprietors in the Lake District at that time.
37. *Blore*: 'blore' could mean 'stormy weather; bluster'.
38. *all was grey*: perhaps from James Hogg, *The Pilgrims of the Sun* (1815), I.120.
39. *Faint ... appearing*: apparently the author's own composition.
40. *ducat*: gold coin, value varying from country to country.
41. *will-o-wisp*: name given to dancing flames on a swamp's surface caused by the gas from rotting vegetation and in legend, sprites luring fools to destruction in the morass.
42. *Yonder ... doom*: adapted from Oliver Goldsmith (1730–74), 'Edwin and Angelina', ll. 11–12.
43. *fidgets*: physical agitation.
44. *Pity ... roam*: apparently by the author.
45. *chapman*: itinerant peddler selling small wares.
46. *Not drunk ... Tara la lay*: a widely distributed ballad originating in the seventeenth century and appearing in the eighteenth century under the title 'The Tankard of Ale' in broadside form, in garlands, or chapbooks of lyrics, sold by street hawkers and in books.
47. *October*: strong ale brewed in October.
48. *catch*: in music, a round for three or more voices, in which each singer takes up the first line when the previous singer begins the second line, and so on.
49. *'Twas ... you!*: also known as 'Kiss and Tell', by Garrett Wesley, Earl of Mornington.
50. *Molly ... only life!*: not identified; possibly the author's lines.
51. *pearl-white*: a cosmetic powder.
52. *Juliet ... Belvidera*: heroines respectively of Shakespeare's *Romeo and Juliet* and Thomas Otway's *Venice Preserv'd* (1682).
53. *Castleton*: a village in the Peak District of Derbyshire.
54. *Your's*: a common alternative for 'Yours' at this time.
55. *The world's ... scorn*: from James Thomson, 'Autumn', *The Seasons* (1730), ll. 233–4.
56. *many ... drown it*: the Bible, Song of Solomon, 8:7.

57. *Bakewell*: village near the Peak District of Derbyshire.
58. *Buxton*: a fashionable spa town in Derbyshire.
59. *turnpike-house*: a building housing the collector of fees.
60. *anatomy*: skeleton.
61. *confusion worse confounded*: Milton, *Paradise Lost*, II.996, describing the rout of the fallen angels from heaven after their rebellion against God.
62. *Richard ... camp-couch*: in Shakespeare, *Richard III*, V.iii.178.
63. *birch*: birch branches bound together to form an instrument for beating a person.
64. *compunctious visitings*: Shakespeare, *Macbeth*, I.v.45.
65. *Job-like patience*: in the Bible, Book of Job, Job persists in his faith despite numerous afflictions visited on him by God.
66. *chew ... fancy*: adapted from Shakespeare, *As You Like It*, IV.iii.101.
67. *Peak*: the Peak District, Derbyshire.
68. *Udolpho*: Ann Radcliffe, *The Mysteries of Udolpho* (1794), a widely read Gothic novel.
69. *bosom'd high in tufted trees*: Milton, 'L'Allegro' (1645), l. 78.
70. *siezed*: usually spelled 'seized' at this time.
71. *mechanics*: labourers, artisans.
72. *jorum*: large drinking vessel.
73. *gentle craft*: cobbling, or repairing shoes.
74. *crown*: five shillings.
75. *Here's ... Brown*: perhaps a variation of the song 'Hearty Tom Brown', published in songsters, or small pamphlets containing the words to several songs.
76. *ascending me into the brain*: from Shakespeare, *Henry IV, Part 2*, IV.iii.95.
77. *Falstaff's sherris-sack*: sherry.
78. *shealing*: piece of pasture.
79. *The stars ... to me*: apparently by the author.
80. *Ariosto*: Lodovico Ariosto (1474–1533), Italian author of the verse romance *Orlando Furioso* (1516).
81. *Despairing ... laid*: ballad by Nicholas Rowe (1674–1718), title as first line.
82. *Wilton*: perhaps a play on 'will' meaning willfulness or impetuosity and 'ton' meaning fashion or trend, suiting Wilton's character.
83. *shamoy*: or chamois.
84. *Egyptian*: gipsy, because gipsies were thought to have originated in Egypt.
85. *Savoyard*: inhabitant of Savoy in the French-Italian Alps and familiar elsewhere as itinerant musicians with monkey and hurdy-gurdy.
86. *O give ... crystal wall*: adapted from John Dryden, *Don Sebastian* (1690), II.i.367–9.
87. *hundred guineas*: £105, worth about £7,000 in 2005, following the retail price index.
88. *nabob*: name applied to a person who acquired a fortune in India, from Urdu nawab, a viceroy or ruler.
89. *Through forests ... mountain glen*: apparently the author's composition.
90. *plump down*: immediately.
91. *damsels in durance*: young women in confinement, humorously echoing terms from chivalric romance.
92. *charge of seduction*: such a legal action could be brought by a parent or guardian for seduction of an unmarried woman causing loss of the woman's services to the plaintiff, the woman herself deemed innocent.
93. *castle-building*: building imaginary castles, fantasizing.
94. *Theocritus*: third-century BC Greek bucolic poet.

95. *Despairing ... head*: another ballad by Nicholas Rowe (1674–1718), title as first line.
96. *Ossianic*: characteristic of the semi-factitious 'Poems of Ossian' published in the 1760s, represented by their fabricator James Macpherson as translations of fragmentary ancient Gaelic epics.
97. *Hollands*: Dutch gin.
98. *Ramsay*: on the Isle of Man in the Irish Sea.
99. *Mother Bunch*: spurious author of books of divination and fairy tales.
100. *I wander ... my dear*: adapted from Robert Burns, 'Their Groves o' Sweet Myrtle', ll. 15–16.
101. *lov'd a lass and lov'd a glass*: echoing a song in Isaac Bickerstaffe's comic opera *Lionel and Clarissa* (1768), end of I.ii.
102. *Scale Force*: the highest waterfall in the Lake District.
103. *Langley Pikes, and Helvellyn*: notable high places in the Lake District.
104. *Lowood ... Ambleside ... Rydal Water*: places in the Lake District.
105. *Then hie ... liberty*: apparently by the author.
106. *love's* willing *fetters*: Robert Burns, 'Their Groves o' Sweet Myrtle', l. 16.
107. *Love ... flies*: adapted from Alexander Pope, *Eloisa to Abelard* (1717), ll. 75-6.
108. *merry-andrew*: clown.
109. *letter of credit*: a letter recommending the bearer.
110. *Bleak ... Mary*: apparently by the author.
111. *rath*: early blooming.
112. *Abraham ... Hittite*: the Bible, Genesis 49:29.
113. *Northern Minstrel*: James Beattie, *The Minstrel* (1771–2), 2.149–53.
114. *quondam*: former (Latin).
115. *Morn ... breathes*: apparently by the author.
116. *Warwick*: the county town of Warwickshire in central England.
117. *Leamington*: a spa town in southern Warwickshire.
118. *gins and springes*: traps.
119. hors de combat: disabled (French).
120. *to hover about the enemy*: adapted from John Home, *Douglas* (1756), act 2, l. 56.
121. *black-jack*: tar-covered leather beer jug.
122. *climbing boy*: chimney-sweep, a boy small enough to climb up and down inside chimneys to clean them.
123. *inn-keeper of Warwick*: apparently a proverbial figure.
124. *dickens*: devil.
125. *Bow-street*: site in central London of a magistrates court.
126. *Cambridge*: university town in east central England.
127. *Oxford*: the other university town at this time, in south central England.
128. *green lane*: a bridle-road or horse path.
129. *like ... both*: Shakespeare, *Measure for Measure*, III.i.33-4.
130. *Cantabs*: of Cambridge University, from Cantabrigensis, the Latin name of Cambridge.
131. *steeped ... to the very lips*: adapted from Shakespeare, *Othello*, IV.ii.51.
132. *blood horse*: pedigree or thoroughbred horse.
133. *tow*: flax fibre.
134. *in bed*: that is, while in bed.
135. *Punctual ... sworn:* E. Young, *The Complaint; or, Night Thoughts* (1742–5) Night III, l. 4.
136. *rushlight*: a dim candle made by dipping a rush pith into grease.

137. *rowing*: rowdy; quarrelsome.
138. *Trinity*: a very wealthy Cambridge college.
139. *post-obiting*: borrowing money, usually at high interest, to be repaid after the death of someone who is to leave the borrower a legacy.
140. *smoked*: suspected.
141. *play*: gamble.
142. *debts of honour*: debts incurred without a formal contract.
143. *hunter*: fine horse used for hunting.
144. *Buonaparte ... Marengo*: Napoleon Bonaparte (1769–1821), leader of France, won a famous victory at Marengo in northern Italy in 1800, and gave the name to his own horse; there were many spurious Napoleonic relics in circulation.
145. *four thousand pounds*: about £270,000 in today's money, using the retail price index.
146. *lottery ticket*: the lottery for public revenue ended in England in 1826.
147. rouge et noir: red and black (French), card game played on a table with two red and two black diamond shapes on which players place their stakes.
148. *smack*: at a stroke; thirty thousand pounds would be about £2,000,000 today, using the retail price index.
149. *Byam Finch*: 'Byam' could be a play on 'buy 'em' or 'buy them'; 'Finch' could mean 'gullible person'.
150. *Newmarket*: most famous race course in southern England at this time.
151. *foxers*: hounds for fox hunting.
152. *guineas*: a guinea was twenty-one shillings or one pound and one shilling.
153. *repeater*: an expensive pocket watch that repeated the hour when a button was pushed.
154. *blank*: not winning a prize.
155. *take to his pistols ... laudanum*: that is, kill himself; laudanum: opium dissolved in alcohol.
156. *dark lantern*: a lantern with sliding panels that could conceal the light.
157. *theatrical lightning*: an effect of lightning made behind the scenes by igniting sulphur powder.
158. *fête*: festival (French).
159. *rustication*: temporary dismissal from university.
160. *Hampstead Heath*: a piece of open ground on the north of London.
161. *vestry*: a parish assembly, with certain powers over local affairs.
162. *beggars, gipsies, and other vagrants*: phrase used in notices regulating vagrancy.
163. *Norwood ... Wimbledon*: Norwood Green, to the west of London, and Wimbledon Common, to the south.
164. *ecstasy*: Possibly Wilton is taken in certain respects from the poet Shelley.
165. *The midnight ... ETERNITY*: apparently by the author.
166. *notice to quit*: an official notice to vacate or leave a place, with penalties for failure to comply.
167. *too many for*: too clever for.
168. *Bishop's Wood*: village north of London.
169. *practise upon*: scheme against.
170. *Three Spaniards*: a public house on Hampstead Heath known as The Spaniards.
171. *every muscle quivered with delight*: not identified.
172. *general utility*: reference to utilitarianism, or the view that social and state policy should be based on the principle of pursuing the greatest good for the greatest number.
173. *jobbing*: performing small tasks.

174. *set a thief to catch a thief*: proverbial, from the mid seventeenth century.
175. *helped himself ... common*: Enclosing or appropriating of formerly common lands by individual proprietors accelerated during the late eighteenth century, and was deeply resented by the lower classes for denying them access to land they regarded as a 'traditional' or customary right.
176. *Higglesworth*: 'to higgle': 'to dispute petty details'.
177. *job*: turn a public office to personal benefit.
178. *mare's nest*: an illusory discovery.
179. *additional rate*: increased assessment of property for local tax purposes.
180. *under the rose*: in confidence, privately.
181. *nose is out of joint*: scheme is spoiled.
182. *cob*: stout horse.
183. *out and out*: completely.
184. *to the nines*: to perfection.
185. *cock-and-bull*: rambling, tedious.
186. *Wrestliana*: a play on Piers Egan's popular account of boxing, *Boxiana* (1818).
187. *Carmen Triumphale*: song of victory (Latin).
188. *trim*: character.
189. *waunds*: wounds, for 'God's wounds', an oath.
190. *smack*: certainly, completely.
191. *hair in my neck*: source of trouble for me.
192. *hook or by crook*: by any means legitimate or otherwise.
193. *deuced*: devilish.
194. *prosing*: tedious discourse.
195. *catastrophe ... denouement*: the conclusion or resolution of a story's plot.
196. *Highgate ... Finchley*: villages on heights to the north of London.
197. *Lud*: euphemistic form of 'Lord', an oath.
198. *Gad-a-mercy*: euphemistic form of 'God have mercy'.
199. *perpendicular*: upright position.
200. *on*: of (dialect).
201. *ninny-hammers*: blockheads.
202. *cloud of witnesses*: title of several early books about of Protestant martyrs, especially *A Cloud of Witnesses for the Royal Prerogatives of Jesus Christ* (1714), reprinted several times in the early nineteenth century.
203. *ears ... ass*: in ancient legend, the god Pan punishes Midas by giving him ass's ears.
204. *Holloway*: village north-east of London.
205. *Mother Red-Cap*: A pub of this name existed at the time and still exists in Holloway; the nickname dates back to the sixteenth century, at least; according to one legend, mother Red-cap was the nickname of a woman whose husbands mysteriously disappeared; in the early nineteenth century, the poet 'Peter Pindar' (James Wolcot, 1738–1819) used the name as a figure for female revolutionaries.
206. *pugilists*: Boxing, like horse-racing, became very popular as a spectator sport in the early decades of the nineteenth century, though it was illegal.
207. *flash*: insiders' slang.
208. *Moulsey Hurst*: popular sports venue near the river Thames to the west of London.
209. *wrestling*: A popular sport since the Middle Ages, wrestling was coming to be regarded by many as vulgar and outdated, while others promoted it in the name of 'national' culture and 'tradition'.

210. hipping ... striking: wrestling holds or moves.
211. *By jingo*: an interjection, a euphemistic substitution for 'by God'.
212. *pretty pup*: fine beginner.
213. *Goles*: euphemistic substitution for 'God'.
214. *main prime*: strongly insistent.
215. game: spirited, brave.
216. *tip the blunt*: furnish the money (slang)
217. *come it for this here chip*: come up with it for this quarrel.
218. *Belcher's, Castle Tavern, Holborn*: celebrated venue for boxing matches at this time; Thomas Belcher (1783–1854), keeper of the Castle Tavern from 1814 to 1828, was a retired prizefighter, the younger, less famous brother of the boxer Jem Belcher (1781–1811).
219. Clk. pro temp: temporary clerk.
220. Jolly Miller: traditional song also known as 'The Miller of Dee', often adapted; the following lines in the novel are based on the opening part of the song:

> There was a jolly miller once
> Lived on the river Dee,
> He danced and he sang from morn till night—
> No lark so blithe as he.
> And this the burden of his song
> For ever used to be,
> I care for nobody, no, not I,
> If nobody cares for me.

221. *perdie*: *par dieu*, by God (French).
222. *Sir John Barleycorn*: malt liquor, made from barley.
223. *Hibernianism*: Irishism, meaning a verbal paradox or contradiction, to which the Irish were thought by the English to be susceptible.
224. *Litany*: prescribed form of public prayer in the Church of England, read aloud by the parish clerk during services.
225. *Dr. Slop in Tristram Shandy*: a character in Laurence Sterne's popular comic novel *The Life and Opinions of Tristram Shandy, Gentleman* (1759–67).
226. *uncle Toby's Lillibullero*: Toby is another character in *Tristram Shandy*; 'Lillibullero' was an anti-Irish traditional song used as a kind of anthem by those favouring the politics of the Whigs, or supporters of the interests of the landed gentry against monarchical and court power.
227. *dickens*: euphemistic substitution for 'devil'.
228. *braggadocio*: braggart, based on a character in Edmund Spenser's verse romance *The Faerie Queene* (1590–1609).
229. palsy-touch *and the* fank: palsy: paralysis; fank: coil of rope, or sheep-pen.
230. *apprentice to the driver of a mail-coach*: At this time fashionable well-to-do young gentlemen would affect the dress, talk and attitudes of coach drivers.
231. *Honourable*: courtesy title accorded to sons of noblemen below the rank of marquess.
232. *CHIP*: meaning 'quarrel' but also 'small bit or piece' and 'something worthless'.
233. *Wimbledon Common*: large open ground south of London.
234. *St. George's Fields*: an area in Southwark, south of the river Thames from London.
235. *swell*: self-consciously fashionable person.
236. *full feather*: fine spirits.
237. *prime go to do him*: first-rate exploit to overcome him.
238. *easy as a glove*: perhaps 'perfectly suited'.

239. *pluck*: rob, despoil.

240. *blown up*: ruined.

241. *plume*: set up.

242. *blues*: low spirits; gloomy prospects; also a kind of pigeon.

243. *pigeon*: swindler's victim.

244. *entered rook*: entered: placed in a register; rook: black bird resembling a crow; swindler.

245. *Chesterfield*: Philip Stanhope, Fourth earl of Chesterfield (169–1773), author of a famous advice book on gentlemanly behaviour in the form of *Letters* to his son (1774).

246. *flat*: dull person; dupe.

247. *hankered*: In wrestling a hank is a restraining hold.

248. *gulls*: dupes.

249. *falls*: A 'fall' occurs when one of the combatants is thrown, or deemed to have been overcome.

250. hors de combat: see note 119.

251. incog: incognito: unknown, or disguised (Italian).

252. *Mivart's Hotel*: fashionable establishment frequented by nobility and royalty, founded in 1812, now Claridge's.

253. *usher*: teacher's assistant.

254. *livery*: uniform worn by certain servants, especially of the wealthy and aristocratic.

255. *St. James's Park*: long-established elegant park adjacent to fashionable part of central London.

256. *Manks*: Manx; from the Isle of Man, between England and Ireland.

257. *Exeter Mail*: regular coach carrying mail between London and Exeter, a major town in the south-west of England.

258. *Bow Street*: location of a magistrates court in central London, to which were attached the so-called Bow Street runners, a police force founded in 1750, responsible for investigating crimes, gathering intelligence on criminals and carrying out arrests; they were nicknamed Robin Redbreasts from the red waistcoats that were part of their uniform.

Volume II

1. *rummer*: large drinking glass.

2. *shop*: office.

3. *Jehu*: in the Bible, second book of Kings, a rebel and king of Israel.

4. *quality*: well-to-do, upper-class.

5. *on tiptoe*: eager.

6. *Roehampton*: village to the south-west of London.

7. *Putney Heath*: an open ground at this time, on the south-west edge of London.

8. *rank*: noble title.

9. *settled upon her ... Manson*: On marriage, the wife's property or inheritance became the husband's unless a contract set something apart for her use and control.

10. *Battersea*: located on the south side of the Thames river south-west of London.

11. *the affair ... Monsal-Dale*: in vol. 1, ch. 8.

12. at fault: lose the scent or track of the quarry.

13. *footpads*: pedestrian highway robbers.

14. *note of preparation*: in a musical composition, a preparation for a discord.

15. *neck-or-nothing*: regardless of risk.

16. *anatomists*: Study of human anatomy was a prerequisite to medical qualification and was taught at commercial anatomy schools, which were in constant need of fresh cadavers, leading to grave-robbing and even murders committed to obtain bodies for sale to the schools, as in the crimes of William Burke and William Hare at Edinburgh in 1827–8.

17. *whited sepulchres*: Bible, Matthew 23:27, comparing hypocrites to tombs that are white-washed on the outside but conceal rottenness and decay within.

18. *h—*: hell.

19. *shab*: low fellow (slang).

20. *thof*: though (dialect).

21. *d—*: damned.

22. *d—*: damnation.

23. *pink*: stab.

24. *staff*: staff of office.

25. *turn-up*: turning over a card in a game of chance.

26. *coroner's inquest*: a court of investigation, usually into deaths occurring in unusual circumstances.

27. *sit ... on*: deal with.

28. *birth-mark ... longed for*: a common kind of folk belief.

29. *circulating library*: Most people obtained current fiction, such as this novel, from commercial circulating libraries, which charged subscription fees and rental fee for each volume borrowed.

30. *gammon*: talk, humbug.

31. *chinkers*: coins.

32. *Lud*: euphemistic substitution for 'Lord'.

33. *blue*: the colour of constancy.

34. *'peach*: impeach, betray.

35. *stuff*: property, valuables, or money.

36. *goles*: euphemistic substitution for 'God'.

37. *neat*: exact.

38. *pulled up*: arrested.

39. *under hatches*: under restraint.

40. *New Forest*: a large wooded area in Hampshire near the south coast of England.

41. *Monseer's country*: 'monsieur's country' – France.

42. *smoked*: detected.

43. *bankers*: bankers' bills, paper money.

44. *Wandsworth*: at that time a village south-west of London.

45. *palming*: fraudulently passing off.

46. *boots*: generic name for all-purpose servant of a hotel or inn, from his principal task of blacking the boots of guests.

47. *Windmill Street*: in central London, location of a famous anatomy school.

48. *dissected alive*: Dissection was so detested by the common people that many fictitious stories about it were readily credited.

49. *trim*: readiness, preparation.

50. *old 'un*: old one – the devil.

51. *Lambeth side*: south bank of the Thames.

52. *coal-luggers*: A lugger is a small sailing ship.

53. *maid*: 'girl or young woman' or more narrowly 'young virgin'.

54. *Borough*: Southwark.

55. *Bacchus*: ancient Greek god of wine.
56. *fall on his neck and weep*: echo of three Bible passages, for example, Genesis 33:4, 45:14.
57. *baseless fabric of a vision*: Shakespeare, *The Tempest*, IV.i.151, spoken by Prospero.
58. *great pith and moment*: Shakespeare, *Hamlet*, III.i.86: 'great pitch and moment', from Hamlet's soliloquy, 'To be, or not to be'.
59. *ample verge and scope enough*: T. Gray, 'Ode: "Ruin seize thee"', l. 51: 'ample room, and verge enough'.
60. *Twining's Souchong*: The famous tea packaging firm of Twinings dates itself back to 1706; Souchong: a variety of fine black tea with a smoky flavour, originally from Fujian, China.
61. *Epping sausages*: Epping forest in Essex was famous as a source of pork sausages, but there were claims that not all sausages going by that name were made at that place.
62. *aboveboard*: into the open.
63. *Gumping*: 'To gump' means 'to grope about (for something)'.
64. otium cum dignitate: leisure with office.
65. *posse*: *posse comitatus* (Latin), a force with legal authority.
66. *stuck ... Jews*: perhaps referring to a prejudice of that time against Jews as persistent in pursuing sales, business, or repayment (after Shakespeare's portrayal of Shylock in *The Merchant of Venice*).
67. *Cockspur*: a kind of thorny bush, after the spur, or sharp point in the legs of the cock.
68. *finishing her education*: 'Finishing' schools emphasized elegant accomplishments to fit girls for the marriage market and were widely regarded as teaching young women to disdain domestic skills and household management.
69. *the great*: the wealthy and upper-class.
70. *La*: emphatic exclamation.
71. *ravening wolf*: a phrase found in several poets.
72. *Crome*: 'To crome' means 'to seize with a hook'.
73. *griped*: gripped, grasped.
74. *racking and drawing*: charging excessively, extorting, draining.
75. *pound*: worth about £68 in 2005, using the retail price index.
76. *advowson*: right to appoint a clergyman to a church living, or appointment with income; before church reform, advowsons could be bought and sold.
77. *tithes*: church right to a tenth of the produce of those in a parish, often commuted to a cash sum, liable to decline in real value with time or in relation to increased agricultural productivity and incomes.
78. *Grotius De Veritate*: H. Grotius, *De veritate religionis Christianae* (*Concerning the Truth of the Christian Religion*, 1632).
79. *University credentials*: Normally a priest in the Church of England had to have a degree from Oxford or Cambridge.
80. *D.D*: Doctor of Divinity (theology).
81. *in kind*: as produce, which Cockspur would sell.
82. *cubit*: measure used in the Bible, being the length from elbow to fingertips.
83. dumpish: dull, stupid.
84. *Goody*: term of address for an older married lower-class woman.
85. in the dumps: melancholy, depressed.
86. *cross-grained baggage*: contrarious good for nothing woman.

87. *predial, personal, and mixed tithes*: predial tithes: tithes from produce of the soil; personal tithes: tithes from trade or manufactures; mixed tithes: tithes partly predial and personal.
88. *de jure and by custom*: by law (Latin) and by established tradition.
89. *agistment*: pasturage of another's cattle.
90. *subbois*: small trees or shrubs.
91. *sylva cædua*: small trees or shrubs.
92. *bell-wethers*: sheep with bells.
93. *folded*: penned in a sheep-fold.
94. *laying*: putting to rest.
95. *colour*: kind.
96. *goblins damned*: echoing Shakespeare, *Hamlet*, I.iv.43 (Boswell/Malone edition, 1821).
97. *black spirits and grey*: echoing the Witches scene in Shakespeare, *Macbeth*, IV.xiii.44–5 in the Boswell/Malone edition (1821).
98. *travelling out of the record*: going off the subject.
99. *Get thee behind me, Satan*: in the Bible, spoken by Christ in response to Peter's urging him not to sacrifice himself, for example Matthew 16:23.
100. *Bunyan's Pilgrim's Progress*: Christian is the protagonist of John Bunyan's widely read salvation allegory, *The Pilgrim's Progress* (1678).
101. *Rejoice ... arise*: the Bible, Micah 7:8.
102. *Though ... evil*: the Bible, Psalms 23:4.
103. *witching time of night*: Shakespeare, *Hamlet*, III.ii.379.
104. *sybil*: in ancient legend and literature, a female oracle or prophetess.
105. *imp ... breechling*: imp: devil's child; breechling: offspring.
106. *o'erstept the modesty of nature*: Shakespeare, *Hamlet*, II.ii.19.
107. *fifteen thousand*: worth about £1,100,000 in 2005, using the retail price index – the sexton is clearly exaggerating.
108. *to cut before the point*: to draw a conclusion without full knowledge; a Scottish expression.
109. *all the Capulets*: referring to Shakespeare, *Romeo and Juliet*, IV.i.111–12: 'that same ancient vault / Where all the kindred of the Capulets lie'.
110. *trap has nosed us*: detective has discovered us.
111. *gammon*: see note 30.
112. *serve 'im with notice to quit*: kill him.
113. *Windmill Street*: see note 47.
114. *screens*: bank-notes.
115. *leery cove*: suspicious fellow.
116. *Down to*: aware of.
117. *darkey*: night.
118. *kiddy*: lad.
119. *fly*: coach built for speed.
120. *ding*: smash.
121. *cold meat consarn*: trade in cadavers.
122. *blunt ... ready down*: money.
123. *cage*: small jail or lock-up.
124. *shilelah*: or shillelagh; wooden cudgel.
125. *spalpeens*: rascals.

126. *drums beating and colours flying*: John Dryden, *The Spanish Fryar*, V.i.153, but an often repeated phrase.
127. *tories*: robbers.
128. *Thady*: the same name as that of the Irish narrator of Maria Edgeworth's widely read novella, *Castle Rackrent* (1800).
129. *white-boys*: organized Irish agricultural labourers defending their interests against exploitative landlords, or others perceived to be enemies, by acts of vandalism and violence.
130. *make ... child*: the Irish custom of holding a wake or celebration in honour of the deceased.
131. *bammed*: bamboozled, fooled (slang).
132. *Cadenham ... Christmas*: a folk legend disproved in the late eighteenth century.
133. *Castle Malwood*: in fact, the remains of an Iron Age hilltop fort.
134. non pros: non prosequitur (law Latin); judgment against a plaintiff on grounds that his or her action has not been prosecuted within the allowed time limit.
135. *William Rufus ... Tyrrel*: William II of England (1056–1100) was apparently shot accidentally by Walter Tyrrel.
136. *Nimrod*: Syrian king mentioned in the Bible, and pen-name of Charles James Apperley (1777–1843), author of popular magazine articles on hunting in the 1820s.
137. *swain-motes or forest-courts*: instituted by a charter of 1217 to administer the New Forest as a royal hunting reserve.
138. *Ascot, Epsom, or Doncaster*: famous racecourses in Berkshire, Surrey, and Yorkshire, respectively.
139. *forest breed*: the so-called New Forest ponies, a breed dating back to the eleventh century and still in existence.
140. *under-keepers*: assistant forest-keepers.
141. *Greeks*: cheats.
142. *This ... place*: Shakespeare, *A Winter's Tale*, IV.iv.157-58, said of Perdita.
143. *Where ... maid*: a nursery rhyme, but also a ballad, 'Rolling in the Dew'.
144. ma chere: or ma chère: my dear (French).
145. *Maria*: name of a love-crazed young woman in Laurence Sterne's widely read novel *A Sentimental Journey* (1768).
146. *grig*: grasshopper.
147. *Jacques in the play*: referring to Jaques in Shakespeare, *As You Like It*, act II, scene v.
148. mauvaise ton: unfashionable (French).
149. *quips, and cranks, and wreathed smiles*: conflation of phrases in Milton, 'L'Allegro' (1645), ll. 27–8.
150. *Softly ... pain*: apparently by the author.
151. *gentleman eccentric*: Purposely odd and whimsical behaviour, pursuits, and tastes became fashionable at this time.
152. *ton*: fashion (French).
153. *chuck-farthing*: a coin-throwing and tossing game, recorded from the late seventeenth century.
154. *crack*: first-rate.
155. *the Derby, the Oaks, or the St. Leger*: famous races still run today, the Derby and Oaks at Epsom and the St Leger at Doncaster.
156. *rook*: cheat.

157. *twelve, fifteen, or twenty pounds*: twelve pounds would be worth about £800 in 2005, using to the retail price index.
158. *raff*: worthless fellow, but 'raff' could also refer to foreign timber, perhaps a slight on Blizzard's West Indian origins and mixed race.
159. *put money in his purse*: echoing Shakespeare, *Othello*, I.iii.381.
160. N' importe: no matter (French).
161. *cutting the* haut ton: ignoring fashionable society (French).
162. *pigeoning*: plundering.
163. *deuced*: euphemistic substitution for 'devilishly'.
164. *chip ... off*: perhaps 'cut away'.
165. comédie larmoyante: weeping or sentimental drama (French).
166. *Zounds*: euphemistic substitution for 'God's (i. e., Christ's) wounds', an oath.
167. *her's*: an accepted variant of 'hers' at this time.
168. *Turk*: At this time western Europeans believed Turks to be characterized by extreme cruelty.
169. tonic: a restorative drink or substance—here, probably a piece of money.
170. gunpowder: fine green tea, with leaves rolled resembling grains of gunpowder.
171. *confab*: confabulation, conversation.
172. alias: literally 'otherwise' (Latin): assumed name.
173. outré: beyond the normal or accepted (French).
174. *galloways*: breed of small strong horses.
175. *guineas*: a guinea is twenty-one shillings, or one pound and one shilling.
176. *Eclipse, Highflyer*: Eclipse (1764–89): undefeated racehorse owned by the Duke of Cumberland; Highflyer (1774–93): also undefeated and sire of numerous winning horses, owned by Viscount Bolingbroke and then Richard Tattersall.
177. *gratis*: free (French).
178. *preventive service*: arm of the revenue service charged with preventing smuggling.
179. *The Cottager ... Content*: John Cunningham, 'Content: A pastoral' (1771), ll. 31–2.
180. *all are fellows in their need*: Byron, *Mazeppa* (1819), l. 52.
181. *eye-glass*: monocle, later referred to here as a 'quizzing-glass', from dandies using it to stare at or 'quiz' women or anyone.
182. *Bond Street*: place of fashionable shops in London.
183. *renounce ... society*: 'Fallen' women, married or not, were not considered acceptable company by those who styled themselves 'respectable'.
184. *Norley ... Beaulieu*: on the Solent, Hampshire coast.
185. *devil's tatoo*: drumming with the fingers on a tabletop or other surface out of boredom.
186. *Gretna Green*: town in Scotland just across the border with England, where couples could marry quickly, without the formalities required in England.
187. *'Gad*: Egad: euphemistic substitution for 'A God' (by God), an oath.
188. *manna*: in the Bible, book of Exodus, food dropped from heaven by God to save the Israelites in their flight through the wilderness from bondage in Egypt.
189 *phiz*: physiognomy: face.
190. niaiserie: foolishness (French).
191. *Lothario*: womanizing character in Nicholas Rowe's play *The Fair Penitent* (1703).
192. en regle: en règle: in due form (French).
193. *Connaught*: eastern region of Ireland, regarded by the English as very Irish.
194. *Shrove-tide*: a time of festival just before Lent.
195. *leprighaun*: leprechaun: in Irish legend a small sprite.

196. *cratur*: creature: humorous term for whisky.
197. *gathered unto their fathers*: the Bible, Judges 2:10.
198. *Since ... wrong*: adapted from Robert Burns, 'A Prayer in the Prospect of Death', ll. 9–12.
199. cads: low-level associates.
200. *preventives*: officers of the revenue responsible for preventing smuggling.
201. doing up: getting the better of.

Volume III

1. *ducat*: gold coin, value varying from country to country.
2. *smoked*: discovered.
3. *Each ... whip*: Robert Burns, 'The Jolly Beggars: A Cantata', Recitativo, ll. 25–6.
4. *pith and moment*: 'great pitch and moment', Shakespeare, *Hamlet*, III.i.86.
5. *Lot's wife*: In the Bible, Genesis 19:26, Lot's wife ignores the angel's order not to look back at the destruction of Sodom for its sinfulness, and she is turned into a pillar of salt.
6. *Mother Carey hatching her chickens*: The appearance of 'Mother Carey's chickens', or storm petrels, was thought by sailors to forebode bad weather.
7. *derbies*: handcuffs (slang).
8. *coronach*: dirge or lament.
9. *ha'p'orth*: halfpenny's worth.
10. *shavers*: young fellows.
11. *peelers and tories*: peeler; at this time, a member of the Irish constabulary, created by Robert Peel; later, an English policemen; tories; outlaws.
12. *Dad*: euphemistic deformation of 'God', an oath.
13. *jinked*: eluded.
14. *potheen*: illegally distilled whisky.
15. *skiver*: skewer, stab.
16. *frog and the harrow*: A number of proverbs involving a frog or toad and a harrow could be referred to; the general sense seems to be that Thady does not have a choice.
17. *spalpeens*: rascals.
18. *strike their colours*: surrender, from a defeated ship lowering its flag in sign of surrender to its opponent.
19. *beat up*: disturb.
20. *Day and Martin*: manufacturers of blacking, a paste giving a shiny black surface to boots and shoes.
21. *quondam*: former (Latin).
22. *topped*: hanged.
23. *shab*: low person.
24. *buttered*: flattering.
25. *murphies*: potatoes.
26. *Throth*: troth, in truth.
27. *hobby*: hobby-horse: obsession, favourite subject.
28. setout: spread.
29. *fallen from his high estate*: John Dryden, 'Alexander's Feast' (1697), l. 78.
30. *a longing, lingering, look*: echoing Thomas Gray, 'Elegy Written in a Country Church-yard' (1751), l. 88.
31. *moral*: likeness.

32. *Sampson*: Hebrew strongman in the Bible, book of Judges, tricked by Delilah and captured by his enemies.
33. *platoon*: volley of shots.
34. *stock*: neckcloth.
35. *Forty pounds*: worth about £2,700 in 2005, using the retail price index.
36. *Thomson*: James (1700–48), libertarian poet.
37. *honest, harmless, oxen ... peaceful flocks*: referring variously to James Thomson, 'Spring' (1728), *The Seasons*, ll. 362–3: 'the plain ox, / That harmless, honest, guileless animal, / In what has he offended?' and ll. 357–9: 'The beast of prey, / Blood-stained, deserves to bleed: but you, ye flocks, / What have ye done? ye peaceful people ...'.
38. *Justice Greedy*: mentioned in Philip Massinger's play, *A New Way to Pay Old Debts* (1625), popular throughout the eighteenth and early nineteenth centuries.
39. *a loin of veal*: spoken of highly by characters in a number of plays, and associated with middle-class tastes.
40. *tabula rasa*: 'erased tablet' (Latin), ready to be written on again.
41. *Coulraine*: referring to Coleraine in northern Ireland, regarded at that time as producing the finest linen.
42. *Milesian*: Irish, from the name of a legendary early king.
43. *raising the wind*: obtaining money.
44. *pigeoning a flat*: cheating a dupe.
45. *high life below stairs*: title of a farce (1759) by James Townley; 'below stairs': in a large house, the servants' work area.
46. *Inishowen*: the northernmost part of Ireland, producing a lightly peated blended whisky.
47. *go snacks*: have a share.
48. *trap-stair apartment*: accommodation reached by a ladder or movable steps.
49. *watch-house*: police station and overnight lock-up.
50. *thirteen*: Irish silver shilling, worth thirteen pence, whereas the English shilling was worth twelve pence.
51. *malted*: made drunk by malt liquor.
52. *merry England*: the English as they perceive themselves.
53. *pucker*: state of agitation.
54. *suburban villa, or cottage ornée*: Suburban development was becoming fashionable, with Loudon's designs for semi-detached houses resembling mansions, and decorated (orneée) pseudo-cottages.
55. *rule the roast*: hold sway.
56. *Abigail*: common term for a female domestic servant.
57. *March hare*: hare in the spring breeding season, exhibiting agitated behaviour and so considered mad.
58. *Bedlam*: an asylum for the insane in London.
59. *spring-guns*: guns that discharge when a wire is tripped.
60. *natural*: someone born with impaired intelligence.
61. *farther ... thickness*: The law at this time permitted a husband to beat his wife to this extent.
62. *drilling*: disciplining.
63. *mort*: great deal.
64. *the winds of heaven itself to pay a visit to her rough face*: clumsy version of Shakespeare, *Hamlet*, I.ii.141-42, Hamlet speaking of his father's love for his mother.

65. *'Fore George*: before George: an oath.
66. *horn mad*: enraged enough to gore someone, as a horned animal would do.
67. *rumbustical*: rumbustious: turbulent, unruly.
68. *Petruchio*: male lead in Shakespeare's *The Taming of the Shrew*.
69. *virtue in a lock and key*: John Tobin, *The Honey Moon: A Comedy* (1805), II.i.117.
70. *softly! you stir not hence except to breathe with me*: Tobin, *The Honey Moon*, II.i.66–7: 'You stir not hence, except to take the air; / And then I'll breathe it with you'.
71. *swore the sun was the moon*: referring to an incident in Shakespeare, *The Taming of the Shrew*, IV.v.
72. *non compos mentis*: not of sound mind (Latin).
73. *pretending ... what not*: the incident and phrases occur in *The Taming of the Shrew*, beginning of IV.i.
74. *pluck up ... patient*: an incident in *The Taming of the Shrew*, IV.iii.
75. *sweeting ... honey-love*: phrases in *The Taming of the Shrew*, IV.iii.36, 52.
76. *no rest for the wicked*: the Bible, Isaiah 57:21: 'There is no peace, saith my God, to the wicked'
77. *school for wives*: Jean-Baptiste Molière's comedy, *L'École des femmes* (1682)
78. *Laugh ... best*: John O'Keeffe, *The Castle of Andalusia: A Comic Opera* (1784), beginning of III.i.
79. *Xantippe*: wife of the fifth-century BC Greek philosopher Socrates, reputed to have been the only person to defeat him in argument, and proverbial figure for the scolding wife.
80. *prepense*: premeditated.
81. *Hotspur*: Sir Henry Percy (1364–1403), called 'Hotspur' from his impulsiveness in battle.
82. *mad doctors*: Treatment of the insane was a rapidly developing practice at this time.
83. *strait waistcoat*: a jacket with extra long sleeves and straps for securing the arms of the prisoner or patient.
84. *order of the day*: way of doing things, prevailing system (from military orders, or order of parliamentary business).
85. *crazy*: unsound.
86. *high estate*: a common phrase.
87. *bandboxes*: light boxes for hats and so on.
88. *patience on a monument*: Shakespeare, *Twelfth Night*, II.iv.115.
89. *spoken no more than was set down for him*: adapted from Shakespeare, *Hamlet*, III.ii.39.
90. *Od*: euphemistic substitution for 'God'.
91. *Whistle-chops*: 'Whistle' could mean 'entice, allure', as for example in selling goods; 'chops' could mean 'jaw' in the sense of 'talkative person'.
92. *Tickel*: 'Tickle' could mean 'appeal to' but also 'touch up, make to look better', either applying satirically to a seller of fashions.
93. *moral*: counterpart.
94. *Lady's Magazine*: there were several with this title, containing miscellaneous editorial matter and featuring illustrations of the latest fashions.
95. *rum*: strange; bad.
96. *kennels*: street gutters.
97. *gammon*: humbug.
98. *in the multitude of counsellors there is safety*: the Bible, Proverbs 11:14 and 24:6.
99. *Quarrel ... porridge*: Samuel Butler, *Hudibras*, part 1 (1663), I.225–6.

100. *a change came o'er the spirit of his dream*: echoing a refrain in Byron's 'The Dream' (written 1816).
101. *Turkish harem … sack or bowstring*: It was a common European belief that the several wives and concubines of a Turkish ruler were treated ruthlessly, and that methods of punishment included being tied in a sack and thrown into the sea and being strangled with the string of a bow.
102. *by the lump*: all together.
103. *I love … house*: different phrases and lines from Shakespeare, *The Taming of the Shrew*, IV.iii.
104. *Then … moon*: *Taming of the Shrew*, IV.v.1–2.
105. *a whoreson … knave*: *Taming of the Shrew*, IV.1.116, 145.
106. *We're beset … million*: *Taming of the Shrew*, III.ii.234, 236–7.
107. *salvo*: self-exculpating evasion.
108. *Red Book*: book listing state office-holders and pensioners.
109. *Ludgate Hill*: in the centre of the City of London.
110. *twenty pounds*: a very large note for the time, worth about £1,400 in 2005, using the retail price index.
111. *risk of life and reputation*: forgery was a capital offence.
112. *Bank*: Bank of England, which began issuing banknotes in the late seventeenth century.
113. *utterer*: person who passed the notes.
114. *approver*: someone proving another to be guilty.
115. *strong*: 'stong' in the original text.
116. *Hyde Park*: large park on what was then the west edge of London.
117. *Serpentine River*: now covered except for a long pond in Hyde Park, a place where the desperate committed suicide by drowning.
118. *public prints*: newspapers and magazines.
119. *a poet … heart*: The narrator invokes the Romantic figure of the poet as essentially a self-expressive artist, in contrast to earlier figures of the poet as commentator on public issues and affairs.
120. *Percy*: in fact, the last name of a long-established, wealthy, and titled family that included the earls and dukes of Northumberland.
121. *projectors*: speculators.
122. *none-so-pretty*: in fact, the name of a fabric used in dressmaking and upholstery, and of the flowers Heartsease and Sweet William Catchfly.
123. *coup de main*: surprise attack (French).
124. *non-plussed*: baffled, literally 'not further' (Latin).
125. *eclaircissement*: or éclaircissement: enlightenment, disclosure (French).
126. *romping*: frolicking, as in love-play.
127. *few and far between*: a phrase used by several writers.
128. *unvarnished tale*: Shakespeare, *Othello*, I.iii.91.
129. *unbronzed*: not hardened.
130. *ten thousand pounds*: about £670,000 in 2005, using the retail price index.
131. *trim*: condition.
132. *toils*: net.
133. *Astley's*: an amphitheatre, opened in 1773, putting on displays and dramas featuring horses.
134. *Grosvenor Street*: near Grosvenor Square in the fashionable Mayfair district of the west end of London.

135. *waterman*: man who plies the Thames river for hire.
136. *Philistines*: in the Bible, a people hostile to the Jews, thus any group of foes.
137. *handsome*: considerable.
138. *flat*: dupe.
139. *the frauds of London*: various handbooks were published at the time outlining these frauds, here absorbed into the novel's narrative.
140. *flash*: underworld or in-group jargon.
141. *order of the day*: normal course of events.
142. *rubber at whist*: rubber: set of games, a certain number of which must be won in order to win the match; whist: card game played by four, in two pairs, in which one suit is trumps, each round or trick consisting of playing one card each, won by being able to play a particular card, and the pair winning most tricks winning the game.
143. *tête-a-tête*: or tête-à-tête; intimate chat, literally 'head to head' (French).
144. *West End*: fashionable part of London, to the west of the City of London proper.
145. *weeds*: mourning clothes.
146. *pigeon*: cheat.
147. *blue devils*: depression.
148. *castle-building*: building castles in the air or in Spain, that is, fantasizing.
149. *the lazy foot of time*: Shakespeare, *As You Like It*, III.ii.299.
150. *soirées*: evening parties (French).
151. *criminal intrigues*: illicit love affairs.
152. *Against ... charms*: Milton, *Paradise Lost*, IX.998–9, describing Adam, in the Bible the first man created by God, falling in love with Eve, the first woman.
153. *Curzon Street*: in Mayfair.
154. *liaisons*: connections, especially amorous (French).
155. *King David and the Trojan Prince*: In the Bible, 2 Samuel 11:2–5, King David of Israel falls in love with Bathsheba, the wife of one of his officers and commits adultery with her; in Homer's *Iliad*, the Greeks' siege and destruction of Troy originates when the Trojan Paris elopes with Helen, wife of the Greek king Menelaus.
156. *catastrophe*: conclusion of the plot.
157. *plum*: £100,000: about £6,700,000 in 2005, using the retail price index.
158. *roué*: person of debauched life (French).
159. *funds*: government stocks.
160. *one fell swoop*: Shakespeare, *Macbeth*, IV.iii.219, Macduff lamenting the destruction of his family by Macbeth; fell: cruel, savage.
161. *in the gall of bitterness*: the Bible, Acts of the Apostles, 8:23, Peter rebuking Simon.
162. *Jezebel*: In the Bible, 1 Kings, Jezebel is a queen who persuades her husband king Ahab to admit worship of the god Baal into Israel, eventually sparking a revolt in which she is killed.
163. *lieu*: place (French).
164. *salvo*: self-absolving bad excuse.
165. *ottomans*: backless and armless seats.
166. *mangle*: machine for squeezing water from cloth, paper, etc.
167. *quietus*: extinction, as found in Hamlet's soliloquy, Shakespeare, *Hamlet*, III.i.75.
168. *'sterner stuff'*: Shakespeare, *Julius Caesar*, III.ii.93, spoken by Antony: 'Ambition should be made of sterner stuff'.
169. *vails*: gratuities.
170. *bugbear*: imaginary terror, such as used to frighten children into obedience.

171. *punctilio*: overly refined point of honour or conduct (Italian or Spanish).
172. *approver*: one who proves the guilt of another.
173. *non est inventus*: not to be found (Latin).
174. *well ordered and sure*: echoing the Bible, 2 Samuel 23:5: 'an everlasting covenant, ordered in all things, and sure', but also used by many religious writers.
175. *fams*: fambles: hands.
176. *understrapper*: underling, assistant.
177. *all dickey*: all over.
178. *derbies*: handcuffs.
179. *chaff*: banter.
180. *in at the death*: present at the capture and death of the hunt's quarry.
181. *laudanum*: opium dissolved in alcohol.

For Product Safety Concerns and Information please contact our EU
representative GPSR@taylorandfrancis.com Taylor & Francis Verlag GmbH,
Kaufingerstraße 24, 80331 München, Germany

Batch number: 08153780

Printed by Printforce, the Netherlands